Y0-AWH-502

THE EPISCOPAL CHURCH
IN
THE UNITED STATES

THE EPISCOPAL CHURCH IN THE UNITED STATES

1789-1931

BY

JAMES THAYER ADDISON

ARCHON BOOKS
1969

Copyright, 1951, by Charles Scribner's Sons
Reprinted 1969 by permission of Charles Scribner's Sons
in an unaltered and unabridged edition

sbn: 208 00741 5
Library of Congress Catalog Card Number: 69-15786
Printed in the United States of America

TO

THE REVEREND ROBERT HATCH

AND

THE REVEREND SAMUEL NORMAN McCAIN, JR.

PREFACE

THIS history ends with the year 1931 for three reasons: the record of a further twenty years would either unduly lengthen the book or require a general treatment too condensed; during fifteen years after 1931 the work of the national Church (especially in the mission field) was so restricted by economic depression and by war that to end with a story of this era would give a false impression of decline; more important than either of these reasons is the fact that it is unwise, except for journalists, to try to write history too near one's own time.

I am much indebted to the Rev. Charles L. Taylor, D.D., and to the Rev. Walter H. Stowe, S.T.D., for their generous consent to read this book in manuscript and to offer many suggestions and criticisms. From their learning and good judgment I have gratefully profited.

JAMES THAYER ADDISON

Boston, Massachusetts
December, 1950

Contents

PART II

THE CHURCH FROM 1789 TO 1835

PART III

THE CHURCH FROM 1836 TO 1865

PART IV

THE CHURCH FROM 1866 TO 1900

PART V

THE CHURCH FROM 1901 TO 1931

PROLOGUE

"EPISCOPAL Convention Starts Today," ran the headlines of the *San Francisco Chronicle* of September 26, 1949. And in the next issue its readers learned that "San Francisco's Civic Auditorium became a cathedral yesterday for close to ten thousand Episcopalians from all parts of the world, gathered for the fifty-sixth General Convention of the Protestant Episcopal Church of the United States." For this triennial meeting there were met nearly 150 bishops and more than 600 clerical and lay deputies representing 74 dioceses and 28 missionary districts, domestic and foreign, with a baptized membership of two and a half million. It was not one of the largest Churches in Christendom, but its influence in every State in the Union and in the lands of its oversea missions was out of all proportion to its numbers.

Here was an event which might easily prompt the man in the street to ask, "What is this Episcopal Church? Where did it begin and how did it get here?" These were questions, too, which many Episcopalians might well raise without being able to answer fully. For the Episcopal Church has its roots deep in the past and its history is long. That is why we cannot fairly begin the account of the Church with the years when the United States entered upon their career. What we now call the Episcopal Church was once the Church of England in the colonies, and what was happening in the Church of England for more than two hundred years before the Revolution is a portion of its rich inheritance. So its background in the Anglicanism of the mother country and in generations of colonial experience is that part of the story which must come first.

PART I

THE BACKGROUND

Chapter I

ANGLICANISM IN ENGLAND, 1559–1789

THE Church of England is as old as Christianity in Britain; it reaches back perhaps to the third, and certainly to the fourth century. In days before the Emperor Constantine died and before our Nicene Creed was formulated the Catholic Church was securely planted in that distant island. But "Anglicanism" is a result of the Reformation. It is the form which the Catholic Church in England took after it had been reformed in the reigns of Henry VIII, Edward VI, and Elizabeth. It is the type of Christianity which we find in the national Church after the "Elizabethan Settlement," and which has been evolving ever since through four centuries of history.

Under the leadership of Luther in Germany and Zwingli in Switzerland the Reformation of the Church had been in progress since the early years of the reign of Henry VIII, who ascended the throne in 1509. This movement involved the separation from the Catholic Church of the existing churches in large parts of Germany and Switzerland, and the adoption of new liturgies, doctrines, and forms of government. By the year 1529 the Reformation had earned the name "Protestant" and had begun to split into two branches. One was the "Lutheran," which eventually controlled Scandinavia and most of Germany; the other was the "Reformed," soon dominated by Calvin and ultimately including Switzerland, the Netherlands, Scotland, and the Protestant elements in France. It was this wing which after 1559 had by far the stronger influence in England.

The revolt of England from the control of the papacy resembled the German revolt in one particular: it was supported and partly inspired by a strong and growing nationalism which resented foreign control and the power of a clergy increasingly corrupt. In other respects the two movements were markedly different. The Lutheran and Reformed Churches broke with Rome under the guidance of great religious leaders who expressed and promoted deep religious convictions. The changes they effected depended for success on any number of mixed motives; but the chief issues proclaimed and debated were religious issues, such as justification by faith alone and the supreme authority of a divinely inspired Bible. The movement consequently stirred the Church to its depths and resulted in reforms not only of doctrine but also of discipline, worship, and organization. In England, on the contrary, the leader of revolt was Henry VIII, whose motives were partly personal, partly political, and (as none knew better than he) not in the least religious.

England, however, had not been wholly lacking in movements of genuine reform. The protests uttered by Wycliffe against abuses in the Church a century and a half earlier had never died out; the influence of Christian humanists like Colet and Tyndale had recently been reviving similar longings for a cleansing of the Church; and the writings of Luther himself had entered England and were being read by the King and many of his subjects, especially in the universities. These were some of the spiritual forces which were preparing England for adjustment to the shock that was soon to come.

Henry VIII, profoundly disturbed at the lack of a male heir after many years of marriage, wanted to divorce his wife Catherine of Aragon. Having failed to obtain the necessary papal annulment of his marriage, he determined to break with the Pope. The Church of England, it must be remembered, had long maintained considerable independence of Rome. To cite in evidence but two points among many, the King practically controlled the appointment of bishops, and a law nearly two centuries old forbade the prosecution of suits in foreign courts (such as the papal) without the King's leave. Thus fortified by the independence he already enjoyed and banking on the patriotic nationalism then strong among his subjects, Henry obliged the clergy in their Convocations to declare him the Supreme Head of the Church and to agree to pass no laws without his permission (1531 and 1532). The Court of the Archbishop of Canterbury declared Henry's marriage to Catherine null and void and his recent marriage to Anne Boleyn valid. The formal severance of all bonds with the papacy was accomplished in 1534 when Parliament passed a series of acts prohibiting the payment of money to Rome and declaring the King Supreme Head of the Church. To deny him this title thereafter was treason.

The Reformation in England was thus not doctrinal but constitutional. The Church of England had reformed itself in one respect only. It had denied the supremacy of the Pope and had broken relations with Rome. In doctrine and liturgy and orders, however, it remained a Catholic Church. To mark the fact that its new head was not to be numbered among the reformers, Parliament passed in 1539 an "Act Abolishing Diversity of Opinion" in six articles with a death penalty. Among the doctrines and practices it was now fatal to attack were transubstantiation, the administering of the Communion in one kind, and the celibacy of the clergy. During Henry's remaining years, then, Romanists were in danger of execution for treason and Protestants for heresy. Between these two extreme wings was the great mass of Englishmen, content to leave things as they were.

With the accession of the young Edward VI in 1547 the pendulum swung sharply to the left. The Protector and other nobles who determined England's policy were strongly in favor of reformation along Continental lines. Their zeal was all the warmer when surveys of the dioceses revealed a scandalous degree of ignorance and inefficiency among the clergy. During the six years of this reign Protestant-minded priests were appointed to bishoprics, the clergy were permitted to marry, the use of the Bible in English was encouraged, and a set of Forty-two Articles of belief, much influenced by Continental Confessions, was authorized by the King. As a further step of permanent value the Liturgy was translated into English in two successive versions (1549 and 1552)—the foundation of our present Prayer Book. Nor were the changes of this period merely formal and legal. The "new learning" of Renaissance humanism continued to spread among the educated classes; men like Bishops Hooper and Ridley were active in Protestant propaganda; and the first signs of what was later to be known as Puritanism began to be evident.

With the death of Edward came a sudden and violent movement to the right. In 1553 Edward was succeeded by his elder sister, the Roman Catholic Mary, daughter of Catherine of Aragon. Under the new sovereign Parliament at once declared Henry's marriage with Catherine to have been valid and Mary to be the legitimate heir to the throne. All the religious legislation of Edward's reign was repealed, and the Church was restored to its condition at the death of Henry. The following year Mary married King Philip of Spain, and the process of restoration was carried to its limit. Parliament repealed the anti-papal laws of Henry's time and united with the Queen in acknowledging the supremacy of the Pope and imploring his absolution for the years of heresy and schism. Medieval legislation for suppressing heresy was revived, and so ruthlessly enforced that during the five years of this reign nearly three hundred persons were burnt alive for heresy, including the bishops Ridley, Latimer, Cranmer, and Ferrar.

When Elizabeth came to the throne in 1558 the people were prepared to welcome a change. They had begun to hate what Romanism had now come to mean—bloody persecution and the subjugation of English interests to Spain. The new Queen and her ministers were aware that the English were then very far from being a Protestant people; but in view of the dangerous ambitions of the great Catholic powers of Europe, France and Spain, they realized that England's safety lay in the adoption of the cause of the Reformation. Peace at home, too, called for the same remedy. The religious issue was thus determined on political grounds and settled by political means. But the famous "Elizabethan Settlement" was not another sharp reaction like that under Edward. It was a deliberate compromise, providing the legal setting and secular framework within which Anglicanism could develop as a *via media.* This characteristic note of Anglicanism was struck early in the Queen's reign by legislation which declared in effect that the Church of England was both Catholic and Reformed. Reflecting the sovereign's temperate mind and moderate policy, the Church was neither to revert to Rome nor to advance to meet Protestant Geneva. Yet because this Settlement embodied the deepest traits and tendencies of a great people it was far more than a temporary remedy invented by statecraft. It gave outward shape to what has since been recognized as essential in the nature of Anglicanism—loyalty to a Catholic past in creeds and polity, and glad appropriation of the fruits of reform not only in freedom from papal control but in the central place assigned to the Scriptures and in definite changes in doctrine and ritual.

During the year 1559 Parliament enacted a new Act of Supremacy, making the sovereign "Supreme Governor" of the Church. Other laws restored the Communion in both kinds, adopted as tests of orthodoxy the Holy Scriptures and the decisions of the first four General Councils, and authorized a new Book of Common Prayer differing but little from the second Prayer Book of Edward VI. To implement this last provision an Act of Uniformity compelled all subjects of the Queen to worship according to the new liturgy. Four years later the doctrine of the Church as to controversial questions raised by the Reformation was expressed in the Thirty-nine Articles.[1]

This fourth major change in religious policy within one generation was carried through by the State in defiance of the bishops and of Convocation. It was a laymen's settlement forced upon the clergy. It is, in fact, a true statement that "the sanction which the Elizabethan compromise may rightly claim to have from the Church is not that of formal acceptance but of subsequent acquiescence." Thirteen of the fourteen bishops then in office refused to take the oath of supremacy abjuring the Pope; and so many new bishops were required that the Elizabethan Episcopate (headed by Matthew Parker, Archbishop of Canterbury), though validly

[1] This exposition, strongly tinged with Calvinism, did not receive the royal assent until 1571, at which time subscription to the Articles was required of clergy by act of Parliament.

consecrated, was largely a new creation. The other clergy, however, submitted more readily to their new governor and their new liturgy. Probably no more than two hundred of them had to be deprived of their livings for failure to conform, and many more were prepared for further advance toward the ritual simplicity of Continental Protestantism.

In dealing with religion during forty-five years Elizabeth was forced by events to be steadily active in protecting the country from Romanism, and the Church from Puritanism. The former was a political, the latter an ecclesiastical danger.

Despite existing laws which laid them open to charges of heresy and treason, Elizabeth followed a mild policy toward Roman Catholics for the first twelve years of her reign. But a change came in 1570 when Pope Pius V issued a bull excommunicating and deposing Elizabeth and releasing her subjects from their allegiance. Romanists at the same time were forbidden to attend Church of England services. When war had thus been declared, Roman Catholics had to choose between disloyalty to the Church and disloyalty to the State. The Pope and the Jesuits had made it impossible to treat Romanism as purely a religion. It was a political force enlisted in a determined effort to overthrow the ruler and the state religion of England. Recognizing this fact and stimulated by a series of plots, which included attempts to assassinate the Queen, Parliament passed new and harsher laws against members of the Church of Rome. Popular hatred of the papacy became intense, and reached an extreme of bitterness in the war with Spain which ended in the defeat of the Armada (1588). By the year 1603 about two hundred Roman Catholics had been executed in England.

Early in the reign of Elizabeth Puritanism became a powerful movement and its representatives grew bolder every year. These Puritans of the sixteenth century were the Protestants who found the Elizabethan Settlement inadequate in purpose, method, and result. Inspired by the example of Calvinism flourishing in Geneva, they were eager to go *further* in the reformation of doctrine and worship and to go *deeper* in the moral reformation of clergy and people. In its earliest phase the movement was chiefly concerned with apparently trivial ritual details. Finding no warrant for them in Scripture, Puritans objected to vestments, the ring in marriage, the sign of the cross in Baptism, and other ceremonial usages. By the year 1570, however, they began to lay increasing stress upon the need for more drastic changes. In 1572 appeared "An Admonition to Parliament" and "A Second Admonition to Parliament." The first was a vehement denunciation of the Church of England as having a ministry and a polity contrary to God's will and a Prayer Book "culled and picked out of that popish dunghill . . . the Mass book." The second document prescribed the remedy—a complete reorganization abolishing the Episcopal Establishment as hitherto known and substituting the main features of the Presbyterian theocracy of Geneva. One result was the suppression of these tracts by the government; another was five years of public controversy chiefly between John Whitgift, later archbishop, and Thomas Cartwright, the Puritan divine. Several attempts were made, moreover, to obtain these reforms by action of Parliament, efforts which might well have succeeded had it not been for the opposition of the Queen.

Yet increasing discontent and controversy did not then involve any purpose of secession. Everyone in that era accepted the principle of compulsory uniformity within one State Church, and therefore even the more advanced leaders desired not separation from the Church of England but the remoulding of the Church in accordance with the Presbyterian pattern. Before long, however, they went so far as to remodel the churches in many places along Presbyterian lines by a more or less secret process concealed under the forms of Anglican order. And along with other reforming activity went continuous agitation for the promotion of preaching and the raising of standards for the clergy. Here, from any point of view, the Puritans were justified in their loud complaints, for preaching had been almost abandoned by most of the priests, and the ignorance and inefficiency of the majority and the immorality of a minority were notorious.

The issues were sharpened and discipline was enforced after the elevation of Whitgift to the Archbishopric of Canterbury in 1583. Both then and thereafter the central thesis of the Puritan was that God had revealed in the Bible the form which church order should take, that the Church of England was defying that revelation, and that the Puritans were zealous to conform to it. For them the issue was, "Shall we obey God or man?" But for Whitgift and Elizabeth, in whose eyes Presbyterianism was not necessary to salvation, the issue was, "Shall the religious life of England continue to be expressed in the historic Church of England with its Catholic heritage, or in a system like Calvin's at Geneva?" Since the Queen and the Archbishop had no doubt about the answer, they set themselves to suppress with rigor all signs of rebellion in speech and action. Henceforth with greater strictness was enforced the law that no one should be allowed to perform any ecclesiastical function unless he had subscribed to the royal supremacy and accepted the Prayer Book and the Thirty-nine Articles. Most Puritans proceeded outwardly to conform; but among the members of their most radical wing the first "Independents" arose. The followers of Robert Browne and others, the earliest Congregationalists, repudiated both Canterbury and Geneva, and flatly refused to conform. Beginning in 1593 all such Separatists were banished. But some who emigrated to Holland were later to be heard from in America.

Happily for the future of the Church the development of Anglicanism at this period was not to be measured entirely in terms of laws and legal compulsion. Thanks to Richard Hooker, the greatest of thinkers in the Church of England, Anglicanism was not only enforced but also interpreted. In days when force was being applied on one side and resisted on the other there appeared a classic of persuasion. Hooker's *Laws of Ecclesiastical Polity,*[2] raised the whole contest with Puritanism to a higher plane by investing it with dignity and charity and a sober appeal to reason. Its author denies the Puritan assertion that the Bible is the *only* source of authority; in his view Reason and Tradition are other sources, and Reason serves to interpret both Scripture and Tradition. A similar breadth marks his treatment of the "visible" Church as composed of all those who have been baptized and profess loyalty to Christ and the Christian faith. He thus believed that both the Roman Church and the Presbyterian Church were true parts of the universal Church, for convictions about Church government, he taught, were not to be regarded as matters of faith; and even Episcopacy, though ordained by God, is not absolutely necessary where bishops cannot possibly be obtained. This massive common sense of Hooker, his wealth of scholarship, and his ardent piety are among the reasons why Anglicanism is not merely a political compromise or a straddling of issues but a live organism positive and vigorous. In his intense conservatism, in his predominantly intellectual emphasis, and in his convincing fusion of Protestant and Catholic elements Hooker remains the normative Anglican.

When James I became the first Stuart King of England in 1603 there began a troubled period in English history which lasted for nearly two generations and in which religion and politics were closely entangled. For the first forty years until the outbreak of the Civil War the agitating question in politics was the seat of sovereignty. Where, in the last analysis, did the ultimate power lie? Was it with the King, and was Parliament only an advisory council, or was it with Parliament? The problem never became acute under Elizabeth, whose actions were often quite as arbitrary as those of any Stuart, because in contrast to her successors the Queen was gifted with common sense; she never dogmatized about the power of the Crown; and she was trusted and loved. But James and his son Charles, who were never trusted by the wise, maintained a version of the divine right of kings which involved a royal absolutism quite as complete as that which then prevailed in France and Spain. They proclaimed it on many occasions and expected their subjects to agree with them and to abandon all thoughts of resistance.

In the increasingly bitter struggles between King and Parliament

[2] The first five of its eight Books appeared between 1593 and 1597.

which marked the period before the war began in 1642, religion played an active part. A minor feature was the fact that the kings were inclined to be lenient toward Romanism while Parliament was violently anti-Roman. But the primary cause of intensified feeling and deepening cleavage was the more important fact that James and Charles sided whole-heartedly with the anti-Puritan element in the Church, and the Church returned the favor by endorsing with enthusiasm all the claims and even all the actions of would-be absolute monarchs. Thus Puritanism and Parliament came to unite in the cause of English liberty, while the Church paid a heavy penalty for trying to save itself by an alliance with two of the least valuable kings in English history.

In 1603 no step had been taken which would prevent a statesmanlike solution of the problem created by Puritanism. What was lacking was not the opportunity but the statesman. There were then no Nonconformists. There were High Churchmen, like the saintly and lovable Bishop Andrewes—those who emphasized the Catholic aspect of Anglicanism and laid stress upon episcopacy, apostolic succession, the Sacraments, and the priestly power of the clergy. At the other extreme were the Puritan Low Churchmen who worshipped an infallible Bible and objected to much in the Prayer Book, and whose moral vigor was their strongest point. Both groups alike were then Calvinistic in theology; but many on the left wing would gladly have followed Calvin further by restricting or even abolishing episcopacy. Yet up to this point, and well beyond it, all these varied types counted themselves members of the Church of England, and if all could have been retained within its fold, the Church would not only have remained national but would have been permanently enriched.

What actually happened, however, led to consequences far different. James began his reign by holding a conference in response to a petition signed by eight hundred Puritan clergy. At Hampton Court in 1604 he and some of his bishops and other clergy met with representatives of these radical Low Churchmen, including a cathedral dean. The King and Bancroft, Bishop of London, set the tone of the conference by treating these serious Puritans with a mixture of rude contempt and cheap humor. The demands of the petitioners ranged from permission to discard the surplice all the way to the transformation of the Articles into complete Calvinism. It was even suggested that bishops should not only be more restricted in authority but perhaps actually eliminated.

In view of the increasingly radical changes proposed, it was fortunate for Anglicanism that these Low Churchmen were not allowed to get all they wanted; but statesmanship, we cannot but think, would have found some means to help both sides by a wise measure of compromise and concession. The fundamental trouble was that both parties believed in uniformity and both considered themselves infallible. Yet even supposing all the right was on one side (which happens less often than partisans imagine), at least these fellow-Churchmen might have been treated with Christian charity. But James insisted upon complete submission in every detail, and in the tone of a scoffing bully declared of the Puritans, "I will make them conform, or I will harry them out of the land, or worse." And to show that the threat was not idle, a new set of canons was promptly formulated, riveting upon all clergy precise conformity to the royal supremacy, the Prayer Book, and the Thirty-nine Articles. One consequence was that three hundred clergy were ejected from their livings.

The strife with Parliament and with Puritanism which was characteristic of the reign of James I reached its fatal conclusion in the reign of his son Charles, who became King in 1625. His chief religious adviser was William Laud, who was made Bishop of London in 1628 and Archbishop of Canterbury in 1633. These two were active partners for fifteen years. Laud supported Charles in his fight against Parliament to make monarchy absolute, and Charles supported Laud in his campaign against Puritanism to achieve uniformity of belief and practice in the Church. By treating all types of Puritans as rebellious opponents who must be disciplined, King and Archbishop did all they could to make it inevitable that the national Church should lose not only the Separatists, whom it was hopeless to retain, but also the uncounted number of moderate Puritans who were permanently alienated by the policies of Charles which Laud upheld and the policies of Laud which Charles upheld.

Even with all these handicaps England might have escaped years of civil war if the religious problems had not been so involved with political problems. Questions of Christian doctrine and church polity became entangled with constitutional questions as to the powers of Parliament and the King's prerogative. And the interweaving of these elements, instead of blurring the issues, merely sharpened them. The reason, of course, was that on the whole the Puritan party in religion, which insisted on radical reforms in doctrine and polity and resisted episcopal domination, was the same party in politics which magnified the rights of Parliament and sought to limit the royal prerogative. It is conceivable that if the two controversies could have worked themselves out separately, peace might have been maintained; but once each had inflamed the other, war was probably inevitable.

With Charles as King and with Laud representing the Church, the probability of conflict became a certainty, since Charles stood for the extreme claims of monarchy and Laud spoke for what had by that time become an unpopular minority in the Church. In every step the bishop took he could count on royal support, and in return he gave his warm approval to those arbitrary acts of the King which were leading to political revolution. These two men, wielding great power in a period of crisis, were indeed a lethal combination.

The record of Charles from 1625 to 1642 is a well-known chapter in history too long for full recital in a brief sketch of Anglicanism. After dissolving two Parliaments because they would not vote him the supplies he wanted until the national grievances had been redressed, the King had to deal with a third Parliament, which forced his signature to a Petition of Right denouncing his use of martial law, arbitrary taxation, and arbitrary imprisonment. Thenceforward he ruled for eleven years without a Parliament, in the course of which time he violated all his promises and aroused throughout the nation a deep sense of injury. While thus making the summoning of Parliament highly perilous, he proceeded to make it necessary by trying to force the Prayer Book upon Presbyterian Scotland. After one war with the Scots, which was hardly more than a feeble gesture, he was confronted with the need to finance a second war. Then Parliament had to be convened; but as it would vote no money until reforms had been approved, it was dismissed, and the King went on to lose a second little war with Scotland. With the Scottish army quartered in England until indemnity should be paid, money from Parliament became a necessity. Thus the "Long Parliament" was summoned in November, 1640, and began its career first with remedial, and then with revolutionary legislation. Within seven months the King's chief minister, the Earl of Strafford, was executed, those instruments of tyranny the Courts of Star Chamber and High Commission were abolished, and all taxes made without Parliamentary authority were condemned and prohibited. Though Charles signed these measures, he later entered Parliament in force and attempted to arrest his chief enemies there. After this action and his subsequent flight from the capital, preparations for war began, and the first battle was fought in October, 1642.

During the fifteen years in which these political events were developing Laud was the vigorous leader in a campaign to root out all forms of Puritan resistance and to secure uniformity in the Church of England. For five years in the see of London and for seven as Archbishop he controlled the religious policy of the King and with intense energy and brusque manners attempted to enforce the program of reform in every quarter of the country. In this effort he was the champion of efficiency, decency, and order in an era when slack and lazy disarray was a shameful mark of the Church of England. But he went much further to "harry the Puritans," for in their great movement he could see only heresy and rebellion to be suppressed by compulsion.

In the spirit of an academic martinet Laud enforced the laws of the

Church with the continuous use of secular power, and appealed to the King whenever additional aid was needed. Preachers, writers, and professors were forbidden to discuss the meaning of the Thirty-nine Articles. Bishops were required to limit or to forbid "lecturers" and the indiscriminate employment of private chaplains—the two roles in which Puritan clergy could make headway. Ritual details were insisted upon with rigor. And of course such extreme heretics as Anabaptists and Brownists were proceeded against to the legal limit. The censorship of the press, too, engaged his attention; and libels attacking episcopacy and bishops were eagerly prosecuted, and sometimes (as in the case of the famous Prynne) savagely punished with mutilation and long imprisonment. In all this prolonged campaign, moreover, public resentment was aggravated by the constant resort to the Court of Star Chamber and the Court of High Commission—tribunals which had been active since Tudor times and which were so arbitrary and inquisitorial in their procedure as to be dangerous to English liberties.

Many of the purposes which Laud pursued were wholly worthy from the Anglican point of view. Ritual beauty and order, reverence toward things holy, devotion to duty on the part of the clergy, and above all the emphasis upon the sacraments and the preservation of episcopacy and of the apostolic succession—these were inherited values for which he rightly contended and for the perpetuation of which he is partly responsible. As to other aims for which he fought opinions will always differ. But when we judge the *methods* he employed it is hard to escape the conclusion that he did more harm than good. Whatever his ideals may have been, the practical result of his career was to make bishops the most intensely hated group of men in the country. In the effort to defend episcopacy he made it abhorrent to successive generations of Dissenters in England and America. In all Church reform his continuous appeal to secular force and royal authority proved a costly and clumsy method of vindicating Anglicanism. Yet we ought not to forget that the passion for uniformity and the ready resort to compulsion were characteristic of nearly all parties. Only those rarer souls who were in advance of their age could plead for toleration and persuasion; and Laud was more nearly behind the times than ahead of them.

One consequence of the Laudian policy was the religious legislation of the Long Parliament, for the Church was not spared when that body set to work. Laud was soon sent to the Tower, impeached as a traitor, unjustly condemned by a bill of attainder, and executed in January, 1645. Two years before he died Parliament had abolished episcopacy. Such action was all the easier because by that time all the bishops, most of the lay peers, and many members of the House of Commons had joined the

King at Oxford. This migration left a Parliament deprived of its loyal Anglicans and composed of Presbyterians, Independents, and those so-called Erastians who were anticlerical in temper and chiefly concerned to see that the State remained supreme even in spiritual affairs.

The next move of this reduced but still divided Parliament was to summon the Westminster Assembly which met on July 1, 1643. Composed of a hundred and twenty-one English divines and thirty laymen, it proceeded to formulate a system of Presbyterian government and Presbyterian discipline, to compose a "Directory" to take the place of the Prayer Book, and to write the Westminster Confession and Catechism, which have ever since maintained their place as Presbyterian standards. Before this work was completed the cause of Parliament in the field of battle had become so dubious that an alliance with Scotland was sought and obtained. The high price to be paid was conformity to a Solemn League and Covenant in which Parliament agreed to "reform the Church of England according to the word of God and the example of the best reformed churches." This pledge was carried out so reluctantly that not until 1646 did a modified form of Presbyterianism become the state religion of England; and such it remained officially for the next fourteen years. The new Church, however, was never fully established except in London and Lancashire, for the great majority of the people viewed it either with indifference or with hostility. But the Prayer Book was pretty successfully proscribed and large numbers of the clergy were ejected from their livings. After the execution of Charles in January, 1649, the condition of the Church in England became even more disorderly. Some benefices were filled by Presbyterians, some by Independents, and some by men who were not ordained at all.

When Cromwell dissolved the "Rump" of the Long Parliament and became Lord Protector in 1653 a greater degree of toleration ensued, but not to the advantage of Anglicanism. In the Army the sectarian varieties known as "Independency," which were congregational in polity, had become a powerful majority. They were, by their own principles, more disposed to tolerance and far less zealous for uniformity than the Presbyterians. Moreover, Cromwell himself was by nature averse to persecution. In the confused situation which he faced he found it hard to keep all the Puritans united. He knew that the great majority of the people were Anglican by tradition and in their sympathies, but for political reasons their Church could not be tolerated. The Independents in his "new model" Army hated both Anglicans and Presbyterians. The Presbyterians, in turn, though a small minority, could claim that their sect was established by law. It was clear, then, that toleration *within Puritanism* was the only feasible policy. During the Protectorate, therefore, from 1653 to

1660, all Christians who believed in the Trinity and the Scriptures were allowed to worship freely, but Roman Catholics and Anglicans (as well as Quakers and "antinomian blasphemers") were denied that privilege. "Popery" and "prelacy" were put in the same class and ruled out.

During this period of the Interregnum it was the loyal clergy of the Church of England who were the Nonconformists. More than three thousand of them were deprived and obliged to live on pensions so small and irregular that they were reduced to poverty and sometimes almost to starvation. For a time they were allowed to practice liturgical worship in private; but after 1655 the Prayer Book was more strictly banned and Anglican priests were not even permitted to serve as tutors or teachers. By that time Cromwell's major-generals were governing the country, and legislative acts and their enforcement were making crimes of all sins. In the process of "discouraging and discountenancing all profaneness and ungodliness" the Puritan government added moral intolerance to religious intolerance and broadened the range of inquisition and compulsion. With a stern minority firmly in power, there was far less liberty in England than under Charles.

When Cromwell's grip on affairs was released by his death in 1658, his son Richard proved unable to hold back the tide of reaction. After his fall in May, 1659, the Army first restored, then ejected, and once more restored the "Rump" of the Long Parliament. By this time Presbyterians were ready to join with Royalists in bringing to an end "the rule of the saints." Unwilling to trust its fortunes to the remnants of an assembly elected twenty years earlier, the nation welcomed the coming of General Monk with the army which had been occupying Scotland. He and his forces reached London early in February, 1660, and proceeded to arrange for the election of a new Parliament; and once in session this Parliament voted to recall Charles II to the throne. After long exile the King had come into his own. He landed in England on May 25, 1660, and the days of the Restoration began.

If the vast majority of the English people were hoping for drastic changes, they must surely have been satisfied. In place of an ardent Puritan for their ruler they now had a sensual and selfish monarch who has been well described as "half an infidel and half a papist." Yet he was clever and politically shrewd. Unlike his father, however, he was no devout Churchman, and the advantages which the Church began to reap were primarily due to the "Cavalier" Parliament (1661–1679) which was thirsting to take revenge on its Puritan predecessors. In addition to the restoration of the King and the House of Lords, the Church too was restored to the status and to the property which it had held twenty years before. The Laudian Juxon became Archbishop of Canterbury, the surviving bishops were restored to their sees, and new bishops were consecrated. As the Church historian Patterson expresses it, "Squire and parson were to be the dominant factors in English life for the next hundred and fifty years."

A year after the King's return an attempt was made at the Savoy Conference to discuss the differences between Presbyterians and Anglicans with a view to possible changes which might unite the groups. Twelve representatives from each side conferred at length; but when it proved that the Presbyterians were demanding no less than the concessions called for at the Hampton Court Conference fifty-seven years earlier, the bishops rejected their proposals. In the atmosphere which then prevailed it seemed impossible to satisfy the Presbyterians without sacrificing what was vital and essential in the Church of England. Though the Conference failed, the year 1661 witnessed the achievement of Prayer Book revision. The Convocations of Canterbury and York produced a new version without substantial changes, and after it had been approved by Parliament, it became the one authorized *Book of Common Prayer* and has so remained ever since.

Any plan for comprehension or union having been almost doomed from the start, the only policy which Parliament could understand or endorse was that of compulsory uniformity. It had the added attraction of being retaliation for a like policy adopted by the Puritans. In 1662, therefore, was enacted the Act of Uniformity. This law compelled every minister not only to use the Prayer Book but also to declare he agreed to what it contained and to renounce the doctrine that arms could ever be rightly borne against the King. All lay persons, moreover, were required, under penalties, to attend Anglican services. As a result of these rigorous enactments nearly two thousand Puritan clergymen were removed from their livings without compensation. Later acts forbade Nonconformists to assemble for worship in numbers greater than five, and prohibited ejected ministers from coming within five miles of any corporate town.

Charles, being a Roman Catholic at heart, was interested neither in the welfare of the Church of England nor in protecting the Nonconformists. Instead, he was disposed to intrigue for the restoration of Romanism. In 1670 he signed a secret treaty with France promising to re-establish the Church of Rome in England with the aid of French money and French soldiers. As a first moderate move in the process he issued in 1672 the Declaration of Indulgence, which suspended the execution of the laws against Dissenters and permitted Mass to be said in private houses. At this alarming action Parliament was indignant, and their firm petition to the King obliged him to withdraw the Declaration. But the legislature was not satisfied with this merely negative step. It proceeded to pass in 1673 the

Test Act, which demanded of all holders of civil and military office that in addition to taking the oath of supremacy they should make a declaration against transubstantiation and receive the Holy Communion in accordance with the rites of the Church of England. Both these actions, of course, were impossible for loyal Roman Catholics, but participating in the Communion was also objectionable to many Nonconformists. Thus the holiest of sacraments was prostituted to serve as an inadequate test to keep certain classes out of public service. So dear to the hearts of Churchmen was this Act degrading the Eucharist that it was not repealed until 1828. The fact reminds us that a State Church which has to submit to secular control and to serve political purposes is bound to be soiled in the process.

The historical explanation of what looks to the modern mind like inexcusable intolerance is that, whether we approve it or not, religion and politics in those days were inseparably intertwined. "If a Puritan Commonwealth did not dare to tolerate the Churchman because he was likely to be a friend of the monarchy, still less could the monarchy tolerate the Puritan Dissenter who had been one of those who had established the Commonwealth. In the confusion of the times the vital distinction between the imposition of civil and religious disabilities was forgotten. It was assumed that if a Puritan was permitted to retain his Puritanism he would retain his disloyalty too, and Parliament in its terror and its revenge took blindly up the old weapon of repression which it found ready to its hand. . . . The dread of a return to military rule and the fear of the establishment of Roman Catholicism [were] the dominant factors in English affairs during this period." [3]

The earnest effort to suppress Romanism was not successful in preventing the "Popish plot" of 1678, which may have been in part a hoax but which certainly led to the execution of many innocent Roman Catholics. Nor could any act of Parliament withhold King Charles from being baptized into the Roman Communion on his deathbed. But far worse was still to come, for his brother James II, who came to the throne in February, 1685, was fiercely determined to establish Romanism in England by the speediest possible methods. He appointed Romanists to important commands in the Army and to political and judicial posts, and even thrust them into university office. And to provide himself with a sharp weapon he revived the hated Court of High Commission.

In spite of rising resentment no explosion came until the infatuated King issued in April, 1687, his Declaration of Indulgence. The decree gave freedom of worship to Dissenters and Roman Catholics and suspended all laws which debarred them from office. A second Declaration,

[3] H. O. Wakeman, *History of the Church of England,* 382, 385.
The full titles of all books referred to, together with place and date of publication, will be found in the Bibliography.

issued in May, 1688, not only repeated the provisions of the first but was accompanied by an order commanding all the clergy to publish it from their pulpits. The final purpose of these actions, of course, was not to secure universal toleration but to make Romanism the religion of England. Well aware of this ultimate aim, seven bishops met in haste at the call of William Sancroft, Archbishop of Canterbury. They composed a respectful petition to James, pointing out that the dispensing power he was exercising had been declared illegal by Parliament, and affirming that they would not read the Declaration in church. As a result, scarcely any priests published that document at their services. But the bishops were prosecuted at once for seditious libel, and the whole nation watched to see the outcome. Their acquittal was greeted with a general tumult of enthusiasm, and proved that except among Roman Catholics the King had not a friend in the country. Its leaders had already resolved that his reign must end.

Acting upon a written appeal signed by notable peers, including the Bishop of London, William of Orange, Stadtholder of Holland, landed at Torbay on November 5, 1688, and some weeks later James escaped to the Continent. William (the son of Mary, daughter of Charles I) and his wife Mary (the daughter of James II) became joint sovereigns at the invitation of a duly elected Convention; and, on April 11, 1689, they were crowned. The coronation oath included for the first time a clause it has ever since contained—that the sovereign would maintain "the *Protestant* reformed religion established by law." Two immediate results of the change of rulers were the Toleration Act and the rise of the Nonjurors.

When the time came to take the oath of allegiance to William and Mary five bishops refused to swear and were deprived of office. Their example was followed by about four hundred clergy and a considerable number of laymen. This large group seceded from the Established Church and formed the body known thereafter as the Nonjurors. Their consciences, stimulated by a devout belief in the divine right of kings, would not permit them to transfer their allegiance from a living anointed sovereign to any synthetic successors. By no means all of them were Jacobites in the active political sense of plotting the return of James or his son; but none the less all the clerical Nonjurors were deprived of their livings. According to their own view their little band was truly the Catholic Church in England, and it was the rest of the Church that was in schism. In course of time, therefore, they consecrated a number of bishops and maintained a succession which did not expire until the end of the eighteenth century. Whatever judgment may be passed upon the wisdom of their action, there is general agreement that the Church suffered a serious loss in having these Nonjurors isolated from the corporate life of the Establishment. Among their bishops, priests, and laymen were to be found the best living examples of Anglo-Catholic piety, for want of which the Church was impoverished. Thanks to their retirement the typical High Churchman for the next thirty years was simply a boisterous Tory.

In the words of Trevelyan, "At last the time had come when English Protestants were ready to let one another worship God. All their parties were exhausted with fifty years of revolution, bloodshed, and terror, culminating in the recent narrow escape of their common religion." The outcome of this new situation was the Toleration Act of 1689. Freedom of worship was accorded to all orthodox Protestant Nonconformists; but Roman Catholics and the few Unitarians then visible were excluded from the benefits of the Act. The liberty granted to Dissenters, however, was only religious liberty, for their civil rights were limited by the Test Act, so that the governing class consisted only of Anglicans until well into the nineteenth century. The national Church had thus definitely ceased to be national, and permanent recognized dissent had begun and still continues.

Before the close of the seventeenth century there had clearly taken shape the division of parties both in State and Church which was to prevail for a hundred years and more. As early as the reign of Charles II there had arisen the Whig and Tory parties. The Whigs were concerned to maintain the rights of Parliament and the limitations of the Crown. They favored toleration of Nonconformists, and they were intensely anti-Roman. The Tories, on the other hand, favored the support of Anglicanism by compulsory uniformity, and their principles included belief in the divine right of kings and passive obedience to the monarch under all circumstances. Though the nobles were to be found in both parties, the landed gentry were mostly Tory, as were also nearly all the country parsons. In the Whig party were to be found the financial and commercial classes, and of course the Nonconformist minority.

Within the Church there were three parties. The first and least important were the Low Churchmen, who resembled the orthodox Protestant Dissenters, but had decided to stay just inside the Church instead of just outside it. The second were the Latitudinarians, who were sometimes called Low Churchmen but were really Broad Churchmen. They constituted a group which foreshadowed the thought and the attitude of the eighteenth century. Reacting sharply against the fierce dogmatism of the seventeenth century they detested emotion and fanaticism in religion, advocated wide toleration, and emphasized on every occasion the rule of reason. They laid great stress upon conventional morality but tended more and more to neglect what was characteristic or difficult in the Christian religion. The High Churchmen dwelt upon the sacraments as indispensable means of grace and stood fast for episcopacy as ordained by Christ and perpetuated by the apostolic succession. They hated the Toleration Act and sought to limit its operation.

The Church would not have suffered serious injury from the existence of these almost unavoidable groups if they had been simply *ecclesiastical* parties; but to the grievous hurt of the Church these corresponded identically to the political parties. The Latitudinarians and Low Churchmen were all Whigs and the High Churchmen were all Tories. Since the period covered by the reigns of William and of Anne (1689–1714) was an era of intense party strife and since divisions in the Church coincided almost exactly with divisions in the State, the Church was inevitably involved and begrimed in all political contests; and religion—or what passed for religion—was again and again an issue in Parliamentary struggles. The cleavage was deepened by the fact that William gave the important bishoprics to Latitudinarian Whigs like Tillotson and Burnet, while the large majority of the country clergy were High Church Tories. Thus for a whole generation there was continuous ill-feeling between the episcopate and most of the priests. Nowhere was this more disgracefully obvious than in the meetings of Convocation, in which constant bickering between the two Houses prevented any work of value from being accomplished.

As we pass from the seventeenth century, with its story of action and reaction and of civil and military strife which always colored and often determined the fortunes of the Church, we have need to remember that from the point of view of Anglican development the redeeming feature of the age was the production of theology—chiefly the work of "the Caroline Divines." Under this term we generally cover the theologians who wrote during the two generations between 1625 and 1689—such honored names as Ussher, Bramhall, Sanderson, Hall, and Jeremy Taylor, or, in later decades, Pearson, Bull, Stillingfleet, and the Cambridge Platonists. While others were fighting about Anglicanism these wise thinkers were interpreting it. Both by their agreement in essentials and their interesting variety in nonessentials they enriched the thought of the English Church. If more of those who refer to them would read them, modern theology would benefit.

"The religious life of England in the reigns of William III and Anne was better than its ecclesiastical history. It did not produce a single martyr, nor a saint, nor a devotional classic; but it was fruitful in all those charitable and humane activities which are the religious aspect of English practical sense. The forces which were bringing into being the great humanitarian movement of the eighteenth century were deeper and wider than the disputes of sects, as wide as the desire for reasonableness which was appeasing the wranglings about creeds." [4] That the devotional life was not

[4] G. N. Clark, *The Later Stuarts,* 151.

being neglected at the turn of the century is proved by the rise and development of the "religious societies," groups of young Churchmen organized to deepen the devotional life and to promote public worship, especially the celebration of the Holy Communion. By the year 1710 there were forty-two of these societies in London and many others in the larger towns. The earnest zeal of their members was expressed not only in worship but in works of charity. To them, for example, more than to any other groups we may attribute the founding of over one hundred Charity Schools for the education of poor children.

Still flourishing are the two greatest tributes to the vitality of religion in that era—the Society for Promoting Christian Knowledge, founded in 1698, and the Society for the Propagation of the Gospel in Foreign Parts, founded in 1701. The former was organized to support three causes then almost wholly neglected by the Church—religious education in elementary schools, the circulation of good literature at low prices, and the provision of libraries for the clergy, especially in the colonies. "The S.P.G." as the later Society is universally known, was established to assist the work of the Church in the colonies both among Englishmen and among natives. How richly the Church in America benefited from its activities we shall soon see.

The eighteenth century was a period when England took a rest from the seventeenth century. Whatever in the earlier age had been admired and pursued—idealism, fierce loyalties, ecclesiastical and political strife pursued to the point of bloodshed, controversy bred of dogmatic theologies—all these became taboo. "Nothing too much" was the cautious motto of several generations which condemned any warmth of feeling as "enthusiasm" and which demanded in all spheres of life conventionality, rationality, and order. During the whole century this temper prevailed. But especially in the reigns of the first two Georges it was accompanied by corruption in politics, immorality at Court, decay in the universities, and spiritual lethargy in the Church.

"The fat slumbers of the eighteenth century" is a mordant phrase which not unfairly describes the somnolent condition of the Church of England. Reason, religion, and good breeding were regarded as very much on a level. No religion that could not be sandwiched between reason and good breeding was acceptable. Such being the general attitude, it is not surprising that worldliness, place-hunting, and a deplorable lack of spiritual earnestness were characteristic of the clergy. Any sign of zeal was frowned upon not only by society and the State but by the bishops. Because Convocation appeared to be capable of nothing but fruitless wrangling, it was suppressed by George I in 1717 and was not revived for 145 years. In consequence the Church had no forum for discussion and no means of consulting about religious affairs or about those moral and social questions which ought to have been raised by the miseries of poverty in the cities and such social evils as the prisons at home and slavery abroad.

During the first half of the century the religious temper of the age and its prevailing interests were displayed in apologetic controversy, especially in the contest between the Deists and their orthodox opponents. The rapid growth of rationalism, the development of science, and the dry coolness of the atmosphere, all tended to overemphasize the intellectual aspect of religion and to reduce it to belief in a series of propositions. This meagre version of religion and the kind of arguments employed in dealing with it were characteristic of both the Deists and the Churchmen. The two groups, in fact, were far more alike than they were aware. The Deists believed in an omnipotent and omniscient Creator who since creation had been practically an absentee God. For them the only dependable religion was "natural religion"—the religion with which nature was supposed to have endowed all men—and so far as the Christian revelation goes beyond this it is not only useless but untrue. "Deism," as Christopher Dawson once wrote, "is nothing but the ghost of religion which haunts the grave of dead faith and lost hope." But the Christianity for which the theologians spoke was not much warmer or more stirring than Deism. The orthodox apologists attempted by appeals to prophecy and miracles to prove the truth of the Christian revelation; but even for them God was not the living God of the New Testament, nor was His Holy Spirit an unpredictable present force in the lives of believers, nor was His Church the the Body of an ever active Christ. In trying to distinguish between the degrees of anaemia represented by the Deists and by their adversaries modern Christianity has little interest.

The most hopeful and fruitful religious movement of the eighteenth century was that which began with the work of John Wesley. To God's use of his genius and power we owe an evangelical revival comparable to the Franciscan in Italy and the Pietist in Germany. In 1729 Wesley was a Fellow of Lincoln College, Oxford, a priest of the Church of England holding High Church views. In that year he became the leader of a small group of dons and undergraduates who were banded together for the development of the devotional life. The strict regularity of their regimen earned them the title of "Methodists." But it was not for another ten years, after a visit to the colony of Georgia and association on the voyage and in London with brethren of the Moravian Church, that Wesley was converted and became an ardent evangelist.

Thenceforward for the next fifty years Wesley was ceaselessly active in preaching to hundreds of thousands throughout England. For the first time within the memory of the living, men and women in vast numbers began to hear of personal religion, to experience religious emotion, and to know the meaning of conversion. Aided by that marvellous preacher George Whitefield, Wesley had launched one of the great revivals of history, which, like other such revivals, was welcomed chiefly by the hard-working poor. But the evangelist was too far-sighted to be content with rousing enthusiasm. Wherever he went he organized local societies and class meetings and planned for the activity of itinerant lay preachers. Thus there gradually grew up in England a widespread organization which ignored not only parish lines but parish priests—a systematic network of which Wesley was in full control. Though to his dying day he combatted every proposal to secede from the Church, the pressure to create a separate church life became too strong to resist. As early as 1760 lay preachers administered the Holy Communion, and Wesleyanism began to approach the status of a nonconformist sect. Soon after Wesley's death in 1791 separation became complete, and Methodism was added to the number of Protestant denominations.

If the Church of England was the poorer for having lost the Puritans in the seventeenth century, it was again the poorer for losing the Methodists in the century which followed. It may well be that Puritanism could not have been assimilated without concessions that would have been fatal to the integrity of Anglicanism. But no such danger from Methodism ever threatened the Church, for no vital difference of doctrine or polity was involved. There may be good reason to believe that once a distinct organization had been formed within the Church ultimate separation became ever more likely; but it was made necessary only by the treatment accorded to Methodists. Thus for the loss of these elements in the life of the Church the blame rests chiefly upon the eighteenth-century bishops. In their eyes the activities of Wesley and his followers were emotional and irregular; and nothing worse could have been said about them. They did not conform to the humdrum pattern of the Church's tame existence. Instead of studying the movement, guiding it, using it, and absorbing it, the bishops simply opposed it; and by their attitude did what they could to make schism inevitable. It is true, no doubt, that Wesley lacked the obedient humility of St. Francis, but he was intensely loyal to the Church. What was chiefly wanting, however, was the wise and discerning Christian statesmanship of an Innocent III.

Yet the warming effect of the Wesleyan revival left deep marks upon the Church. It was maintained long after the secession of the Methodists by the members of the Evangelical party. Toward the close of the eighteenth century and the beginning of the nineteenth, they were "the salt of the Church of England." Their leaders constituted a notable group of men who had been converted and inspired by the Wesleyan movement but, believing that schism was a sin, they had determined to remain within the Established Church—men like John Venn, William Wilberforce, and Charles Simeon. Though individualistic in their religion and unable to contribute anything of value to the theological thought of the time, they won renown by the enthusiasm and efficiency with which they put Christianity into practice. In missionary activity and in social reform they opened a new era.

So condensed a summary of the course of Anglican history during nearly two and a half centuries dealing, as it must needs do, very largely with external facts, may well seem to be chiefly concerned with political conflicts and religious controversy. Two reasons justify this almost inevitable emphasis. In the first place the main facts of history in these critical centuries (as students of the period can testify) are the product of conflict and controversy. In the second place, it is just these very conflicts and controversies which best serve to illuminate the story of the Church of England in the colonies, for which it is the aim of this chapter to prepare.

Yet it would be a serious error to let the record of political and religious strife overshadow the positive achievements of Anglicanism between the accession of Elizabeth and the reign of George III. Through those seven generations a strong religious tradition was in process of slow but steady growth. As George Macaulay Trevelyan puts it, "In 1559 Anglicanism had been hardly so much a religion as an ecclesiastical compromise decreed by a shrewd, learned, and moderate young woman, with the consent of Lords and Commons. But at the end of her reign it had become a real religion; its services were dear to many, after more than forty years of use in the ancient churches of the land; and its philosophy and spirit were being nobly set forth in Hooker's 'Ecclesiastical Polity.' George Herbert (1593–1633) is the poet of an Anglican religion that is something better than a convenience of State." [5] And after the Queen's death, in spite of the discord and distress that marked a century full of contrasts, there continued beneath the surface the same evolution. It was the evolution of a form of Catholic Christianity which ceased to be national in the strict sense of embracing all the people of England, but which remained national in the deeper sense of reflecting in its sobriety, its restraint, its dignity and beauty of ritual, and its capacity for ample development without the change of ancient forms, certain of the lasting mental and moral traits of the English people.[6]

[5] G. M. Trevelyan, *English Social History,* 181.

[6] A Table of Dates in English Church History from 1558 to 1799 will be found on p. 382.

Chapter II

THE CHURCH OF ENGLAND IN THE THIRTEEN COLONIES, 1607–1775

THE majority of those who emigrated to the American colonies in the seventeenth century were not members of the Church of England. They were either Nonconformists from Great Britain or Protestants from continental Europe. Only in Virginia and Maryland was the Church of England fully and effectively established. Elsewhere, in the midst of communities more or less substantially Nonconformist and usually anti-Anglican, the Church in America had to be liberally assisted by the Church in the mother country, chiefly through the Society for the Propagation of the Gospel.

To put it in a sentence, the story of the Church of England in the thirteen colonies before 1776 is the story of what happens to an episcopal Church when it tries to live and thrive without a bishop. The record on the whole is not a happy one.

A. COLONIES WHERE THE CHURCH WAS OFFICIALLY ESTABLISHED

1. *Virginia*

The Church of England took root in America with the founding of the first permanent colony in Virginia. It was in 1606 that King James I gave charters to two companies to plant colonies in the New World. To the London Company was granted the exclusive right to settle in the region between 34° and 38° of north latitude. This area between the present Wilmington, North Carolina, and Charlottesville, Virginia, was part of the wide territory already named Virginia by Queen Elizabeth in honor of herself. The company was to be governed by a Council of thirteen members in England, which was to appoint a similar Council to manage affairs in America. Unlike the colonies of other countries before and since, the emigrants to Virginia were to enjoy all the liberties and privileges of Englishmen in the homeland. Part of this heritage, of course, was the Established Church.

On December 20, 1606, three ships, bearing about one hundred passengers, sailed from the Thames. Since they voyaged by way of the Canary Islands and the West Indies, it was not until May 6, 1607, that the storm-worn vessels reached Chesapeake Bay. A week later the weary colonists disembarked on the north bank of the river which they named the James, about thirty-two miles from its mouth; and there they began to build their first settlement, James Fort or Jamestown.

The main aims of this expedition were to get rich quick by finding gold and silver and to discover the northwest passage to the Orient. To that extent its members were not true colonists who sought to build homes and to earn their living. But the declaration of a pious purpose was not wanting in the instructions supplied by the governing Council, in which it was provided that "the Word and service of God be preached, planted, and used, not only in the said Colonies, but also, as much as might be, among the savages bordering among them, according to the rites and doctrines of the Church of England." As an earnest of the purpose of King and Council that religion should be an integral part of the life of the settlement, the emigrants were accompanied by a chaplain, the Rev. Robert Hunt, whom his fellow-colonist Captain John Smith called "an honest, religious, and courageous divine."

Six weeks after landing Chaplain Hunt celebrated the Holy Communion in a setting which still remains real for us through the picture drawn by John Smith in after years. "We did hang an awning," he wrote, "(which is an old sail) to three or four trees, till we cut planks, our pulpit a bar of wood nailed to two neighboring trees. This was our church till we built a homely thing like a barn, set upon crotchets covered with rafts, sedge, and earth. . . . Yet we had daily Common Prayer morning and evening, every Sunday two sermons, and every three months the Holy Communion."

Bitter hardships and suffering were the lot of these earliest Virginians. In the first three years of the colony more than nine hundred emigrants had landed; but by the summer of 1610 only one hundred and fifty were still alive. A few had been murdered by Indians, but most of them had died of fever and starvation. By that time there was a second charter in operation which provided for the formation of the Virginia Company, a corporation independent of the King and empowered to send out its own governors. Shiploads of reinforcements brought settlers of varied types representing all classes; private ownership of land was agreed to by the

Company; the growth of tobacco began to be profitable; and by 1614 the permanence of the colony was assured.

The year 1619 became famous for two events, each big with consequences for the remote future. A Dutch ship landed the first Negro slaves, and there was held at Jamestown a general assembly of elected burgesses, the first popular legislative body in America. Among other enactments the burgesses passed laws confirming the authority of the Church of England and providing that everyone should attend divine service twice on Sundays. Ministers were to be furnished with a "glebe," or tract of farm land, of one hundred acres, together with a fixed salary generally paid in tobacco. At this time, however, there were only three priests and two deacons in the colony so that the need for more clergy was urged upon the Bishop of London.

Five years later, when Virginia had a population of more than twelve hundred, scattered in nineteen settlements, the Assembly passed new laws concerned with Church affairs. Once again uniformity was decreed, and provision was made for building churches. That the clergy were not always models for their parishioners is suggested by a further ordinance that disparagement of a minister should be a punishable offence. And just why they might be disparaged is explained by a law passed seven years later forbidding parsons to give themselves to excessive drinking or riot or to spend their time idly day or night, playing at dice or cards.

In June, 1624, King James procured the annulment of the charter of the Virginia Company, and thenceforward, until the Revolution of 1776, Virginia was a royal province governed by officials appointed by the King. The House of Burgesses, however, remained a part of the constitution, and a royal governor with a popular assembly became the standard American pattern. During the next ten years of comparative prosperity and contentment the population increased to five thousand.

Except for a five-year interval during the Protectorate, Virginia was governed for thirty years by Sir William Berkeley, who was sent out in 1641 with instructions to see that the Church was firmly maintained and no innovations permitted. Since he agreed with Charles and Laud in all their policies, he was a natural champion of the established order. Soon after his arrival the House of Burgesses passed an act organizing the Church with vestries, much as parishes were then organized in England. Ministers who could certify that they were episcopally ordained and had pledged themselves to conformity were nominated by the vestries and inducted by the governor. Tithes were collected by law, and no one was allowed to vote unless he was a member of the Church of England. In short, Nonconformity did not prosper in Virginia; and even as late as 1645 there were probably not more than two hundred Dissenters out of a population of nearly fifteen thousand. Quakers especially were given a rough reception, and a small group of Puritans from Massachusetts reported in 1648 that Governor Berkeley had banished two of their leaders.

Though strongly royalist in its sympathies, the province had to submit to the control of Parliament after the execution of Charles; but distance made Puritan decrees too difficult to enforce, and there was no attempt, as in England, to prohibit Anglican worship. For eleven years, however, during the Commonwealth and Protectorate, the Church at home could give no aid to Virginia, and religious life in the colony deteriorated. When the Restoration came in 1660 there were not more than ten ministers left to serve the fifty parishes, and means for their support were almost everywhere lacking. But with the return to power of Governor Berkeley the Assembly took steps to carry out the instructions he had received "for building and due furnishing of churches, for the canonical performance of the liturgy, for the ministration of God's word, for a due observance of the Sunday, for the baptism and Christian education of the young."

Yet the masterful governor was not content with the effect of his influence, for when he reported to the government in England in 1671 (when Virginia had a population of 38,000 whites and 2,000 Negro slaves) he had this to say of religion:—"There are forty-eight parishes, and the ministers well paid. The clergy by my consent would be better if they would pray oftener and preach less. But of all other commodities, so of this, the worst are sent us." "But," he adds, "I thank God there are no free schools nor printing, and I hope we shall not have [them] these hundred years." Berkeley may have had no high opinion of the local clergy, but at this time they were superior to their successors in the eighteenth century. Throughout the whole colonial period, however, their average quality was low and their morale poor, for most of them were viewed with scant respect by the laymen who really controlled them. Only the right kind of bishop could have upheld their standards and espoused their cause.

With the accession to the throne of William and Mary in 1688 and the passage of the Toleration Act in the following year, the Church in Virginia felt no marked change, save for a new leniency toward Dissenters and the arrival of a "commissary." From the earliest days of the colony the Bishop of London had been regarded as having a somewhat vague responsibility for the welfare of the Church in America, perhaps because John King, then Bishop of London, was a member of the first Council of the Virginia Company. He and his successors had been accustomed to license candidates for the colonial ministry; but not until 1675, when Henry Compton became Bishop of London, did the government instruct the colonial governors that such certificates were necessary. Compton, who regarded his overseas duties seriously, took the further step of sending "commissaries" to America, the first of whom was James Blair, appointed to serve in Virginia.

A commissary was the agent or deputy of the bishop, with power to perform all episcopal functions except Confirmation and Ordination. In other words, he was theoretically authorized to make visitations, call conventions, suspend clergymen, and otherwise exercise discipline. Partly in defence of his own rights and partly on behalf of the clergy, Blair succeeded, during more than fifty years, in quarrelling with a series of governors, few of whom were his match. But, though he was a stubborn and strong-minded Scot, he could exercise no jurisdiction that was really coercive; and to warn and to scold proved to be all that most commissaries could accomplish. One achievement, however, of lasting value to State and Church, may be credited to Blair—the founding of William and Mary College, of which he became the first president.

The low estate of the Church in Virginia in 1724 may be estimated from two valuable documents—the replies to a set of questions sent out by Bishop Gibson of London and the terms of a "Proposition" submitted to the Assembly by a group of earnest clergy and laity. From both sources we learn that many parishes were too small to support a minister and not a few declined to receive one, that they might use their money for other purposes. Nearly all the ministers were ill-paid at irregular intervals, and disputes between pastors and people were scandalously frequent. The vestries usually refused to allow clergymen to be formally inducted and would generally consent only to yearly contracts. Clergy, in fact, were completely at the mercy of vestries, and there was no proper system for maintaining discipline. Since few strong and self-respecting men would accept office, the majority of the priests were of poor quality, and a deplorable minority were given to drink and vice.

In view of these conditions it is not surprising that the Church neglected to provide for the pioneers who were moving westward, and that Dissenters supplied the missionary energy demanded by a moving frontier. In the older portions of the colony, too, Nonconformists made rapid headway in the eighteenth century. Especially Baptists and Scotch-Irish Presbyterians so increased in numbers that, with Quakers and others, the Dissenters in 1776 outnumbered the members of the Established Church. Moreover, as tension between the mother country and the colonies began to grow from 1760 on, the Church which represented the Crown and its authority was certain to suffer in influence and in repute.

2. *Maryland*

Sir George Calvert, who became the first Baron Baltimore, wanted to found a great family estate in America. Although he was a Roman

Catholic, he secured from Charles I the promise of a tract of land roughly corresponding to the modern Maryland, a name then given to it in honor of Charles's Queen, Henrietta Maria. Before the necessary charter had been sealed and the patent issued Calvert died in April, 1632; but two months later the grant was made to his son Cecil Calvert, Lord Baltimore, who was also a Roman Catholic. Because the new colony was really the property of Baltimore, it belonged (like Pennsylvania) to the special class of provinces known as "proprietary." Some clauses of the charter, indeed, appear to give to the owner the most absolute power. By other provisions, however, he is limited. The laws, for example, must not conflict with those of England, and they must receive the consent of the freemen of the province.

In November, 1633, two small vessels, carrying about twenty gentlemen and two hundred laboring men, sailed from the Thames. More than half the emigrants were Protestants; but for the benefit of the Roman Catholics, three Jesuit priests were taken aboard at the Isle of Wight. At the end of March this little company made their first settlement at St. Mary's on the St. George River. The religious situation in the infant colony was peculiar. Though the owner of Maryland was a Roman Catholic, his charter gave him the right to appoint clergy in all churches. Yet these churches, it is clear, were supposed to be organized according to the ecclesiastical laws of England, and when the patent refers to "the Church" it means the Church of England. Theoretically, then, the status of Roman Catholics ought to have been the same as in England, and on paper at least they were still subject to the Act of Uniformity. Baltimore's primary aim, however, was to found a colony where his persecuted fellow-Catholics might find a secure refuge. As a consequence, there were Jesuit priests to minister to those of their own faith, but no Anglican clergy to serve the still larger number of Protestants.

Lord Baltimore, a man of tact and wisdom, was fully aware of all the factors involved. With his brother Leonard, who was to represent him as Governor, he sent explicit instructions that Roman Catholic services were to be conducted with as much privacy as possible in order to avoid offending the Protestants. For some time, however, the Jesuits acted as if their church law had superseded Parliamentary law, and it was not for seven or eight years that he succeeded in reducing their mission to proper subordination. The proprietor realized that only general toleration and religious freedom could serve his cause; for if Catholic persecution of Protestants were to be the only alternative to Protestant persecution of Catholics, his charter would soon be revoked and his enterprise suffer ruin.

The matured religious policy of Maryland was clearly formulated in the years 1648 and 1649 when Lord Baltimore appointed a Protestant Governor and a law was passed to the effect that no person believing in Jesus Christ should be molested in the exercise of his religion or compelled to any other than his own belief. But the death penalty awaited any who denied the Trinity or the divinity of Christ. As an interesting illustration of the rich religious diversity then prevalent in the province and an indication of how the different varieties of Christians had gradually got on each other's nerves we read a further clause in this legislation which provides a penalty of a fine and whipping and imprisonment for anyone who should call another "an heretic, schismatic, idolater, Puritan, Independent, Presbyterian, popish priest, Jesuit, Jesuited Papist, Lutheran, Calvinist, Anabaptist, Brownist, Antinomian, Barrowist, Roundhead, Separatist, or any other name or term in a reproachful manner relating to matter of religion." Mutual mud-slinging was so characteristic of seventeenth-century English religion that it naturally reappeared in Maryland. Toleration may have been legally achieved, but tolerance seems not to have been one of the social virtues.

Though unaccompanied by any minister of their own, the Anglicans in the community built a chapel, and the more earnest among them maintained services there with the aid of a lay reader. Not until sixteen years after the founding of the colony do we hear of a resident clergyman of the Church of England—the Rev. William Wilkinson, who arrived in 1650. He received such meagre support, however, that he had to make his living by trade. Even twenty-five years later there were only three Anglican priests in Maryland. One of these, the Rev. John Yeo, wrote to the Archbishop of Canterbury in May, 1676, to report that "the province of Maryland is in a deplorable condition for want of an established ministry. Here are ten or twelve counties, and in them at least 20,000 souls and but three Protestant ministers of the Church of England. The priests [i.e. Roman Catholics] are provided for . . . but no care is taken to build up churches in the Protestant religion. The Lord's day is profaned; religion is despised; and all notorious vices are committed." But so little attention was paid to this plea for help that, though new clergy were sent out at intervals, the total remaining in 1689 was still only four.

By that time a revolution had taken place in Maryland. The great Protestant majority had long been ill-content with the toleration of Roman Catholics and with the rule of a Romanist proprietor. When news came in 1689 of the accession of William and Mary the Protestants in the colony seized the reins of government and addressed to the new King a petition to end the proprietary regime. Two years later William agreed, and Maryland became a royal province. It remained in that class for twenty-four years, until in 1715 it was returned to the Calvert family, whose representative was then a Protestant. One of the earliest results of the new status of the colony was an act of the Assembly providing for the establishment of the Church of England, the division of the province into parishes, the organization of vestries, and taxes in the form of tobacco for the support of clergy. These provisions began to be enforced with the coming of Sir Francis Nicholson as Governor in 1694. A high-tempered and zealous supporter of the Establishment, he set himself to the building of churches and to finding clergy for the newly founded parishes.

In answer to a petition from the Governor and Assembly, the Bishop of London in 1696 agreed to send out to Maryland as his commissary the Rev. Thomas Bray. During the four years which elapsed before he arrived in his new field Bray was eagerly active not only in recruiting clergy for the province and raising money to establish libraries for them, but in founding in 1698 the Society for Promoting Christian Knowledge, which serves today the Anglican Communion throughout the world. Soon after landing in Maryland in March, 1700, Bray attended a meeting of the Assembly. He probably shares responsibility for an act which they then passed making attendance on Anglican worship compulsory for every member of the colony. In the hope that he might secure the approval of this intolerant legislation by Parliament, Bray sailed for England after only two months and a half in America. Yet he had been responsible for increasing the number of ministers to seventeen, and he had held an effective visitation. But his real claim to fame is not the impulse he gave to a stronger church life in Maryland but his leadership in founding soon after his return to England the Society for the Propagation of the Gospel in Foreign Parts, from which the colonial Church was to draw rich benefits.

Parliament rightly rejected the legislation from Maryland so far as it conflicted with the Toleration Act enforced in England; but the three thousand Roman Catholics were still subject to harsh restraints; and the Church of England was to remain the Established Church of the province. Yet not until 1716, after a period of discouraging disorder, did another commissary appear. In that year two commissaries were appointed—both of them citizens of Maryland, one to serve the Eastern and the other the Western Shore. The activity of these deputies was sometimes mild and sometimes zealously intrusive, but whatever their methods, they remained in the long run largely impotent. Most of the clergy refused to acknowledge their jurisdiction, and they had no power to remove ministers who had been duly licensed by the Bishop of London and inducted by the Governor. No discipline, therefore, could be maintained. As the Rev. Hugh Jones reported to Bishop Gibson in 1741, "Enthusiasm, Deism, and Libertism (with all which we abound) make no small advantage"; and things were little better in 1764 when the Rev. Thomas B. Chandler wrote the Bishop of London that though some of the Maryland clergy were exemplary, "their number seems to be very small in comparison, they appearing here and there, like lights shining in a dark place."

It is well to remember, nevertheless, that the evil of any time or place is likely to be more easily recorded and remembered than the good. Whatever form the headlines of any era may take, they do not often celebrate the praises of inconspicuous piety. Though eighteenth-century Christianity was no more vigorous in Maryland and Virginia than in England, there were devoted pastors in these provinces, living on wretched salaries paid in tobacco, riding twenty and thirty miles on Sunday to celebrate the Holy Communion and to catechize the children, visiting the sick and aged, and sometimes preaching every day during one week of the month in order to reach the more distant Church members. In any decade of the century what Governor Calvert wrote in 1724 was probably true—that the majority of ministers "behaved themselves very well as good clergymen and good subjects."

Yet compared with other Protestant bodies in Maryland the Established Church was plainly wanting in vitality and expansive power. More vigorous were the spirit and the program of dissenting bodies like the Presbyterians. Though these Nonconformists were not as numerous and aggressive as in Virginia, they were steadily increasing in numbers and influence as the time for the Revolution drew near, and as hostility to Britain magnified the dislike and suspicion with which the Church of England was regarded.

3. *South Carolina*

In 1663 Charles II granted an extensive territory south of Virginia to the Earl of Clarendon and seven other favorites. Two years later a second charter set the limits of the new colony as the present northern boundary of North Carolina and a line running almost through the present Orlando, Florida. The proprietors were authorized to legislate for the province with the consent of the freemen, and they were empowered to grant religious freedom to Dissenters. In 1669 a "Fundamental Constitution" was adopted by the Proprietary Board. Composed in rather academic fashion by the philosopher John Locke and Lord Ashley Cooper, it was too elaborate and impractical ever to be enforced in detail; but it provided for the establishment of the Church of England and the support of its ministry, with liberal treatment for Nonconformists. In the following year the first permanent settlement was made at Albemarle Point near Charleston; but within another two years Charleston itself became the centre of the community and soon the seat of government. With every year the numbers of the colony were increased not only by immigrants direct from England but also by new arrivals from the Barbadoes, by Scotch-Irish, and after 1685 by many Huguenots from France.

Though the application to the King for a charter alleged among other motives "a zest for the propagation of the Christian faith," the Proprietors neglected for a generation to take any steps toward establishing the Church. Dissenters in the colony were at least equal in numbers to members of the Church, and religious variety was too great to encourage general taxation for the benefit of an establishment. But Churchmen were in control of the Assembly, and in 1698 they succeeded in passing an act for the maintenance of an Anglican minister in Charleston. Six years later, encouraged by a High Church Jacobite governor, the Assembly enacted much more radical and disturbing legislation, providing that no Dissenter should be a member of the Commons House of Assembly; that a commission of laymen should sit in judgment on ministers and remove them when they saw fit; and that the colony should be divided into parishes, and churches built and ministers employed at the public charge. To the first two of these provisions opposition was so vigorous that representatives were sent to London to urge their annulment. In consequence of these protests the Whig House of Lords advised their repeal; the Proprietors consented; and in 1706 the legislature in Carolina rescinded the measure and passed a new and better law.

The Act of 1706—the permanent basis of Church life for the next seventy years—omitted the objectionable features of its predecessor but retained those providing for public support of the Church, the building of churches, and the calling of ministers. Dissenters still remained free to worship as they desired. When the act went into force there were only three Anglican priests in South Carolina, including one missionary of the Society for the Propagation of the Gospel. During the following year, however, the Society sent out two more men, and the Bishop of London despatched the first commissary to South Carolina, the Rev. Gideon Johnston, who served as rector of St. Philip's, Charleston. Though he came to have a low opinion of the colonists in general, whom he described as devoid of honesty and religion, he had good words to say for the clergy. "There is not a better set of clergymen," he reported, "in all America than what is to be met with in this place." For the worthy quality of ministers then and thereafter the relatively high standards of the S.P.G. were responsible. Their representatives, however, were almost never successful in carrying out one of the declared aims of the Society—the conversion of Indians and slaves. Only one man, the Rev. Francis Le Jau, achieved notable success in the instruction and Christianization of Negroes. But there could be no general progress in work on their behalf in the face of opposition from the planters. By the middle of the eighteenth century the

Negroes in South Carolina outnumbered the whites two to one; but of course the greater their number the more suspicious were their masters of any plans for their enlightenment.

In 1719 a bloodless rebellion overthrew the existing regime. The government in England accepted the results of this popular revolt and proceeded to administer South Carolina as a royal province. Sir Francis Nicholson was appointed provisional governor and equipped with instructions to maintain the worship of the Church of England, to keep the churches in repair, and to provide for the support of the clergy. By 1723 there were thirteen parishes in the colony, nearly all with substantial churches and parsonages. Most of the clergy were missionaries chosen and partly paid by the S.P.G. An added source of strength to the Church was the appointment in 1726 of the Rev. Alexander Garden, rector of St. Philip's Church, Charleston, as commissary, an office which he filled with high distinction for the next twenty-two years. Partly because of the quality of clergy and commissary and partly because the laity were more active supporters of the Church than in the other southern colonies, the Church in South Carolina probably deserved the words of praise with which John Wesley described it when he attended an annual Visitation at Charleston in 1737. "Such a conversation on Christian righteousness," he wrote in his journal, "as I have not heard at any Visitation, or hardly on any other occasion." After another twenty years, however, when the Assembly had relieved the S.P.G. of responsibility for the support of the clergy, a gradual deterioration in their character and standards began to be felt, and during its remaining years the colonial Church was less effective. Though they had been reinforced by the accession of large numbers of French Huguenots, the Episcopalians constituted less than half the population. In contrast with the Presbyterians and other Nonconformists, moreover, the Church continued to neglect the frontier. Indeed, only one man is known to have ministered in that uninviting area, and he was a layman.

4. *North Carolina*

Though theoretically North Carolina and South Carolina were for half a century parts of a single province, the settlements were so far apart that the two governments were always separate. Until 1691 each area had its own governor; for the next twenty-two years a deputy of the governor at Charleston served in the north; and thereafter there were again two governors. After 1713, in fact, we may rightly speak of North Carolina and South Carolina as two distinct colonies, though not for another sixteen years did the former come under royal rule. In the northern province the population was very much more scattered than in the southern, slaves were far less numerous, and relations with the other colonies were closer.

There were fewer settled communities and less of the comforts of civilization in the northern territory; and Dissenters, especially Quakers, were aggressively active at an early date. For both these reasons the Church was slow in gaining a foothold; not more than one Anglican priest served there in the seventeenth century; nor before the Revolution were there ever as many as twenty. During the first two decades of the eighteenth century, however, a few S.P.G. men were sent out at intervals, though none remained long. One who had the persistence to work for three years wrote of "the world of trouble and misery" he had suffered in "so disorderly and barbarous a place." The contrast between the smooth and somnolent clerical life in England and rough pioneering in America was too painful for most of these missionaries. Though one of them took to drink and stayed, nearly all the others returned to the old country. By 1730 there was not a single Church of England minister in the colony, and even eleven years later there were only two. But soon thereafter we can credit the Church with the admirable career of the Rev. Clement Hall, who worked for fifteen years on a salary of £30 a year. In 1752 he reported that after eight years he had travelled 14,000 miles, preached 675 sermons, and baptized 5,783 white children and 243 black. He may not have been typical, but he was probably not the only one of his kind.

The Assembly of North Carolina was slow in passing acts to implement effectively the Anglican establishment, which long existed only in theory. In 1755 and 1760 such legislation was enacted; but chiefly because it gave too much power to vestries and ignored the rights of the Bishop of London, it was annulled by the Crown. Soon after the famous Governor Tryon assumed office in 1764 a more acceptable law was passed with his assistance and later approved by the King. The right of presentation was given to the governor, and the salaries of the clergy were raised. Aided by these provisions, Tryon's effective interest in the Church resulted in increasing the number of ministers from five to eighteen. The Episcopalians, however, remained a minority group; for the Dissenters had always outnumbered them, and there were now added to the numerous Baptists and Quakers a growing body of Methodists, and in the western part of the colony Presbyterians and Lutherans.

5. *Georgia*

In June, 1732, General James Edward Oglethorpe and several other noted philanthropists obtained from George II a charter granting them land between the Savannah and Altamaha rivers for a colony to be known as Georgia. The chief aim of the founder and his associates was to establish a refuge for imprisoned debtors, whom English laws condemned to filthy jails. Life in this youngest of the thirteen colonies began with the arrival of Oglethorpe and 130 chosen emigrants at Savannah in February, 1733.

Though religious freedom was to be offered to all Christians except Roman Catholics, the Proprietors were Churchmen, and it was expected that the Church of England would be established. The leaders of the colony had brought with them not only prayer books and a set of Communion vessels presented by John Wesley's father, but also an Anglican chaplain. The latter, however, remained for only three months, and his successor, Samuel Quincy, for less than three years. But before Quincy, complaining of much "hard usage," left for England, there had arrived in Georgia, as a missionary of the S.P.G., the already famous John Wesley. He was then only thirty-two years old, and so far from being an evangelical Nonconformist, was so rigid a High Churchman that his overzealous ministrations and exacting discipline came to an end after a year and nine months. Upon his departure there appeared another leader who was later to win equal fame as a Methodist preacher—George Whitefield. Already a deacon, he returned to England at once to be ordained priest, and began in 1740 a brief term of service as rector of Christ Church, Savannah. His chief contribution to the Church in Georgia, however, was the founding of the orphanage which became Bethesda College. Settled parochial work was not for him, and after 1742 he gave himself to those evangelistic tours which produced so magical an effect throughout the colonies and in England.

After eighteen years of struggle the colony proved so plainly unsuccessful that the Proprietors surrendered their rights to the Crown, and Georgia became a royal province. Even as late as 1760 there were only five or six thousand white settlers, whom one minister reported as having "very little more knowledge of a Saviour than the aboriginal natives." By that time, however, the Assembly had divided the colony into eight parishes, and had appropriated money for the support of clergy, whose maintenance was in several cases supplemented by grants from the S.P.G. Yet in 1769 there were still only two Episcopal churches in Georgia—at Savannah and Augusta.

B. COLONIES WHERE THE CHURCH WAS NOT OFFICIALLY ESTABLISHED

1. *Massachusetts*

For two generations Massachusetts consisted of two separate colonies from both of which the Church of England was debarred—the Plymouth Colony and the Massachusetts Bay Colony.

The Pilgrims who sailed on the *Mayflower* and landed at Plymouth in December, 1620, were Separatists—Puritans so extreme in their views that they counted the Church of England too far gone in sin and error to commune with. As followers of Browne, Barrowe, and other radical reformers, they believed that only the Congregational form of government was true to Scripture; and the famous Mayflower Compact, signed on the soil of the New World, was really a Separatist church covenant. Fifty years later this colony consisted of fifty towns and 8,000 people, but nowhere was there any trace of Episcopalians or of Episcopal influence.

In March, 1628, the Massachusetts Bay Company was formed by a patent given in England by the Council for New England to John Endicott and five others, granting them land between the Charles River and the Merrimac River. Though originally designed as a commercial venture, the enterprise soon led to a great emigration sustained by a motive primarily religious. The founders and most of their followers were conservative Puritans, who had a reverent regard for the Church of England as their mother and who did not wish to separate from her. They were, however, Nonconformists, for many Anglican practices were repugnant to them and seemed in their eyes to call for further reform. Antagonized and sometimes persecuted by Laud and other bishops, they sought in America, as the historian Channing puts it, "to establish a Bible Commonwealth in which they should play the principal parts and bend others to their will."

Beginning at Salem under Endicott in 1628, the influx of Puritans rapidly increased in numbers. In June, 1630, there arrived eleven ships under Governor John Winthrop, who bore with him the charter of the new Company and established its authority at Boston. Three years later the strong tide of immigration set in, dating (not wholly by accident) from the elevation of Laud to the Archbishopric of Canterbury. At the end of the next decade the population of the Bay Colony was over 16,000, outnumbering all the rest of British America put together. Thanks to the opponents of Charles and Laud in the mother country the liberties of the people were preserved, and "Massachusetts came to be an aristocratic republic substantially independent of England."

Though in origin and convictions the Plymouth and Boston groups were different, it was not long before their church organization and practices were assimilated. The Puritans who landed in Massachusetts Bay, despite their earlier protestations of Anglican loyalty, promptly formed a church on the Congregational model. Winthrop declared that "no church [i.e. local congregation] can have power over another church," and Boston soon became as intolerant as Plymouth of any signs of "prelacy" or any use of the Prayer Book. The franchise was restricted to the members of

Congregational Churches, and "Dissenters" who were obstinately devoted to the usages of the Church of England were shipped home or voluntarily departed. Religious toleration was thus accounted as sinful as it was in England. In the year 1664, when Charles II sent over a commission to order affairs in New England, its members failed to obtain in Massachusetts any toleration for the use of the Prayer Book, and all similar efforts during the next twenty-seven years were equally unsuccessful. In 1679 there was not one Episcopal clergyman in all New England. Having deliberately identified itself not only with royal absolutism but with unrelenting hostility to every variety of Puritanism, the Church of England was now paying the price in America.

Aiming to maintain a firmer discipline in his overseas dominions, Charles II in 1684 had the charter of the Massachusetts Bay Company vacated and proceeded to form plans for making the colony a royal province. These arrangements, however, were not completed until after James II had succeeded his brother in February, 1685. On May 14, 1686, Joseph Dudley, the newly appointed "President of New England" sailed into Boston harbor on the frigate *Rose,* accompanied by the Rev. Robert Ratcliffe, an Anglican clergyman. Ratcliffe symbolized the fact that the King proposed to rule the province and that the King (although a Roman Catholic) was Supreme Governor of the Church of England. But the doors of every church in town were closed to this unwelcome stranger, and he could conduct services only in a room in the Town House. Even after the arrival in December of the Governor, Sir Edmund Andros, Puritan opposition continued to be unyielding, and the little Episcopalian minority could do no better than force an agreement to worship in the South Meeting-House when its congregation was not using it. But a parish was organized with wardens and with Ratcliffe as rector, and within three years its members had built for their use the first King's Chapel. The attitude of the local clergy is expressed in a pamphlet written by their dominant leader Increase Mather and entitled, "The Unlawfulness of the Common Prayer Worship." After referring with contempt to "those broken responds and shreds of prayer which the priests and people toss between them like tennis balls," he affirms that Anglican worship is both papacy and idolatry.

At the end of March, 1689, the people rejoiced at the news that James was King no longer and that William and Mary had ascended the throne. Unable to resist an uprising in Boston, Andros was imprisoned and later sent back to England. The change of rulers in the home-land, however, brought few advantages to the province and none to the opponents of the Church of England. The new charter, set forth in 1691, destroyed for the time being that connection between Church and State which had been characteristic of Massachusetts for more than sixty years. The franchise was now granted on the basis of property regardless of religion, and of course the royal governors were nearly all members of the national Establishment, prepared to support its interests. Even the Plymouth Colony could no longer remain exclusive, for at this time it was annexed to Massachusetts.

The entry of the Church into Massachusetts was thus due to the King's authority, exercised through the royal governor. Just as in England, the Church was to be associated with the power and prerogative of the Crown. But though its status was guaranteed by these means, it was chiefly indebted for support and nourishment to the Society for the Propagation of the Gospel, which was organized in London in 1701. For these reasons the story of the Anglican Church in colonial Massachusetts is almost entirely confined to the first three-quarters of the eighteenth century.

One of the first important acts of the new Society was to send to America two emissaries, the Rev. George Keith and the Rev. Patrick Gordon, for the purpose of making a tour of inspection. At that time there were probably only six Anglican clergymen in all the colonies outside of Virginia and Maryland. Soon after their arrival at Boston in 1702 Gordon died, but his place was taken by the Rev. John Talbot, chaplain of the ship on which they had sailed. For the next two years Keith and Talbot were engaged in energetic travel from Maine to North Carolina; and from the time when Keith returned to England and reported, the S.P.G. played an active and generous part in sustaining the Church in America until the outbreak of the Revolution. Its contribution was particularly large in colonies where the Church was not established. Massachusetts and Connecticut, in fact, owed to the S.P.G. the financial support of most of the Episcopal clergy, for whose relatively high quality the standards and the discipline of the Society were in large measure responsible. Partly through such aid from England and partly through local efforts the Church made gradual progress during the next half century, so that by 1748 there were three churches in Boston and nine in neighboring towns.

2. *New Hampshire*

The colony of New Hampshire originated in a grant made in March, 1622, by the Council for New England to Captain John Mason. Some of its early settlers came from England and others from Massachusetts. In September, 1679, it was constituted a separate province, though during most of the years before 1741 New Hampshire and Massachusetts had the same governor. Religion in this area was so dominated by the Puritans of the Bay Colony that the only Anglican minister to serve there in the seventeenth century was soon suppressed and obliged to return to England. The church founded at Portsmouth in 1640 was revived in 1734, and later another was organized at Claremont. But in these parishes or as itinerant missionaries only five clergy were at work in the colony during the forty or more years before the Revolution.[1]

3. *Rhode Island*

Roger Williams, a Separatist minister of extreme views, proved so objectionable to the rulers of Massachusetts that in 1636 he was forced to leave the colony. Seeking an opportunity for greater freedom, he established a small settlement at Providence. Shortly afterward Anne Hutchinson, accused of heresy, was banished from Massachusetts, and she and her followers migrated to Rhode Island, where they founded the towns of Portsmouth and Newport. In 1643 Roger Williams obtained from the Commissioners of the Long Parliament a patent of incorporation on the basis of which the people of "Rhode Island and Providence Plantations" proceeded to organize; and twenty years later a royal charter from Charles II securely established the colony. As might have been expected from its origins, Rhode Island was hospitable to heretics, and, with the exception of Roman Catholics, welcomed all kinds of Christians. Abjuring any connection between Church and State, the government made no attempt to regulate the religious lives of the citizens. From the point of view of the orthodox communities of Massachusetts and Connecticut the new colony was a religious dump, composed, it was said, of "the Lord's débris." A scornful jester, indeed, once remarked that "if a man had lost his religion, he would be sure to find it in some Rhode Island village." But from this laissez-faire individualism the Church of England could profit, for among the varieties of religion to be tolerated was Anglicanism.

As early as 1702 Trinity Church in Newport was organized, and in 1704 the S.P.G. sent to the parish the Rev. James Honeyman, who served as rector for forty-five years with notable devotion and success. At Bristol the ministry of John Usher, a convert from Harvard College, was even longer. Other churches were founded at Providence, Warwick, and Narragansett—all with substantial aid from the Society, which is estimated to have expended in Rhode Island as much as £20,000.

4. *Connecticut*

In the same year (1636) that Massachusetts expelled Roger Williams a group of respected and orthodox Puritans left the Bay Colony of their

[1] The frontier region of Maine was not one of the thirteen colonies and did not become a state until 1820. Between 1652 and 1658 it was gradually annexed to Massachusetts. During the seventeenth century only one Church of England clergyman is recorded to have ministered there, and in the eighteenth century before the Revolution hardly more than four.

own accord to found settlements in Connecticut. Headed by the Rev. Thomas Hooker, these first westward pioneers established the towns of Hartford, Windsor, and Wethersfield. Though one of their motives to migrate had been a growing distaste for the rigor of the Massachusetts "aristocracy of righteousness," the constitution which they adopted in 1639 was in substantial agreement with that of Massachusetts on matters of Church and State, and no Anglican would have been tolerated.

A second colony owes its origin to the leadership of the Rev. John Davenport, who had been ejected by Laud from his cure in England. Accompanied by his friend Theophilus Eaton and by the greater part of his congregation, Davenport reached Massachusetts in 1637. In the following year the little group set out for the shores of Long Island Sound, where they began the settlement of New Haven. There they organized a Bible commonwealth or ecclesiastic republic quite as strict as that of the Massachusetts theocracy. Until 1662 neither colony was recognized by the English government, but in that year Charles II granted to Connecticut a charter which included New Haven within its limits.

In 1702 George Keith, the agent of the S.P.G., reported that the thirty-three towns of Connecticut contained a population of thirty thousand, all of whom were Dissenters. Congregationalism being the State Church there was no room for other types of Christianity until in 1708 the Assembly of the colony granted the benefits of the English Toleration Act to various qualified persons, provided they continued to contribute to the support of the regular ministers. Taking advantage of this limited but valued freedom, the Church in Connecticut began its slow growth, founded and supported for the most part by the S.P.G. The process was aided by the fact that more Anglicans appear to have migrated to Connecticut than to Massachusetts. It was a further advantage that since Connecticut never had a royal governor, the advance of the Church was not associated with the exercise of arbitrary power. The first parish was organized at Stratford in 1707, just before toleration became legal; but it was not until 1723 that the Rev. Samuel Johnson became its first settled rector. He was one of those who had been ordained in England that year as a result of the most famous event in the Church history of colonial Connecticut—the incident of "the Yale converts."

Yale College had been founded in 1701 as a perfectly safe alternative to a Harvard already regarded as liberal. Its president in 1722 was the Rev. Timothy Cutler, a Congregational minister; and Daniel Brown was the only other instructor of its thirty-five students, among whom Jonathan Edwards was numbered. To the dismay of the community, and ultimately of all New England, there was presented on September 13, 1722, to the Trustees of Yale College a paper signed by Cutler and Brown and five highly respected Congregational pastors in neighboring towns, one of whom was Samuel Johnson. The document declared that some of them doubted the validity of their orders and others were persuaded of their invalidity and that therefore they were greatly disturbed by the fact that they were not "in visible communion with an Episcopal Church." As Josiah Quincy wrote a century later, "This event shook Congregationalism throughout New England like an earthquake, and filled all its friends with terror and apprehension." Considering that the community and its new college were supposed to be proof against any allurements of heresy and that there was but one little Episcopal parish in the whole colony, this alarm was only natural. Nor did it abate when it became known that four of the signers, including Cutler and Johnson, were soon to depart for England that they might there receive episcopal ordination.

After their return to New England Cutler became rector of Christ Church, Boston, and Johnson remained in charge of the Stratford parish until late in life he was chosen to be the first President of King's College, New York, the future Columbia University. He was the only Yale convert to remain in the colony and the only Church clergyman within its borders for the next four years. At this early period one obstacle to further growth was the legal requirement that members of the Church of England, in addition to supporting their own pastor, must contribute to the maintenance of the local Congregational church. In 1727, however, as the result of a petition of a Churchman at Fairfield, the legislature passed an act permitting the taxes of Churchmen to be applied to their own rector if he were near enough to minister to them. This new privilege, of course, made further progress easier. The second Anglican church in the colony was organized in Fairfield in 1727 and a third at New London three years later. In 1742 there were fourteen churches built and building, though they were served by only seven ministers. At the outbreak of the Revolution, however, these small numbers had increased to forty churches and twenty clergy.

5. *New York*

After the voyage of Henry Hudson in 1609 Dutch fur traders began to frequent the Hudson River, using the island of Manhattan as their centre. In 1621 the States-General (the Dutch Parliament) chartered the West India Company, which was to rule the future colony; and two years later a group of Belgian Protestants, or Walloons, became its first permanent inhabitants. During the next forty years the colonists of New Netherland settled not only at New Amsterdam on Manhattan Island but at Albany, at various points on Long Island, and in Connecticut, New Jersey, and Delaware. The government of the colony was a despotism which admitted no representative government and no religious toleration. The Reformed Church was the only form of Christianity allowed. Even Lutheranism was banned, and Quakers were cruelly persecuted. So slowly did the colony grow and so few were the Dutch immigrants that by 1647 there were not more than two thousand inhabitants, more than half of whom were English.

On March 12, 1664, Charles II granted to his brother James, the Duke of York, the territory lying between the Connecticut and Delaware rivers, and shortly despatched a small naval and military expedition to enforce the grant. Taken by surprise, the Dutch authorities surrendered to its commander; New Netherland became the province of New York, and New Amsterdam the town of New York. Though the Dutch, in the course of war with England, regained their colony for sixteen months during the years 1673 and 1674, it remained thereafter secure in English possession. Following the Dutch tradition and conforming to the natural disposition of James, its proprietor, New York continued to submit to an absolute form of government, until after the accession of William and Mary, when in 1691 a popular assembly was granted to the colonists. Two years later this assembly passed an act for the establishment of religion—a law which was defective in two respects. It applied to less than half the counties in the colony, and it was so worded that the rights of the Church of England over the other Christian bodies were so uncertain as to be frequently a matter of dispute.[2] Successive governors, however, interpreted it to favor the Establishment.

Until 1697 the only Anglican priest in the province was the garrison chaplain, but in that year Trinity Church was founded as the first parish of New York. In later years a royal gift enriched its corporation with a large tract of land which has since brought to the parish both the advantages and the disadvantages of great wealth. During the following century the Chapel of St. George's (1752), now an independent parish, and the Chapel of St. Paul's (1766) became the first of the churches which have looked to Trinity as their mother. At the suggestion of its first rector, the Rev. William Vesey, the Society for the Propagation of the Gospel decided in 1702 to send missionaries to New York. The first of these, the Rev. John Bartow, organized the church at Westchester in the same year, and by the end of 1704 parishes had been founded at Rye, Hempstead, Jamaica, Oyster Bay, and Staten Island. Five years later a representative of the S.P.G. began work at Albany. So continuous was the generous activity of the Society that in the period between 1702 and 1776 it assisted in maintaining in the province, for terms longer or shorter, as

[2] It is for these reasons that New York is here included among those colonies in which the Church of England was not established.

many as fifty-eight missionaries. Partly to the credit of the Church, moreover, we must assign the founding of King's College, chartered in 1754. Most of its trustees were Churchmen, and the acres of land donated to the college by Trinity Church were given with the proviso that the President of the College should always be a communicant of the Church of England and that the services of the Prayer Book should always be used in the chapel.

6. *New Jersey*

In June, 1664, before New Netherland had surrendered to the English forces, James, the Duke of York, assigned to Sir George Carteret and Lord John Berkeley that portion of his new possessions which lay between the Hudson and Delaware rivers. In honor of Carteret, who had been governor of Jersey, this proprietary colony was named New Jersey. The owners proceeded to offer lands to colonists on liberal terms and pledged themselves to provide for a popular assembly and for liberty of conscience and of worship. In 1676 the province was divided into East Jersey (really northeast Jersey), to be owned by Carteret, and West Jersey (really southwest Jersey), to be owned by a group of Quakers, including William Penn. Six years afterward Penn and other Quakers bought East Jersey; but in 1702 the two divisions were united, and though the rights to the soil remained with the proprietors, all rights of jurisdiction were transferred to the Crown. Royal governors were thereafter appointed, between whom and the colonial assembly there were bitter disputes and constant friction.

The northeastern part of New Jersey was settled largely by people from New England and Long Island, with the result that it was dominated by Puritans, to whom were later added many Scotch Presbyterians. Southwestern New Jersey, on the contrary, was controlled almost entirely by Quakers. In neither section, therefore, was the Church of England early represented. No sustained work of the Church was to be found before 1702. In that year George Keith and John Talbot, then at work for the S.P.G., preached at Amboy, Burlington, and other towns; and in 1705 Talbot became rector of St. Mary's Church, Burlington. There he labored for twenty years, serving in addition, by his frequent tours, as an apostle for all New Jersey. Acting, so far as was legal, as a kind of missionary bishop, he was foremost among those who were continuously urging upon the mother Church the need for an American episcopate. In 1705, too, the church at Elizabethtown was founded; and its rector after 1751, the Rev. Thomas B. Chandler, was likewise active in the controversy about appointing bishops for America, a project which he zealously promoted and defended. Though Anglican growth was slower than in several other colonies, by 1770 there were, according to Chandler, "eleven missionaries in the district, none blamable, some eminently useful." And churches had been organized in Salem, Newark, New Brunswick, Shrewsbury, and other towns.

7. *Pennsylvania and Delaware* [3]

William Penn, to whose deceased father, Admiral Sir William Penn, Charles II owed a heavy debt, petitioned the King in 1680 for a tract of land in the New World where he and other Quakers might found a settlement. He was soon granted an immense region west of the Delaware River, which he named Sylvania, but which Charles, in honor of the admiral, called Pennsylvania. Though the new province was to be one of the proprietary type, its charter contained the unusual stipulations that the English Parliament should have the right to tax the colony and that the Church of England should be tolerated. Penn, indeed, gave complete religious freedom to all, including Jews and Roman Catholics, and made provision for a democratic assembly. Philadelphia was shortly established as the capital, and immigrants began to pour into the province in such numbers that during the first half of the eighteenth century the population grew from 20,000 to 200,000. Though Penn himself spent only about four years in America, the colony remained in the hands of his children and grandchildren until the Revolution. Quakers, however, were by no means the only settlers. There was a great influx of Protestants from the north of Ireland, who were Presbyterians, and of Germans from the Rhine country (the "Pennsylvania Dutch"), among whom were included not only Roman Catholics but Mennonites, Moravians, and other sectarians.

Owing to the origin of Pennsylvania and the immigration it attracted, Anglicans were not numerous, and even after the middle of the eighteenth century they constituted only two per cent of the population. The first parish, organized in 1695, was Christ Church, Philadelphia. When its second rector, the Rev. Evan Evans, was sent out in 1701 by the S.P.G., he found that the Church members in the town numbered not less than five hundred. For the next seventeen years he not only served the parish but ministered to Churchmen within a wide radius of the capital. The second church to be founded was at Chester in 1703; and in the two succeeding years missions were begun at Oxford, and at New Castle and Dover in what is now Delaware.

Progress in the smaller towns, however, was not continuous, for twenty years later it was reported to the Bishop of London that for lack

[3] At first the region now included in the state of Delaware was a part of Pennsylvania known as "the Lower Counties" or "the Territories"; but in 1704 Pennsylvania and Delaware separated, though both continued to have the same constitution and the same governor until the Revolution.

of ministers many little churches had long been neglected, and even as late as 1766 twenty missions were vacant. Though the Society in the course of the century provided forty-seven men, one of whom worked on the southwest frontier, there were seldom, if ever, more than six at work at any one time. To these may be added several in Delaware and the ministers of Christ Church and the newer parish (1761) of St. Peter's, Philadelphia. Though the Churchmen at the capital were only a numerical minority, they were instrumental, as in New York, in furthering the cause of higher education. The College of Philadelphia, chartered as such in 1755, was not a Church institution, but three-quarters of the first trustees were members of the Church, and its first provost, the Rev. William Smith, became one of the foremost Anglican clerics in the colony.

C. CONCLUSION

When we review the history of the Church of England in the Thirteen Colonies from the earliest days at Jamestown to the eve of the Revolution, we find ample evidence that all the disadvantages under which it labored were due to its connection with the State either in England or in America. In every respect its official character and political affiliations worked harm. In those provinces where it was supposed to be established the Church enjoyed a variable amount of patronage from royal governors and a certain degree of social standing, neither of which benefits was of any spiritual value. This "establishment," it should be added, did not imply established revenues; it merely gave power to tax all members of the community to support on a feeble scale a Church to which not all owed allegiance. The Church in these southern colonies, moreover, attracted from the home-land the least desirable elements among the Anglican clergy. Few of them emigrated from high missionary motives. The majority had been either unsuccessful or worse. Partly on account of their poor quality and partly because nearly all the clergy were dominated by their lay employers, the standing of the ministry was inferior and their morale low. Though admirable exceptions were notable in every generation, the clergy who were dependent on local support were not of a sort to advance the welfare of the Church or to command the respect of Dissenters.

In colonies where the Church was not established it suffered from quite different troubles. In Massachusetts and Connecticut, for example, at a time when the Church was a tolerated minority, it was always at a grave disadvantage because it was the colonial representative of the State Church of England. The leaders of that Church under James I and Charles I had given warm support to royal absolutism and had made life in England intolerable for the founders of the Puritan colonies. In consequence, throughout a wide area in America the Anglican Church could never be fairly judged on its religious merits because of its organic relation, past and present, with the English government. Thus in all the provinces, for varying reasons, the political aspect of the Church was harmful.

Of the many defects of the Church of England in the colonies none was greater than the absence of bishops. If a Church does not believe in bishops and is so organized as to perform its functions without bishops, history has sometimes shown that it may achieve notable success. But for an *episcopal* Church to attempt to prosper without bishops is certain to produce the kind and degree of failure which marked the Anglican Church in America. The benefits of Confirmation and Ordination could be obtained only at the cost of a long, dangerous, and expensive voyage to England.[4] For want of opportunity for Ordination in America the healthy growth of a native clergy was everywhere retarded. Lack of discipline, lack of leadership, and lack of unity were further results disastrous to the welfare of what might have been a vigorous Church. And, as we shall see in the next chapter, this absence of bishops was only another consequence of the fact that the Church of England was a State Church dominated by a government to which the interests of religion were always of secondary concern.

The one steadily beneficent factor in the life of the colonial Church was the one element which had no connection with the government at home or abroad—the Society for the Propagation of the Gospel. It was not even an official agency of the Establishment. It was an independent private society, composed of zealous Churchmen (mostly High Churchmen), and its fundamental purpose was missionary. It represented all that was best in the Anglicanism of the day, and of that best it gave liberally to the Church in America. In the course of the seventy-five years between 1701 and 1776 the Society maintained in the colonies as many as 310 ordained missionaries, assisted 202 central stations, and spent £227,000, or over one million dollars. Outside of the southern colonies, and even in many parts of them, the Church could hardly have sustained its life without this continuous support.[5]

[4] It cost £100 for an American to travel to England for ordination and return, a sum now equal in purchasing power to $2,500. One out of five who attempted this journey died because of disease or shipwreck.

[5] The S.P.G. also "stimulated and supported missions to the Negroes and the Indians as well as to the white colonists." The net result of these has been summarized by Dr. Manross, after careful study, in the following terms, "The Church of England in the colonies worked with some effect among the Mohawk Indians, and it made spasmodic efforts for the conversion of other tribes. Among the Negroes its labors were more persistent, and, in spite of numerous difficulties, were attended with some success. Nevertheless, it is probable that only a very small minority of them had been reached by that or any other denomination before the Revolution." (W. W. Manross, *History of the American Episcopal Church,* 153, Morehouse-Gorham Co., copyright 1950.)

Chapter III

THE CHURCH DURING REVOLUTION AND REORGANIZATION, 1776–1789

A. THE CHURCH DURING REVOLUTION

IN 1776 there were in the Thirteen Colonies less than 300 parishes and missions of the Church and about 250 clergy, more than half of whom were in Virginia and Maryland. "No other religious body was seriously injured by the American Revolution, [but] the Church was almost destroyed." [1]

When the Revolution began probably less than half the people favored independence, though far fewer were ardent loyalists. Yet the loyalists (or "Tories") were numerous enough to supply 40,000 soldiers to the King during the war, and a still larger number found refuge in Canada, Nova Scotia, the West Indies, and England. Among these loyalists Episcopalians were especially prominent, and of their clergy a very large majority sided with the King. Though two-thirds of the men who signed the Declaration of Independence were Churchmen, there were good reasons why few of the ministers of the Church espoused the cause of the Revolution. Outside of Virginia and Maryland, most of them were wholly or partly supported by the Society for the Propagation of the Gospel. In addition to the fact that their livelihood depended on their loyalty, they (like all the Anglican clergy) had taken, at ordination, an oath of allegiance to their sovereign. For nearly all of them this solemn oath took precedence over any sympathy with discontented colonists. Though in most cases they would gladly have remained neutral, they would almost never agree to omit the prescribed prayers for the King, and wherever rebels were in control these were forbidden. Since they were easily identified and their practices were readily observed, they were among the most obvious targets for patriots. Through five years of warfare scores of them

[1] G. Hodges, *Three Hundred Years of the Episcopal Church in America*, 78.

were deprived of their property, mobbed, shot at, starved, imprisoned, and banished.

Most of the southern revolutionary leaders were Churchmen, and two-thirds of the ninety-two Anglican clergymen in Virginia supported the American cause. That so many took sides for independence may be partly explained by the fact that, being locally supported, they were more inclined to sympathize with their parishioners than were the imported missionaries. Yet even in Virginia by the end of the struggle twenty-three parishes had been wholly extinguished and thirty-four others had no ministers. In Maryland, two-thirds of the clergy remained steadfast in their allegiance to the King, and more than half of the two score of ministers left the colony, and their churches were closed. Only one minister in Georgia and one in North Carolina could be counted for the Revolution, but in South Carolina fifteen out of twenty were patriots who sided against the King.

In New England, outside of Connecticut, the effect of the Revolution was more devastating than in the South. By the time the war ended there were only four Anglican ministers left in Massachusetts, one in New Hampshire, and none in Rhode Island. Connecticut, however, was much less enthusiastic about the Revolution than was Massachusetts, and a larger proportion of her population, including many Congregationalists, were loyal to the King. All the twenty Anglican clergymen were loyalists; and though several were imprisoned for a time and three left the country for good, most of them remained at their posts.

After the capture of New York by the British in August, 1776, the city became a place of refuge for many loyalists, including clergy from other colonies. The only Anglican minister in favor of the Revolution was Samuel Provoost, who later became the first Bishop of New York. The rest of the clergy were all on the other side, and once the British were in control, the life of the Church proceeded much as in peacetime. Only in Manhattan, Staten Island, and Long Island, however, could protection be offered, and the few clergy resident elsewhere were eventually driven out. In New Jersey, too, the ministers were loyalists, and all but one of the churches were closed. Pennsylvania, like New York, produced one famous pro-Revolutionary cleric—the Rev. William White, who was appointed chaplain of the Continental Congress, and was later elected the first Bishop of Pennsylvania. At one time he was the only Episcopal minister in the State, for the others were sooner or later expelled.

The effect of the Revolution upon the Church has here been described chiefly in terms of its effect upon the clergy, not only because no accurate account could ever be given of what happened to the masses of Church members but chiefly because the attitude of the ministers, and the choices they made, and the fortunes which they encountered, reveal with some precision the position and the fate of a Church which had a minimum of organization and no central authority.

The Critical Period of American History is the title of a well-known book by John Fiske which treats of the years between the close of the Revolutionary War and the inauguration of Washington as President in April, 1789. A similar title would well describe the same period in the life of the Episcopal Church. These years, indeed, were even more critical for the Church than for the State, since the State had emerged as victor in a long contest, while the Church had met with nearly every form of disaster. The question of its survival in the new Republic had yet to be answered, and the days of gradual reconstruction were dark and difficult.

The process of reorganization which now ensued may best be understood if we first review the earlier history of the quest for bishops.

B. THE QUEST FOR BISHOPS

The effort to obtain an American episcopate did not begin in the Revolutionary era; it had been in process throughout the century. To a certain ineffective degree, during most of the colonial period, the Church in America had had episcopal supervision, for, as we have noted, the Bishop of London was supposed to exercise this oversight. But his shadowy authority was almost never brought into action until Henry Compton occupied that see in 1675. He then induced the government to instruct colonial governors not to induct any minister into a benefice unless the Bishop of London had provided him with a certificate. The provision of such certificates and the ordination of candidates for the ministry overseas were thereafter the chief functions of the Bishop of London in relation to the colonies. Compton is further responsible for initiating the practice of sending out commissaries to represent him. When Edmund Gibson became Bishop of London in 1723 he persuaded the King to grant him a patent which made definite his power to inspect the Anglican churches in America, to correct and punish their clergy, and to appoint commissaries. Taking advantage of this authority, he took steps to learn the condition of the Church in the provinces, to remedy evils, and to secure the choice of worthy ministers. But his successor, Thomas Sherlock (1748–1761), adopted a contrary policy. He declined to assume any colonial responsibility, and, by way of compensation, exerted himself to obtain an American bishop.

The Church in America was continuing to grow, and the supervision of the Bishop of London was always either limited or lacking. These were reasons enough for efforts to give the colonies a bishop; and throughout the eighteenth century before the Revolution such endeavors were earnest and frequent.

The first and most nearly successful attempts were made by the S.P.G., beginning with its earliest days. Among its representatives Thomas Bray in 1701 and John Talbot for many years thereafter urgently pressed upon the Society the need for a bishop; and these pleas were reinforced by successive petitions from parishes and groups of clergy. Responding to such appeals, the Society was so successful in convincing Queen Anne of the importance of favorable action that only her death in 1714 prevented the achievement of the project. Similar efforts to persuade George I were fruitless. In spite of numerous petitions from the colonies, signed by vestries and their ministers and by clergy met in convention, the S.P.G. then gave up what seemed a hopeless enterprise. The campaign was renewed, however, when Bishop Sherlock in 1748 determined to secure a colonial bishop. Though he was aided in his endeavors by several other prominent bishops, he never succeeded in making any impression on George II or on the members of the thoroughly worldly Whig ministries. After four years of repeated failure he abandoned further attempts as useless.

The third and last phase of the campaign for a bishop took the form of a series of efforts by the clergy of the colonies during the decade before the Revolution. To cite but three examples, a convention of the clergy of New Jersey in October, 1765, a meeting of fourteen clergy from New York and New Jersey in May, 1766, and a larger convention of clergy from New York, New Jersey, and Connecticut held in November, 1766—all resulted in petitions to the King, the Archbishops, and the S.P.G., begging for bishops in America. The movement for an episcopate, of which these resolutions were an expression, created widespread notice at the time and led to a series of prolonged and violent public controversies. The most famous was that between the Rev. Thomas B. Chandler, rector of St. John's Church, Elizabethtown, New Jersey, and the Rev. Charles Chauncy, a Congregational minister of Boston, who aimed pamphlets at each other for four successive years. Even more widely noticed was the controversy carried on in newspapers of New York and Philadelphia during the years 1768 and 1769. In the columns of these journals partisans of both sides belabored each other under cover of such pen names as "American Whig," "Timothy Tickle," and "The Anatomist." But though much talk was stirred up in America, in the mother country no action was taken. As long as England ruled the Thirteen Colonies they were never given a bishop.

We have already reviewed the many reasons why bishops were needed and desired; we must now try to explain why they were never sent. Perhaps the least important reason was the economic reason: no fully reliable plan for the permanent support of bishops was ever presented to the government of England; and yet it was taken for granted on both sides that bishops were an expensive luxury. Another minor reason was the fact that in Virginia and Maryland, where the Church was strongest, there was little general enthusiasm for an American episcopate. In 1771, for example, the House of Burgesses in Virginia passed a resolution which referred to "the pernicious project of a few mistaken clergymen for introducing an American bishop." If the colonists themselves could not agree on the subject why should the home government act? Yet these retarding causes did not really determine the result. The two decisive reasons were psychological and political.

The psychological reason for inaction was the English conception of a bishop. Though a bishop was regarded as a successor of the Apostles, he was not supposed to *be* an apostle. He was an official of State with a large income derived from endowments, with a palace, a coach, and a corps of servants. He was expected to live in style, and this expectation was seldom disappointed. His functions and status were appropriate to an Established Church in an ancient and settled social order. The last thing a bishop was thought to be, or would have wanted to be, was a missionary pioneer. He might eventually be the final crown and reward of a younger Church; he was certainly not meant to be the spearhead of a vigorous advance. Until his retinue could be properly supported and his dignity safely preserved he had better stay at home. Given, then, this somewhat unscriptural idea of a bishop, it is not surprising that the government of England balked at the proposal to grant the privilege of the episcopate to a lot of raw colonials, most of whom lived more or less in the woods surrounded by Indians, or in towns of deplorable crudity. It was a project almost as fantastic as a plan to ask our government to send a symphony orchestra to the natives of Guam. A few of them might enjoy it, but it would be quite inappropriate to their level of culture.

Most effective of all, however, in determining official decision, was the political factor. Bishops being what they were and having been what they had been, the great majority of the colonists did not want them; and since the British government was having enough trouble with Americans about more important matters, it declined to add fuel to the fire. It is true, of course, that whenever the episcopate was demanded provisos were always attached to make it clear than an American bishop would have no legal power over the laity; that he would not interfere with the authority of governors; that he would not be supported by the State; and that he would not be resident in colonies where Dissenters were in control. But these pledges were never taken at their face value, because opponents believed either that they were not seriously meant or that they would be soon forgotten. In the eyes of all Nonconformists and of many Churchmen a bishop inevitably called up the image of William Laud, and no argument could dispel the spectre. The resulting outcries, chiefly Puritan, were more than enough to deter the King's ministers.

Congregational and Presbyterian adversaries agreed with Cotton Mather when he wrote, "Let all mankind know that we came into the wilderness because we would worship God without that Episcopacy, that Common Prayer, and those unwarrantable ceremonies with which the land of our forefathers' sepulchres has been defiled." [2] His views were echoed many years later by another Boston pastor, Jonathan Mayhew, who declared in 1750, "People have no security against being unmercifully priest-ridden but by keeping all imperious bishops, and other clergymen who love to lord it over God's heritage, from getting their feet into the stirrups at all." Similar forebodings were voiced in the course of the newspaper controversy. "A modern English bishop," wrote one combatant, "would be dangerous to the religious rights and privileges of all the non-Episcopalians in America." Or, in the more biblical language of another, "You are yet to be chastised only with whips, but depend upon it, when the apostolical monarchs are come over, and well established in their American dominions, you, and such as you, will be chastised with scorpions."

Nor was it only private warnings which reached the British government. On January 12, 1768, the Massachusetts House of Representatives authorized a letter to its agent in London which included the words, "We hope in God such an establishment will never take place in America, and we desire you would strenuously oppose it." John Adams was correct when he stated in later years that the plan for a colonial episcopate "spread an universal alarm against the authority of Parliament. It excited a general and just apprehension that bishops and dioceses and churches and priests and tithes were to be imposed on us by Parliament. It was known that neither King nor ministry nor archbishops could appoint bishops in America without an act of Parliament; and if Parliament could tax us, they could establish the Church of England with all its creeds, articles, tests, ceremonies, and tithes, and prohibit all other churches as conventicles and schism shops." [3] When we add to the protests from the colonies the persistent opposition of Dissenters in England—a powerful element in the electorate—the government's refusal to act seems almost

[2] The successive quotations in this and the following paragraph are from A. L. Cross's *The Anglican Episcopate and the American Colonies,* 139, 145, 202, 197 f., 235 f.

[3] A. L. Cross, *Anglican Episcopate,* 159, quoting a letter to H. Niles, dated Feb. 13, 1818.

inevitable. Once more we find that the Church as the body of Christ had to suffer because it was for all practical purposes a department of State.

C. THE BEGINNING OF REORGANIZATION

With the defeat of Great Britain the Church of England in America had been completely disestablished and could no longer count on any form of government aid. Even the Society for the Propagation of the Gospel was prevented by its charter from ministering anywhere except in British possessions. The last link with the Bishop of London had been broken. Great numbers of the laity had left the country. Furthermore, the one bond—loyalty to the King—which had united the colonies, was now destroyed, and they found themselves thirteen independent units. Facing this situation, the Church had to develop self-support, to plan for unity, and to provide an episcopate. The endeavors to achieve these goals fill the decade from 1779 to 1789.

Attempts to preserve in Virginia and Maryland some of the privileges of an established Church proved to be fruitless, for the influence of the non-episcopal churches was too strong and the general temper of the Revolutionary leaders was opposed to any State aid for religion. Thus even in the South the Church at once became chiefly dependent for support upon the voluntary contributions of its members. With varying degrees of success that system was gradually adopted in all the States, and in course of time the change was seen to be not only necessary but wholesome and invigorating.

Less readily recognized for some time was the need for cooperation and unity. Since no American *nation* had yet come into being and the final relation of the States to each other was still undetermined, the Church naturally thought in provincial terms. In each State, in fact, the Church regarded itself as a separate organization. It was in Maryland, at a small conference of clergy and laity in November, 1780, that the title "Protestant Episcopal Church" was first used. Later, at the first representative convention of the Church in Maryland held at Annapolis in August, 1783, the name was officially adopted, and before long became widely accepted. But the new name implied no united Church for all the States. At this period there were few who saw further than "The Protestant Episcopal Church" in Maryland, or in New Jersey or Virginia.

It is to the leadership of William White in Pennsylvania that we owe the first impetus toward a national Church and the wise guidance which aided its evolution. This rector of Christ Church, Philadelphia, had profited from intimate association with some of the statesmen who were soon to mould our constitution, and in a spirit akin to theirs he had been thinking about the future of the Church. In the summer of 1782, after actual fighting had ceased, he published anonymously a pamphlet entitled, "The Case of the Episcopal Churches in the United States Considered." No higher praise could be given this historic document than to say that most of its ideas were eventually incorporated in the constitution of the Church. Among these were the proposal for a *federal* organization of the Church and the principle of lay representation in its governing bodies.

Before these projects had been considered and acted upon by any Church bodies, representatives of the Church in Connecticut had taken the first steps to obtain what appeared to them more plainly essential than any schemes for cooperation and union—an American episcopate. Meeting secretly at Woodbury on March 25, 1783, ten of the fourteen clergy in the State voted to ask either the Rev. Jeremiah Leaming or the Rev. Samuel Seabury to go to England for consecration as their bishop. Leaming declined the election on account of advanced age, but Seabury accepted.

Dr. Samuel Seabury, then fifty-three years old, was a missionary on Staten Island, New York. Born in Groton, Connecticut, he had been educated at Yale and later ordained in England. After ministries at New Brunswick, New Jersey, and Jamaica and Westchester, New York, he had served as a chaplain in the British army during the war. As a High Churchman and an active Tory he was thoroughly representative of the clergy of his State, and his sterling character, sound learning, and devotion to the Church qualified him for a bishopric. The fact, however, that he well deserved the half-pay which he continued to receive from the British government injured his reputation in the eyes of those who had not worn the King's uniform during the Revolution.

Equipped with the necessary testimonials Seabury arrived in England on July 7, 1783. For more than a year he earnestly sought consecration at the hands of English bishops. But the Church of England was not free to help the Church in America. Without an act of Parliament no bishop could be consecrated who would not take the oath of allegiance to the King. Moreover, since it was inconceivable that a Bishop should not be a State-official, it was observed with distrust that the legislature of Connecticut had not endorsed the election of Seabury.

When it became clear at length that the Church of England could do nothing for him, Seabury proceeded to Scotland and found a welcome there among the non-juring bishops. These men were the successors of those bishops who had refused in 1688 to take the oath of allegiance to William III. Since the Nonjurors had continued to be ardent Jacobites, they had been persecuted in earlier years as political rebels and they were still the leaders of a private unofficial Episcopal Church, but they were all the more free to act, and the validity of their orders was undeniable. Thanks to the fact that these bishops had to consider nothing but the welfare of the Catholic Church and its future expansion in America, Seabury was consecrated at Aberdeen on November 14, 1784, by the Bishop of Aberdeen, the Bishop Coadjutor of Aberdeen, and the Bishop of Ross and Moray. At the end of the following June the new bishop landed at Newport, and on August 3, 1785, he presided at the first convention in the State of Connecticut, and ordained at that time four candidates for the diaconate.

Thanks to the Church in Connecticut there was now a bishop in the United States; but much remained to be accomplished before the unity of the Church could be achieved. During the absence of Seabury, however, important events had occurred. The movement to organize one Episcopal Church for the United States began at an informal meeting of several clergy from New York, New Jersey, and Pennsylvania held at New Brunswick, New Jersey, on May 11, 1784, a gathering at which William White presided. There it was agreed to arrange for a meeting of representatives from as many states as possible to be convened in New York on the sixth of October following. Thirteen days later in Philadelphia White presided at a convention of Pennsylvania clergy and laity which adopted a set of fundamental principles that served to shape the policy of later conventions and were eventually embodied in the final constitution of the Church. This statement declared that the Protestant Episcopal Church in the United States was independent of all foreign authority, civil or ecclesiastical, and had full power to regulate its own affairs; that so far as possible its liturgy should conform to that of the Church of England; that its ministry should consist of the three orders of bishops, presbyters, and deacons; that canons should be made by representatives of both clergy and laity acting jointly; and that no powers should be delegated to a general ecclesiastical government except such as could not be conveniently exercised by State conventions.

The meeting which occurred in New York after another five months (*i.e.* October, 1784) was not a formally authorized convention; its members were not regarded as official delegates; and its resolutions took the form of recommendations. The group, however, was widely representative, for it included men from Virginia, Maryland, Delaware, Pennsylvania, New Jersey, New York, Connecticut, and Massachusetts. The chief action taken was to adopt a declaration of principles essentially the same as that agreed upon at the May meeting in Philadelphia. But there was added the proposal that there should be bishops in each State and that they should have seats in the General Convention. These recommendations were communicated to all the Churches, and a date was set for a General Convention—September 27, 1785, at Philadelphia.[4]

On that day there met the first General Convention of the Protestant Episcopal Church in the United States of America. It consisted of sixteen clergy and twenty-four laymen, duly elected to represent Virginia, Maryland, South Carolina, Delaware, Pennsylvania, New Jersey, and New York. White was chosen as presiding officer. There were no delegates from any of the New England States. Connecticut, their leader in Church affairs, objected to the principles set forth in New York chiefly because they failed to provide for the presidency of a bishop. Connecticut, in fact, believed that an Episcopal Church was a Church in which the bishops controlled everything; and it was to be some years before her clergy could be persuaded to think less of the powers of the episcopate and more of the blessings of unity.

Though working at a disadvantage because of the lack of representatives from four States in the north and two in the south,[5] the convention proceeded to do business with diligence and wisdom. Committees were appointed to deal with the episcopate, the liturgy, and the constitution. As a necessary step toward obtaining bishops the delegates approved an address, written by White, which presented to the archbishops and bishops of the Church of England an account of the state of the Church in America and earnestly requested them to provide for the episcopal succession. In order to be prepared for the response, the Churches in all the states were asked to elect their bishops. The committee charged with revising the liturgy made no final report to the convention, but continued to work after adjournment. "The Proposed Book" which it eventually produced went beyond the needs and the sentiment of the time and was never approved. The Ecclesiastical Constitution which the convention sent to the Churches in all the States was largely the work of William White. In all important respects its provisions were reproduced in the final form adopted at the General Convention of 1789, of which an account will be given in the next chapter.

It appeared to many at the time not only in New England but elsewhere that to formulate a constitution and a liturgy before the episcopate had been fully established was to begin at the wrong end. The outcome, nevertheless, fully justified the policy pursued at Philadelphia, since the actions taken there averted the formation of many independent Churches

[4] A month before this important action, looking toward an independent national organization, John Wesley had made the decision which led to the ordination of presbyters by presbyters in the United States, and the definite secession of a body of at least 15,000 Methodists which till then had regarded itself as part of the Church of England. If bishops had been available earlier in America, this split need never have taken place.

[5] In North Carolina and Georgia the Church was too weak to respond officially to the call for a convention.

in the different States and made almost inevitable within a few years one Church for the whole country.

The Address to the archbishops and bishops of the Church of England, accompanied with certificates from the President of the Continental Congress and its Secretary for Foreign Affairs, was presented by John Adams, our minister to Great Britain. Their reply was communicated to the General Convention of twenty-six members which met in Philadelphia on June 20, 1786. Though the message was friendly, it expressed doubts about the changes in the Prayer Book as to which private information had already reached England. The deputies, after voting down two attempts to impugn the validity of Seabury's orders, approved a conciliatory reply to the bishops, which was despatched with copies of the Ecclesiastical Constitution and the "Proposed Book."

During the interval which now ensued three bishops were elected—the Rev. Samuel Provoost, rector of Trinity Church, for New York; the Rev. William White, rector of Christ Church, Philadelphia, for Pennsylvania; and the Rev. David Griffith, rector of Fairfax parish, for Virginia. But since the Churchmen of Virginia lacked either the interest or the energy to provide funds for his journey, Griffith was never consecrated.

To hear the next response from the Anglican hierarchy, the General Convention reassembled at Wilmington, Delaware, on October 10, 1786. It appeared that the principal objection raised by the Primates and other bishops was concerned with the omission from the Prayer Book of the Nicene Creed and the Athanasian Creed, together with certain doctrinal changes in the Ministration of Holy Baptism, in the Thirty-nine Articles, and elsewhere. Since the "Proposed Book" was already thoroughly unpopular in America, where its more drastic amendments met with strong opposition, it was not difficult for the convention to remove the features which had raised doubts in England. But one plea they denied. As to the Athanasian Creed perhaps they anticipated the verdict of Matthew Arnold, who once described it as "learned science with a strong dash of temper." At any rate they insisted on its omission.

Certain now that they would be cordially received, and encouraged by news that Parliament had passed the necessary enabling act, White and Provoost sailed for England on November 2, 1786. Three months later, on February 4th, they were consecrated in Lambeth Chapel by the Archbishop of Canterbury, the Bishop of Bath and Wells, and the Bishop of Peterborough. By Easter Sunday they were once more in New York.

Now that the Church in the United States had three bishops, a constitution, and a Prayer Book, the next step would seem to have been a union of the Church in New England with the Church in the other colonies. Yet this conclusion, so desirable on all grounds, was not to be reached until another two years had passed—the same two years which witnessed the formation and ratification of the Federal Constitution. For this delay there were deep-seated causes, some more worthy than others. In New England the laity then played almost no part in Church affairs, and most of the clergy were High Church ex-Tories whose bishop had been consecrated by Jacobite Nonjurors. They viewed with grave distrust their fellow Churchmen in the Middle and Southern States partly because laymen were so prominent in the councils of the Church in those parts and partly because of the doctrinal lapses which had appeared in the "Proposed Book." Leaders of the Church in New York and Pennsylvania and the States to the south were equally suspicious of their northern brothers. Bishop Provoost, who had been an outspoken champion of the Revolution, despised Bishop Seabury and would not even answer his letters. His conviction, though quite groundless, that Seabury's orders were not valid, was shared by others and served to increase ill-feeling. More widespread and more justifiable, however, was the strong distaste of the democratic Low Church dioceses for the Connecticut policy of magnifying the powers of the bishop and excluding the laity from sharing in the business of the Church. So marked, indeed, was this difference in policy that even so diplomatic a statesman as White felt obliged to decline overtures from Seabury because the latter insisted on having the three bishops decide all matters in dispute, while White and Provoost desired a settlement in which bishops, priests, and laymen would all participate. With such a serious prospect of a permanent schism, each side began to plan for the consecration of more bishops, so that if union were to prove impossible, each might be safely independent of the other. Such, then, was the unhappy and unstable situation when the third General Convention met in Philadelphia on July 28, 1789, three months after the inauguration of President Washington.

PART II

THE CHURCH FROM 1789 TO 1835

Chapter IV

THE GENERAL CONVENTION OF 1789: CONSTITUTION, CANONS, AND PRAYER BOOK

THE General Convention which met in Christ Church, Philadelphia, on July 28, 1789, was the most important convention ever held by the Episcopal Church, for it considered and adopted a constitution and a set of canons, it authorized a Book of Common Prayer which continued in use for more than a century; and it achieved the unity of the Church. Yet these creative achievements were the work of only twenty-two clergymen (including Bishops White and Seabury), together with sixteen laymen. The convention met in two sessions—from July 28th to August 8th and from September 30th to October 16th. During the earlier sittings there were no representatives from New England, but deputies were present from New York, New Jersey, Pennsylvania, Delaware, Maryland, Virginia, and South Carolina. Bishop White presided over the single chamber.

Of this famous synod it has sometimes been asserted by church historians that the membership was much the same as that of the convention which formulated the Federal Constitution. "The same men," it has been said, "were engaged in the two transactions." As a matter of fact, however, none of the fifty-five participants in the Federal Convention was a deputy in the General Convention of 1789. Only three delegates who shared in the formation of the Federal Constitution bore any official part in the moulding of the Church constitution. David Brearly of New Jersey was a member of the General Convention of 1786, which adopted the constitution later amended and ratified in 1789; John Rutledge of South Carolina took part in the second session of the same convention; and Charles Pinckney of South Carolina represented his State in the General Convention of 1785, which spent much time in considering the future constitution.[1] (Pinckney, by the way, was only twenty-eight years old at the time, and supplied an element of youthful enterprise not always perceptible in many later and more elderly conventions.) Yet if the composition of the two bodies was quite different, the influence of the Federal Convention and its members was undoubtedly marked. So many of the latter were Episcopalians that their counsel must often have been sought. More weighty, however, in its effect upon General Convention was the impressive fact that thirteen independent States had recently consummated a federal union. Successful action in the political field gave strength and stimulus to the cause of union in the ecclesiastical field.

FIRST SESSION: JULY 28–AUGUST 8

The task of the convention was to achieve unity and to adopt a constitution and canons and a liturgy. The two objects were so closely linked that the effort to secure unity determined to some degree the form taken by the constitution and the Prayer Book.

The first step looking toward union was taken on July 30th when it was resolved unanimously "that it is the opinion of this Convention that the consecration of the Rt. Rev. Dr. Seabury to the Episcopal office is valid." There would have been no possible chance of winning the adherence of the Church in New England if this action had not been taken; for Seabury had a right to such recognition, and only ignorance and prejudice had prevented its earlier expression. Fortunately for this resolution and for the welfare of the convention Bishop Provoost of New York was absent on account of illness. His only contribution to the peace and unity of the Church, eight years after Yorktown, was no compromise with former Tories and a cold shoulder for any who had trafficked with Nonjurors.

Further endorsement of Seabury's status was rendered by the convention in their reply to a message from five clergy in Massachusetts and New Hampshire, addressed to Bishops Seabury, Provoost, and White. The letter informed the bishops of the election of the Rev. Edward Bass of Newburyport as bishop and requested them to proceed to his consecration. After prolonged consideration the convention passed a series of resolutions declaring 1.) "that a complete Order of Bishops, derived as well under the English as the Scots line of Episcopacy, doth now subsist within the United States of America" (and Seabury, Provoost, and White are then named); 2.) "that the said three bishops are fully competent to every proper act and duty of the Episcopal office"; and 3.) that these three

[1] See Jonathan Elliot (Ed.), *Debates in the Several State Conventions on the Adoption of the Federal Constitution,* vol. I.

bishops are requested to comply with the prayer of the clergy of Massachusetts and New Hampshire for the consecration of the Rev. Edward Bass. Two further resolutions provide that before such action is taken representatives from New England should meet with those from the other States in an adjourned convention and that the archbishops and bishops of the Church of England should be consulted. A long missive was later addressed to the Anglican bishops; but Bass was never consecrated by these three bishops, because Bishop Provoost declined to participate.[2]

One obstacle to union with the Church in New England had been removed: Bishop Seabury was accepted by the convention as equal in status to the other bishops. But several other doubts remained to be cleared away. Not only the clergy but even the leading laymen of Connecticut were disturbed to learn that the constitution, as hitherto approved, demanded that laymen as well as clergymen should be members of General Convention. They were offended, too, at the want of any provision for a separate House of Bishops; and Seabury and his clergy had voiced their objections to a number of changes in the proposed Prayer Book. Bearing in mind these impediments to complete agreement, the convention postponed any action on the Prayer Book, and after passing a body of ten canons, amended the constitution to make the election of lay deputies only permissive and to provide for a House of Bishops. But this upper House could not initiate legislation, and its veto upon action by the other House could be overridden by a three-fifths vote. With these conciliatory motions to its credit, the General Convention adjourned to meet again at the end of September.

Before adjournment the deputies voted their approval of a letter to President Washington, then in the fourth month of his first administration. "When we contemplate the short but eventful history of our nation," the message declares; "when we recollect the series of essential services performed by you in the course of the Revolution; the temperate yet efficient exertion of the mighty powers with which the nature of the contest made it necessary to invest you; and especially when we remember the voluntary and magnanimous relinquishment of those high authorities at the moment of peace; we anticipate the happiness of our country under your future administration. . . . We devoutly implore the Supreme Ruler of the Universe to preserve you long in health and prosperity,—an animating example of all public and private virtues—the friend and guardian of a free, enlightened, and grateful people,—and that you may finally receive the reward which will be given to those whose lives have been spent in promot-

[2] He was consecrated seven and a half years later by Bishops White, Provoost, and Claggett.

ing the happiness of mankind." Equally stately was the President's reply, which concluded with these words, "I request, Most Reverend and respectable Gentlemen, that you will accept my cordial thanks for your devout supplications to the Supreme Ruler of the Universe in behalf of me. May you, and the people whom you represent, be the happy subjects of Divine Benediction both here and hereafter!"

SECOND SESSION: SEPTEMBER 30–OCTOBER 16

During the interval of two months before General Convention reassembled, a committee appointed for that purpose conferred with Bishop Seabury and supplied the clergy of New England with full information as to what had been done at Philadelphia. Bishop White, too, acted as intermediary; and all joined in presenting a warm invitation to the bishop to attend the next session and to bring with him clerical deputies from the eastern States. Though Seabury was rigidly conservative, and firm in temper to the point of obstinacy, he was a devout Christian and a thorough gentleman. The actions of the convention had not given him all he wanted, but he gladly agreed to take part in its future proceedings; and at its first session on September 30th the deputies had the profound satisfaction of greeting the Bishop of Connecticut, together with two clerical delegates from that State and a representative of the Church in Massachusetts and New Hampshire. Bishop Provoost, deeply offended at these signs of harmony (bought, as he believed, at too high a price) refused to preach at the opening service, and sulked in his New York tent during the whole session.

On the third day of meeting the convention moved into the State House, where the Federal Constitution had been signed, and in those historic surroundings proceeded to take further action conducive to union with the Church in New England. The constitution was amended to give the House of Bishops the right "to originate and propose acts for the concurrence of the House of Deputies" and a veto on legislation by the lower House which could be overridden only by a four-fifths vote. At this point Bishop Seabury, the two deputies from Connecticut, and the deputy for Massachusetts and New Hampshire signed the following statement: "We do hereby agree to the Constitution of the Church, as modified this day in Convention." Thereupon the signers became members of the convention and took part in all its subsequent actions. It was at this moment, too, that the House of Bishops came into being. With Provoost absent it had only two members, but since that was enough for a quorum, White and Seabury withdrew and met thereafter as a separate House. As the senior in point of consecration, Seabury presided.

THE CONSTITUTION

Before adjournment eleven days later the constitution was adopted and signed by all members present. Though it was a brief document, comprising only nine articles, it recorded decisions upon all the main points of the government of the Church, and it has ever since supplied the groundwork of that structure. The first article established a triennial General Convention as the central and supreme governing body, with provision for special sessions when necessary. The second article, describing the House of Deputies, declares that each State is "entitled" to send not more than four clerical and four lay deputies. (So strong was State feeling and so long were dioceses coextensive with States that the term "diocese" was not substituted for "State" throughout the constitution until 1838.) The House of Bishops, as we have seen, could initiate legislation; but its full status as an upper House was not achieved until 1808, when its power to veto action by the deputies was freed of all restriction. The following article states that bishops are to be elected according to rules to be fixed by the Convention of each State, and the bishops so elected must confine the exercise of their episcopal functions to their own dioceses. With an eye to future expansion it is announced in the next article that the Episcopal Church in any State may be admitted to the Protestant Episcopal Church in the United States of America by acceding to the constitution. Article VI deals with the question of the trial of bishops and other clergy. The details are left to the Conventions in each State; but it is required that at least one bishop must be present at the trial of a bishop and it is affirmed that only a bishop may depose a bishop, a presbyter, or a deacon. Next in order is an article providing for the examination of candidates for the ministry by a bishop and two presbyters and for the subscription by the ordinand of a declaration of belief and conformity. The use of the *Book of Common Prayer* is made compulsory by Article VIII, and the final article states that amendments to the constitution can be made only by favorable action in two successive General Conventions.

THE CANONS

The first of the seventeen canons "agreed on and ratified" proclaims that "in this Church there shall always be three Orders in the Ministry, *viz.*, Bishops, Priests, and Deacons." The remaining sixteen deal with questions less vital but still highly important, such as rules for the preparation and ordination of candidates for the ministry, the use of the *Book of Common Prayer,* the duty of ministers to prepare for episcopal visitations, to keep registers, etc. Canons like these, of course, have been retained, with amendments and additions; but Canon XIII, no longer part of the Church's legislation, strikes the modern reader with surprise. "No ecclesiastical persons [i.e. ministers] shall, other than for their honest necessities, resort to taverns or other places liable to be abused to licentiousness. Further, they shall not give themselves to any base or servile labor, or to drinking or riot, or to the spending of their time idly." Here we see reflected the unhappy past experience of more than one colony. But if we may congratulate ourselves that the standards of the community today make drinking in taverns less attractive to the clergy than it once was, "spending their time idly" remains a permanent temptation.

THE PRAYER BOOK

Since most of the work on constitution and canons had been accomplished before this autumn session convened, the chief remaining task of the Convention was the revision of the Prayer Book. In view of the unpopularity of the radical "Proposed Book" published four years earlier, no attempt was made to revive it; but it contributed a number of valuable features. Though theoretically the five committees appointed were supposed to be producing an entirely new book, actually the process was a conservative line by line revision of the existing *Book of Common Prayer* of the Church of England authorized in 1662. But though conservative, it was minutely thorough. As is frankly acknowledged in the Preface (which still appears in our present Prayer Book), the changes introduced went far beyond those demanded by the recent Revolution. The limitations of which the revisers were conscious are well expressed by these words at the conclusion of the Preface: "This Church is far from intending to depart from the Church of England in any essential point of doctrine, discipline, or worship; or further than local circumstances require." The accent here, as the alterations prove, was clearly on the word *essential.*

Not more than twenty amendments can be accounted for by the fact that King George no longer ruled in his former colonies. Beyond these few political substitutions there are over two hundred minor verbal changes. Most of these were made for the purpose of modernizing the language, as when "them that" is replaced by "those who"; many others serve to eliminate useless words. In addition to these small modifications there is another group of nearly one hundred variations which might fairly be described as unimportant. The changes really worth noting a hundred and sixty years later are fewer than fifty.

Among the more interesting of the major amendments are the following: (1) The omission from the Calendar of sixty-nine saints' days and other days. Nearly all the days dropped commemorate persons subsequent to New Testament times or events not based on New Testament evidence. (2) The omission of the so-called "Ornaments Rubric," formed from a clause in the Act of Uniformity of 1559 requiring the use of ornaments and vestments used in 1549. The rubric had been generally ignored in England for 230 years and was always a standing invitation to legalistic bickering about non-essentials. (3) In Morning Prayer the omission after the Creed of a second Lord's Prayer and of four sets of versicles and responses, and the addition of the Prayer for All Conditions of Men and A General Thanksgiving, which in the English book are grouped elsewhere among the "Prayers and Thanksgivings." (4) In Evening Prayer the unfortunate omission of the Magnificat and the Nunc Dimittis, which were restored in 1892. As inadequate substitutes, part of Psalm 92 was inserted before the Second Lesson and part of Psalm 103 after the Second Lesson. (5) The omission of the Athanasian Creed. This action brought grief to Bishop Seabury and others, who appeared to believe that faith in the Trinity depended upon its dry clauses and harsh threats. But it was eventually realized that the rest of the Prayer Book offers more than enough testimony to the Church's trinitarian faith. (6) In the Catechism the sentence "the Body and Blood of Christ . . . are verily and indeed taken and received by the faithful in the Lord's Supper" is amended to read "spiritually taken and received." (7) The Solemnization of Matrimony is improved by the omission of various references to carnal lusts, procreation, and fornication, and is shortened by dropping a psalm, four prayers, and a long exhortation. (8) A change distinctly doctrinal in character is to be found in the Office for the Visitation of the Sick, where the revisers leave out the rubric directing that the sick person be urged to confess, and omit the subsequent Absolution which includes the words, "I absolve thee from all thy sins." (9) The omission of the Office entitled, "A Commination, or denouncing of God's anger and judgments against sinners." This is the sulphurous service which contains such lines as "Cursed is he that removeth his neighbor's landmark" and "Cursed is he that maketh the blind to go out of his way." (10) The addition of the following offices, the last two of which have long proved of high value: A Form of Prayer for the Visitation of Prisoners,[3] A Form of Thanksgiving to Almighty God for the Fruits of the Earth, and Forms of Prayer to be Used in Families.

The changes in the Order for the Administration of the Holy Communion may be traced to the fact that Bishop Seabury, in the Concordat with the Scottish bishops which he had signed, had promised to try to

[3] A revised version of a similar office in the Prayer Book of the Irish Church.

make the American Prayer Book conform to the Scottish in this office. Partly for this reason, but still more because of the intrinsic merit of the proposals, the Convention not only added the section beginning "Hear also what our Lord Jesus Christ saith," but enlarged the Prayer of Consecration by making the most impressive addition of all the hundreds embodied in the new book. After the first paragraph in this prayer, concluding with the words of institution, there was added "The Oblation" and "The Invocation." The last section of the Invocation appears in the English Prayer Book after the Lord's Prayer which follows the communicating. But the Oblation and the first part of the Invocation (with a few modifications) come from the Scottish Prayer Book which, in turn, borrowed them from the first Prayer Book of Edward VI (1549). By this notable amendment the revisers enhanced the beauty and enriched the meaning of the heart of the Liturgy.[4]

To account for the remaining material forming part of the Prayer Book before 1892, we may note that at the following General Convention of 1792 there was added "The Ordinal, the Form of Making, Ordaining, and Consecrating Bishops, Priests, and Deacons." Seven years later the Form of Consecration of a Church or Chapel was authorized, and in 1808 there was set forth the Office of Institution of Ministers. It was in 1801, after many postponements, that the Convention finally adopted the Thirty-nine Articles, with a few amendments not concerned with doctrine; but no subscription to them was required by canon.

AN APPRAISAL

Attention to many canonical and liturgical details ought not to obscure the great creative achievements of this General Convention. A small number of leaders within a brief time, working upon material wrought out for five years past, had given to the Anglican Communion in the United States a constitutional and legal setting which the Church had never elsewhere known. Without departing at any point from either their Catholic or their Protestant heritage, the representatives of the Church had produced a constitution which regulated the functions not only of laymen and priests but also of bishops. There thus appeared a limited constitutional episcopate, quite divorced from its long alliance with monarchy and Parliament. "The introduction of the laity into the place assigned to them was a momentous step. . . . From government by bishops, themselves the creatures of the King, to government by a convention made up of popularly elected bishops, priests, and laymen, is a

[4] For full information about the Prayer Book see Parsons and Jones, *The American Prayer Book.*

tremendous leap." [5] In making these courageous innovations the leaders of the Church were certainly aided by the previous labors of their political contemporaries. None can fail to remark the analogies between the ecclesiastical and the federal constitutions—diocesan conventions corresponding to State legislatures, the House of Deputies answering to the House of Representatives, the House of Bishops to the Senate, and the like. But only to statesmen would such statesmanlike models appeal. And among the statesmen of the Church none was wiser or more influential than Bishop William White. He was the Madison of the Church's constitution.

[5] S. D. McConnell, *History of the American Episcopal Church,* 266, 265.

In the words of Francis Wharton (first a famous Professor of Law and later a priest of the Church), "It is difficult to see any limit, on the face of the constitution, to the powers of the General Convention." (W. S. Perry, *History of the American Episcopal Church,* II, 402.)

Chapter V

THE CHURCH CONVALESCENT

WHEN the Protestant Episcopal Church of 1790 began its career as a fully organized body it was small and weak. The clergy in all the thirteen States numbered no more than two hundred, less than we now find in the diocese of Connecticut. Even in 1800, after ten more years of growth, there were only about 12,000 communicants, less than the number in the present diocese of Alabama. Not only was the Church small in numbers; it was weak in relation to the general population. In 1940 one citizen of the United States out of every 90 was an Episcopal communicant; but in 1790 the proportion was hardly better than one in 400.

When we remember how insignificant in size was the Church at the end of the eighteenth century, we must not forget how scanty and thinly distributed was the population of the new United States and how primitive, as we view them today, were the conditions which prevailed.[1] Even including 700,000 Negro slaves, the total population was only 4,000,000, scattered from the northern areas of Massachusetts (later to become Maine) all the way to southern Georgia. Only six cities had over 8,000 inhabitants—Philadelphia, New York, Boston, Charleston, Baltimore, and Salem. Not for another fifty years would the urban population reach ten per cent of the total, for agriculture was the main occupation of the vast majority.

One quarter of all the citizens lived in New England, most of them of Puritan origin and still loyal to their Congregational churches. In New York, despite its Dutch origins, the majority was of English stock. More Tory in sentiment than any other State during the Revolution, New York

[1] For a survey of social and economic conditions in the U.S. in 1790 no better brief account can be found than that of S. E. Morison in *The Oxford History of the United States,* London, 1927, Chapters 1–3. An excellent record on a larger scale is that of J. A. Krout and D. R. Fox in *The Completion of Independence* (*A History of American Life* series, vol. V), New York, 1944.

had been the most aristocratic of the colonies, and the Episcopal Church was the only Christian body to which most gentlemen cared to belong. Philadelphia was the largest city in the country and was to be the federal capital for ten years. In culture, philanthropy, and education, as well as in commerce, it was the foremost centre.

Virginia, then twice its present size, was by far the most populous State, but forty per cent of its inhabitants were slaves. Though the general level of comfort and intelligence was not high, the "first families" among the Virginia planters were supplying more than their share of national leaders, and the majority of these were Episcopalians. To the southward North Carolina, with relatively few slave-owners, was a growing community peopled largely by democratic farmers. Quite different in atmosphere and ancestry was South Carolina, with its gay capital Charleston, the fourth city in the country. By 1793 the cotton gin had been invented, and with that change the growth of cotton was about to begin its huge expansion, bringing with it the increasing importance of slavery as the basis of the social structure. "The west country" had already drawn from the East a population of over 100,000, and within twelve years Kentucky (1792), Tennessee (1796), and Ohio (1803) had entered the Union.

From end to end of this long narrow country, transportation was wearisome and slow. Journeys on land were by stagecoach or horseback, and most of the roads were wretched. Since it took nine days to go from Boston to New York and a month from Philadelphia to Charleston, it is fair to say that travel was distinctly less comfortable and speedy than it had been in the Roman Empire eighteen hundred years before. This tardiness in communications encouraged provincialism and made united action difficult not only for the State but for the Church. It was a constant obstacle to prompt cooperation which we must charitably bear in mind as we watch the slow process by which the Episcopal Church, from a collection of pieces loosely tied together, evolved into a sound organism.

The industrial revolution had not yet become effective in the United States, where shipping and fishing were practically the only industries. In a nation still composed almost wholly of farmers and planters there was a fairly wide diffusion of prosperity. But since the Episcopal Church, then as now, was strongest in the cities, the fact that the urban population was so small a fraction of the total was a disadvantage which the Church had to add to such other hindrances as its English associations and its upper-class flavor.

During the first decade and a half of the Church in the United States the French Revolution ran its violent course. To a generation that has pulled through two world wars and witnessed the Bolshevik Revolution and the Nazi terror, the struggle in France may look small; but it was the most disturbing event since the discovery of America, and it determined to a large degree the course of events in the century which followed. Its impact on the United States was powerful. Especially after the overthrow of the monarchy in 1792, excitement in America was intense. The general current of feeling, of course, was warmly sympathetic; but the more conservative propertied classes, represented by the Federalists, were profoundly disturbed by events abroad. Antagonism at home thus arose between those who favored England and those who favored France, and the epithets "Monarchist" and "Jacobin" were hurled about in much the same spirit as are "Fascist" and "Communist" today.

Throughout this period of party strife Episcopalians, except in parts of the South, would naturally be found on the conservative side, partly because of their English heritage and English ties and partly because so large a proportion of their membership was to be found among the well-to-do. Yet even stronger opponents of republicanism in France, as hostile to religion and morals, were the Congregational clergy of New England. In course of time, in fact, the violent excesses in Paris and elsewhere cooled the first fervor in America, and professing Christians of all denominations awoke to the danger of the spread of "infidelity." Americans might be enthusiastic republicans, but most of them either were orthodox Christians or had inherited a deep respect for religion. Those who were numbered in neither class were swept along for a time by an incoming wave of French free thought. Deistical clubs were formed in the cities; European rationalism invaded the colleges; and Tom Paine's *The Age of Reason* (1796) became a best-seller. Yet, as a careful observer has noticed, "philosophic rationalism could scarcely compete, except among intellectuals, with the emotionalism of evangelical religion"; and liberalism at this point secured no foothold outside of the Unitarian element in Boston and Cambridge.

It was in this period of disturbance in politics and in thought that the Church took its first tentative steps. It was in the same period and subject to the same influences that the new federal government was slowly feeling its way to power under the wise oversight of Washington and the masterful leadership of Hamilton. The Church had found in Bishop White a Madison, but it had to go forward as best it could without the encouraging vigor of a Hamilton.

The closing years of the eighteenth century show the lowest low-water mark of the lowest ebb-tide of spiritual life in the history of the American Church.[2] That verdict, passed upon American Christianity in general, applies truly to the Episcopal Church. In fact, we might extend the period of depression for another decade. From 1790 at least to 1811

[2] Cf. L. W. Bacon, *A History of American Christianity*, 208 f.

the Church showed few symptoms of vitality and made little progress. It seemed hardly aware of the mission and the purpose of a Church. The fundamental causes of this weakness were operative in all the Churches, which reported at the time a spiritual deadness. As the Presbyterian General Assembly expressed it in 1798, "We perceive with pain and fearful apprehension a general dereliction of religious principle and practice among our fellow citizens." The demoralizing effect of a long war and of political and social insecurity was partly responsible for a decline so widely remarked.

There were additional reasons, however, why the Episcopal Church should suffer. In the first place, the Church had just begun the long and painful process of learning how to support itself by a voluntary system. Deprived of the sources of revenue once supplied either by the State or by the S.P.G., Church members had to be trained in giving. They had to learn for the first time that if they did not contribute to the upkeep of their church buildings and to the salaries of their ministers, nobody else would do it for them. And this new call for intelligent generosity came at a time when a large fraction of once prosperous Episcopalians had left the country.

A further reason for hesitation and weakness was the general status of the episcopate. The Church, it is true, had at last obtained bishops. Before the end of 1790 there were four of them—in New York, Pennsylvania, Connecticut, and Virginia; but twenty years later there were only six. That they supplied little or no leadership was partly due to the fact that they were not leaders. White was a saint, a scholar, and a diplomat, but completely devoid of aggressive energy; Provoost, as a bishop, was proving to be a talented amateur botanist; and Madison of Virginia soon found himself less interested in his diocese than in William and Mary College, of which he was president.

Yet in justice to the memory of even the least valuable bishops of the day it should be remembered that their position was insecure and they all had to tread cautiously. No one questioned, of course, the validity of their orders or their power to ordain and confirm. But public opinion in the South had never been strongly in favor of bishops, and the general sentiment in that quarter might be expressed by saying that if there had to be bishops, the less power they had the better. Even in the North, except perhaps in Connecticut, there was a similar tendency to keep a watchful eye on bishops to see that they did not develop symptoms of "prelacy." Until the Church could become accustomed to having bishops and to trusting them it was almost necessary that they should refrain from any bold exercise of power. As a matter of fact, the bishops in question were inclined by nature to play a modest role; and by the time the Church was ready to respond to energetic leadership, bishops who could lead began to appear.

The General Conventions in this period were slimly attended. South Carolina, for example, after the meeting of 1795, sent no more representatives until 1814. In 1789 two bishops, twenty clergy, and sixteen laymen had been present, and twenty-two years later there appeared two bishops, twenty-five clergy, and twenty laymen—no very large increase. Alarmed at this neglect of opportunities the Convention of 1808 (when the House of Bishops, with two members present, met in a small bedroom) passed the following resolution: "That a committee be appointed . . . to make a solemn and affectionate address to the Churches represented in both Orders in this Convention, urging upon them the propriety, necessity, and duty of sending regularly a deputation to the General Convention, and that the said address contain a respectful appeal to every bishop of this Church, on the subject of attendance on his part."

The Conventions were small and uninteresting because the dioceses behind them were weak. Indeed, one of the depressing features of these triennial gatherings was the report from the field describing the condition of the Church in the different States. Massachusetts had a bishop for only six of the twenty-two years between 1789 and 1811, and even as late as the latter date there were only fifteen clergy in all New England outside of Connecticut. During the same period Connecticut was without a bishop for only a year and a half. As early as 1792 there were twenty-two clergy in the State, and at no point did that steady diocese have a discouraging report to offer. Despite its reverence for Bishop Seabury, who died in 1796, it had even sent laymen to represent it in General Convention, and appeared to be none the worse for the experience. Samuel Provoost, the neglectful Bishop of New York, resigned in 1801, despite the strong disapproval of the House of Bishops, and his successor was too mild to prove helpful as a leader. Yet thanks to missionaries like Philander Chase, Daniel Nash, and others, and to unusual activity among the laity, upstate New York could point to encouraging expansion. New Jersey, however, was far from prosperous, for though organized as a diocese in 1785, it had no bishop for another thirty years. It was only in Philadelphia and its environs that the Church in Pennsylvania, with its fourteen clergy, was at all flourishing. In that capital it enjoyed much prestige, especially among the aristocracy, but its capacity for outreach was negligible. Here, as elsewhere, the bishop was rector of a large parish, which not only absorbed much of his time and energy but served to give him the impression that his parochial office was his main function.

From the Church in Virginia was reported "the lethargy of despair." Soil exhaustion at home and the disorders in Europe had so reduced the profits from tobacco that the State was suffering from economic distress. The new bishop Madison, consecrated in England in 1790, found his diocese profoundly disheartening. The clergy were greatly reduced in numbers and miserably poor. So many of them, in fact, were turning away from their duties that a canon had to be passed to prevent their holding military commissions. In January, 1802, the legislature passed an act ordering the sale of the Church's glebe lands for the benefit of the State. The resulting loss of the last remnants of endowment led to the decay of church buildings and to the increasing impoverishment of the clergy, whose ranks were steadily diminished by death and removal and very seldom increased by ordinations. The diocesan convention of 1805 was attended by only fifteen clergy and sixteen laymen and no more were held for seven years. To the first four General Conventions of the nineteenth century Virginia sent no deputies. It is therefore not surprising that the General Convention of 1808 should report that "the Church in Virginia is, for various causes, so depressed that there is danger of her total ruin unless great exertions, favored by the blessing of Providence, are employed to raise her." Remembering this era of depression, during which he was ordained, William Meade, the future Bishop of Virginia, wrote, "In every educated man whom I met, I expected to find a sceptic, if not an unbeliever."

In Maryland conditions for a time were almost as bad as in Virginia, but improvement came somewhat sooner. When its new bishop, Thomas J. Claggett, was consecrated in 1792 he found nearly half the parishes vacant, Church property everywhere neglected, the glebes run to waste, and the clergy decreasing in numbers and so feebly supported by voluntary subscriptions that many had to leave the State or to take secular work. Six years later, however, when conditions had already begun to improve, the Church was cheered by an act of the legislature which permitted to organized vestries the legal right to own the churches and glebes which had once been the property of the Church of England. Thus the Church in Maryland profited by acquiring the kind of property which the Church in Virginia was soon to lose. Yet at the close of another five years half the parishes were vacant, and General Convention in 1808 was informed that "the Church in Maryland is still in a deplorable condition." For the next few years, however, before the war broke out, the continued efforts of an earnest bishop began to show favorable results.

The Church in Delaware, in North Carolina, and in Georgia was barely alive. In 1792 only three clergy were reported in Delaware and General Convention received no figures from the other States. Delaware, though organized as a diocese in 1786, had no bishop of its own until 1841. In North Carolina, despite several earlier efforts, the Church was not formally organized until 1817, nor in Georgia until 1823. But the Church in South Carolina was so far developed that its first bishop, Robert Smith, was consecrated in 1795. An elderly man, who evidently shared the opinion of his diocese that bishops were unimportant, he never administered Confirmation, and during four of the six years of his episcopate there were no diocesan conventions. Not until eleven years after his death did his successor take office.

An inevitable consequence of the low vitality of the Church at this period was the almost complete lack of expansive power. The era of revolution and reconstruction had brought the Church in most areas so close to extinction that during the ensuing twenty years it had enough to do merely to survive. There was no surplus energy available for that missionary activity which is the unfailing symptom of a vigorous institution. Energy and ambition can hardly be expected of a convalescent.

But though this general weakness was the fundamental defect which delayed expansion, there was a secondary reason why the Church failed to move forward, especially in the growing West. The Episcopal Church in the United States still regarded itself as a loose confederation of dioceses, and the dioceses were still co-terminous with the States. As Dean Hodges once put it, "The Church did not consider itself as a single Church responsible in the land for the extension of the Kingdom of God." There was little power at the centre and no organ by which the Church could act as a unit. Partly because no means had yet been invented for supporting bishops, except by making them rectors of large parishes, bishops were never thought of as pioneers. As in earlier days, they were still regarded not as the first, but as the last stage in the development of any area. The unfortunate result was a kind of duplication of the very troubles from which the Church had suffered in the colonial period. In the new lands of the West the Episcopal Church could not flourish without bishops, but there appeared to be no way of providing bishops; so other Christian bodies which did not depend on bishops proceeded to supply the demand which the Episcopal Church was either too weak or too dignified or too badly organized to meet.

For a century or more we have been so accustomed to thinking of the missionary bishop as the first man to enter new territory that it requires an effort to imagine the methods which prevailed from 1790 to as late as 1835. During that epoch the usual course of events began with the admission of a Territory as a State. Then anywhere from ten to thirty or more years later a handful of priests and laymen would organize a diocese, and the diocese would be admitted to union with General Convention. As a third step, sometimes delayed for years, the diocese would elect a bishop. In the whole process the General Convention played only a passive role.

To cite but two examples, we find that these three stages in Tennessee were reached in 1792, 1829, and 1834, and in Ohio in 1803, 1818, and 1819.

These dates and others like them reveal how negligible was any progress before the second decade of the nineteenth century. Opportunity, of course, was urgent and obvious, especially on the frontier. Even as early as 1790 five per cent of the population was living west of the Alleghanies, and this western movement went on, with increasing volume, for another generation. Admitted as a State in 1792, Kentucky had 221,000 inhabitants in 1800, and Tennessee almost half as many. Ohio had attained a population of 40,000, and was to be a State within three years.

The earliest sign that this movement—one of the great migrations in modern history—had caught the attention of General Convention was the appointment by the Convention of 1792 of a Joint Committee to "prepare a plan of supporting missionaries to preach the Gospel on the frontiers of the United States." On the basis of their plan an act was passed which recommended to all the clergy that there should be in each church an annual missionary sermon accompanied by an offering, and that diocesan treasurers should collect these offerings. It was further provided that there should be a Standing Committee of two bishops, four presbyters, and four laymen, and that "the Bishop of this Church in Pennsylvania," together with this Standing Committee, should have power to appoint a treasurer and a secretary and to employ missionaries to be paid by the funds raised. As an aid to the proposed offerings the Bishop of Pennsylvania and the Committee were asked to "frame an address to the members of the Church recommending this charitable design [3] to their particular attention, which address shall be read by every minister on the day appointed for the collection." Here in rudimentary form we have a kind of Department of Domestic Missions, with a secretary and treasurer, and even (if we count the "address" to be published) an embryonic Department of Promotion.

At the General Convention three years later this earliest attempt at a central organization was abandoned; the responsbility for spending what money might be raised was transferred to the several dioceses, which were probably jealous of their rights; and the subject of western expansion was not allowed to disturb General Convention for another thirteen years. The only recorded result of these resolutions and committees appears to have been a lone missionary sent to Kentucky by the Church in Maryland.[4]

[3] Those whose ignorance leads them to believe that the Church long ago was much more missionary-minded than it is today should notice that the expansion of Christianity in the United States is here referred to in terms appropriate to the founding of an orphanage or of an Old Ladies' Home. It is no wonder that the response was on a corresponding scale.

[4] F. L. Hawks, *Contributions to the Ecclesiastical History of the United States*, II, 334.

Meanwhile, among the Protestant Churches, a series of revivals marked the closing years of the eighteenth and the opening years of the nineteenth century. More sober and gradual than the "Great Awakening" of an earlier generation, these revival movements resulted not merely in emotional camp-meetings in frontier settlements but in constructive advance in the life of the Churches in the East. Before the eighteenth century ended missionary societies had been organized by the Congregational churches in Connecticut, Massachusetts, and New Hampshire; in 1802 the Presbyterian General Assembly appointed a standing committee to supervise its missionary work; and within a few years there were Baptist missionary societies in New England, Pennsylvania, and New York.

Westward expansion by these Churches, however, had never had to wait for these formal steps. The first Baptist Association west of the mountains had been established in 1785. The Baptists, in fact, were usually first on the ground in the western settlements, for their preachers, lay and ordained, were settlers themselves and shared the lot of their fellow-migrants. Working in the fields or the woods five or six days a week, they were able to support themselves with but little assistance. They were ill-educated and often crude in their manners; but they had one undeniable advantage over more refined representatives of Christianity: they were on the spot when they were needed. As a result, between 1800 and 1803 the Baptist churches added 10,000 to their membership in Kentucky alone. Quite as successful in adapting their methods to western conditions were the Methodists, with their itinerant preachers riding the circuits, meeting with the people where they were to be found, and delivering in cabins or taverns or in the open air a message of warm evangelism. As early as 1789 there were ten Methodist circuits in the new West, and by 1812 these had increased to sixty-nine and the membership to more than 30,000.

Less fitted for rapid advance through the use of laymen, the Presbyterians were soon far outnumbered by the Methodists and Baptists. Yet their denominational zeal—or perhaps we should say their church consciousness—was so much stronger than that of the Congregationalists that after these two groups had adopted a "Plan of Union" (1802) for cooperation especially in the West, the final unexpected result was that 2,000 churches, originally Congregational, became Presbyterian. Congregationalism, in fact, was destined never to flourish outside New England. But through their emphasis upon a trained ministry and their success in founding schools and colleges both Presbyterians and Congregationalists made by far the largest contribution to the educational and cultural life of the frontier.[5]

While Baptists, Presbyterians, and Methodists were occupying a field

[5] W. W. Sweet, *The Story of Religion in America,* 311.

in which they have prospered ever since, the leaders of the Episcopal Church were explaining to each other why such expansion was impossible. The General Convention of 1808 passed a resolution appointing a committee to plan for the proper mode of sending a bishop into States and Territories where the Church was not yet organized. Three years later at the next Convention the committee reported that "there was no reasonable prospect of accomplishing the object contemplated." Not dismayed by this verdict, the Convention passed a further resolution "that the bishops in Pennsylvania and Virginia be requested to devise means for supplying the congregations of this Church west of the Alleghany Mountains with the ministrations and worship of the same, and for organizing the Church in the western States." These two bishops were chosen to lead a forward movement because their dioceses included frontier territory; but they were otherwise ill-qualified. Bishop Madison of Virginia was not even interested in caring for his own diocese, and Bishop White of Pennsylvania, during his twenty-four years as bishop, had never felt any responsibility for visiting the western parts of his State. It is not surprising, therefore, that after Madison's death in 1812, White reported to the General Convention of 1814 that this unhappy event had "arrested further progress."

If the story of the Church as a missionary body during these decades offers no occasion for pride, its record in the field of Christian education is slightly more encouraging. The Church's responsibility for teaching the truths of Christianity to its members was far more widely understood and accepted than its responsibility for aggressive expansion. Just as here and in England missionary activity was not carried on by the Church as a whole in its corporate capacity but by private societies, so educational advance was likewise promoted by voluntary associations. There was then in existence none of that National Church organization or that diocesan machinery which now assumes the direction of religious education. If there was to be progress in this field it had to be the product of private, and often of lay, initiative.

The opening years of the nineteenth century saw the formation of many societies devoted to the advancement of Christian learning. They were chiefly concerned with the publication and distribution of Christian literature, and to a lesser extent with the support of diocesan missions and of theological students. Their names often have an antique flavor, such as that of the Maryland organ known as "The Society for Confirming and Extending the Interests of the Christian Religion in General and of the Protestant Episcopal Church in Particular." Its title was longer than its life, and it published only a few tracts. Of more permanent value was the Protestant Episcopal Society for the Promotion of Religion and Learning founded in New York and liberally supported by Trinity Church. Its activity included not only aid to candidates for orders but the financial support of missions in the diocese. To the zeal of the assistant minister at Trinity, John H. Hobart, of whom more will be heard we may also trace the origin of the Protestant Episcopal Theological Education Society and the New York Protestant Episcopal Tract Society. In the same diocese there was even a Protestant Episcopal Society of Young Men for the Distribution of Religious Tracts—a group which today would hardly survive the publication of its name. Elsewhere similar associations arose during the same years—the Protestant Episcopal Society for the Advancement of Christianity in South Carolina, "to promote knowledge and piety"; the Episcopal Society of New Jersey for the Promotion of Christian Knowledge and Piety; and the Episcopal Female Tract Society in Baltimore.

To the modern mind "Christian education" immediately suggests the Sunday school, but before 1814 there were no Sunday schools in the Episcopal Church. Except for irregular catechizing in church, children received no religious training outside of the home, and the home could not always be relied upon. Sunday schools began in England in 1780 as a result of the initiative of an Anglican layman. At that time, and for a generation or more thereafter, these charity schools were intended to teach poor children to read and write. Though they met on Sundays and made some use of the Bible, they were not primarily concerned with teaching religion, and in consequence they were likely to be interdenominational. To promote such schools in Philadelphia, Dr. Benjamin Rush, a Presbyterian physician, led in the organization of the First Day Society in 1791, and Bishop White became its president.

During the earliest years of the newly organized Episcopal Church the problem of Church unity presented itself. The attempts at that time to promote union with other Christian bodies were no more successful than various subsequent attempts, but they ought to be recorded because they show that the questions involved and the typical attitudes evoked by these questions were not unlike those which we find today.

To note the first example, Bishop Seabury published in 1790 an "Address to ministers and congregations of the Presbyterian and Independent [i.e. Congregational] persuasions in the United States of America." [6] On the ground that the sects to which these people then adhered had departed from the Church and thereby were guilty of schism, the bishop invited them to take the first step toward return. He assured them that this action would not involve the abandonment of the religion of their forefathers, but only "relinquishing those errors which they, through prejudice, most unhappily imbibed." Toward the close of this

[6] The address was probably occasioned by overtures from certain Congregationalists suggesting the possibility of union on the highly insecure basis of "taking the Holy Scriptures for our Creed and rule of discipline."

appeal he informed his readers that he doubted the validity of their orders and hence the validity of their sacraments, and that therefore he refused any opportunity to join in worship with them. By referring to the bodies to which they belonged as "persuasions" he was careful to deny that they were Churches.

To this not very seductive plea there was naturally no favorable response. The document is worth recording, however, because it is an excellent example of one familiar type of Episcopal attitude toward reunion with Protestants. It expresses what is essentially the Roman Catholic position, and might have been issued by the Pope with hardly a change of wording. It says in effect, "So far as you differ from us, you are all wrong. The sooner you awake to this fact the better. If you will humbly acknowledge your errors and present yourselves for readmission to our Church on our terms, you will not be rejected."

In the following year, quite independently of Seabury's action, negotiations were held on the initiative of the Methodist "superintendent" Thomas Coke. Though in no sense representing his Church, Dr. Coke wrote to Bishops Seabury and White offering a method for uniting Methodists and Episcopalians. He proposed that all who were then Methodist ministers should receive episcopal ordination and all future candidates for the ministry should receive the same; but that these ministers should remain under the government of the existing Methodist superintendents and their successors. The letter to Seabury contained the further proposal that since Episcopal bishops might refuse to ordain uneducated lay preachers, Coke and his fellow-superintendent Francis Asbury should be consecrated as bishops and thereafter do their own ordaining.

To these overtures Seabury made no reply, but White subsequently had three conferences with Coke in Philadelphia. Before these took place news of the death of Wesley had been received; and since his approval had been a necessary preliminary to action, no further steps were taken. An even stronger obstacle arose from the fact that Asbury, the most powerful figure in the Methodist Church in America, had never been informed of these plans, and it was acknowledged by Coke that he would not approve of them. Regardless of the merits of the design, then, no action was possible. But as a matter of fact the proposals were sadly defective. They amounted neither to federation nor to organic union. Methodism was to receive episcopal orders but otherwise was apparently to continue its independent career. White believed, moreover, that the plan gave Methodist ministers access to Episcopal congregations but prevented Episcopal clergy from having access to Methodist congregations. Yet in a letter to Coke, White reveals an open-minded attitude and a generosity of spirit which might be held to set a standard for future negotiations. After referring to the infidelity and heresy then so widely evident, he continues: "In this situation it is rather to be expected that distinct Churches, agreeing in fundamentals, should make mutual sacrifices for a union, than that any Church should divide into two bodies without a difference being even alleged to exist, in any leading point. For the preventing of this, the measures which you may propose cannot fail of success, unless there be on one side or on both, a most lamentable deficiency of Christian temper." [7]

At the next General Convention of 1792 the subject of Church unity was introduced by Bishop Madison of Virginia. He succeeded in persuading his three colleagues in the House of Bishops (Seabury, White, and Provoost) to vote for the adoption of the following declaration: "The Protestant Episcopal Church in the United States of America, ever bearing in mind the sacred obligation which attends all the followers of Christ, to avoid divisions among themselves, and anxious to promote that union for which our Lord and Saviour so earnestly prayed, do hereby declare to the Christian world, that, uninfluenced by any other consideration than those of duty as Christians, and an earnest desire for the prosperity of pure Christianity, and the furtherance of our holy religion, they are ready and willing to unite and form one body with any religious society which shall be influenced by the same Catholic spirit. And in order that this Christian end may be the more easily effected, they further declare, that all things in which the great essentials of Christianity or the characteristic principles of their Church are not concerned, they are willing to leave to future discussion; being ready to alter or modify those points which, in the opinion of the Protestant Episcopal Church, are subject to human alteration. And it is hereby recommended to the State [i.e. diocesan] conventions, to adopt such measures or propose such conferences with Christians of other denominations as to themselves may be thought most prudent, and report accordingly to the ensuing General Convention."

When the resolution containing this statement reached the House of Deputies, "they were astonished, and considered it as altogether preposterous; tending to produce distrust of the stability of the system of the Episcopal Church, without the least prospect of embracing any other religious body. The members generally mentioned, as a matter of indulgence, that they would permit the withdrawing of the paper; no notice being taken of it. . . . The bishops silently withdrew it, agreeably to leave given." [8] Considering the cautious safeguards included in Madison's proposal, the shocked horror of the Deputies at what they regarded as the bishop's incredible *faux pas* gives some indication of the contemporary

[7] W. White, *Memoirs of the P.E. Church,* 3rd ed., 413.
[8] *Ibid.,* 195 ff.

sentiments regarding Church unity. They are perhaps a little easier to understand, however, if we remember the extreme weakness of the Church at that moment. At all events, it was many a long year before the subject of Church unity received serious attention from General Convention.[9]

[9] "In 1797 the Rev. Thos. Ellison, Rector of St. Peter's Church, Albany, communicated to the Convention [of N.Y.] the interesting intelligence 'that some Lutheran clergymen had, in the name and on behalf of the Consistory of the Lutheran Church in the State of N.Y., intimated to him a desire to have it proposed to this Convention that their Church might be united with the Protestant Episcopal Church in this State, and that their ministers might receive episcopal ordination.' A committee, of which the Rev. Dr. Benjamin Moore was chairman, was appointed 'to meet such gentlemen of the Lutheran Church as may be duly appointed by their ecclesiastical authority to confer with them on the subject.' Provision was made for bringing the matter, should it be found advisable, before the approaching General Convention, and the committee was instructed to report to the next State [i.e. diocesan] Convention." Perry, *History*, II, 150 f. This proposal was attended with no results.

Chapter VI

NEW LEADERS

AFTER the war of 1812, which ended in the year of Waterloo, there was peace at home and abroad. Despite some years of depression in the early twenties, the short period which followed the battle of New Orleans (1815) and ended with the retirement of Andrew Jackson (1837) produced an expansion of national energy.

By 1830 the population of 4,000,000 in 1790 had more than tripled. The State of New York alone had nearly 2,000,000 inhabitants and the city of New York over 200,000. During the first three decades of the century 8,000 miles of canals had been completed, and in 1830, 200 steamships were operating on the Ohio and Mississippi. Urban communities then represented about one fifteenth instead of one thirtieth of the population, and factory towns had begun to develop. In politics the era from 1812 to 1837 covered the greater part of the long reign of Chief Justice Marshall in the Supreme Court and the rise to power of Henry Clay in Congress. It included the second administration of Madison and those of Monroe, John Quincy Adams, and Andrew Jackson. It witnessed such events as the liberation of most of Latin America from Spain, the proclamation of the Monroe Doctrine (1823), the Missouri Compromise (1820), Webster's famous Reply to Hayne (1830), and South Carolina's experiment with Nullification (1832). In literature the years were made memorable by the work of Irving, Bryant, and Cooper, and by the immense popularity, especially in the South, of those greater figures, Scott and Byron. The careers of Gilbert Stuart and Charles Bulfinch produced masterpieces of lasting quality in painting and architecture. Indeed, in almost every field of endeavor, except in science, it was a creative epoch.

In the general movement of progress American Christianity was vitally engaged, and almost every denomination made notable advances. With the year 1811 signs of life in the Episcopal Church began gradually to appear. Every few years thereafter brought encouraging evidence that the Church was awakening to its opportunities and planning for the future with growing wisdom and firmness. This increasing vigor was largely due to the rise of new leaders, men of very different types but all endowed with contagious energy. Foremost among these were three bishops—Griswold of the "Eastern Diocese," Hobart of New York, and Chase of Ohio. If we would follow the growth of the Church in those days we could find no method more effective than to survey their varied careers.

By the time these men were active and influential, groups or parties in the Church had become prominent, and neither men nor movements of that time can be fully interpreted without a knowledge of these schools of thought. Moreover, since the types of Churchmanship then evident were to persist, with certain variations, from that day to this, their characteristics ought to be summarized briefly at this early period. A more adequate understanding of their beliefs and policies will emerge as our story goes on.

Ever since the Elizabethan Settlement it has always been true that in any branch of the Anglican Communion there exist, in a greater or less degree of tension, two elements or factors—the Catholic and the Protestant. That is the kind of Church that the Church of England then set out to be—a Catholic Church which had undergone a vigorous reformation. Though the Anglican Communion, taken as a whole, may keep these elements in proper balance, it is asking too much of human nature to expect all its members to view them with impartial eyes. It is almost inevitable that individuals, and even dioceses, in their thought and practice, should incline to favor one factor more warmly or readily than the other. The High Churchman expresses his loyalty to the Anglican Communion by stressing the Catholic element in it. The Low Churchman expresses his loyalty by stressing the Protestant element.

To heighten the Catholic factor in the Church is to magnify the importance of those characteristics which the Church possesses in common with other Catholic Churches—for example, episcopacy conceived as of apostolic descent; a strong emphasis upon the Sacrament of the Eucharist; a relatively elaborate ritual; and in general a tendency to express the *corporate* side of Christianity and the *objective* aspect of religion.

To emphasize the Protestant factor in the Church is to magnify the importance of those characteristics which the Church possesses in common with other Reformed Churches—for example, the heaviest stress upon the Bible as the source of authority; devotion to the doctrine of salvation by faith in Christ alone; a high value set upon preaching, especially upon preaching to produce conversion; and in general a tendency to express the *individualistic* side of Christianity and the *subjective* aspect of religion.

To these constant factors in the two groups there were other features familiar in those days. Both groups, for instance (unlike either today), believed in a verbally infallible Bible, and the theology of both was of an Evangelical type, often strongly tinged with Calvinism. The High Churchman was not then greatly concerned with ritual, and he was vigorously anti-Roman. As an aid to maintaining the position of his Church, he avoided cooperation with Protestants and played but a small part in promoting the various humanitarian causes of the period.

The Low Churchman or Evangelical, like his counterpart in England, was likely to be earnestly active in philanthropic undertakings and always ready to work with Christians of any denomination. Though loyal to the Prayer Book, he declined to confine himself on all occasions to liturgical services and written prayers. To a degree that is hard to appreciate today he was intensely anti-sacerdotal, having a real abhorrence of such terms as "priest," "altar," and "sacrifice." Also to an extent that would make him unpopular in modern life he was markedly Puritanical in his attitude toward social morality.

Taking all the facts into consideration, it would not be unfair to say that the High Churchmen of 1820 were more moderate than many of their group today, while the Low Churchmen of 1820 were more extreme in their views than any party now existing. For that reason the average Episcopalian of today would probably feel more at home with the older type of High Churchman than with the older type of Evangelical. In between the two main types there were of course a large number of middle-of-the-road Episcopalians; but in the era of Griswold, Hobart, and Chase there were no "Broad Churchmen," and "Liberalism" as later known was still below the horizon.[1]

ALEXANDER VIETS GRISWOLD

The gentlest and finest character of the three bishops we have named —and the least interesting—was Alexander Viets Griswold. His long life from farmer's boy to Presiding Bishop began in 1766 when he was born at Simsbury, Connecticut. Thanks chiefly to his maternal uncle, Roger Viets, a priest of the Church in charge of the local parish, his education in boyhood was more thorough than might have been expected, and his devotion to the Church dated from his earliest years. Though he was prepared by the age of nineteen to enter Yale and had read nearly all the books in his uncle's library, his marriage in that year (1785) put an end to any further advance toward higher education. For the next ten years he

[1] It may be said, however, to have appeared in England, if we may rightly so label men like Richard Whately and Thomas Arnold.

had to earn his living as a farmer. Yet he never ceased to crowd his few spare moments with study, and the thought of the ministry was never long absent from his mind. In the words of his son-in-law, "His early marriage and his condition as a working farmer rendered his education a series of difficulties. He has told us that when he was attempting to prepare himself for the ministry he was obliged to labor all the day on the farm; and not being able to afford himself adequate lights, he was in the habit of stretching himself on the hearth, with his books before him, and by the light of pine-knots, as they blazed in the chimney corner, pursuing his studies for hours after his wife and children were asleep."

At length, in 1794, Griswold was admitted as a candidate for orders, and in the following year was ordained both deacon and priest by Bishop Seabury. For the next nine years he served as the minister of three small Connecticut parishes, at Plymouth, Harwinton, and Litchfield. They were so small, in fact, that even in combination they could not fully support a priest, and Griswold sometimes had to work as a hired farming hand, and in winter taught in the district school. Yet he wrote long after, "No years of my life have been more happy than the ten which I passed in those three parishes."

In 1804, after twice declining the call, he accepted the rectorship of the little church at Bristol, Rhode Island. The vestry had been insistent not only because they had met Griswold and taken his measure, but because they had learned what his parishioners thought of him. As one of them had put it, "He is an uncommonly perfect man; you can find no fault with him, no way." He was leaving many dear friends and exchanging two hundred and twenty communicants for only twenty, but with a growing family he had great need of a larger salary. What he had previously been content with we may infer from the fact that Bristol gave him only $600 a year, and he had to run a large school to make both ends meet. But within a few years the church had to be enlarged to hold the growing congregations. Thenceforward for a quarter of a century Bristol remained his beloved home, and in ministering to its people his character deepened and his powers expanded.

To find himself in a new community and in a different atmosphere wrought changes in Griswold's own attitude and temper. It was at Bristol that he learned more fully the meaning of evangelical Christianity and came to deserve his future reputation as a leader of the Evangelical group. But his natural instincts and his Connecticut training always kept him conservative.

During the year when Griswold moved to Bristol the second bishop of Massachusetts died three months after his consecration, and for more than five years thereafter the diocese was too weak and discouraged to provide for his successor. But on May 29, 1810, at a convention in Boston, representatives of the Church in New Hampshire, Vermont, Massachusetts, and Rhode Island organized "the Eastern Diocese," and on the 31st they elected Griswold to be its bishop. This Eastern Diocese was not a diocese in the full sense. It was a kind of holding company formed to maintain four dioceses, none of which could afford a bishop. Curiously enough, though the bishop chosen was to be the bishop of the Eastern Diocese and not of any one of its component parts, the four dioceses continued to operate as such. Each held its own separate annual convention, and each was represented, under its State title, in the General Convention. Yet there was also a convention of the Eastern Diocese, held at first biennially and later annually. "The effect of these peculiarities," as the bishop's biographer notes, "was to beget a kind of ecclesiastico-'States-rights' feeling, drawing almost all the proper efficient action of the Church from the diocesan to the State institutions."

It was this kind of episcopate that Griswold accepted, and a year later he was consecrated in New York. Fortunately for his own peace of mind and the welfare of his extensive see, he was humble-minded and conciliatory in his methods. Though his fibre was tough and he had plenty of backbone, he was no martinet; he never worried about his own rights and privileges; and he was no vigorous organizer with a passion for system. What this sketchily federated "diocese" needed was a moderator of a calm disposition who would accept limitations and inconsistencies for the good of the cause, and who would prefer persuasion to force. Griswold filled this difficult role to perfection. His achievements, as we shall see, were less striking than those of Hobart, but they were accomplished in the face of greater obstacles.

The years of his election and consecration brought heavy sorrow to the new bishop. Within that short time two of his daughters died and one of his sons. His life, indeed, was to be scarred with many domestic losses, for ten of his twelve children died of consumption, and for ten years he was a widower before his second marriage at the age of sixty-one.

Griswold had still to retain his rectorship at Bristol in order to provide the modest measure of support to which four dioceses were unashamedly unequal. Yet without neglecting his parish he could report to the first convention of the Eastern Diocese in 1812: "With very few exceptions I have visited the churches of this diocese once, and some of them a second time; and the present appearance is that most of them are increasing in numbers, piety, and attention to the doctrines and discipline of the Church. I have administered the holy rite of Confirmation to 1212 persons." His first three years as bishop, however, were the three years of the war with Great Britain, which not only aroused fierce partisanship in New England but brought many of its towns close to ruin. Yet in spite of local depression, which is too often the excuse for refusing to share in any advance, Griswold was insistent upon the need for missionary expansion at home and abroad.

To the convention of the Eastern Diocese held at Portsmouth, New Hampshire, on September 28, 1814, the bishop addressed a Charge, which was published in the following year together with a Pastoral Letter. In these documents he has some severe words to say about the indifference of his people to the cause of missions. He calls their attention to "the painfully discouraging results" of the annual Easter offerings for diocesan missions and frankly declares that "there is probably no other Church by which missionary work is so much neglected as by ours in this diocese. . . . The efforts made by other denominations of Christians to propagate the Gospel are a reproach upon us." He asserts that though the reputation of the Church of England has been sullied by her "apathy in regard to propagating her faith," there are now encouraging signs of her awakening. But he adds, "There is one portion of the Christian Church still delinquent, and however humiliating may be the confession, truth will compel us to acknowledge that it is this portion to which we belong, even the Protestant Episcopal Church in the United States of America." [2]

That Griswold's hopes and plans reached beyond his own area is evident from his correspondence with the secretary of the English Church Missionary Society, to whom he reported in 1821 the organization of that national Domestic and Foreign Missionary Society which he himself had been active in promoting. But his immediate responsibility was for Church extension in New England. In the Eastern Diocese, with its population and its parishes thinly scattered over a wide area, progress was slow. After the hardships entailed by the war, New England began to suffer from the heavy migration westward which then set in. Yet in spite of drawbacks like these, the number of communicants had doubled by 1818. Two years later, when Maine became a State, the Church there joined the Eastern Diocese as its fifth member.

Except for a controversy during the 'twenties on the subject of prayer meetings, which served to warm up several Church periodicals and to produce not a little ill-feeling, the churches in the diocese had been remarkably united, and there had been few signs of party spirit. But with the opening years of the next decade, soon after the bishop had moved to Massachusetts to become rector of St. Peter's Church, Salem, he began to be distressed by growing evidence of antagonism between High Church and Low. It appears to have shown itself chiefly in hampering the work of "The Massachusetts Episcopal Missionary Society," upon which the

[2] J. S. Stone, *Memoir of Griswold,* 594 f., 610.

welfare of diocesan missions depended. His own impartial attitude is well expressed in one of his letters. "If a bishop will become the head of a party," he wrote, "or strenuously enforce the views and promote the interests of one designation of religionists, by them of course he will be highly extolled. . . . Whether I am called High Church or Low Church, I am totally indifferent; for I cannot easily decide which I most dislike. The former, it is well known, are the most impatient of control and the least willing to be governed." And to show how he hated to be involved in such struggles, he concludes by saying, "The canting language a few years since so much used in Pennsylvania, about the bishop's *friends* and the bishop's *enemies,* was in my view very contemptible; and my prayer is never to hear it in this diocese." [3]

What Griswold objected to on both sides of these controversies was the display of party animosity and the resulting harm to the advance of the Church. But though he was usually careful to take an impartial stand as an official, he was in no doubt as to where his own sympathies lay. He was an ardent Low Church Evangelical. Ten years later, for example, he was rebuking a parish severely for treating the holy table as an altar and for using candles, flowers, and pictures; and in reply to the ensuing protests he stated his views on what was then the new Oxford Movement. "I am well aware," he declared, "that there is a new sect lately sprung up among us called Puseyites, or Low Papists, who have, chiefly in England, written and preached and published much against the Reformation, and are endeavoring to bring back into the Church of England many of those superstitious mummeries and idolatrous practices, for protesting against which so many of her pious bishops and other ministers have been burnt at the stake." [4] Of his attitude toward other Churches his biographer, John Seely Stone, has written: "He never thought that the Church of Christ cannot, in any sense, exist without episcopacy. . . . He saw and felt the dangers to which other denominations are exposed; but he considered them Christian Churches, and rejoiced in all the good of which they were instruments." [5]

When we remember with what an easy rein the bishop's five "dioceses" had to be guided, and how difficult it was to be efficient with the machinery available, we shall not be surprised that Griswold had to wait long for his most encouraging rewards. From the beginning, it is true, there was a slow growth in communicants and in parishes; but not until after twenty and more years could he rejoice in the two surest signs of success—the development of a sound and lasting missionary organization

[3] *Ibid.,* 372 f.

[4] *Ibid.,* 442. The influence of the Oxford Movement on the Church in the U.S. will be treated later in Part III (1836–1865).

[5] *Ibid.,* 221.

in Massachusetts and the achievement of self-support by the parts of his own diocese. In 1836 the diocesan convention of Massachusetts organized a Board of Missions which was to be the official organ of the diocese representing all its members. The Church in Massachusetts, as a united body, thus formally accepted its missionary responsibility. Under Griswold's guidance it was following, as we shall see later, the example of the General Convention, for there too he had been among the leaders in promoting the same wholesome change.

The Church in Vermont was the first to withdraw from the Eastern Diocese. In 1832 its diocesan convention proclaimed its independence and elected John Henry Hopkins as bishop. This sign of maturity was really a tribute to Bishop Griswold, who received from the members of the convention a message of warm affection which included these words: "It may be truly said that the Lord has so multiplied the seed sown under your ministry that the fruits have become more than you can gather. . . . Be assured that towards you we shall never cease to cherish a filial regard; nor will it cease to be our heart's desire that the Lord will have you in His holy and special keeping."

In 1836 Bishop White died and Griswold, by seniority, became Presiding Bishop, a post which he had never coveted and which he never enjoyed. During the previous year he had retired for the first time from parish work and had moved to Boston. Now that he was more than ever identified with Massachusetts, the people's devotion to him prevented them from taking Massachusetts out of the Eastern Diocese. As a matter of fact, all the churches in this federation were a little tired of the Eastern Diocese, but they all loved Griswold. To express both feelings, the convention of the Eastern Diocese in 1838 voted that it should be dissolved upon the death of Griswold. New Hampshire in the same year and Maine in 1839 withdrew from the diocese but insisted on remaining under the jurisdiction of Griswold. Thus the diocese by this time amounted to little more than an annual convention addressed by its beloved bishop.

On February 15, 1843, Griswold died at the age of seventy-six. A few weeks earlier he had taken part in the consecration of Manton Eastburn of New York as Assistant Bishop of Massachusetts, and that diocese resumed its independent career. In the course of another year Rhode Island and New Hampshire had elected bishops, and Maine followed in 1847. During his episcopate the parishes in Griswold's diocese had increased five-fold, and soon after his death there were five dioceses in place of one. He had labored as bishop with unfaltering devotion for thirty-two years, and the fruits of his labor were admirably apparent to the whole Church. Yet even with such a record it was the man who was remembered more than the bishop. Though deliberate and reserved, he was capable of cordial and lasting friendships. His simplicity was almost childlike. Constantly and naturally self-denying and self-effacing, he was an ideal pastor, and as such, rather than as a prelate, he was beloved in every State of New England. As one Congregationalist admirer expressed it, "He is the best representative of an apostle I have ever seen, particularly because he does not know it."

JOHN HENRY HOBART

John Henry Hobart was a dynamo of constructive energy. He was the first bishop to show the American Church how to run a diocese.

Hobart was born in Philadelphia on September 14, 1775. When he was nine, his father, who was a well-to-do business man, sent him to the newly founded Episcopal Academy. Later, after two years at the University of the State of Pennsylvania, he joined the Junior class at Princeton, and in 1793 received his bachelor's degree with high honors at the age of eighteen. Yielding to family pressure he then entered the office of his brother-in-law with the aim to begin a business career; but after a year's trial his love of study led him to abandon the attempt and to accept the offer of a tutorship at Princeton. Though he was not made to be a professional scholar, his executive ability and his personal magnetism were already evident, and he was highly popular with the students. He could undoubtedly have continued for life in the academic world; but during the four years he spent as a teacher his devotion to the Church had deepened, and he had reached the firm decision to enter the ministry. In 1798 he left Princeton and was ordained deacon by Bishop White, who had long been his friend and adviser.

After less than a year in charge of a group of small churches in the neighborhood of Philadelphia, he accepted a call to Christ Church, New Brunswick. It was there that he married Mary Chandler, daughter of the Rev. Thomas B. Chandler, that stout defender of episcopacy in the previous generation. By the middle of May, 1800, he had moved again, this time to Hempstead, Long Island, and six months later we find him in New York as assistant minister in Trinity Church. Since this was his fourth assignment in two years and a half, it began to look as if his restlessness would keep him from steady work. But this fourth move was his last, for as assistant, as rector, and even as bishop, he remained at Trinity for the rest of his life.

Trinity Parish, already more than a century old, then consisted of three large congregations, so that the members of its staff had heavy responsibilities. Even these, however, were not enough for Hobart's energy. From the very beginning of his career he was never content with less than the maximum of varied activity. While still a deacon he was appointed secretary of the House of Bishops, and in 1801, just after he had reached New York, he was elected secretary of the diocesan convention. In the same year he was a deputy to the General Convention, and for the next two conventions was secretary of the House of Deputies. In 1801, moreover, at the age of twenty-six, he joined Alexander Hamilton and others on the Board of Trustees of Columbia College.

His power of initiative and his organizing ability could not be satisfied with sharing in work already in operation. Always he was busy starting something new, and generally it was something of which the Church was badly in need. At that moment the Church was equally neglectful of missionary expansion and of Christian education. In view of his past experience and of his present opportunities it was the lack of means for education which Hobart was especially eager to remedy. As a first step he became one of the chief promoters of the Protestant Episcopal Society for Promoting Religion and Learning in the State of New York, which was formed in 1802. Four years later the Protestant Episcopal Theological Society was organized. Its constitution and by-laws were drawn up by Hobart, and its purpose was to bring together the clergy of the diocese for weekly meetings, which included not only devotional periods but the reading of sermons and essays. Finding religious journalism at a low ebb, he took over *The Churchman's Magazine,* the only periodical in the Church, moved it from New Haven, and edited it for the next three years. It was in that year that the first interdenominational Bible Society in the United States was founded at Philadelphia; and prompt to improve upon a good idea, Hobart took the lead in establishing in 1809 the Bible and Common Prayer Book Society of New York, which still flourishes.

Through these same years of his early ministry Hobart became known not only as an organizer of educational societies but as an author of educational works. He was among the first American Churchmen to produce religious literature. In 1804 appeared *A Companion for the Altar.* In this devotional manual, partly compiled from English sources, Hobart strikes the notes which were to be characteristic of all his future writings. As he was often to describe them, these were "Evangelical Truth *and* Apostolic Order." The Gospel of salvation through the divine merits of a crucified Redeemer was the evangelical element upon which he was always warmly insistent. Equally firm, however, was his conviction that the grace of Christ was mediated and "applied to the soul of the believer" through the sacraments of the Church administered by a priesthood episcopally ordained. So far as he dwelt upon the Gospel message he was in accord with the Evangelicals of his own Church and with Protestant preachers and writers. But since he never missed a chance to proclaim with the same emphasis the indispensable factors of episcopacy and the priesthood, he was frequently engaged in controversy. Though he found support only from a growing minority in his own Church and met with opposition everywhere else, he never wavered.

Soon after the publication in 1805 of *A Companion for the Festivals and Fasts of the Church,*[6] Hobart became involved in a long newspaper controversy aroused by his High Church views. For some months the *Albany Centinel* bristled with anonymous essays and letters on both sides, and in the next year Hobart published his own papers as *A Collection of Essays on the Subject of Episcopacy.* His convictions, familiar enough in earlier and in later times, were then so novel in America as to shock the Protestant world. The public seemed not to have suspected these elements in the Episcopal Church. So Hobart's book was reviewed by a powerful Presbyterian divine, who described the author's beliefs as "of such deep-toned horror as may well make one's hair stand up like quills upon the fretful porcupine and freeze the warm blood at the fountain." Language like this was relatively mild in those days when religious disputations were seldom modified by Christian manners. But in any case Hobart would not have been daunted by the doughtiest of foes, and in the spring of 1807 he set forth a vigorous retort in *An Apology for Apostolic Order and its Advocates.* That ended what may be called the first round; but the appetite for controversy was to be as characteristic of his future career as were his zeal and his whole-hearted consecration to his chosen task.

The diocese of New York had made too little progress when Bishop Provoost resigned in 1801. His successor, Benjamin Moore, though highly respected and of saintly character, was no leader. When he was stricken with paralysis in 1811, the chance had come at last to find a bishop who was able not only to confirm and to ordain but to govern and to pioneer. Hobart was the obvious choice, and on May 29, 1811, he was consecrated as Assistant Bishop of New York. Five years later, upon the death of Moore, he succeeded him both as rector of Trinity and as diocesan. From the beginning, however, he was solely responsible for administering the Church in New York, a diocese which then covered 46,000 square miles.

Every corner of the diocese was soon aware that there was a new bishop, for in the second full year of his episcopate he travelled over 2,000 miles, visited 33 parishes, and confirmed 1,100 persons. Hundreds of Episcopalians who had long wondered what a bishop was like soon grew to know their chief pastor. "In personal appearance he gave the impression of vigor and agility. Below the average stature, his figure was well knit

[6] This book was founded on Robert Nelson's work, which bore the same title and had been published in England a century earlier. In adding other material Hobart acted chiefly as a compiler.

and muscular; his head large, his voice strong and flexible. Near-sighted from youth, he always wore spectacles of more than ordinary power. . . . In consequence of his defective sight, he dispensed as much as possible with manuscript, committing his sermons to memory, and preaching with rapidity and energy. Like most men of lively temperament he had intervals of depression; but it was generally said of him that his presence in a room was like a ray of sunshine." [7] His frankness, vivacity, and warmth of manner won him friends everywhere.

When he first took office Hobart found only two diocesan missionaries. At his death nineteen years later there were fifty. That record is enough to show that he was not only a militant Churchman and an enthusiastic educator, but also an eager promoter of missionary advance. In addressing his diocesan convention in 1813 he dwelt primarily on the importance of Church extension. He recommended the adoption of a canon (in place of a pious "resolution" commonly ignored) making it obligatory on all parishes to contribute to diocesan missions. This action was among those which laid the foundation for the expansion of the Church through the northern and western parts of New York. Behind him, moreover, he had the wealth of Trinity Parish and its heavy endowments, a share of which was always available for the enterprises of a bishop who was also a popular and persuasive rector.

A symptom of new life in the diocese might be found in the journals of General Convention. The committee which reported triennially on the state of the Church produced brief accounts of each diocese, many of them rather depressing. After Hobart became bishop the story of New York grew to be nearly as long as all the others put together, and the space was filled not with pious language but with factual evidence of unresting activity. After only four years, for example, the number of clergy in the State had doubled, and the number of missionaries had more than quadrupled; and after twenty years nearly every important town in the State had an Episcopal church and a rector. Trinity Church received more attention than ever; yet at the same time there was new work among the distant Oneida Indians, whose chiefs corresponded with their Father the bishop and received from him long letters of paternal advice beginning, "My children."

The effect upon the community of this movement of expansion was marked. Combined with Hobart's outspoken statements of what the Church meant to him, it gave to those Americans who observed it a new idea of the Episcopal Church: "The whole tone of public feeling toward the Church changed. It was no longer tolerated as an amply endowed institution too respectable to be disturbed, but too torpid to be feared. It

[7] Morgan Dix, *History of Trinity Church,* II, 208.

become a living factor, dreaded by some, admired by others, but acknowledged and respected by all. . . . He made the Church in New York a living power." [8]

It was not New York alone which felt the impact of Hobart's ardent vigor. In General Convention his leadership was evident. Dr. William Berrian of New York, who wrote his life, has noted his talent for public business. "Fond of its excitement, patient of all its details . . . prompt in action, full of resources . . . always self-possessed, confident of his own powers, prepared for any emergency." [9] Though he was naturally domineering, with what Bishop Coxe called "an almost military air of command," he could draw out the strongest affection and loyalty, because of the warmth of his temperament and his personal charm. He seems to have been equally effective whether he was using force or persuasion.

His most important contribution to the general Church was in the field of theological education. Like Bishop White and others, he was at first opposed to the idea of a General Seminary for the whole Church. He preferred diocesan seminaries where bishops could count on having their own way. But as we shall see in a later chapter, when General Convention had determined on a General Seminary he gave support to the plan, and when the new school was finally established in New York and he had secured a dominant voice in its management, it continued to owe much to him both as a teacher and as a trustee. The little seminary he had organized at Geneva, in connection with Geneva College, was abandoned in 1824; but the college, for whose revival and expansion he was largely responsible, now bears his name and testifies to his lifelong concern for higher education.

Among those who stood in need of higher education Hobart always counted his clergy. Partly for their sake and partly to guide the laity he was accustomed to deliver episcopal "Charges" at his diocesan conventions. A glance at one of these will reveal certain basic convictions of the bishop and of the school of thought of which he was leader.

There was published in 1819 "The Principles of the Churchman stated and explained, in distinction from the corruptions of the Church of Rome and from the errors of certain Protestant sects." Hobart's main thesis is here stated clearly: "The Churchman . . . adheres in all essential points to the faith, the ministry, and worship which distinguished the apostolic and primitive Church, and particularly to the constitution of the Christian ministry under its three orders of bishops, priests, and deacons." Though he endorses heartily the belief in justification by faith in Christ alone, he rejects such Calvinistic doctrines as those of total depravity and

[8] C. C. Tiffany, *History of the Protestant Episcopal Church,* 414.
[9] W. Berrian, *Memoir of Hobart,* 382 f.

election to reprobation. At the same time he condemns the practice of invoking the saints, repudiates "the horrible doctrine of transubstantiation," and insists that the bread and wine of the Eucharist are "symbols" and that the term "Sacrifice" as applied to them is "unknown to our liturgy." His words about confession would not satisfy many modern Anglo-Catholics. "The Churchman," he declares, "justly deems auricular confession and private absolution an encroachment on the rights of conscience, an invasion of the prerogative of the Searcher of Hearts, and, with some exceptions, hostile to domestic and social happiness, and licentious and corrupting in its tendency." [10]

Hobart is firm, however, in his teaching that "the Churchman is distinguished by the great stress which he lays on the sacraments, ordinances, and ministrations of the Church. . . . He would think that he hazarded his salvation if he refused or neglected to receive these means and pledges of the divine favor." And he does not hesitate to affirm that the Churchman believes that in separating himself from the order of bishops he is cutting himself off from the communion of the Church and is guilty of the sin of schism. Yet in a later charge he adds this modification: "So far indeed from confining salvation to a state of visible union with Christ's mystical body, the Churchman extends the benefits of the Redeemer's merits and grace to the pious and sincere of all sects and of all nations. But a divine society being established as the regular and ordinary channel of salvation, his duty is plain to unite himself to that society and to seek to induce others sincerely to do so." [11]

These beliefs often led Hobart into taking unpopular stands which sometimes resulted in hot controversies. He used all his resources to keep his clergy and laity from cooperating with the newly founded interdenominational American Bible Society. He condemned such non-liturgical services as prayer-meetings and evangelistic meetings, believing that they led to disorder and "enthusiasm." By severe pressure he managed to extinguish a "Clerical Association" of some of the New York clergy because he feared it would prove to be merely a party organ of the Evangelicals. In short, he was opposed to any organization which he could not control, for, like most powerful characters with intense convictions, he identified himself with his cause. But in his best moments what he really

[10] Hobart, *Principles of the Churchman*, etc., 15, 19 ff.

[11] *Ibid.*, 16, 23 f., *The High Churchman Vindicated*, p. 32.

More than a century earlier the famous High Churchman of Queen Anne's reign, Dr. Sacheverell, had written a similar statement of his faith. "The High Churchman," he said, "is High for the divine right of Episcopacy, High for the uninterrupted Succession, High for the Liturgies against extemporary prayers, High for the primitive doctrine and discipline of the Ancient Church." But what the historian Trevelyan says of these early eighteenth century High Churchmen was true of Hobart—"There was no approach towards Rome, and no tendency to ritualistic innovation." (G. M. Trevelyan, *England under Queen Anne*, I, 52.)

meant was that he could not endorse movements or groups whose actions violated his principles.

Even Hobart's strong constitution could not indefinitely survive labors that were both intense and extensive to an amazing degree. In 1832, when he was only forty-eight, his health had become so seriously impaired by what was then described as "bilious fever" that he was obliged to cease all work and to spend two years of rest and travel in England and on the Continent. Though he described France as an "uninteresting" country, he was enthusiastic about Italy, and especially about England, where he was received and entertained by many bishops and other leaders of note. Most memorable of all these occasions from our point of view was the day he spent with Wordsworth walking over the great hills near Rydal Mount.

The long vacation brought him renewed strength, and he resumed his exacting office with a vigor which seemed almost undiminished. Yet he was never quite the same man again. For five years with growing effort he kept at his work and maintained his leadership; but in 1830, while on a visitation of the western parts of his diocese, he died suddenly at Auburn two days before his fifty-fifth birthday. He was buried in the chancel of Trinity Church in New York.

In appraising Bishop Hobart one is tempted to compare him with Archbishop Laud. Their beliefs about the Church were in pretty close agreement; and both of them, with intense and self-forgetful energy, devoted their lives to realizing in action their ideals for the Church. Both men were fearless and aggressive, resenting opposition; both were quick tempered, impatient, and restlessly active. Yet there were important points of difference. Hobart had a sense of humor; he was always ready to apologize when his impulsiveness had led him into any injustice; and above all he was not only socially winning but essentially lovable. His death was mourned by countless friends.

PHILANDER CHASE

Another farmer's boy who became Presiding Bishop was Philander Chase; but in his temperament, in his methods, and in the scope of his career he stands in striking contrast to his contemporary Griswold. Far from working quietly and persuasively in one corner of the country, Chase was an aggressive and dominating pioneer in areas as far apart as New York, Louisiana, Ohio, and Illinois. And in days when trans-Atlantic voyaging was painful and insecure he found time and occasion for two trips to England.

Chase was born on December 14, 1775, at Cornish, New Hampshire. All his boyhood was spent on his father's farm, and the experience he won in those years he put to good use throughout his life; for, as has been remarked, "he remained to the end of his days, despite his varied ecclesiastical occupations, an enthusiastic and successful farmer." Yet by the industrious use of spare time he was able to prepare himself for college, and in 1791 he entered the Freshman class at Dartmouth. During his Sophomore year the Church's *Book of Common Prayer* came into his hands, and the study of it produced in him so profound an effect that he became devotedly attached to the Episcopal Church. More than that, he proceeded to show his instinctively missionary spirit by winning his Congregational family to this new allegiance. It was only an early instance of his lifelong practice of overpowering persuasion. For the next sixty years he was constantly successful in getting people to do things which they had never dreamed they would find themselves doing.

Chase took his B.A. degree in 1795, and in the following year he married Mary Fay of Hardwick, Massachusetts. By this time he had served for several years as a lay reader, and had slowly reached the determination to enter the ministry. In those days, however, preparation for holy orders was irregular and uncertain, for there were no theological schools, and where Chase lived there was no local rector to whom he could turn. Quite undeterred by such obstacles he proceeded to make inquiries, and was recommended to consult an Englishman, the Rev. Thomas Ellison, rector of St. Peter's Church at Albany. He made his way to Albany, rang Ellison's doorbell, and respectfully proposed that this unknown clergyman should prepare him for the ministry. Finding the newcomer both powerful and prepossessing (a vigorous specimen, six feet four in height and broad in the shoulders) Ellison agreed. Having secured a teaching position at a local school, Chase then moved his young wife to Albany, and there in 1797 his first son was born.

It required less than two years for Chase to prepare himself for his profession, and on May 10, 1798, he was ordained deacon by Bishop Provoost. At once he was assigned to missionary work in central New York. Within a year he had organized small groups that were later to be parishes at Auburn (where there was then one house and a tavern), at Utica, Canandaigua, and Batavia, but not at Syracuse, where then "there was but a dreary salt marsh." It was during this year and a half in 1798 and 1799 that he travelled over 4,000 miles, preached 213 times, and baptized 319 infants and 14 adults. This record was achieved twelve years before Hobart took hold of the diocese, and New York had hitherto seen no such display of missionary energy.

Chiefly in order to satisfy the canonical requirement that a priest must occupy a settled and salaried post, Chase became minister of the churches at Poughkeepsie and Fishkill, and was ordained to the priesthood on November 10, 1799. So feeble, however, was the support provided for him that he had to add to his labors by teaching school. The strain of supporting his family was increased by the discovery that his wife was developing tuberculosis. He was more than ready, therefore, to welcome in 1805 a message from Bishop Moore of New York asking him to respond to a call from New Orleans where Church folk were looking for a rector.

After a long and very rough voyage Chase arrived in New Orleans—the first Protestant minister to enter that city. Within a few months he had organized a vestry and founded what is now Christ Church Cathedral. Having obtained a formal call on his own terms, he returned to Poughkeepsie, placed his sons in school in Vermont, and brought his wife back to New Orleans. At the close of nearly six years in this unfamiliar environment, during which he not only built up a strong parish but also founded and maintained a school for Protestant children, Chase decided to return to the North, chiefly to provide for the further education of his boys.

Soon after he had placed George and Philander in the new Episcopal Academy at Cheshire, Connecticut, Chase accepted a call to be rector of Christ Church, Hartford, where he served for six years until 1817—"the most peaceful part," he declared, in the history of his life. His happiness there is evidence that he could be successful and contented in prosperous and cultivated surroundings, and that his future missionary career was sustained less by a crude instinct for pioneering than by a zeal that was genuinely apostolic.

At the age of forty-two, when most men have ceased to be venturesome and are preparing to settle down, Chase made the bold decision to head for the frontier. It was the period after the second war with England when a great stream of western migration was in full flood, and the traffic to Ohio from New England, and especially from Connecticut, was heavy. Some of these emigrants were known to Chase; and inspired by their example and by his own past experience in central New York, he determined upon a career as a free-lance missionary in Ohio. These, in fact, were the only terms upon which such a project could be undertaken, for there was no missionary society to guarantee salaries and other forms of paternal care. Leaving his wife and children, he journeyed by stage to the little village of Buffalo, and travelled thence across the perilous melting ice of Lake Erie until he landed safe in Ohio. On March 16, 1817, to the occupants of a few log houses in what is now Salem, he preached his first sermon in the western country.

Throughout the weeks of a slow spring he rode on horseback over bad roads, always heavy with mud and often deep in snow, establishing little congregations in the new communities of Windsor, Ravenna, Zanesville, and Columbus. In early June he bought a large farm in Worthington (a settlement founded by Churchmen from Connecticut) and agreed to become the minister of the church there and of the churches at four other points including Columbus. To make his position still more secure he accepted the principalship of the rudimentary "academy" at Worthington. By that time it was possible for his wife to join him; but her health began to fail so rapidly that within less than a year she died of tuberculosis.

Ten months after his arrival the diocese of Ohio was organized by nine laymen and two clergymen, including Chase; and at a later convention held on June 3, 1818, Chase was elected bishop. He accepted the election and prepared for the long journey which must precede his consecration. On February 11, 1819, he was consecrated in Philadelphia by Bishop White and three other bishops, and in bitter weather set off once more upon the lonely road to Ohio. Four months after his return he married Sophia May Ingraham, whom he had known at Poughkeepsie and who remained thenceforth his able and steadfast fellow-worker in all his laborious undertakings.

Since he received no salary as bishop, he still retained the care of his five churches, but his son Philander soon relieved him of responsibility for the Academy. In addition to all his heavy obligations as bishop and pastor he had to work hard on his farm to maintain his wife and family. Yet he was able in the second year of his episcopate to travel nearly 1,300 miles and to preach 182 times. By 1821 he was so hard pressed for money that he accepted the presidency of the college at Cincinnati and moved there in the fall of that year.

Chase was much less deeply concerned, however, with his own low estate than with the desperate condition of the Church in Ohio. Too poor to meet its own growing needs, the diocese received almost no support from the Church in the East, and no machinery then existed by which the general Church could give such aid. After five years as bishop, Chase had nearly reached an impasse. But in 1823 his son Philander read in the *Philadelphia Recorder* extracts from an English periodical praising the achievements of the Church in Ohio, and the young man suggested to his father that money from England might prove the salvation of the struggling diocese. Chase embraced the proposal with all the force of his enthusiasm, resigned his post at the college, and began at once to plan a campaign in the mother country.

After writing to all the American bishops about the needs in Ohio and his new proposal for supplying them, Chase sailed for England, arriving at Liverpool on November 2, 1823, after a stormy passage. He entered on his venture with every disadvantage. Only two bishops had given him any encouragement. White had thrown cold water on the project; and Hobart, condemning it in strong language, had warned his brother from

Ohio that he would do everything he could in England to frustrate the plan. Being energetic and influential he was as good as his word. His opposition was partly directed against Chase's design to found a theological school in the West, which Hobart thought would be harmful to the new General Seminary; but both he and White were also agreed that any pleas for money in England were undignified and unnecessary. In addition to being thus disowned and opposed by the leaders of his own Church, Chase was completely unknown in Britain. It was as a bishop from the backwoods that he had to win the favor of British aristocrats. His only tangible weapons were letters from Henry Clay to Lord Gambier and Alexander Baring, in which he was described as "a learned, pious, and highly esteemed clergyman." But this clergyman had the bearing and the manners of a gentleman, and his greatest asset was his own vigorous and engaging personality.

Chase's story of his eight and a half months in England would fill a small volume. For our purposes it must be summarized by saying that after a slow and discouraging start his campaign rapidly became a huge success. Before long he was being everywhere lionized, and his list of subscribers was growing daily. By the time he left for home he had raised $20,000, a sum later increased from the same sources to $30,000.[12] On November 3, 1824, at his diocesan convention he made his triumphant report, and in the following month the legislature of Ohio passed an act to incorporate "The Theological Seminary of the Protestant Episcopal Church in the Diocese of Ohio." Thirteen months later this act was amended to give the president and faculty of the seminary power to confer academic degrees as "President and Professors of Kenyon College." And "Kenyon College" soon became the popular name for the institution.

What had happened was that the seminary, which had been the original project chiefly advertised in England, had need to be supported by a grammar school and a college in which students for the ministry could be prepared. In the course of a brief time the college came rapidly to overshadow the theological school, where few students were enrolled. In fact, the seminary did not attain a distinct faculty of its own and a separate building until 1839.

The new school, which taught everything from spelling to systematic divinity, was first opened at Chase's own home in Worthington, and within a year thirty students were accommodated in the farmhouse and in two small temporary buildings. Where it should be permanently settled

[12] When Chase had returned after brilliant success, Hobart withdrew his opposition, and (his sense of humor failing him for the moment) made the impudent suggestion that part of the money raised in England should be given to him for use in New York! Chase's *Reminiscences,* II, 262.

was a question long and actively disputed. The sensible plan would have been to accept an offer from one of several competing towns; but Chase insisted with increasing obstinacy that only in the open country could young men be trusted to overcome "temptations." Finally, against the opinion of many of his advisers, he persuaded his diocesan convention in June, 1826, to authorize the purchase of 8,000 acres in Knox County as the site for the college. The settlement which grew up there around the institution was called Gambier after Admiral Lord Gambier, a generous donor. The college named after Lord Kenyon and the seminary (with its later title Bexley Hall) named after Lord Bexley perpetuate the names of other liberal Englishmen who made possible this frontier venture. Their gifts, however, were insufficient to sustain the new seat of learning, and the bishop, by travel and correspondence, had to continue to raise money in the East.

In June, 1828, the school was moved from Worthington to its new home at Gambier, where temporary quarters were ready to shelter sixty-five students and several professors. Its charter provided that it should be "under the immediate charge and superintendence of the bishop of the diocese" and upon that basis academic life proceeded for the next three years. But during that period trouble was steadily brewing. There was no harm in the fact that Chase was the kind of man who would get up at four in the morning and answer all his letters before breakfast. It must be confessed, however, that he was not only fiercely energetic but also domineering. He treated the students and even the faculty as children, and would tolerate no form of opposition or criticism. He insisted that the government of the college must continue to be patriarchal, with himself as permanent patriarch. In mitigation of judgment against him, however, it must be remembered that the diocese not only paid him no salary but had never raised a cent for Kenyon. Nearly every dollar raised in the United States "he had raised at the expense of hard, wearing, uncongenial labor. Every bit of constructive work on Gambier Hill he had planned and supervised and found the money to pay for. . . . And on him alone rested the responsibility of meeting the great and pressing demands for money not only to advance the work but even to keep the institution alive from day to day." [13] Even a less aggressive man than Chase might well have come to regard Kenyon as wholly under his own control.

But his faculty of four professors and two schoolteachers was composed of well-educated young Americans with a pioneer spirit. They did not intend forever to be superintended and browbeaten. At the diocesan convention of 1831 their rebellion took effective form. Undoubtedly with the moral support of the student body of nearly two hundred, they pre-

[13] G. F. Smythe, *Kenyon College,* 96.

sented to the delegates a formal petition accusing the bishop of exercising "absolute and unlimited power." Chase defended himself at great length, denying the charge and referring to the charter as justifying his exercise of authority. After hearing both sides the convention appointed a committee, which reported that the troubles at Kenyon had resulted from the want of a proper code of laws to define the duties of all parties. It recommended that the requisite statutes be formulated by a new Board of Trustees, and it pointed out that the bishop had no right to "invoke his episcopal functions or any powers or authority other than the customary functions of president." This report, which Chase characterized as "evasive, ignorant, malignant, and hypocritical," was unanimously adopted by the convention.

Having counted upon vindication, the bishop was bitter in his resentment. Long afterwards he wrote: "He [i.e., himself] beheld the whole diocese for whom he had labored so much and so faithfully, now as one man combined against him, not a voice being heard in his behalf. . . . Could he, with a safe conscience, identify himself any longer with a people like this? To walk in their paths would be to partake of their sins." [14] Never at any point did it occur to him that he might have been wrong in the smallest particular. His immediate resignation was accepted, and the convention proceeded at once to elect as his successor the Rev. Charles Pettit McIlvaine. The new bishop was a young Evangelical, thirty-two years old, who had been chaplain at West Point and rector at St. Ann's Church in Brooklyn. He ruled the diocese for the next forty years.

Such an experience, suffered at the age of fifty-six, might well have ended the career of an ordinary man; but there was something invincible about Chase, and his superabundant vitality seemed to endow him with almost nine lives. Six months after his resignation he accepted the invitation of a friend to visit Michigan, and there he soon bought a farm of a thousand acres in Branch County near the Indiana border. If he was not to be allowed to manage a diocese, at least he would manage a farm. With the aid of hired men he built a house, where "wolves in the daytime came and looked on the carpenters at their work," and when it was finished he sent for his family. Within three years he could view a prosperous estate containing more than a hundred cattle and a busy lumber mill.

Though skillful as a farmer, Chase was too valuable and too famous to spend the rest of his days in a corner. He had not long to wait for a new opening. On March 9, 1835, at Peoria three clergymen and a few laymen held the first convention of the diocese of Illinois and elected Chase as their bishop. By way of inducing him to accept, they could offer

[14] Chase, *Reminiscences*, II, 107.

him thirty-nine known communicants, no salary, and not even a parish to provide for his support. But though he was now approaching sixty, he took up the challenge, and seven months later, despairing of any adequate help from resources at home, he sailed for a second time to England.

It is an amazing tribute to the force and attraction of Chase's personality that his adventures at Gambier should not have prevented him from reaping a second harvest in Britain. "Here he is again," they must have said, "asking for more money for another college in the midst of still wilder woods four thousand miles away." Yet in May, 1836, he arrived in New York with pledges of nearly $10,000.

The life he led in Illinois and the problems he faced are described in a letter which he wrote in 1837 to Lord Kenyon. The setting in all its features is so typical of what the Church encountered nearly everywhere on this frontier that it deserves quotation at some length.[15] "I was once more commencing the work of founding a new diocese. Few, very few, were the hands to assist me in this Herculean work. A vast territory was to be traversed, more in extent than all England and Wales united [a very slight exaggeration]; the soil exceedingly rich, but the inhabitants but thinly scattered, in some parts the distance between the settlers being from ten to fifteen miles. Few or no bridges were erected over the streams, and the sloughs sometimes extremely difficult to pass. Add to this state of things the heterogeneous characters of the inhabitants pouring in from all quarters of the world, and the consequent impossibility of uniting but a very small portion of them together to build the walls of our primitive Zion.[16] Those persons who had emigrated from New England brought with them the prejudices of their ancestors, the Puritans, against the Episcopal Church. . . . The Romanists, too, had been indefatigable in trying to keep alive the seeds of heresy which the French had sown along the banks of the Mississippi river and its tributary streams, and although their numbers were not so great as others, yet their clergy were more learned, and their efforts more united. Great as these obstacles were, yet still more formidable were others. A spirit of worldly-mindedness, amounting to an idolatry of wealth, involving a recklessness of all moral and religious principles in the attainment of it, had spread itself over the whole land." [17]

Unlike Kenyon, which was rapidly established and is still flourishing, the new "Jubilee College," which Chase was so eagerly planning, took many years to found and enjoyed but a short life. The land was bought near Peoria in 1838 and the cornerstone laid in the following year, but a

[15] *Ibid.,* II, 437 f.

[16] During the first half of the nineteenth century all pious clergymen were wont to refer to their Church as "our Zion."

[17] These were the times of wild speculation and inflation preceding the great Panic of 1837.

subsequent tour by Chase through all the South and East was needed to keep construction going. Though it was in operation with fifty students two years earlier, it was not chartered till 1847, and during the 'sixties and 'seventies it gradually expired.[18]

While still hopeful of the success of the college and still untiring in the service of his diocese, Chase died on September 20, 1852. "Two collegiate institutions and two dioceses, started and consolidated, are a monument which few have ever erected to their own memory." [19] He had the faults which often attend impetuous zeal and tenacity of purpose; but his truest epitaph will still remain the words with which Bishop Doane greeted him in 1835, when he resumed his seat in the House of Bishops: "A veteran soldier, a bishop of the Cross, whom hardships never have discouraged, whom no difficulties seem to daunt."

RICHARD CHANNING MOORE

Another bishop, if perhaps less notable than the trio we have been describing, brought to his see the same kind of invigorating leadership from which Ohio, New York, and the Eastern Diocese were benefiting—Richard Channing Moore of Virginia.

Moore was the New Yorker who revived the Church in Virginia. The son of a local merchant, of considerable wealth until the Revolution, Moore was born in 1762. Educated as a youth under a private tutor, he later studied with a distinguished physician, and by the time he was twenty-one he had begun the practice of medicine in New York City. For the next six years he enjoyed success in his calling and a substantial income; but as the result of inner changes of which he left no record, he resolved to abandon his profession and to devote his life to the Church. During the year 1787 he was ordained both deacon and priest by Bishop Provoost. After two years at Grace Church, Rye, New York, he served for ten years as rector of St. Andrew's Church, Staten Island, and in 1809 became rector of St. Stephen's in New York City. His ministry there brought him immense popularity and a commanding influence in the town. He was so widely and favorably known, in fact, that in 1814 he was elected Bishop of Virginia and rector of the Monumental Church in Richmond.

As we have noted on a previous page, the Church in Virginia at this moment was almost moribund. The diocese had had no bishop for more

[18] It is probable that Chase's habit of exercising absolute control and of raising funds at a distance had a paralyzing effect upon local self-support. Even after he had been Bishop of Illinois for eight years he received from his diocese in 1843 only $179, scarcely one-quarter of his mere travel expenses. (E. Waylen, *Ecclesiastical Reminiscences*, 451.)

[19] Tiffany, *op. cit.*, 437.

than two years, and no real episcopal care for a much longer time. Its roll of active priests then listed hardly more than half a dozen, and men had begun to wonder whether it could survive. For a Church thus wasting away Channing Moore was just the right remedy. Though he was not a Virginian, he possessed the qualities which Virginia produces and admires. He was a thorough gentleman and a warmly emotional Evangelical. Hardly had he entered his new field when his enthusiasm and vigor met with an instant response. The effect of his hopeful vitality was everywhere enlivening. A process had begun which was to make the future dioceses of Virginia one of the strongest Church centers in the country and to set the tone of Virginia Churchmanship for a century to come.

At his diocesan convention in 1816 the bishop was justified in the optimistic report which he made. He had confirmed 750 persons and supplied clergy for twenty vacant parishes. "The Protestant Episcopal Church in the diocese of Virginia," he declared, "presents to the view of her friends a prospect truly encouraging. The clouds of adversity, which for years have overspread her horizon, appear to be dispersing, and our Zion, animated by the beams of the Sun of Righteousness, is recovering from her desolations, exhibiting the most heart-cheering evidences of returning health and vigor."

Every quality and trait of the typical Evangelical of the day shone in the character and career of Moore. For one thing, his attitude toward "worldliness" and his standard of morals were Puritanical. In his New York parish no one had been admitted to Holy Communion who was not prepared to give up dancing, card-playing, and the theatre. Virginia, however, had never been noted as a center of Puritanism. Yet in 1818 Moore succeeded in persuading his convention to pass a resolution declaring that gambling, horse-racing, attending theatres, and dancing in public "stained the purity of the Christian character" and should be avoided by all communicants.

Typical again was his policy in relation to interdenominational projects. He accepted the presidency of the Virginia branch of the American Bible Society. Here he found himself in friendly opposition to the views of Hobart, who insisted that Churchmen should never help to distribute Bibles unless Prayer Books went with them. "Could a Prayer Book," he wrote, "accompany every volume of the Sacred Writings, I should be rejoiced; but as that was not the case when the Scriptures were first given to the world, I cannot see the propriety at the present day of making it the condition of their dissemination." [20] In works of philanthropy, too, he was not afraid to cooperate with Christians of other bodies. As he expressed it in one of his convention addresses: "We stretch forth the right

[20] J. P. K. Henshaw, *Memoir of Richard Channing Moore,* 178.

hand of fellowship to all who in sincerity call upon the Lord Jesus Christ; we expect to meet in heaven with Christians of all denominations; and while we labor in our department, we wish prosperity to all the Saviour's friends." [21]

Moore was true to type, moreover, in the forms in which he expressed the spirit of Evangelicalism. He heartily approved of ministerial and other associations for the development of personal religion. He encouraged extra-liturgical services and prayer-meetings; and even his diocesan conventions displayed a touch of the right kind of revivalism, so plainly were they designed to inspire as well as to legislate.

After Moore had served as bishop for fifteen years and had reached the age of sixty-seven, he was given the aid of an assistant bishop, William Meade, who proceeded to relieve him of his heavier duties, and who survived him by twenty years. But the old man lived until 1841, when he died in his eightieth year. Gifted with personal charm and persuasive eloquence, he had always been loved for his gentleness, his courtesy, and his abounding charity and good-will. He had found a diocese almost on the point of disappearing, and he left it with 170 churches served by nearly a hundred clergy. To good purpose he had preached and practised the Gospel of Christ crucified.[22]

[21] *Ibid.,* 181.

[22] For a similar revival, on a smaller scale, North Carolina was indebted to the leadership of John Stark Ravenscroft, who entered the ministry at the age of forty-five. During the seven years of his vigorous episcopate the four parishes he found in 1823 increased to twenty-seven, and the Church in North Carolina began to flourish.

Chapter VII

THE CHURCH BEGINS TO TEACH

OUR survey of the activities of certain new leaders will have made it evident that in the period from 1814 to 1835 the Church had begun to take with increasing seriousness its neglected duty to teach. For the first quarter of a century after 1789 Christian education had been confined to an irregular use of the Catechism in parishes and to the publication of literature, largely second-rate, by societies representing a small fraction of the Church's membership. No adequate provision had been made for the training of children, young people, or candidates for the ministry.

In recording the encouraging advance of the next two decades we may begin with the progress of Sunday schools. In 1814 two of Bishop White's assistants at Christ Church, Philadelphia—Jackson Kemper (the future Bishop of Missouri and Indiana) and James Milnor—started a Sunday school in the township just north of Philadelphia. This was the first Sunday school under the auspices of the Episcopal Church and is said to have been the first one officially incorporated by any religious body in America. Almost at once the example of these pioneers was followed by the more alert rectors in parishes elsewhere. In the following year the first schools appeared in Massachusetts, New York, New Jersey, and Maryland. By 1817 there had been formed Protestant Episcopal Sunday School Societies in New York and Philadelphia, aiming to promote the further organization of schools and to improve their quality. Before another year had passed the Sunday school movement was in full career, with the support of influential bishops. And at every General Convention during the 'twenties there were reports from the dioceses of the establishment of schools as well as of Sunday School Unions or Societies.

The important place which these schools had then come to hold in the life of the Church is indicated by the formation in 1826 of the General Protestant Episcopal Sunday School Union. In this action, completed at the General Convention of that year, Hobart and White played prominent parts; but the new Union had no official relation to the Convention. It was a private association, with a membership consisting of representatives of those Sunday schools which wished to join it. Its useful aims were stated as follows: "The object of the General Protestant Episcopal Sunday School Union is to combine the resources of Episcopalians into one great whole, which, by its concentration of power, may be enabled to give life and vigor to the multitude of branches which now pine in solitude and neglect. The talent and experience of the most active supporters of Sunday schools will be united in the invention of efficacious systems of instruction; and their combined wisdom exerted in the choice of proper books." Though modern "promotion" would never permit any reference to our least valuable schools as "pining in solitude and neglect," the aims stated by the Union are substantially the same as those of our Department of Christian Education today. That Department is the latest stage in the process of cooperation of which the Union was a rudimentary beginning. The establishment of the Union marked the end of the evolution of the Sunday school from a charitable lay enterprise for the instruction of needy children in reading and writing to a recognized Church institution for the training of the children in every parish.

The system and the methods of the Sunday schools of a century and a quarter ago may be illustrated by some of the publications of the Sunday School Union. The material it produced and the standards it aimed to set will give the fairest estimate of those far-off schools at their best. During the year after its foundation the Union issued a pamphlet entitled, "System of Instruction for the Use of Protestant Episcopal Sunday Schools in the United States," a handbook which not only supplied a curriculum but dealt also with such subjects as the government of schools, the keeping of records, etc.

From this booklet and from other sources we learn that the superintendents of the schools were generally laymen, and often men who had not been appointed by the rector—a survival of the recent past when Sunday schools were not Church institutions. The schools, especially in the larger centers, usually had sessions both in the morning and in the afternoon, one or both of which included attendance at church! Grading was seldom systematic, and few parishes adopted any regular plan of promotion. The material for instruction was the Bible, the Prayer Book, and the Catechism, and the almost invariable method of teaching was catechizing—that is, memorizing followed by recitation. That was also the chief method in day schools; and since it requires only a minimum of intelligence on the part of both pupil and teacher it prevailed with little improvement for several generations to come. It included, of course, the learning by heart of the Catechism and of texts, so that typical Sunday school reports would read—"Many recite their Catechism accurately, and repeat from ten to fifty verses of the New Testament with hymns," or "A child in one week learned and recited to her teacher 1046 verses in the Bible."

There may still be those who can see advantages in this mode of education; its contribution to the mind of the child had a certain definiteness. But there can be no doubt as to the low quality of the Sunday school hymns and the library books as compared with what children are offered today. Instead of training them to appreciate the best, the effort was always made to write down to their supposed level and to substitute piety for literary quality. Here, for instance, is a verse sung by the children to the teachers in St. George's Church in New York:

When wandering far astray
 In paths of vice and sin
You kindly pointed out
 The danger we were in.

And at the close of the service the congregation sang:

O, what a pleasure 'tis to see
Christians in harmony agree!
To teach the rising race to know
They're born in sin, exposed to woe!

As these stanzas indicate, no effort was spared to impress upon the children their corrupt and sinful condition. This realization would be aided by such lines as these:

Happy the child whose youngest years
 Receive instruction well;
Who hates the sinner's path, and fears
 The road that leads to hell.[1]

Sunday school books of the earlier type have long since become a standard subject for gibes, yet some of the worst of them were published by the Church Sunday School Union. Passing over such titles as *The Robber's Daughter, or the Sunday School Convert* and *Nosegay of Honeysuckles,* we may note, for example, *Procrastination, a Story by Mrs. Sherwood,* wherein we find a warning against youthful neglect of religion, including a harrowing picture of Edward Crawford, who was "lying under sentence of death in one of our country gaols." More suited to feminine needs was *The Miller's Daughter, or the Lord's Prayer Applied*

[1] C. H. Brewer, *History of Religious Education,* 173 ff.

to Practice, which told of a girl named Ellen who became deeply pious through reading a Bible containing the Lord's Prayer with illustrations, given to her by a dying friend.[2]

Drilled for hours in memory work and provided with little or no chance for free expression, the children, we might assume, would have found Sunday school pretty dreary. But much of their day school work was drudgery just as colorless; and in Sunday school at least punishment was rare indeed, and rewards were many. For attendance, for diligence, and for excellence in lessons there were many prizes and "premiums"—inscribed cards and medals and tracts, and even Bibles and Prayer Books.

During its first nine years of existence the Sunday School Union succeeded in enlisting in its membership only half of the 700 Sunday schools in the Church.[3] Even those which belonged to it often failed to adopt its plan of organization and study. It had more than justified itself by its extensive publication of books and of a widely used periodical, and it had undoubtedly raised the standard of education. But it made the mistake, repeated by national Church organizations in more recent times, of producing too elaborate plans and failing to make flexible allowance for the needs of small schools with meager resources. At the General Convention of 1835, therefore, the Union reported that it was abandoning its more ambitious schemes, but declared itself committed to promoting the acceptance of three main principles: that every school should be under the supervision of the rector, who should control the curriculum and methods; that except for pupils unable to read, all instruction should be religious, with the Bible as the foundation; and that the Scriptures should be interpreted through the Prayer Book and the Catechism.[4]

Educational progress since 1835 has been so phenomenal that it is easy to speak disrespectfully of our ancestors' Sunday schools. Yet it would be unsympathetic and unimaginative judgment which would underestimate the vast measure of good accomplished by these early schools. They were not only an immense improvement upon no schools at all, but they made to the religious life of the age a contribution hard to estimate but none the less solid. However great the contrast between the older methods and ours, the textbooks were the Bible and the Prayer Book, and contact with them, even when unskillfully mediated, must again and again have proved an enriching experience. And to that undeniable fact we must add the further point that then no less than now teachers were born and not made; and whatever the setting and the material might be, the con-

[2] *Ibid.,* 191–195.

[3] In these schools in 1835 there were about 3,000 teachers and 28,000 scholars, of which New York and Pennsylvania supplied nearly half.

[4] Brewer, *op. cit.,* 207 ff.

secrated Christian man or woman transmitted by contagion the meaning and the joy of the Christian way of life.

Since the Church is still trying to solve the problem of adult education, we need not be surprised that it was far from a solution in the early decades of the nineteenth century. The most obvious and natural extension of the Sunday school beyond the age of Confirmation was the Bible class. These classes had begun in Episcopal churches of the Evangelical type and were becoming a feature more and more familiar in parish life. Yet of course only a small minority of those who attended church would enlist for such study. The chief mode of training adults in the meaning of Christianity was then, as it has been ever since, the services of the Church and the sermons which they included.

The arrangement and the conduct of the services differed from modern practice more extensively than did the actual text of the Prayer Book itself. Nearly all parishes had services both on Sunday morning and on Sunday afternoon, each with its sermon. The morning service generally included not only Morning Prayer but also the Litany and the Ante-Communion. Vestments, ornaments, and ritual were all simpler than they have since become. The minister wore a long surplice without a cassock and usually without a scarf or stole. For the sermon he put off the surplice and donned a black gown. The choir was never vested and commonly sat in a gallery in the rear of the church. At the altar Churchmen today of whatever type would note an unfamiliar bareness. The priest celebrating the Holy Communion wore no vestments but the surplice and generally stood at the north end of the holy table. On the altar there were no flowers or candles or cross, at most a linen cloth; and the elements were ordinary bread and unmixed wine. The Eucharist was seldom administered more than once a month. Though High Churchmen often observed the holy days, weekday services were more likely to be of the Evangelical type—prayer meetings or gatherings for "lectures" or informal sermons.[5]

Sermons in those days were longer than the modern congregation would tolerate and usually more concerned with doctrine. Though some of the Evangelicals were given to extempore preaching, the written sermon was the accepted type both in this country and in England. It was naturally in Evangelical circles that preaching should receive the strongest emphasis, especially preaching to arouse the emotions and produce conversion; yet Bishop Hobart was noted for the fervor and free delivery of his homilies. Perhaps the most notable contrast with the best sermons of our time would be found in the constant reference to Scriptural author-

[5] For an excellent account of services at this period see W. W. Manross, *The Episcopal Church in the U. S., 1800–1840,* ch. 6.

ity, the frequent quoting of texts, the ponderous formality of the language, and the general want of simplicity and directness. But as that was the kind of preaching which people expected and often enjoyed, it must be counted as a powerful influence in the Christian education of adults.

Usually less impressive and effective than the sermons, yet distinctly a factor in the slow education of the churchgoer, were the hymns sung at the services. The General Convention of 1789 had approved a metrical version of the Psalms by Tate and Brady and had added twenty-seven modern hymns. For nearly twenty years this collection was the only official hymnbook. Of its contents there are still retained in the Hymnal of 1940 five of the twenty-seven hymns, including "The spacious firmament on high" and "While shepherds watched their flocks by night" and five other hymns which were originally metrical versions of Psalms, such as "O 'twas a joyful sound to hear" and "Lord, forever at thy side."

Today we find it hard to understand the strange fear of hymns which then prevailed and the stranger attachment to Psalms often versified in mere doggerel. But the historical explanation, though curious, is simple. The Protestants of Scotland and England in earlier days had confined their singing to metrical versions of the Psalms because only such hymns were truly Scriptural. In the United States in 1789, however, and for long thereafter, these metrical Psalms were strongly preferred to hymns because in the eyes of Bishop White and many others of his cool type of Christianity hymns were dangerously Evangelical and likely to encourage "enthusiasm" or what White called "animal sensibility." In such a judgment there was this much truth, that nearly all the hymns of the period were written by fervent Evangelicals. That type of hymn, in fact, gave its color to our hymn-books until the days of the two most recent revisions, when a larger number of more objective and robust hymns, written in the Middle Ages or in the twentieth century, has somewhat redressed the balance.

In 1808 thirty hymns were added to the first collection; and in 1826 a new Hymnal, destined to serve the Church for forty years, was authorized by General Convention. It contained 212 hymns, of which a majority were by non-Anglicans and only twenty-six by Americans.[6] Forty-nine of them still survive in the Hymnal of 1940.

The promotion of adult religious education was one of the avowed purposes of the many societies for the advancement of Christian learning, some of which we have noted in an earlier chapter. By the publication and distribution of tracts and books of different types they aimed to reach both young people and older people of all classes. We cannot avoid the

[6] Among the best new American hymns were "Softly now the light of day" by G. W. Doane, later Bishop of New Jersey, and "How wondrous and great thy works, God of praise!" by H. U. Onderdonk, later Bishop of Pennsylvania.

conclusion, however, that they met with little success, and that for at least two reasons: they were so feebly supported that they had little money to spend; and their publications, outside of Prayer Books and a few standard religious classics, were of poor quality. In the earlier years of the century the societies depended largely upon importing the English tracts of the S.P.C.K. No doubt Archbishop Tillotson's *Persuasion to Frequent Communions* had its merits, for his style had been admired a century before; but what are we to think of "An Earnest and Affectionate Address to the Poor, more particularly in regard to the prevailing Sin of Drunkenness," or of Bishop Gibson's "Caution against Enthusiasm"? And surely few converts could have been made by "A Serious Address to Seceders and Sectarists who exist in Separation from the Church of England."

For those who were capable of more advanced study the material offered became increasingly respectable. To a growing degree the writings of American clergy were made available. The devotional works of Hobart, sermons by Griswold and Ravenscroft, and the Commentary on the Prayer Book by Bishop Brownell of Connecticut showed that the Church was no longer dependent on English authors. Even in the more scholarly field of Apologetics Episcopalians could point to Bishop Hopkins' *Christianity Vindicated* and to Bishop McIlvaine's *Evidences of Christianity* of which an English edition appeared, and even a translation into Italian.[7]

Helpful auxiliaries to adult education in those days as in ours were the Church periodicals. Most of them were short-lived; their circulation was small; and they appealed chiefly to those who were already devout; but they served none the less a useful purpose. During the years before 1826 a score may be listed, including *The Churchman's Magazine* (1804+) from which the present *Churchman* is somewhat irregularly descended, and *The Southern Churchman* (1835+).

The quality and flavor of these early journals may be tested by sampling the contents of three of them. Here, for example, is part of what we find in the first number of *The Gospel Advocate, conducted by a Society of Gentlemen* (Newburyport, Massachusetts, January, 1821): A sermon on the New Year; Bishop Griswold's address to the convention of the Eastern Diocese, September 27, 1820; a sermon on St. John 21:22; "Remarks on Baptism"; a paper "On the Landing of the Pilgrims"; religious intelligence, including a report from the famous Baptist missionary Adoniram Judson in Burma, together with items of Episcopal domestic missionary news.

Perhaps even less popular in tone is the material in the first number (January, 1804) of *The Churchman's Monthly Magazine or Treasury*

[7] For a treatment of the Church literature of the period see Brewer, *op. cit.*, especially pp. 122–129 and 314–325.

of Divine and Useful Knowledge, edited by a Committee appointed by the Convocation of the Episcopal Church of Connecticut: articles on the Church, on the Collects, Epistles, and Gospels for the Sundays in Advent, on the Constitution of the Protestant Episcopal Church, and on Religious Experience; a poem "written by the learned and ingenious Dr. Ogilvie at sixteen years of age" (the contents of which would have justified the author in dying young) ; and at the close a group of three "Anecdotes," the cleverest of which is the following: "A military officer, who was so unfashionable as to profess religion, being challenged by another, coolly returned this answer, 'Tell him that though I fear not man, I am afraid of offending God, and though I want not courage to face a cannon, I dare not venture to rush into the mouth of hell.' "

Twenty years later at Charleston, South Carolina, appeared for the first time *The Gospel Messenger and Southern Christian Register, by a Society of Gentlemen Members of the Protestant Episcopal Church.* Here may be found, among other articles, an account of the new General Theological Seminary in New York; "The Church's Advice to her Clergy"; "On Man's Accountableness"; "Meditations Divine and Moral"; a list of new religious publications; and a letter protesting against giving to foreign missions on the ground that "there is more than enough to do in the United States" and "charity begins at home." (This species of Christian thinker has evidently been familiar in every generation, though nowadays he seldom finds his way into the Church press.)

Making all due allowance for the change in taste from one age to another, it is plain that Church journals of a century ago catered chiefly for clergymen and the serious-minded laity, and could hardly have played a part in winning the attention, still less the allegiance, of the unconverted whether young or old. They bear ample testimony, however, to the fact that in those days readers were not easily bored.

As a means of controlling the religious education of the young most of the Churches in this era were active in founding schools and colleges. There was all the greater inducement to offer these advantages because during the first third of the century the educational performance of towns and States lagged far behind American theory. Free schooling for all was still unknown, and no part of the country had a comprehensive school system except on paper. Secondary and higher education was far more dependent then than now upon private enterprise. "As late as 1830, public support of education was still largely 'a gift to the destitute.' "[8]

To meet a need which was thus both religious and secular, the Church had established during these years a considerable number of boarding-schools, most of which proved to be financial failures. Among

[8] J. A. Krout and D. R. Fox, *Completion of Independence,* 183, *cf.* 179–181.

the very few which are still flourishing may be listed the Episcopal Academy of Philadelphia (1785+), the Hannah More Academy in Maryland (1832+), St. Mary's Hall at Burlington, New Jersey (1837+), and the Episcopal High School of Virginia (1839+). The Episcopal Academy at Cheshire, Connecticut, chartered in 1801, served as a diocesan institution for more than a century. Much briefer but still useful careers were those of the Flushing Institute on Long Island (later St. Paul's College), which did not long survive the depression of 1837, and the preparatory school attached to Kenyon College in Ohio.

The first sign of interest in college work displayed by the national Church appears in the General Convention of 1823, when a resolution was adopted calling for a Joint Committee to report answers to the following questions: (1) What colleges have Protestant Episcopal clergymen on their faculties? (2) What colleges have adopted a system of religious instruction? (3) What colleges are so situated as to permit their students to attend Episcopal worship? These inquiries reveal the same problems and opportunities which the present Division of College Work of the National Council is successfully encountering. But for adequate answers the Church had to wait for more than a hundred years. In the 'twenties and 'thirties of the nineteenth century the chosen method of influencing young men in college was to establish Church colleges.

The founding of Kenyon College at Gambier we have already described in reviewing the career of Bishop Chase. Two other Church colleges organized at about the same time are likewise active today. Thanks to the energetic initiative of Bishop Hobart, a provisional charter was granted in 1822, and a permanent charter in 1825, to Geneva College in the little town of Geneva, New York. Though the college had been established by a group of which the majority were Churchmen, the charter provided that no rule should exclude any person of any denomination from any privilege. Episcopalians received no special favors, and there was no attempt to proselytize. But the trustees have always had a decided majority of Episcopalians and for a century the president was always an Episcopal minister. In 1852 the name of the institution was changed to Hobart Free College and in 1860 to Hobart College.

The diocese of Connecticut was not far behind New York, for in 1823 the legislature of the State granted the petition of certain Churchmen by passing an act incorporating Washington College, which opened its doors at Hartford in 1824. By the end of its first academic year it was composed of four professors, one tutor, and fourteen students; but within another two years the undergraduates numbered fifty. Like Hobart, the college has had a majority of Episcopalians on its board of trustees and a clergymen for president until very recent times; yet no religious test has ever been required of any officer or student. The former Washington College has been known since 1845 as Trinity College.

In founding five colleges before 1840, two of which died, the Episcopal Church was only following the tendency of that epoch in American life. Colleges were rapidly increasing, and nearly all of them were more or less under clerical control. There were fifty-six degree-granting institutions in 1830; and it has been estimated that during the previous forty years nine-tenths of the college heads were ministers.

The same decade which saw the founding of these three colleges witnessed also the origin of three theological seminaries—the General Theological Seminary in New York City, the Theological Seminary at Alexandria, Virginia, and the theological course at Kenyon, later evolving into Bexley Hall. Twenty years before these developments, however, the Church had begun to pay some attention to theological education.

At the request of the House of Deputies as early as 1801 Bishop White prepared a syllabus of theological education which was approved by the House of Bishops in 1804 and remained for some two generations the official standard.[9] This "Course of Ecclesiastical Studies" begins with a reminder (interesting to readers in a later century) of the extreme variations in applicants for holy orders as to endowments, previous preparation, access to books and teachers, and time available for study. The bishops found their candidates highly diverse and unequal in their attainments and opportunities; and the only way to provide for their professional education was to place them under the care of some learned clergyman—a form of apprenticeship which in these same years was producing the lawyers and doctors of the community.

The syllabus composed by White provided for a course of study which, in the epoch in which it appeared, could scarcely have been improved. Its long life, in fact, testified to the wisdom of its contents. Perhaps its most noteworthy feature was the arrangement of subjects by which every student had a long and thorough training in the Bible and Church history before he began theology. The quality of the books recommended maintained a high standard by the inclusion of the best Anglican writers of the previous two centuries—men like Hooker, Pearson, Hammond, Stillingfleet, Taylor, Bull, Paley, and Butler. Nor did the bishop omit subjects so heavily dwelt upon today as homiletics and pastoral care. These, together with the study of the Prayer Book and the Constitution and Canons, gave the prospective minister an effective training in "practical theology." Yet wise as was White's selection of material, conditions have so greatly changed since 1804 that a modern theological student might easily graduate *cum laude* without ever having read any

[9] *Journals of General Conventions,* Ed. W. S. Perry, I, 315–320.

of the long list of books in the syllabus, except the Bible, the Apostolic Fathers, parts of Hooker, and perhaps a few pages of Jeremy Taylor.

Quite properly this outline of "Ecclesiastical Studies" represented a maximum. It was far too elaborate and exacting to fit an average course. Indeed, Professor Turner at the General Seminary later declared that the requirements were more than twice as much as anyone could meet. In view of this acknowledged fact, the syllabus as finally adopted included a statement of the *minimum* demanded, which amounted to little more than the study of eight or ten standard works in different fields.

Ten years after the adoption of this program of education in divinity there was presented at the General Convention in 1814 a resolution, sponsored by the diocese of South Carolina, proposing that a committee be appointed to consider the establishment of a general theological seminary under the control of the national Church. Like so many other good ideas, upon their first appearance in Church circles, the proposal met with a cool reception. The most outspoken opponent was Bishop Hobart, who was already planning for his own seminary in New York, and who expressed his fear of "committing a power so vital to the Church as the control of the education of its candidates, to a body so fluctuating and irresponsible as the General Convention, at least in the House of Delegates." It would indeed be a bold bishop in these times who would refer to the House of Deputies as "irresponsible," but for Hobart the authorities who really counted were the eight prelates then in the House of Bishops. As a result of this objection and those of others no action was taken except to refer the matter to the bishops with the request that they report to the next General Convention.

When the Convention met in 1817 favorable opinion had so far developed that resolutions were adopted approving the establishment of a General Theological Seminary in New York and providing for committees to raise funds for it and to make plans for its organization. The group of planners was to consist of White, Hobart, and Croes of New Jersey. The choice may not seem to have been happy, since White and Hobart strongly preferred diocesan seminaries and Croes wanted no such school at all. But they honestly accepted the decision of the Church and worked to such good purpose that on May 1, 1819, teaching actually began. There were two professors, including Samuel H. Turner, who gave a lifetime of service to the institution, and six students, among whom were the future bishops George W. Doane and Manton Eastburn. Though land on which the Seminary is now located had just been given by Clement C. Moore, no buildings were ready; and in the course of the next ten months the classes met in two different chapels and finally in one of the rooms of a house used in other hours by a girls' school.

After a year and a half in New York it had become quite clear that the school as then constituted was not a welcome factor in the diocese. By failing to support it either with money or with men Hobart was expressing his distaste for an institution within his borders but not under his control. Sensing this coolness and learning that outside of South Carolina money for the Seminary was almost wholly lacking, the General Convention in May, 1820, decided to move the new school to New Haven, on the ground that there its expenses would be less and its facilities for study greater. Four months later the Seminary set to work at New Haven with one professor and ten students, adding in the course of the year eleven more.

But this New Haven episode was only brief. A legacy of at least $60,000 was left in March, 1821, to "an Episcopalian Theological Seminary," whenever such an institution should be established in New York State either by General Convention or by the diocese of New York. At that moment a small diocesan seminary in New York City was about to open, and the General Seminary was in New Haven. Aware that the decision as to who should get the money was a vital question for the Church, Bishop White called a special session of General Convention. As a result of the accommodating spirit shown by Bishop Hobart a fruitful compromise was reached. The local school and the General Seminary were merged and their faculties and funds were combined. At the same time it was decided to move the Seminary to New York and to adopt a new constitution. In addition to declaring that all bishops should be *ex officio* members of the Board of Trustees, it provided for further representation in proportion to the number of clergymen in each diocese and to the amount of money which each diocese contributed. This arrangement rewarded Hobart with a preponderating influence in the school and enlisted him among its effective supporters.

Confident of its newly planned future, the Seminary reopened in New York in February, 1822, meeting in the schoolrooms of Trinity Church. Not until 1827 was the first building completed on the present grounds, which could then be described as "a quiet rural retreat." But for some years to come the struggle to raise money kept the school in a precarious state, for from many dioceses there were no contributions at all. By 1835, however, a total of $171,000 had been donated; a second building was being constructed; and the student body numbered about sixty-five.[10] Already there were over a hundred graduates and an equal

[10] Modern parents and students will be interested to learn that the total annual expenses of a student, including board, washing, fuel, and lights, was not more than $80. When Geneva College first opened tuition and room rent amounted to $25 a year and board was $1.50 a week.

number of other former students.[11] The General Seminary had become a power in the Church, pursuing the effective policy of offering theological training of high grade to those equipped for graduate study.[12]

Only a few years younger than the General Theological Seminary is the Protestant Episcopal Theological Seminary in Virginia. The nursing mother of this institution is "The Society for the Education of Pious Young Men for the Ministry of the Protestant Episcopal Church" (usually shortened to "The Education Society") which was organized in 1818 by a group of clergy and laity meeting in Washington. Its earliest attempt to provide theological education in the South was the support of a theological professorship at William and Mary College. The response to this opportunity was so feeble that in 1820 the experiment was given up. In the following year the diocesan convention of Virginia voted to establish a theological school and appointed trustees to raise funds. Within another year $10,000 had been obtained and a constitution adopted, placing the seminary under the control of the diocesan convention. Abandoning the original plan for a school at Williamsburg, the convention resolved in 1823 to place it at Alexandria, Virginia. As a result of this action, and with the continued generous support of the Education Society,[13] the Virginia Seminary opened on October 15, 1823. By the autumn of 1824 the two professors had twenty-four students, and by the end of another three years the Seminary had moved to its present site on "The Hill," three miles from Alexandria. From that day to this its chief contribution to the life of the Church has been an evangelical warmth, only one sign of which has been the founding by Virginia men of nearly all the foreign missions of the Church.

The activity of the Church in organizing seminaries as well as colleges followed again the religious pattern of the age. It was in 1808 that the Congregational seminary at Andover, Massachusetts, was founded. The Dutch Reformed Church opened its school at New Brunswick, New Jersey, in 1810. In 1812 the Presbyterian Seminary at Princeton began; and 1815 and 1822 mark the dates when the Divinity Schools of Harvard and Yale were organized. So many were the denominations and so active their concern for training their ministries that by 1837 there were thirty-five theological schools in the United States. All the Churches had begun seriously to teach.

[11] In 1835 there were 763 Episcopal clergymen in the United States.

[12] The best account of the origin and growth of the Seminary is to be found in a series of articles in the *Historical Magazine of the Protestant Episcopal Church,* for Sept. 1936. An excellent article by Prof. E. R. Hardy, Jr. deals with the early period.

[13] In 1826 the Virginia delegation reported to General Convention that the Theological Seminary looked to the Education Society "as to a precious fount, by whose streams her barren waste shall be watered and made glad."

Chapter VIII

MISSIONARY AWAKENING

THE two decades between 1815 and 1835 witnessed a steady expansion of the Church both in numbers and in area.[1] The triennial reports to General Convention made by each diocese indicate, with a few exceptions, an almost uniform rate of progress. Among the older dioceses Virginia, New York, and South Carolina were responding to the stimulus of new leadership; the Eastern Diocese was steadily approaching the time when it could be divided into its five successors; advance in Connecticut and Pennsylvania, though at a sober rate, was uninterrupted; Maryland suffered at intervals from party strife and regained vitality only slowly; and little Delaware remained a problem child, chiefly for lack of clergy.

During this period dioceses were organized in the two remaining original States—North Carolina (1817) and Georgia (1823). In the newer States more dioceses were formed. In Maine the diocese took shape in the same year in which Maine joined the Union (1820), and Michigan was a diocese (1832) five years before it was a State. But in all the other cases the ecclesiastical organization lagged far behind the political for periods varying from nine to thirty-seven years: Ohio (1818), Mississippi (1826), Kentucky and Tennessee (1829), Alabama (1830), and Illinois (1835). Sometimes a new diocese included as few as four clergy, and as we have noted before, it was often many years before it had a bishop.

Growth within each diocese was frequently due to the direct initiative of the bishop; but other valuable agencies of expansion were the diocesan missionary societies which at this time were growing in number and in activity. Since it was to be long before there was any official diocesan

[1] Reliable statistics of communicants for the earlier date are not available, but in 1817 the clergy numbered 261 and in 1835, 763.

organization, these societies were private and voluntary, but in many respects they served the purpose of modern diocesan departments of missions. Several of the societies which we have already named as promoting the cause of education were helpful also in giving aid to needy missions within their own borders. Others were definitely and entirely devoted to that cause.

As early as 1796 the New York convention had formed what must have been the earliest diocesan board of missions—"The Committee of the Protestant Episcopal Church for the Propagation of the Gospel in the State of New York"—and a generation later this board was supporting in whole or in part 58 missionaries in 70 stations. Pennsylvania's "Society for the Advancement of Christianity" (1812) seems to have been less active, for it reported after fourteen years that it was supplying the salaries of only seven missionaries; but a similar body in New Jersey (1822 +) employed, after thirteen years, as few as four clergy. South Carolina had at least four missionary societies, and in the course of the 'twenties and 'thirties associations of this type appeared also in Vermont, North Carolina, Ohio, and Virginia. It was a favorable sign of the awakening concern for missions that in such new dioceses as Georgia and Mississippi a missionary society should have been considered a prime necessity at the very start and not an after-thought delayed for many years.

Such evidence testifies to the fact that the dioceses were gradually beginning to take seriously their missionary responsibility for their own areas and to devise means for discharging it. The national Church, on the contrary, though faced with vastly greater opportunities, remained almost impotent.

In 1817 a European observer wrote, "All America seems to be breaking up and moving westward." He thus anticipated the fact that for a score of years after 1815 the growth of what we now call the mid-West was phenomenal. In 1816, for example, 42,000 settlers moved into Indiana alone. By 1818 the population of Illinois was already 40,000. Before 1830 Ohio had more inhabitants than Massachusetts and Connecticut combined. The Church's share in this movement might be summarized in the words of an English priest after travel and residence in Ohio, Indiana, and Kentucky: "Throughout the western part of the United States there are multitudes who have been baptized and educated in the Episcopal Church. Yet by far the greater part of these, after waiting perhaps for many years in the hope of obtaining the services of a clergyman, have been swept away by the prevailing current of popular sentiment and have united themselves with dissenting denominations." [2]

What little had been done to represent the Church on the frontier

[2] H. Caswall, *America and the American Church,* 269.

had been largely the work of free-lance pioneers like Chase. In 1815, it is true, Bishop White and some of his clergy organized "The Episcopal Missionary Society of Philadelphia" for the purpose of promoting work in the West; and during the four years of its existence it supported several clergy in Ohio. The earlier "Society for the Advancement of Christianity in Pennsylvania" sent Jackson Kemper in 1815 on a tour of western Pennsylvania, and thereafter maintained a few missionaries in that region. In western New York, moreover, Hobart and his well-supported forces were offering the rare example of a diocese adequate to local needs. Yet nowhere was there to be found any orderly planning or any combined effort on a national scale.

The General Convention of 1814, as we have noted, learned from the Presiding Bishop that no progress was being made toward the support of the Church in the West. To the next Convention in 1817 he presented various documents concerning the Church on the frontier, including petitions from several congregations asking leave to form a convention to include all the western country and to be placed provisionally under the Presiding Bishop. The Convention replied with resolutions which expressed its "lively interest" in their spiritual welfare and its "exceeding solicitude" to extend the Church's ministrations, but which stated that it could not authorize the proposed convention because the constitution of the Church recognized only the convention of the Church in each State. To console these persistent Episcopalians beyond the mountains a further motion was passed to the effect "that it be earnestly recommended to the authorities of the Church in each State respectively, to adopt measures for sending missionaries to our destitute brethren in the western States; such missionaries to be subject to the direction of the ecclesiastical authority of the State or States in which they may officiate." Thus General Convention once more threw the whole problem back upon the dioceses.

So inflexibly was the Church then organized as a mere federation of highly independent dioceses that it was baffled by existing conditions. A State meant a diocese, and a diocese meant a State, and that was all that could be said. That a diocese might comprise more than one State or a State more than one diocese was then a proposition too novel to be considered. Consequently the policy of General Convention was to leave each State or western Territory to qualify as a diocese if and when it could, through the use of its own resources. The Convention assumed no responsibility for helping it to grow. It simply waited for it to appear with a signed certificate proving that it *had* grown.

This paralyzing situation was soon to be improved, and ultimately to be saved, by the organization of a *national* Missionary Society.

In the words of Bishop Lesslie Newbigin, "The New Testament

knows of only one missionary society—the Church. The eighteenth century knew Churches which had totally ceased to be missionary societies and saw the birth of missionary societies which made no claim to be Churches." Such were the English Society for the Propagation of the Gospel (1701) and the English Church Missionary Society (1799), whose income and activities were rapidly expanding during the first third of the nineteenth century. The secretary of the C.M.S. in 1817 wrote to several of the bishops of the Episcopal Church in the hope of obtaining their cooperation in missionary work. He strongly recommended the formation of a Missionary Society by the Church in the United States, and promised that if such action were taken the C.M.S. would contribute £200 as an initial gift. To this friendly pressure from the mother Church was added the example of Protestant Churches here at home. The American Board of Commissioners for Foreign Missions (mainly Congregational) [3] had been organized in 1810, and in 1812 had sent five men to India. In 1814 there had been established the General Missionary Convention of the Baptist Denomination of the United States of America for Foreign Missions.

Realizing at length the growing need for a national Missionary Society and observing how valuable such societies had proved themselves both in England and in America, the members of the General Convention of 1820 had the honor of taking the first step. The constitution which they produced rather too hastily for "The Protestant Episcopal Missionary Society in the United States, for Foreign and Domestic Missions" proved at once to be defective in several respects; but the special session of the Convention in 1821 offered an early opportunity for revising it.

The new constitution, which was to serve for the next fourteen years, changed the name of the Society to "The Domestic and Foreign Missionary Society of the Protestant Episcopal Church in the United States of America," a title which it still bears. The membership was to be composed of (1) the Bishops, (2) the members of the House of Deputies for the time being, and (3) all persons contributing $3 or more annually to the Society. Contributors on a larger scale became "life members" and "patrons." There were to be triennial meetings at the time of General Convention, when a board of twenty-four directors was to be chosen. The Board, which met once a year, included *ex officio* the Presiding Bishop as president, the other bishops (then only nine) as vice-presidents, and the patrons. Provision was also made for the appointment of a treasurer and two secretaries, and for an executive committee.

To further the raising of funds it was designed from the beginning that auxiliary societies should be formed both in dioceses and in parishes, and in the following year these began to appear. Most of them were

[3] For 25 years (1812–1837) it also served nearly all the Presbyterians.

organized by women, thus anticipating by nearly fifty years the Woman's Auxiliary to the Board of Missions. To keep in touch with these local groups and to aid in the effort to obtain subscriptions the Directors sent volunteer agents into the dioceses. The results, however, were discouraging, for most of the bishops declined to support the enterprise, generally on the familiar ground that they did not wish to divert money from cherished diocesan projects. The machinery for nation-wide action was at last available, but the necessary spirit was too often wanting.

At the next General Convention in 1823 it was evident that the diocese of Pennsylvania was among the strongest promoters of the new Society. Yet among its 2,200 communicants only 90 were members; and thus far the organization had not reached the point of employing a single missionary. In that same year, however, two men were sent to Florida and Indiana, and in the course of the ensuing triennium others were appointed for work in Alabama and Missouri, at Detroit, and among the Oneida Indians at Green Bay, Wisconsin (then in Michigan Territory). But in 1829 it was still necessary to report to the Convention that the Society "has not yet received . . . that general and cordial support which was so earnestly to have been desired." No more than meager resources were available because of "the insufficiency of mere casual donations and congregational collections." As an offset to such disappointing news it was decided at this session to send Bishop Brownell of Connecticut on a visit to the States lying west and south of the Alleghanies. This tour the sturdy bishop subsequently accomplished, travelling 6,000 miles by stage and steamboat and on horseback. He estimated that in the nine States and three Territories through which he travelled there was a population of 4,000,000, with only twenty Episcopal congregations and twenty-three clergymen. In fact, throughout extensive inhabited districts there were no signs of a church of any denomination.[4]

One of the few cheerful notes in the report of the Society in 1829 was the news that missionary work on foreign soil had begun. In the previous year the Rev. John J. Robertson had been appointed to open a mission in Greece. It may seem strange that with a non-Christian population throughout the world numbering many hundreds of millions the Church should have chosen Greece for its first venture abroad. It might be counted an early example of the Church's tendency to be sporadic and impulsive in selecting its foreign fields. It has too often happened, we must confess, that a small group has been seized by the conviction that a mission here or a mission there would be a glorious idea; and after a little pressure

[4] In 1940 the ratio of population to one communicant in the diocese of Virginia was about 34 to 1. In Alabama it was 243 to 1 and in Mississippi 257 to 1. There has been little or no foreign immigration to account for this sharp contrast. It is due to the lack of missionary activity in the time of the western movement.

the Church has adopted the proposal with no regard to broader plans or general strategy. As a matter of fact, at this very period there was agitation for missions not only to Greece but also to such unrelated areas as Liberia and Buenos Aires.

Nevertheless, in justice to the Society it must be remembered that Japan was then closed to foreigners, missionaries were proscribed in China, only narrow fringes of Africa were open, and the English Societies were already initiating work in India. Moreover, Greece was then much in the public eye and in command of warm public sympathy. For six years the Greeks had been alternately fighting the Turks and each other, until in October, 1827, the intervention of the Allied Powers, leading to the naval battle of Navarino, freed Hellas from her Ottoman masters. Private aid to the Greek forces and generous contributions to the relief of suffering had already been extended by the American people. It is not so surprising, then, that the Society should have moved to enter Greece and to serve what its report describes as "a people for whose sufferings our countrymen generally have felt great sympathy . . . among whom, being without the Holy Scriptures and destitute of education, a corrupt form of Christianity prevails, except where even this has given place to infidelity."

After a careful tour of inspection in Greece, John Robertson returned to the United States in December, 1829, reported favorably on existing opportunities, and set about raising money for the new project. Within less than a year there had been added to the mission the Rev. and Mrs. John H. Hill and Solomon Bingham, a printer. On September 28, 1830, these three, together with Robertson and his wife, received from Bishop Griswold at a solemn meeting in St. Paul's Church, Boston, a long letter of instruction; and four days later they sailed for Greece. During the next five years the Hills devoted themselves entirely to educationed work at Athens, and Robertson largely to a printing and publishing enterprise which after 1833 was located at Syra. By 1835 the Press had produced 30,000 copies of various books, secular and religious; and the institutions at Athens, numbering 600 students in all, included an infant school, schools for girls and boys, and a school for training teachers. It was encouragingly obvious that the Greeks wanted what the Church had to offer.

In spite of good news from Greece and fragmentary accounts from a few stations in the United States, the General Convention of 1832 could hardly take a cheerful view of the Missionary Society. For nine years in all its official reports a surplusage of ultra-pious language had never succeeded in concealing a general lack of enthusiasm in the Church and a continuous failure to take vigorous action. In all the parishes and dioceses there were only 75 auxiliaries; there were only 251 paying members; and the total income for the previous three years was only $50,000. The growing West was still largely neglected, and the evangelization of the "heathen" was confined to a little group of workers in Greece. But by the end of another three years there was to be a memorable step forward.

A momentous change was wrought in the Society's constitution by abandoning the tradition, which still prevails in England, that a missionary society is a society *within* the Church composed of persons who are interested in missions, just as other societies may be composed of persons who are interested in helping the blind or in building a national cathedral. The decision was made to return to the principle embodied in the New Testament that there is just one missionary society—*the Church*. The new Article II therefore reads, "The Society shall be considered as comprehending all persons who are members of this Church." The ground of membership henceforth was to be not a required contribution but the solemn vow taken at Baptism which grafts the Christian into the Body of Christ and enlists him as Christ's faithful soldier and servant. For leadership in bringing about this revolutionary move the Church is indebted to Bishop Doane of New Jersey, Bishop McIlvaine of Ohio, and the Rev. Dr. Milnor of New York, who found themselves in warm agreement on the principle involved and whose earnest eloquence proved persuasive.

Further revision provided for a Board of Missions of thirty members to be elected by General Convention. Additional members included all the bishops and all who had become "patrons" before the Convention of 1829. The Board, with the Presiding Bishop as president, was given full power to direct the missionary work of the Church; and except for later reduction in its size, it is this Board which controlled the enterprise until the organization of the National Council in 1919. Its meetings at first were held once a year, and between meetings all administration was carried on by two committees—one for Domestic Missions and one for Foreign Missions, each with its secretary, treasurer, and "general agent."

Though Article X of the constitution declared that "the missionary field is always to be regarded as one, *the world*," and though it was explained that the plan to use two committees was simply to promote efficiency, the division was really too sharp to be wholesome. It was the more regrettable because there soon became obvious a tacit understanding that the domestic field was to be assigned to the High Churchmen and the foreign field to the Evangelicals. An English observer, after experience in the United States at this time, recorded as early as 1837 the parts played by High and Low Churchmen. "The former," he noted, "labor with energy in the promotion of missions within their own country; and the latter with equal energy in the propagation of the Gospel abroad." [5]

[5] Caswall, *op. cit.*, 341.

Today, on the contrary, we have cause for gratitude that all types of Churchmanship are represented in both fields, to the marked advantage of a Church in which the promotion of missions is no longer an occasion for partisan contention.

The results of this constitutional revision were to become evident through the rest of the century and are no part of our record in this chapter. But we may well anticipate one point by noting here that the receipts of the Society during the triennium 1832–1835 averaged $26,000 a year, while during the first year after the Convention of 1835 they rose to nearly $56,000. The new sense of responsibility aroused by General Convention had begun promptly to take effect. Yet only a small fraction of Church members had then been trained in giving. They were still accustomed to contributing only in return for what they themselves received. Nearly all the well-organized parishes depended chiefly upon pew rents for their support, and voluntary offerings for which there was no obvious *quid pro quo* were regarded as a most unreliable source of income. If that was true of the local parish it was still more plainly true of giving to diocesan or general missions.[6]

The second great contribution of this Convention was the adoption, long overdue, of a canon creating the office of missionary bishop. It empowered the House of Bishops to nominate and the House of Deputies to elect missionary bishops to serve in States and Territories not organized as dioceses or in any area outside the United States which the House of Bishops might designate. Upon the request of the Board of Missions such bishops might be elected by the House of Bishops between General Conventions, subject to the approval of a majority of the Standing Committees of the dioceses. These missionary bishops, who were given seats in the House of Bishops, were required to conduct their work under regulations prescribed by that House, and were expected to submit regular reports to General Convention. "Thus was brought to pass what to us is a commonplace, but what was then a revolutionary principle, namely, that both jurisdiction and the power of mission belong to the Episcopate as a whole, and that a bishop chosen and consecrated to be the vicar of the American Episcopate should represent that body in places where the constituent members could not go. . . . As Bishop Doane said: 'A missionary bishop is a bishop *sent forth* by the Church, *not sought for* of the Church; going

[6] Bishop Doane of New Jersey seems to have been the first leader to inaugurate on any large scale the modern plan of regular weekly giving by the envelope system. In 1833 he introduced it into his diocese, declaring it to be modelled on St. Paul's command: "Upon the first day of the week let every one of you lay by him in store, as God hath prospered him" (I Cor. 16:2). These contributions were tied in papers or sealed up. After being received in the alms basin they were recorded and later sent to the Board of Missions. In its first year of use, this plan more than tripled the offerings from the diocese.

before to organize the Church, not waiting till the Church has partially been organized; a leader, not a follower.' "[7]

To implement this canon the Rev. Jackson Kemper was at once elected missionary bishop for the States of Indiana and Missouri. With the approval at the same session of the election of Bishop Chase by the convention of Illinois provision had thus been made for the extension of the episcopate to three of the newer States.

Nor had the foreign field been overlooked. In the course of the year preceding the Philadelphia Convention the Rev. Henry Lockwood and the Rev. Francis Hanson had been appointed as our first missionaries to China; and the Convention learned that seven weeks before it assembled these pioneers had sailed from New York for Canton. They carried with them a letter of instruction and advice written by Bishop White. It included these generous words: "In the tie which binds you to the Episcopal Church there is nothing which places you in the attitude of hostility to men of any other Christian denomination, and much which should unite you in affection to those occupied in the same cause with yourselves. You should rejoice in their successes. . . ."[8]

[7] W. H. Stowe, "The General Convention of 1835," *Historical Magazine,* Sept., 1935, 171.

[8] B. Wilson, *Memoir of White,* 250.

PART III

THE CHURCH FROM 1836 TO 1865

INTRODUCTORY

THOUGH the year 1835, so important for the Church, was a year of no particular significance for the country, it remains true that the generation before the Civil War lived in an atmosphere notably different from that of the earlier nineteenth century. Even more plainly than before, "opportunity" and "progress" were the key words of the era, and boundless optimism was its characteristic note. Confident reliance upon the nation's limitless resources and a naive faith in the virtues of unfettered individualism—these traits marked the American of that day. He had become a hustler, who was "much more inclined to believe and feel than to think." Eager readiness for experiment and change produced inventions in the field of mechanics, and in society brought forth reforms and new movements of thought, many valuable and not a few eccentric.

The age at which we have arrived was remarkable for widespread changes in the economic life of the country—westward expansion to the Pacific, the industrial revolution, the rapid growth of cities, and heavy streams of immigration. In the short interval between 1830 and 1850 the value of imports rose from $71,000,000 to $178,000,000; the population nearly doubled; and before 1860 the immigrants (mostly English, Irish, and German) numbered four and a half million. In politics it was a period of great statesmen like Webster, Clay, and Calhoun, and of mediocre presidents like Fillmore, Pierce, and Buchanan. The war with Mexico, the opening of Japan, the Gold Rush to California, the famous Compromise of 1850, and the rise of the Republican Party were great events crowded into only one decade. And the epoch ended with the four tragic years of the Civil War.

If this was the era of "bounce and bluster" which Dickens caricatured in *Martin Chuzzlewit,* it was also the era of educational expansion during which free primary schooling became open to all children in the more settled Northern States. These same decades witnessed "the flowering of New England" in the works of Emerson and Thoreau, of Longfellow and Lowell, of Prescott and Motley, and of Nathaniel Hawthorne. Moreover, "this was distinctly and increasingly a religious period. It was not merely that the interest in religion itself was stronger than in the preceding generation, but that the union between religion and morality was so strong that they became practically indistinguishable, and that almost every subject was invested with the religious qualities of certainty and enthusiasm. . . . In fact during these years the connection of religion with life was more and more emphasized, and preaching took on more and more a humanitarian and social cast." [1] Among the obvious religious developments of the age was the outcropping of freakish sects. In these restless years of experimentation there arose the Mormons, the Millerites who prophesied the immediate end of the world, the Spiritualists with their seances, and many mild communistic groups like those at Brook Farm. But of far more permanent significance was the expansion of the Roman Church, chiefly due to immigration from Ireland. In 1830 there were only about 600,000 Roman Catholics in the country, but in 1865 there were 4,500,000, an increase greater than seven-fold in thirty-five years.

Of the Churches in the United States in 1850 the Episcopal Church ranked sixth in numbers; [2] but the social and economic status of its members may be inferred from the fact that in the value of its property it ranked third. The comments on its constituency published in 1839 by an English clergyman who had served the Church in the United States for ten years were to remain true for some time to come. "The Episcopal Church," he admitted, "exerts at present but little influence on the population at large. Although many of the first families in the United States are enrolled among its members and friends, its field of usefulness is generally limited to the cities and towns. There is, however, a constant improvement in this respect. The number of its clergymen is rapidly increasing, the nature of its church government is becoming better understood . . . and many prejudices are fast wearing away." "The Episcopal congregations," he adds, "are generally composed of highly intelligent and respectable people, many of whom have received an excellent education." [3]

In 1830 there were only 31,000 communicants in the Episcopal Church out of a population of nearly 13,000,000; whereas in 1860, out of a population of 31,500,000, there were 150,000 communicants. From these facts may be drawn the encouraging conclusion that the ratio of population to communicants was about 416 to one in 1830 and about 209 to one in 1860. In other words, Churchmen at the latter date were twice

[1] C. R. Fish, *The Rise of the Common Man,* 179, 183.

[2] The first five Churches were the Methodist, Baptist, Presbyterian, Congregational, and Roman Catholic.

[3] H. Caswall, *America and the American Church,* 64, 296.

as numerous in proportion to the whole population as they had been thirty years earlier. But the *ratio* changed relatively little in the next thirty years because the huge addition to the population brought by immigration provided only a very small increase for the Church. It was the Roman and Lutheran Churches which profited. While this growth in communicant strength was proceeding the total number of clergy grew from 763 in 1835 to 2,450 in 1865—a rate of progress slower than that of Church membership. The difficulty of recruiting for the ministry and the low salaries offered to clergy were constant themes of complaint, especially in the 'fifties.

In a valuable analysis of the causes of the Church's growth during the generation after 1830 [4] Dr. Walter H. Stowe has cited a number of favorable factors upon which most historians would agree. Among these were the decline of prejudice against the Church arising from its English origin and connections, since the Church had by that time become fully Americanized; the intellectual revolt against Puritanism in doctrine and morals; a revulsion of feeling, experienced by many, against crude revivalism; and the spread of education, which enabled an increasing number to appreciate the dignity and beauty of liturgical worship. To these points we may add the fact that the Church was then far better organized to seize new opportunities in the growing West.

[4] W. H. Stowe: "Immigration and the Growth of the Episcopal Church," *Historical Magazine,* Dec., 1942, 341 f.

Chapter IX

MISSIONARY EXPANSION

IN this generation of missionary expansion at home and abroad the Church encountered, then as now, the greatest difficulty in raising the money needed. During the triennium 1835–1838 $157,000 was contributed to the Domestic and Foreign Missionary Society, an average of about $52,000 a year. This sum was given by communicants who numbered only 46,000 in 1838. For the triennium 1856–1859 the average figure was $136,000, and the communicants in 1859 were 140,000. Comparison with modern times, however, would be unfair because in those days the income reported to the Convention by the Board of Missions often included bequests and capital gifts and therefore does not correspond to the money raised by apportionment for current expenses as reported in later years. Anything like assigned quotas, of course, was then not even heard of. General Conventions attempted no more than to pass resolutions pleading for "enlarged liberality on the part of the Church." Yet in 1862 less than half the parishes were contributing to the Board of Missions.

DOMESTIC

The most notable missionary advance of the Church in this era was its westward expansion. Displaying an energy unknown to an earlier generation, its forces were often on the scene as soon as those of any other Church and sometimes as early as the first white settlers. That greater success was not won could no longer be attributed to defective organization or want of spirit, but to the continuous lack of money and especially the lack of men.

Effective leaders, however, were by no means wanting; and to trace the path of progress by following their careers generally proves the most interesting method. Of these pioneers the greatest was Jackson Kemper.[5]

[5] The brief biography of Kemper by Greenough White, entitled *An Apostle of the Western Church,* is less valuable than its subject deserved. The topic has been carefully treated in E. R. Hardy, Jr.'s "Kemper's Missionary Episcopate" (*Historical Magazine,* Sept., 1935) and in E. C. Chorley's "Missionary March of the American Episcopal Church," Part II, Ch. IX (*Historical Magazine,* March, 1948).

Born near Poughkeepsie in 1789 of parents of German stock, Kemper entered Columbia College at the age of sixteen and after graduation studied theology for a year under Dr. Hobart and Bishop Moore of New York. In 1811 he was ordained deacon by Bishop White and became his assistant in the large parish of Christ Church in Philadelphia. Though he remained in this same post for the next twenty years, he was so obviously a born missionary that he was continually exploiting every opportunity for advance even in that rather complacent and comfortable environment. Within a year he had become the moving spirit in the organization of the Society for the Advancement of Christianity in Pennsylvania, and after appointment as its first missionary agent he spent an active summer in traveling widely through southern and western Pennsylvania. In 1814, during the month when the British burnt the White House, he repeated the tour, with an extension into the "Connecticut Reserve" in Ohio.

It was, indeed, through Kemper's respectful but insistent pressure that the aged Bishop White was energized into missionary activity during the last twenty years of his long episcopate. By persuading his saintly but unaggressive chief to visit all the country parishes he was partly responsible for the fact that the number of confirmations in the diocese increased ten-fold in two years. He played an active part, too, in founding the Episcopal Missionary Society of Philadelphia, the main aim of which was to send missionaries into the western States. Nine years later it was with Kemper as encouraging companion that White set out at the age of seventy-seven upon the first tour he had ever made through western Pennsylvania, during which the pair traveled more than eight hundred miles. Much as he loved his ardent assistant, it may well have been a relief to Bishop White when in 1831 Kemper accepted a call to St. Paul's Church, Norwalk, Connecticut, and the old man could spend the last five years of his life in peace.

At the General Convention of 1835, as we have noted in an earlier chapter, Jackson Kemper was chosen to be the Church's first missionary bishop, with Missouri and Indiana as his assigned field. Sending the best men to such a distance was still so great a novelty in Church policy that Bishop Clark of Rhode Island later recorded, "I remember dining with [Kemper] in Boston just before he went out . . . and wondering that such a high-bred gentleman should be willing to exile himself in the far-off regions of the West." The conditions the new bishop encountered were indeed primitive enough. Though Indiana had been a State for twenty years and had half a million inhabitants, log cabins in clearings, roads almost impassable, and bison, wolves, and deer plentiful in numbers were still typical features of mid-western life. In a region where Jacksonian democracy and enthusiastic Methodism were prevalent it is not surprising that the Episcopal minister at Indianapolis was the only one in the State. And when Kemper arrived in St. Louis just before Christmas he found but one parish and no clergy.

In the course of the ensuing year the bishop undertook a difficult journey into Illinois and Iowa and found time for a trip to the East in search of men and money. By the month of January, 1837, his energetic planning had so far advanced that he was able to secure the incorporation of Kemper College, situated five miles from St. Louis. This institution (named for him against his will) was one more example of the Church colleges so eagerly founded in the pioneer era; but it met the fate of Jubilee College rather than of Kenyon, and after running heavily into debt was closed in 1845. Meantime, though Kemper had to struggle with the hardships suffered everywhere during the great depression of 1837, he carried out in that year a westward expedition into Kansas. "I have now experienced a little of western adventure," he wrote, "and really entered into it with much more spirit and enjoyment that I could have imagined. . . Shall I tell you how we were benighted and how we lost our way, of the deep creeks we forded and the bad bridges we crossed, and how we were drenched to the skin, and how we were wading for half an hour in a slough, and the accident which arose from the stumbling of our horses . . . What a proof of the sluggishness of our [i.e., the Church's] movements is the fact that . . . I have been the pioneer from St. Charles up the Missouri!" [6]

By no means exhausted by the wide range of his own territory Kemper promised to join Bishop Otey of Tennessee in a tour of the South and when illness prevented Otey from starting, Kemper spent the firs four months of 1838 traveling through Louisiana, Mississippi, Alabama Georgia, and Florida, visiting and confirming in nearly all the parishes Later in that year the General Convention admitted as new dioceses no only Louisiana and Florida but also Indiana, though the latter include only nine clergy. Kemper, having declined to become Indiana's first diocesan, continued as its acting bishop for the next fourteen years. By th time George Upfold was elected bishop in 1849 there were twenty-thre parishes.

General Convention, so far from relieving Kemper of any of hi districts, proceeded to add to them by putting Wisconsin Territory an Iowa Territory within his jurisdiction. At the same time it elected Leonida Polk missionary bishop for Arkansas with responsibility also for Alabama Mississippi, Louisiana, and the Republic of Texas—an assignment whic he had to travel five thousand miles to cover during the following yea While Polk was traversing the South and Southwest Kemper, havin

[6] White, *Apostle of the Western Church,* 89.

refused election as bishop of Maryland, was entering his northernmost district of Wisconsin, which was to be his center and home in later years. There, in the Oneida Mission at Green Bay, he found the only active work with Indians then conducted by the Church, and there he consecrated the first church building in Wisconsin.

To strengthen the work in this territory Kemper made a brief tour through the East in 1840 in the course of which he visited the General Seminary. There he won three volunteers who came to Wisconsin the next year—James Lloyd Breck, William Adams, and John Henry Hobart, Jr. After a year of pioneering in small stations they settled at the Nashotah Lakes upon a track of some five hundred acres purchased by the bishop. At that lonely spot, in a little frame building, they began the history of Nashotah House, with six men studying for the ministry. Though Hobart left after two years, the school continued to grow, and by the fall of 1844 there were thirty students in residence, of whom eighteen were preparing for holy orders. Within another four years Nashotah had a charter and a board of trustees, and in 1850 Breck was succeeded as president by the Rev. A. D. Cole, under whom the seminary prospered for the next thirty-five years. For any settled executive post Breck was too much like the early Celtic missionaries in Europe—glorying in the isolation and the hardships of adventurous pioneering but too eccentric and temperamental to work well in conventional harness. We shall next meet him blazing trails in Minnesota.

Nashotah, however, was only one fragment of Kemper's huge area. During the year of its founding the bishop was constantly on the march through Wisconsin, Indiana, Missouri, and Iowa, generally spending a week in each parish and mission station. Missouri had become a diocese in 1840, but not until 1844 was the Rev. Cicero S. Hawks consecrated as its first bishop. Thus relieved of the care of his southernmost district, Kemper's interest was drawn the more strongly toward Wisconsin. He bought a house near Nashotah and found himself with a settled home for the first time in eleven years. After another three years (1847) Wisconsin too had been organized as a diocese with as many as twenty-five parishes; but though Kemper declined an election as its diocesan, he continued as its missionary bishop for the next seven years.

As fast as any portion of his field became partly domesticated Kemper always found wilder regions in which to advance, and for some years to come he devoted much time and energy to Iowa and Minnesota. Iowa was growing at such a phenomenal rate that the bishop had only the scantiest resources with which to meet his opportunities. "Were it not," he wrote, "for the sure word of prophecy and the precious promises of the Redeemer, I would wish to relinquish a post which I sought not, and where I have almost thought at times I commanded the forlorn hope." Among his many hindrances were the continuous shifting of population and the unhappy results of Mormon inroads. As one of his workers complained, "The morals and general interests of the place have been sadly injured by the Mormons. It seems past recovering from the baleful effects of their unholy influence." Yet by 1851 he had six missionaries in the State, and four years afterward Iowa was a diocese with its own bishop—Henry Washington Lee. Progress in Minnesota, however, was slower; but in 1857 the first diocesan convention was held, with representatives from thirteen parishes; and in 1859 one of the great Church leaders in the West—Henry Benjamin Whipple—began his career of forty-two years as the first Bishop of Minnesota. Before he was consecrated a mission and schools had been established by Breck at Faribault. Whipple made his home there and proceeded to incorporate the schools and to build a new church. At this center there were soon to develop the Cathedral of Our Merciful Saviour, the Seabury Divinity School, and the Shattuck School for boys.

While the zeal and energy of Kemper were serving to make dioceses out of missionary districts in the West, other leaders no less devoted were developing the Church in the South and Southwest. Among these was the beloved Bishop Otey of Tennessee.

James Harvey Otey was born in 1800 in Bedford County, Virginia, the son of a farmer. At the age of twenty he graduated from the new college at Chapel Hill, which was later to be the University of North Carolina. While serving as tutor in the following year he was converted to the Episcopal Church (like Chase) through the study of a Prayer Book which had been given him by a friend. After his marriage in 1821 he became the head of a boys' academy at Warrenton, North Carolina, and in the course of the next six years he was confirmed by Bishop Ravenscroft and ordained deacon and priest. During the ensuing eight years he labored in the double capacity of minister-in-charge of the little church at Franklin, Tennessee, and master of the local school. At first he was one of only two Episcopal clergy in the State, but by 1829 there were several more; and in that year, under the guidance of Bishop Ravenscroft, the diocese of Tennessee was organized. Four years later his six fellow clergy elected him as their first bishop, and in 1834 he was consecrated in Philadelphia by the aged Bishop White and three other bishops.

Though he never bore the title of "missionary bishop," he was a missionary leader for the next thirty years, serving not only Tennessee but wide areas in the South as pioneer and organizer. For ten years he was responsible for the diocese of Mississippi, and between 1842 and 1844, when Arkansas and Indian Territory were added to his field, he traveled four thousand miles in line of duty. During the last ten years of his life, when ill-health put some restraint upon his activities, his influence in the House of Bishops was steadily increasing. The outbreak of the war he felt as a severe shock, for he had long been a conservative Whig who stood for the Union and deplored secession. But once the South had acted he supported its cause with ardor. Though life in distracted Tennessee during those belligerent days was a continuous hardship, it is recorded that General Sherman treated the bishop with marked respect, declined to compel him to take the usual oath of allegiance, and often attended his services at Memphis. It was in the midst of the campaign for Vicksburg that he died in April, 1863.

Bishop Otey once said, "If I had not been a Christian minister, I would have been a soldier." Six feet four in height, broad-shouldered and vigorous, with heavy dark hair and piercing dark eyes, he was physically a striking figure. Dignity and courage were obvious traits manifest at first sight, but in the eyes of those who knew him better it was his deep and steadfast piety and his genuine humility that entitled him to the honor due to a saint. When his Convention adopted a memorial at his death they knew it was the simple truth to say, "He loved the Church and gave himself to it with deliberate, enduring and ever-increasing devotion."

Though they had become dioceses at a much earlier date, Alabama and Mississippi did not obtain bishops until 1844 and 1850 respectively, and during the interval they were visited not only by Otey but also by Polk as Bishop for Arkansas and wide adjacent regions. The latter became Bishop of Louisiana in 1841, and at the next General Convention in 1844 George Washington Freeman was elected to be "Missionary Bishop of this Church appointed to exercise episcopal functions in the States of Arkansas and Texas [7] and in the Indian Territory south of 36½ degrees of latitude." This would not have been a very neat title to be put in Latin after his Christian name, but it well described his ample responsibilities. He discharged them so fully that within five years Texas was a diocese, and in 1859 Alexander Gregg became its first bishop. In that year Arkansas was made a part of the diocese of the Southwest, but did not obtain diocesan independence until 1871.

Before the close of this period Southern leadership was responsible not only for the development of new dioceses but for the inauguration of a plan for a University of the South. Inspired by previous proposals from Bishop Otey, in the summer of 1856 Bishop Polk took the initiative by writing to nine Southern bishops to urge upon them the need for a university in the South. Their cooperation was so effective that before

[7] Texas was not formally annexed until 1845.

1860 a half a million dollars had been raised, 10,000 acres had been purchased at Sewanee, Tennessee, and the cornerstone of a building had been laid. Though the war wiped out all the financial assets of the university, the land remained, and the firm purpose of the founders was carried to completion despite the dismaying obstacles of the Reconstruction era.

In the year when Polk launched the Sewanee plan Kemper joined with Bishop Lee of Iowa to pay his first visit to Nebraska. Two years earlier, in 1854, he had accepted his second election as Bishop of Wisconsin, but according to the canons of the day that did not prevent him from retaining his missionary jurisdiction elsewhere. After holding services at Omaha—then a town of tents and booths—Kemper journeyed southward into Kansas after an absence of eighteen years. This was the time of strife in "bleeding Kansas," but the days had long passed when the motto of a bishop was "safety first." Instead of peril and adventure, however, he met for the most part with what would have seemed to anyone but an apostle to be wearisome discomfort and unprofitable effort. How little of romance or of immediate reward was the lot of a bishop in Kansas is revealed by a few lines from his diary in that summer of 1856—a journal which he certainly never expected would be reprinted a century later.

"July 22. Met Adams, formerly of the Army, who told a story of placing a preacher on a raft.[8] . . . A few responded at worship. Irish [Rev. William Irish] and I in same room with Adams. . . .

"July 24. Disturbed again by old Adams during the night. Up early. Off in a fair carriage and two young horses for Weston. . . . Rapid driving. . . . Crossed Missouri at Kickapoo in a steam ferry. From there three miles to Weston—a hilly place. At the St. George's, a hot small room. Slept, washed—ice cream &c. Church in an upper room, waited a long time, and then a few came. It was very hot." [9]

When Kansas had attained diocesan status in the same year that Minnesota elected its first bishop, Kemper decided that after twenty-four years of strenuous service he might honorably retire as a missionary bishop and confine his work to the diocese of Wisconsin. At the General Convention of 1859, therefore, he submitted his resignation. With deep regret it was accepted, and resolutions were passed by the Board of Missions recording his achievements—"six dioceses where he began with none, and 172 clergymen where he was at first sustained by only two." For another eleven years he administered his own diocese, and on May 24, 1870, at

[8] This is undoubtedly a reference to the action of a pro-slavery gang in the autumn of 1855, who seized the Rev. Pardee Butler (because he refused to sign a pro-slavery petition) and set him adrift in the Missouri River on a small raft composed of two logs. Miraculously he survived.

[9] "Kemper's Journal and Letters," *Historical Magazine,* Sept., 1935, 234.

the age of eighty, he died at Nashotah. As Bishop Clarkson of Nebraska wrote, "He did more than all other men in the land to mould the churchly life of seven great dioceses. . . . O that every bishop who shall minister on this fair domain may inherit . . . something of his fidelity, his single-mindedness, and his self-consecration!" And Bishop Talbot spoke the truth when he declared that "no bishop in the line of our American episcopate has succeeded in concentrating upon himself more entirely than he the love and veneration of the Church." [10]

The same General Convention of 1859 that accepted the resignation of Kemper elected Joseph C. Talbot to be Missionary Bishop of the North-west, a district which embraced the Territories of Nebraska, the Dakotas, Wyoming, Colorado, Utah (then including Nevada), and Montana—a total of 750,000 square miles. For good measure he was also asked to visit New Mexico and Arizona. Beyond his area were Oregon [11] and Washington which had been united in one missionary jurisdiction under Bishop Thomas Fielding Scott, and California, which by that time was a diocese under Bishop William I. Kip. Now at last the American episcopate had become coextensive with the boundaries of the United States.[12]

FOREIGN

In comparison with the immense areas involved and the large number of missionaries employed in the domestic field from 1836 to 1865, the missionary enterprise overseas was tentative and feeble. Of the districts in question—Greece, Constantinople, Liberia, China, and Japan—two were abandoned, and work in the others was still only in its earliest stages.

The mission to Greece had been the product of temporary impulse rather than of carefully considered strategy, and with the passing of the impulse the Church's support began to wane. In 1838 the printing and publishing center at Syra was given up, but the schools under Dr. Hill at Athens continued to flourish with a total of 800 pupils in 1841. By this time, however, other foreign missions were proving more interesting; Evangelicals were objecting that instead of converting Greeks, Hill was teaching only what their Church approved; and High Churchmen wanted no mission in Greece at all. In 1843, therefore, by way of compromise, the Board of Missions abandoned Athens as an official station and re-

[10] White, *op. cit.*, 230 f.

[11] Oregon then included the later Idaho.

[12] General Convention in 1865, after the election of Talbot as Bishop-coadjutor of Indiana, subdivided the missionary district of the Northwest into three districts—Nebraska (including also the Dakotas), Colorado (including also Montana, Idaho, and Wyoming), and Nevada (including also Utah, Arizona, and New Mexico). New bishops for the first two were elected at that time and one for Nevada in 1868.

duced its obligations to an annual subsidy of $2,000 to the Hill School—a grant which was maintained until 1899.[13]

More grandiose in design and even less effective in its outcome was the Church's first effort to approach the Moslem world. It began in 1835 with the appointment by the Board of Missions of the Rev. Horatio Southgate, an enthusiastic young man of twenty-three, "to an exploring missionary agency to Persia and the adjacent countries"—a choice apparently determined by the fact that that was where he wanted to go. In the following year he reached Constantinople, and the summer and autumn of 1837 he devoted to a reconnaissance of Persia, visiting Tabriz, Teheran, and other cities. After reporting to the Board that the way was open for the evangelization of Persia, he returned by slow stages to Constantinople, whither the Rev. J. J. Robertson of the Greek Mission was sent to aid him. Six years afterward, with undiminished confidence in his ability and his purposes for the future, the General Convention of 1844 elected Southgate bishop for "the Dominions and Dependencies of the Sultan of Turkey." He seems never to have undertaken seriously any direct work among Moslems which, as other missions had discovered, was definitely banned in Turkey and distinctly risky in Persia. But he had been instructed "to seek for friendly intercourse with Eastern Christians and to exert an influence for their enlightenment." His work was widely misunderstood in America, and meagrely supported. After only five years devoted to this endeavor he returned to the United States; in 1850 his resignation was accepted; and nothing more was heard of the mission to the dominions of the Sultan.

The earliest surviving foreign mission of the Church is that in Liberia. Attention had been drawn to that portion of the west coast of Africa because of the activity there of the American Colonization Society founded in 1817 for the purpose of promoting the return to Africa of free Negroes. The Society had bought a large tract of land south of Sierra Leone, which was later named Liberia and which became an independent republic in 1847. Though the venture was never really successful and there was only a handful of American Negroes there in 1821, the Domestic and Foreign Missionary Society then decided to open its work in Africa at that point. Not until 1835, however, did they prove successful in placing a missionary in the field, a Negro layman then resident in Monrovia. It was in the following year that the Rev. Thomas S. Savage was appointed, the first white missionary sent by the Church to Africa. The Rev. and Mrs. John Payne and the Rev. Lancelot B. Minor of Virginia soon followed him; and amid the most harassing difficulties created by climate and by the

[13] The best account of the Mission to Greece is that by E. R. Hardy, Jr., in the *Historical Magazine,* Sept., 1941.

quarrels between natives and colonists the mission was fairly started. In view of the growth of the work and of the increase of the staff despite a number of deaths, the General Convention in 1850 elected Payne "Bishop of Cape Palmas and Parts Adjacent"; and after another five years his district was enlarged to include the whole of Liberia. By that time there were 14 stations, 240 communicants, and at least 15 schools. Even the lack of support caused by the Civil War could not prevent further progress.

The mission to China began, as we have seen, when Hanson and Lockwood sailed from New York in June, 1835. They had been commissioned just before a great crisis in the history of the ancient empire, and their subsequent failure was due to the fact that China was not really open.

Though these earliest messengers may not have known it, Christianity had entered China at least twelve hundred years before, when Nestorian missionaries and their converts introduced the religion and maintained it on a small scale for two or three hundred years. Later, in the thirteenth and fourteenth centuries a Franciscan mission flourished for a time, but likewise faded out, leaving few traces. Finally, in the sixteenth century, Jesuits, followed by other orders, restored Roman Catholic Christianity to China, where it took permanent root. Though the number of Christians at the beginning of the eighteenth century was no less than 300,000, controversies resulting in heavy persecution so greatly reduced these forces that in 1835 there were probably no more than 200,000 in the empire. And severe regulations enforced by the government restricted the residence of foreigners to a single narrow strip of land in the south coast port of Canton.

Such were the unfavorable conditions which confronted the first Protestant missionary, Robert Morrison, when he landed at Canton in 1807. But with the help obtained by securing a position with the British East India Company he persisted at his task and eventually translated the Bible into Chinese and prepared a massive dictionary. Other Englishmen followed, and in 1830 the American Board (Congregational) entered the field. By 1840 there were about twenty Protestant missionaries and perhaps a hundred converts. Hanson and Lockwood, however, were advised by experienced Christian leaders at Canton that they would find in Java much freer facilities for studying the Chinese language. So they sailed for Batavia, which had a large Chinese population, and there set themselves to mastering a difficult tongue. The tropical climate, however, proved so dangerously harmful to their health that Hanson had to return home in 1838 and Lockwood in the following year.

Meantime the Rev. William J. Boone, a graduate of the Virginia Seminary who was also a medical doctor, had been appointed with his wife for service in China and reached Batavia late in 1837. He was to be the real founder of the Anglican Communion in China, for in 1842, having learned in Java the Amoy dialect, he moved to Amoy, and a priest of the Church was at length settled on Chinese soil. His range of action was soon to be broadened by current events.

A naval war between Great Britain and China was brought on in 1840 by the British demand not only for the infamous privilege of selling opium but also for the legitimate right of diplomatic intercourse and normal trade. It ended in 1842 with the Treaty of Nanking which ceded Hongkong to Britain and opened five ports (including Amoy and Shanghai) to foreign trade and residence. Within a few years further agreements had been signed granting to foreigners in China "extra-territoriality"—the right to be governed by their own laws applied by their own officials. It was under these novel and highly encouraging circumstances that immense new opportunities opened out before all the Christian missionary forces.

Realizing already that a great future awaited the Church in China, Boone spent most of the year of 1843 and 1844 in the United States, arousing interest and enlisting workers. At the General Convention of 1844 he was elected bishop, and in the following June he arrived in Shanghai with eight new fellow-workers. The instructions he had been given by the House of Bishops included these words: "So vast is the population of the empire, so great the difficulty of the language, so small the number of missionaries and teachers that we can send out from this country, and so heavy the expense of maintainment that there is an imperative necessity for taking immediate steps for rearing a band of Christian teachers; a body of able translators, and above all, an efficient ministry." This emphasis upon education and upon developing a Chinese ministry of high quality has been characteristic of the Church's mission in China from that day to this.

In taking advantage of the opening of China the two leading missionary societies of the Church of England were somewhat slower; but by 1849 there was an English Bishop of Victoria (Hongkong) sent out by the Church Missionary Society. Later, in 1880, came a bishop supported by the Society for the Propagation of the Gospel. The Church of England and its bishops in China were reluctant to acknowledge the existence of the Episcopal Church in that country by agreeing to any division of territory, and cooperation followed by organic union was not to be achieved until the twentieth century.

Though the new staff of workers was soon diminished by several resignations, and progress at this stage had to be slow, the earliest decade at Shanghai brought the encouragement of the first converts, the first church consecrated, and the first schools for boys and girls. The ensuing years between 1856 and 1858 were disturbed by a second war between Great Britain and China, in which France decided to join. When the unequal contest ended, the Treaty of Tientsin opened ten more ports and secured permission for foreigners to travel in the interior. The whole of China was then theoretically free to missionaries, and by 1864 there were twenty-four Protestant societies at work and nearly two hundred missionaries. In that year Bishop Boone died, a heavy shock to a mission already depleted by deaths and retirements and suffering from the effects of the Civil War at home. His place was not quite filled by the election in 1865 of Channing Moore Williams (then in Japan) as "Missionary Bishop in China, with jurisdiction over all the missionary operations of this Church in China and Japan." For a dozen years he struggled to sustain his heavy double assignment, and was at length relieved of responsibility for China.[14]

Christianity was first introduced into Japan by Francis Xavier and his companions in the middle of the sixteenth century. Before the end of that century there were probably as many as 300,000 Christians in the empire, including many feudal lords. The entry of other orders, bringing rivalry with the Jesuits and strife among Christians, and the fear felt by the Japanese authorities that Christian advance would end in foreign aggression led to strict edicts against the new religion. During the prolonged persecutions that followed, accompanied by tortures and executions, tens of thousands of Christians lost their lives, and only a feeble underground Christianity survived. By the middle of the seventeenth century all intercourse with foreign nations had been cut off except for the occasional visits of a few Dutch ships to one small island. Japan remained thus sealed for more than two centuries until the visit of the American Commodore Perry and his little squadron in 1853 resulted in a treaty permitting commercial intercourse and providing for foreign residence in certain ports. Though the edicts against Christianity were still in force, missionaries began to enter the country in 1859—first among them the Rev. John Liggins and the Rev. C. M. Williams of the Episcopal Mission in China. Like their fellow-workers of other Churches, they could carry on no direct evangelism and had to be content with teaching English to many eager pupils upon whom they could exert an influence that was later to bear fruit.

[14] The best account of the Episcopal Church in China is that by Virginia E. Huntington in *Along the Great River.*

Chapter X

THE OXFORD MOVEMENT AND ITS AMERICAN RESULTS

THE MOVEMENT IN ENGLAND

THE fundamental causes of the Oxford Movement in the Church of England may be traced to the general situation of the Church in the earlier decades of the nineteenth century; the immediate occasion of its opening was the agitation for political and social reform which culminated in the Reform Bill of 1832.

As we have recorded in an introductory chapter, the Evangelical movement arising from the Wesleyan revival of the eighteenth century had brought into the Church of England new vigor, expressing itself in a vital emphasis upon personal religion and upon philanthropic activity. The group which represented that movement supplied most of the spiritual force and earnestness in the Church up to the year 1833. By that time, however, their undoubted virtues were becoming less obvious than some of their defects. Among the latter were a narrow view of "worldliness," a tendency to divorce religion from philosophy, literature and art, and a failure to produce any respectable theology. Evangelicalism had made a contribution of lasting value, but it had never fully permeated the life of the Church, and its effects had begun to wane.

The predominant party in the Church was commonly described as High Church, but most of the clergy who composed it were destitute of the vigorous characteristics either of the early Laudian school or of the later Anglo-Catholics. For them, as for most of its members, the Church was primarily a great national institution, and its close alliance with the State was applauded and promoted. "The notion of the Church as a spiritual body possessing a faith and a conscience like other religious bodies, had died out." It was only natural, therefore, that men should neither expect nor discover any spiritual leadership among the bishops. The Bishop of London, for example, in April, 1829, made a public apology in the House of Lords for having dared to oppose the policy of the Prime Minister who had been responsible for his appointment. The Church, in fact, had but little voice of its own, and there were then held no provincial Convocations or diocesan Synods. Reverent concern for the liturgy, too, was so lacking that its use was often slovenly and its surroundings dishevelled.

The need for a revival that would bring with it idealism and enthusiasm in some new form was plain. That it was widely felt to be urgent at just this time was due to political action and agitation certain to affect a State Church. In 1828 Parliament had repealed the seventeenth-century Test and Corporation Acts, thereby admitting Dissenters to civil and military office. In the following year Roman Catholics were at last made eligible to the House of Commons and to most public offices; and in 1832 the passage of the famous Reform Bill so changed the character of the electorate as to give increased power to the industrial classes and hence to the Dissenters.

Only a diehard Tory would deny that all these changes were long over-due and have ever since proved beneficial. At the time, however, they appeared to spell serious danger to the Church. This fear was naturally increased by public signs that the Church was distrusted and in some quarters despised. Because of their opposition to the Reform Bill several bishops were burnt in effigy; the Bishop of Bristol's residence was set on fire by a disorderly crowd; and the Archbishop of Canterbury was mobbed in his own cathedral town. Meantime the Prime Minister, Lord Grey, was warning the bishops to "set their house in order"; and a Christian as devout as Dr. Thomas Arnold could write in this year of 1832, "The Church, as it now stands, no human power can save," and could advocate as a remedy that *Parliament* should unite all the Protestant denominations with the Church of England. It was high time that men should arise to remind the people of England that their branch of the Catholic Church was more than a department of State.

The first note to be heard was struck at Oxford by a Professor of Poetry, the Rev. John Keble. "On 14th July 1833," wrote John Henry Newman in his *Apologia,* "Mr. Keble preached the Assize Sermon in the University pulpit. It was published under the title 'National Apostasy.' I have ever considered and kept the day as the start of the religious movement of 1833." The sermon expressed the fear of Churchmen that political reform was threatening the rights and even the constitution and creed of the Church. It assailed the utilitarian philosophy of the day to which so many were yielding, and it denounced the prevailing Erastianism which had led the Church to such subservience to the State that its nobler traditions had been forgotten. Later in that month the Rev. Hugh J. Rose (who had been a friend of Bishop Hobart) met with several other clergymen, including William Palmer and Hurrell Froude, to lay plans for a campaign in defense of the Church. Among the first impressive results of their activity were two petitions addressed to the Archbishop of Canterbury, one signed by 7,000 clergy and delivered in February, 1834, the other presented three months later and signed by 230,000 heads of families. Together they marked an outpouring of devotion and loyalty to the Church, especially to her apostolic doctrine and polity.

More widely influential was the phase of the movement in which Newman at once became leader. Believing that simple and bold teaching was what the Church most needed, he began in September, 1833, a series of "Tracts for the Times" addressed to the clergy. In the words of the historian R. W. Church, "the early Tracts intended to startle the world, and they succeeded in doing so." Indeed, they gave to the movement its familiar name of "Tractarianism." Newman wrote most of them, though Keble and others made their contributions. When in 1834 the first forty-six numbers were published, the introduction to the volume declared that "the following Tracts were published with the object of contributing something toward the practical revival of doctrines which, although held by the great divines of our Church, at present have become obsolete with the majority of her members"; and readers were reminded that "the Apostolic succession, the Holy Catholic Church, were principles of action in the minds of our predecessors of the seventeenth century."

The apostolic succession, in fact, was the constant topic of these papers. "Exalt our holy Fathers the bishops," the clergy were exhorted, "as the representatives of the Apostles . . . and magnify your office as being ordained by them to take part in their ministry." Though this theme was central, the subjects were many—Baptismal Regeneration, the Holy Eucharist, Purgatory, Fasting, and many others. The emphasis upon the sacramental life of the Church was steady, and the effort was made in every number to stress doctrines and practices, often long neglected, which the Church of England could be shown to hold in common with the rest of Catholic Christendom. To confirm and enrich the teaching there were frequent quotations from the Fathers and from seventeenth century theologians. Reinforcing these widely read Tracts were the contemporary sermons, preached by Newman at St. Mary's, Oxford.

New prestige and stimulus were given to what had now become a real "movement" by the accession to its ranks in 1834 of Dr. E. B. Pusey, who has been described as "the most venerated man in Oxford"—Regius Professor of Hebrew and Canon of Christ Church. As Newman later expressed it, "Dr. Pusey gave us at once a position and a name." Indeed, in more senses than one he gave them a name, for "Puseyism" and "Puseyite" soon became familiar terms both in England and in the United States, especially among the enemies of Tractarianism. And these enemies were soon numerous and vocal. The liberal Dr. Arnold referred to the leaders as "the Oxford malignants"; all the Evangelicals were indignant at the supposed Romanism of the doctrines taught; and so little Catholic were the so-called High Churchmen that many of them were alienated by the disturbing boldness of the Tracts. Yet with no encouragement from the more or less hostile University authorities, the movement began to grow in power among the students, especially among the younger men.

A turning point in the history of Tractarianism came in 1841 with the publication of Tract Ninety, written by Newman. In this document the subtle author sought to refute the widely accepted idea that the Thirty-nine Articles were incurably anti-Roman. He proved to his own satisfaction that the Catholic doctrines which he and his colleagues were preaching were quite reconcilable with the Articles and that the famous Thirty-nine ran counter only to certain of the perversions and abuses of Roman dogma. In view of the fact that subscription to the Articles was required of members of the Universities and that they had always been regarded as an invincible bulwark against Popery, the outcry aroused by Tract Ninety was loud and long. It was all the more bitter because the "Puseyites" were already beginning to show a sympathy with Rome hitherto unknown in Anglicanism. War was therefore declared against the Oxford Movement by most of the leading authorities in both Universities and by a large majority of the bishops. Branding its members as traitors began to seem justified when in 1845 W. G. Ward, F. W. Faber, John Henry Newman, and others became members of the Roman Catholic Church.

In a history of the American Episcopal Church nothing is to be gained by reciting the persecutions endured by the English Tractarians of a century ago or to note the ups and downs of the movement in early Victorian times. It is more important to sum up very briefly some of the rich advantages eventually won by the Church of England as a result of this revival of religion. Though in its first stages it was not at all concerned with ritual, it brought about a greater reverence, order, and beauty in worship and increased the number of services, especially the celebrations of the Eucharist. Its moral effect was a renewed emphasis upon the devotional life and the meaning of personal holiness and Christian asceticism. In church architecture and music it wrought notable improvements. It stimulated missionary activity at home and abroad. In theology it centered attention upon doctrines held by all three of the main branches of the Catholic Church—the Eastern Orthodox, the Roman Catholic, and the Anglican. Hence it promoted respect for tradition and revived the study of the Church Fathers and the Caroline divines. Above all, it awoke those who had ears to hear to the meaning of the Church as a divine institution. In a word, it initiated with enthusiasm the modern phase of Anglo-Catholicism.

THE MOVEMENT IN THE UNITED STATES [1]

The situation in the American Episcopal Church in 1833 differed from that in England in two respects important from the point of view of the Oxford Movement. In the first place, there was here no question of the dangers of a State Church. The Church was completely independent. In the second place, there was already in the United States an active and influential High Church party which had looked to Hobart as its leader and which was represented by such bishops as Doane, Whittingham, Hopkins, Otey, and Kemper, and by such journals as *The Churchman.* Not only were the perils of "Erastianism" impossible in this country, but Catholic Churchmanship was more definite and vigorous than in England. In other words, the Episcopal Church *needed* the Oxford Movement less than did the Church of England, and for that reason, as well as for others, it produced here less extreme effects.

Since bishops, editors, and other leaders had long been teaching American Churchmen about the meaning of apostolic succession, the nature of the Eucharist, the sin of schism, and the authority of the Fathers, the earlier Tracts, though objectionable to Evangelicals, were not of a kind to cause an explosion. In fact it took the Church in this country a long time to warm up to the controversy. After the Tracts had been appearing for five or six years *The Churchman* and *The Banner of the Cross,* speaking for the Hobartian group, passed upon them a verdict of cautious approval. But by 1839 the opposition between High and Low Church, which had been waning, had been roused to life by the effect of the Oxford Movement. In that year Bishop Moore of Virginia warned his convention that there was a crisis in the Church which "threatened a revival of the worst evils of the Romish system." And in 1841 the ablest of the Evangelical leaders, Bishop McIlvaine of Ohio, published his book *Oxford Divinity.* Maintaining that the Tractarians had completely rejected such precious Gospel truths as justification by faith, he called upon them to go to Rome where they belonged. At the same time *The Church-*

[1] The best accounts of the movement in the U.S. are an admirably written chapter in George E. DeMille's *The Catholic Movement in the American Episcopal Church* and the relevant sections in Chorley's *Men and Movements in the American Episcopal Church.* I am indebted to both sources. They are equally useful for a study of the later Ritualistic Controversy.

man was declaring the republication of the Tracts in the United States to be a blessing to the Church.

With the publication of Tract Ninety the controversy became wider in scope, and its tone grew bitter. Even this advanced step of the Oxford leaders was approved by many. Bishop Brownell of Connecticut and Bishop DeLancey of Western New York welcomed the Tracts and assured their people that this imported material would produce no harmful results. Bishop Onderdonk of New York and Dr. Samuel Seabury (grandson of the bishop and editor of *The Churchman*) strongly advised clergy and laity to read the Tracts. Bishop Doane, too, spoke up warmly in their defence; but the pugnacious Bishop Hopkins of Vermont, who had thought highly of them for a time, turned against the movement after Tract Ninety appeared.

Between those who applauded and those who attacked the principles of the movement was a large group of moderate Churchmen who deprecated strife and ill-feeling and who did not permit themselves to become combative. For that very reason most of their names have left no trace on the records of the period; but two of them were perhaps the greatest Church leaders of their day—Bishop Jackson Kemper, a moderate High Churchman, and Bishop Alonzo Potter, a moderate Evangelical. As a former student under Hobart, Kemper sympathized with many features of Tractarianism, but like all the older group of High Churchmen he was intensely anti-Roman. To his Wisconsin clergy he said, "I am exceedingly solicitous that as a diocese you take a rightminded and conservative stand amid the agitations that now disturb our Zion. . . . I beseech you let no party spirit exist among us." But he denounced "the blasphemies of Rome," whose friendship is "death to our hopes, and our most formidable evil." [2] Though temperate and tolerant in spirit, Alonzo Potter spoke a decade later to his convention in these words: "We may well mourn that instead of accepting the Reformation as a blessing and planting themselves on the liberty and the simplicity of doctrine which that event gave back to the Church, men of thoughtful minds and devout lives can be found who pine after the spiritual bondage and the superstitious worship which our fathers were unable to bear. . . . Should we ever come to hanker after the private confessional and the sacrament of penance, after more power and less responsibility for the clergy, and more responsibility and less liberty for the people,—in such case we should know that we are in imminent danger." [3]

It was of course in the most intensely Evangelical circles that indignation was at its height. In Virginia the Committee on the State of the

[2] G. White, *An Apostle of the Western Church,* 123 f.
[3] M. A. DeW. Howe, *Alonzo Potter,* 254 f.

Church reported that "God has seen fit to permit the spirit of error and Popery, under the guise of suitable 'Tracts for the Times' to array itself against the Church, yet He has been graciously pleased to save the Church of Virginia from the infection of this plague." Bishop Eastburn of Massachusetts described the Tractarian movement as the work of Satan and its adherents as "advocates of the Dark Ages and followers of the Scarlet Woman." Referring to the Tracts *The Gambier Observer* in Ohio uttered this warning: "Let them not be republished, any more than you would offer poisoned meat in the shambles. . . . The meat is putrid to the bone!"

Though language was not always so colorful, agitation on both sides was active in the public addresses of bishops, in the debates of diocesan conventions, in all the Church journals, in lively pamphlets, and even in the newspapers. More dignified and of more permanent value were several serious theological works produced in this and the following decade. These included John S. Stone's *The Mysteries Opened* (1844) and *The Church Universal* (1846) on the Evangelical side, and on the Catholic side, William I. Kip's *The Double Witness of the Church* (1843) and Hugh D. Evans's *The Episcopate* (1855).

In these early 'forties the men most affected by the Tracts were certain of the younger clergy and the students of the General Theological Seminary. The enthusiasm for monastic asceticism which led Breck, Adams, and the junior Hobart to temporary celibacy in the wilds of Wisconsin was but one sign of the response of many in the rising generation. It had already begun to be noticeable that they differed from the numerous representatives of the older High Churchmanship on at least one important point. The latter, like their seventeenth-century models, did not wince at the appellation "Protestant"; they heartily commended the Reformation; and they believed that the Episcopal Church in the United States was so nearly perfect that it could hardly be improved upon. But the younger converts of Newman and Pusey were inclined to be apologetic about the deplorable condition of a Church which had so nearly forgotten its Catholic heritage. For them the Reformation was a *de*-formation; and the ancient Church of Rome, instead of being a target for their abuse, began to exert upon them an uneasy fascination.

Signs that all was not well in the General Seminary, which the diocese of South Carolina had done so much to establish, produced resolutions from the convention of that diocese in February, 1844, calling upon its trustees to investigate the Romish teachings and practices rumored to be found there. But a committee of the trustees reported in September that the tone and sentiment of the students "appeared to be in perfect accordance with the doctrines, discipline, and worship of the

Church, and such as were calculated to sustain its elevated character and command the public confidence and respect." Yet even after this vindication some of the Low Church trustees, including Bishops McIlvaine and Eastburn, filed a dissenting statement. They felt all the more certain that the majority report had whitewashed a sepulchre because in the preceding year a recent alumnus of the seminary, Arthur Carey, after declaring to his canonical examiners that the Thirty-nine Articles could be reconciled with the decrees of the Council of Trent, had later been ordained by Bishop Onderdonk of New York. The incident caused widespread excitement in the Church, and there was cordial support for the insistence of the Evangelicals that General Convention should demand an official investigation of the General Seminary.

At the General Convention which met in October, 1844 the House of Bishops, as constituting the "Visitors" of the Seminary, appointed a committee which submitted a list of forty questions to each member of the faculty, a high-handed procedure much resented at the time and never since repeated. Among the queries which professors had to answer in this inquisition were these: What have you taught concerning the Church of Rome, as being in error in matters of faith? In what manner is the doctrine of the Eucharist taught in the Seminary? Are the students publicly or privately taught to regard the English Reformation of the sixteenth century as a useless or unjustifiable proceeding? Are the Oxford Tracts adopted as text-books in the Seminary? Are the superstitious practices of the Roman Church, such as the use or worship of the crucifix, of images and saints, and the invocation of the Blessed Virgin and other saints adopted or publicly or privately recommended?

After a thorough study of the replies and an investigation on the premises by the committee, the House of Bishops passed these reassuring resolutions: "*Resolved,* that the Bishops as Visitors, having visited the Seminary and inspected the same, do not find, in any of its interior arrangements, any evidence that superstitious or Romish practices are allowed or encouraged in the institution. *Resolved,* that the Bishops deem the publication of the questions of the Bishops and the answers of the professors the most appropriate reply to the current rumors respecting the doctrinal teaching of the Seminary."

Quite aside from the condition of the Seminary, the General Convention of 1844 was deeply stirred by American reaction to the Oxford Movement. It was the chief topic of debate at that session. Those who fully supported what the Tractarians stood for were so obviously a minority that there was no chance of any public pronouncement in favor of "Puseyism." But the more indignant Evangelicals were hoping that the Convention would denounce the movement. A Virginia deputy offered a motion which referred to the Tracts as "Popish poison." A more restrained resolution was expressed in these terms: "Whereas, the minds of many of the members of this Church . . . are sorely grieved and perplexed by the alleged introduction among them of serious errors in doctrine and practice, having their origin in certain writings emanating chiefly from members of the University of Oxford in England; and whereas, it is exceedingly desirable that the minds of such persons should be calmed, their anxieties allayed, and the Church disabused of the charge of holding in her Articles and Offices doctrines and practices consistent with all the views and opinions expressed in said Oxford writings, and should thus be freed from a responsibility which does not properly belong to her: therefore *Resolved,* that the House of Bishops be respectfully requested to communicate with this House on this subject, and to take such order thereon as the nature and magnitude of the evil alluded to may seem to them to require." Though the language of this resolution was mild, it was voted down, perhaps partly for the sound reason that it would be unwise to set up the House of Bishops as a court of inquisition with the mission of hunting heretics.

Refusing to be led by extremists of any type and displaying just when it was needed a saving common sense, the House of Deputies passed by a heavy majority the following resolution: "*Resolved,* that the House of Clerical and Lay Deputies consider the Liturgy, Offices, and Articles of the Church sufficient exponents of her sense of the essential doctrines of Holy Scripture; and that the canons of the Church afford ample means of discipline and correction for all who depart from her standards, and further, that the General Convention is not a suitable tribunal for the trial and censure of, and that the Church is not responsible for, the errors of individuals, whether they are members of this Church or otherwise."[4] Though this resolution was deliberately noncommittal as to the controversial issues, the Pastoral Letter of the bishops was more definite. Having declared the Roman doctrine of the Mass to be a deadly error, it went on to say: "We feel it our duty to declare that no person should be ordained who is not well acquainted with the landmarks which separate us from the Church of Rome; and being so, who will not distinctly declare himself a Protestant, heartily abjuring her corruptions, as our Reformers did."

It was well for the Church that in 1844 the General Convention took the wise position that it was not its duty to make triennial pronounce-

[4] That it was not always easy to keep General Convention from fretting about matters of doctrine is shown by the introduction of a resolution (fortunately not passed) in the Convention of 1847: "*Resolved,* that it is to be referred to the . . . Committee to inquire into the expediency of providing by Canon, 'that no persons shall be allowed to testify at ecclesiastical trials in this Church who do not first declare their belief in a future state of rewards and punishments.' " Just why this particular dogma should have been selected as a shibboleth is not clear.

ments on great questions of doctrine and polity. If the question had come up for decision a few years later, the balance might possibly have tipped the wrong way. For by the year 1845 a few American clergy had begun to follow the English extremists into the Church of Rome. The faculty of the General Seminary had to acknowledge that disciplinary measures had become necessary to keep students from such practices as the use of the Breviary, devotion to the Virgin Mary, and private confession. Prizing these privileges as highly as they did, seven students and newly ordained priests submitted to Rome and six students at Nashotah took the same step. Those who seceded, however, were very small in number compared with the exodus in England. As a matter of fact it has been carefully estimated that throughout the thirty years before 1855 not more than thirty clergy entered the Roman Catholic Church. Two of these were necessarily conspicuous. The Rev. John Murray Forbes made what might be described as a round trip. After fourteen years as rector of St. Luke's Church, New York, he entered the Church of Rome in 1849. There he eventually received high honors including an honorary doctorate. In 1859 he returned to the Episcopal Church, having discovered somewhat tardily that Rome required that "all individual liberty must be sacrificed." After another decade he was elected Dean of the General Theological Seminary! A still more famous case was that of Levi S. Ives, Bishop of North Carolina, who notified his diocese in December, 1852, that he resigned his office, and announced his "submission to the Catholic Church." In the following year at the session of the General Convention he was formally deposed by the Presiding Bishop.

As with any strong injection of ideas (whether brand new or long neglected) the immediate reactions to the Oxford Movement were violent and undiscriminating. The old antagonism between High and Low Church was aroused and intensified. Most of the clergy and a vast majority of the laity soon came to associate Tractarianism with Romanism and to be more suspicious than ever of those who bore an Anglo-Catholic label. As George E. DeMille has pointed out in his discerning study of the question, out of fourteen bishops elected between 1830 and 1840 eleven were High Churchmen of one sort or another, while in the following decade only five out of fifteen elected could be so termed. The fear felt by Evangelicals took another active form in the organization in 1847 of the Society for the Promotion of Evangelical Knowledge, established to counteract the influence of Tractarianism and "to maintain and set forth the principles and doctrines of the Gospel, embodied in the liturgy and Articles of the Protestant Episcopal Church." Even in the mission field rivalry was heightened. In 1851 there was established an unofficial missionary society, the Episcopal Missionary Association for the West, with the aim to secure the appointment of Evangelicals for work in that region; and eight years later the American Church Missionary Society was formed by Evangelicals, one of whose achievements was the initiation of work in Latin America. Not until 1877 did these extra societies become completely auxiliary to the Board of Missions.

Opposition from Low Churchmen was to be expected. More surprising was the antagonism provoked among many representatives of the older High Church group—"a rift so wide and deep that an advanced High Churchman of the next decade asserted that the great enemy of true Catholicism was not the Low or the Broad Church, but the old High Church party. . . . Thus the Tracts, or rather the outcry against the Tracts, drove Hopkins for a time into the arms of the Evangelicals; they made Whittingham . . . a persecutor of ritualists; they led Kemper to attack party spirit and 'the blasphemies of Rome' . . . From 1840 on, then, we find in the American Church not one, but two High Church movements; the one native, conservative, centering largely in the East, with the General Seminary as its nursery; the other imported, advanced, finding its strongest support in Nashotah and the mid-Western dioceses. The difference persists to this day."[5] The divergence thus described, beginning a century ago, was undoubtedly caused by the fact that the conservative High Churchmen represented by Hobart and his disciples (like Laud and his followers two centuries earlier) were just as strong as any Tractarian in upholding the apostolic succession and the sacramental conception of the Church; but they were never interested in elaborate ceremonial, and their abhorrence of "Popish" errors and perversions was just as intense as that of any Presbyterian. Hence arose their suspicion and even persecution of a group of which many members aimed to be as nearly Roman as their status in the Episcopal Church would permit. The result of the overemphasis on ritual was soon to be displayed in the heated controversies of the 'seventies.

When we view the Oxford Movement in the United States after the lapse of a century, undisturbed by the warm reactions to which it immediately led, we must acknowledge that since it supplied only one stream in the current of American Anglo-Catholicism, we cannot safely attribute to it all that we find in the Anglo-Catholicism of the twentieth century. Nevertheless it was undoubtedly the strongest single factor in developing and strengthening these elements in the American Church. Like other religious revivals, of course (including the Quaker and Wesleyan movements), it indulged in extremes and in trivialities. But like other religious revivals, it imparted increased vitality to many groups and to many phases of Church life, emphasizing principles and practices in normative Angli-

[5] G. A. DeMille, *Catholic Movement in the American Episcopal Church,* 42.

canism that needed to be restated and restored. And from its influence have flowed the same varied benefits which we have noted in the English movement, benefits which consciously or unconsciously have been gradually shared and absorbed by nearly every group in a comprehensive Church.

Chapter XI

TYPES OF LEADERSHIP: WILLIAM AUGUSTUS MUHLENBERG AND ALONZO POTTER

WILLIAM AUGUSTUS MUHLENBERG

MUHLENBERG was born in Philadelphia in 1796. His grandfather had been the first Speaker of the House of Representatives in Washington's administration, and his great-grandfather had been a famous missionary leader of the Lutherans in Pennsylvania and New York. Though brought up in the Church of his ancestors, he was soon drawn into the Episcopal Church, and under the influence of Jackson Kemper was confirmed by Bishop White when he was seventeen. Two years later, upon his graduation from the University of Pennsylvania, he began the study of theology with White and Kemper, and in 1817 he was ordained deacon. The next three years he spent as assistant in the united parishes of Christ Church, St. Peter's, and St. James's in Philadelphia. His active concern with the Sunday school at St. James's and his success in completely reforming the church music there revealed in these earliest years of his ministry his two most marked characteristics—his intense interest in education and his powers of imagination and initiative. Until the last years of his long life he was always starting something new. Since the general tendency of the Episcopal Church in his day and long thereafter was never to start anything new, we need not be surprised that Muhlenberg was soon to be a notable and often a lonely figure.

After his ordination to the priesthood in 1820 he served for six years as rector of St. James's Church in Lancaster, Pennsylvania, then a little parish in a state of ill repair. Here again, both in the church and in the community he became a leader in education. He revealed, too, at this time another talent which he never long neglected to use—a deep appreciation of poetry and a facility in writing verse. Judging from the published specimens of what is accounted his best verse, the less said about it the better. The Church is grateful to him, however, (among many other things) for the hymn seldom forgotten at Christmas—

> "Shout the glad tidings, exultingly sing,
> Jerusalem triumphs, Messiah is King!"

And the Hymnal of 1826 contained four others he had written.

So strongly did Muhlenberg now feel drawn to the Christianizing of education as his central vocation that in 1826 he resigned his parish, though as yet he had no definite plans. Having agreed to serve the parish of St. George's at Flushing, Long Island, for a few months, he met there several prominent men who were already actively interested in founding an academy for boys. It was a providential coincidence. They were wise enough to accept his offer to cooperate by becoming headmaster; the cornerstone of "Flushing Institute" was laid within a year; and the school opened in the spring of 1828. Here for the next eighteen years he became the pioneer and the inspiration of Church schools in America. More than a century later we have grown accustomed to Church boarding schools and to the ideals which the best of them represent—the ideals of a wholesome Christian atmosphere, of a community in which the sense of family life prevails, and a spirit of comradeship between masters and boys. But that kind of school was an unknown novelty in 1828, and Muhlenberg made it real not only at Flushing, but by contagion and example at many another center. The most famous of the later schools which can trace its ancestry to Flushing is St. Paul's School, Concord, New Hampshire, incorporated in 1855. Its rector from then until 1895 was the Rev. Henry Augustus Coit, a former pupil of Muhlenberg and one of his devoted admirers.

During its first eight years the Institute had been so clearly successful that Muhlenberg felt able to carry out the second part of his plan—the founding of a Church college. He bought a large trace of land along the East River north of Flushing, and there at College Point wooden buildings were erected, and St. Paul's College was opened in 1838. Flushing Institute was transferred to the new site, and within two years the college had over one hundred students. Of the life there we have an authentic picture drawn by Henry C. Potter, the future Bishop of New York, who was closely in touch with Muhlenberg in later days and knew much of his methods.

"The whole system of teaching," he wrote, "was brought into healthfull subordination to sound principles of Christian nurture. The college chapel, that bugbear of most youths in our ordinary American institutions, was made at once the center of the whole school life and a place of genuine attractiveness. The Church Year, which has so much in its beautiful order to appeal to the young mind, was made practically the school year; and today, among hundreds of men in all ranks of life . . . who have gone forth from College Point, there is scarce one who does not date his first appreciation of the Church's feasts and fasts from the solemn and glowing services in its chapel. . . . The secret of this success was not any system, however excellent, nor any skill, however thorough. It was in the rare and happy qualities of the presiding mind. That mind possessed the magnetism of [Thomas] Arnold without his impatience; the religious earnestness of Arnold without his tendency to speculation. And the boys caught and reflected the master's spirit. . . . The principles of College Point have taken shape in many other schools since then, and its pupils have, in more than one instance, risen to be among the most successful educators of our day; but there is not one of them that would not gladly and gratefully own his indebtedness to the venerable friend and father whose loving wisdom and patient labors inaugurated a new era in the Christian nurture of our youth, and lifted the Church in that matter to a higher level both of effort and of aspiration." [1]

After Muhlenberg had strenuously served his school and college for fifteen years (before teachers ever thought of sabbaticals) he sailed in the spring of 1843 with two young alumni for five months of vacation abroad. Letters of introduction helped him to enjoy hospitality in England, especially at Oxford, where he came to know Newman and Pusey. It was the latter who said, "Dr. Muhlenberg was the most interesting visitor we ever had from the other side"; and of Newman his American visitor wrote, "He is not transparent, yet seems to be artless. If he were an accomplished Jesuit (which God forbid I should say he is) his manner would be, I fancy, just what it is." [2] Those were the days when agitation aroused by the Oxford Movement was at its height, and ever since its first echoes in America Muhlenberg had been strongly influenced, yet it was more by its atmosphere than by its dogmas. He was a poetic, imaginative individualist who loved color and beauty and drama in religion. Many of the forms and ceremonies which enriched the worship of his school were of his own creation. In fact it was temperament rather than tradition which moved him. And so he could honestly write in later years, "I was never a High Churchman," and after his months in England he felt that he had been "neither confirmed nor disenchanted by Tractarianism."

Three years after his return from his holiday Muhlenberg dared at the age of fifty to make what seemed a complete change in his profession.

[1] A. Ayres, *Life and Work of Muhlenberg,* 144 f. The only other life of Muhlenberg is that by W. W. Newton.

[2] *Ibid.,* 166.

He became the rector of a new parish in New York. Yet he would not have regarded the change as radical, for his ardent Christian purpose was central in both his earlier and his later calling. The parish was in the fullest sense his own, or he would never have taken it. It was to be an original organization where no elderly members could say, "We have never done it that way here before." His sister, Mrs. Mary A. Rogers, had recently become a widow of considerable wealth, and in conformity with the wishes of her husband she planned to build a church that should be free to all its members, unhampered by owners and renters of pews. She had asked her brother to be the rector, and he had agreed, for he "had long been dreaming of what an ideal city parish would be like." Here he saw a God-given opportunity to break loose from the rather stiff bonds of the traditions of the day, to give his imagination free play, and to let the warmth of his sympathy for all sorts and conditions find full expression. The new Gothic church designed by Upjohn was consecrated in 1846. It stood, and still stands, on the corner of Twentieth Street and Sixth Avenue. And in the same year, with a former pupil as his assistant, Muhlenberg began his happy years as rector of "the Church of the Holy Communion."

Though the church was in surroundings half rural and thinly settled, it soon attracted a growing congregation in which all social types were mingled. What drew so many into its fellowship was perhaps most of all the rector himself, a leader of unusual charm, keenly intelligent, and selflessly devoted in his pastoral ministrations. The church, moreover, could offer many new features common enough today but then not to be found elsewhere in the city. These were practices and customs introduced by Muhlenberg, such as daily Morning and Evening Prayer, the separation of the services of Morning Prayer, the Litany, and the Holy Communion, a weekly celebration of the Eucharist, systematic weekly offerings for the support of the church and the care of the poor, a boy choir, the parish children's Christmas tree, and the special emphasis laid upon Holy Week.

Among other innovations were new activities which foreshadowed the work of those "institutional churches" which were to thrive toward the end of the century—a "fresh air" fund to send sick and weary men, women, and children to the country in summer; an employment agency to help poor women find work in a city where "sweating" sometimes obliged them to sew fourteen hours a day for thirty-five cents; a parish infirmary and dispensary; and day schools for boys and girls. The sense of family unity which bound together the parishioners was symbolized by the rector's custom of taking members of the congregation with him, after the Sunday service, to visit the sick who were in need. In short, Muhlenberg, having shown the Church how to run a school and having found imitators far and wide, now proceeded to show the Church how to run a parish; and within a generation most of his practices and methods had been tested and accepted.

The next product of his active and fertile mind was a monthly Church journal, *The Evangelical Catholic,* launched in 1851. The term was not intended to stand for any mere compromise. As his assistant editor, Dr. Harwood, put it, "Catholic he claimed to be because he held to the historic Church with its creed and sacraments and ministry and type of worship; Evangelical, because the Scriptures were the sole ultimate rule of faith and practice. He advocated great freedom of thought within the faith of Christ." [3] At the center of his purpose in maintaining the paper was his eager and growing desire to promote union with the Protestant bodies of Christendom. Though that desire never weakened, *The Evangelical Catholic* lasted only two years. Yet it cannot be said to have failed, for it culminated in the "Memorial" presented to the General Convention of 1853, of which a full account will be found in the following chapter.

Plans for his next institution had begun to take shape in Muhlenberg's mind almost as soon as he began work in New York. From his pastoral experience he became painfully aware how wretched were the hospital accommodations in a city of nearly half a million inhabitants. There were only two hospitals, one chiefly used for seamen and for casualty cases, the other given over to paupers. New York needed a hospital, and Muhlenberg determined that it should be a Church hospital. Beginning with offerings taken up in his own church he proceeded to enlist the help of leading businessmen and to make a wide appeal to the entire community. In 1850 St. Luke's Hospital was incorporated, and in the following year a site was chosen on Fifth Avenue at Fifty-fourth Street, then "a dreary weed-covered area"; but not until May, 1858, was the first ward publicly opened.

Six years earlier Muhlenberg had completed the organization of "the Sisterhood of the Holy Communion." Though long eyed with suspicion as a symptom of "Puseyism," this small community of women, demanding no lifelong vows, really resembled an order of deaconesses rather than one of nuns. The sisters became the head nurses in the hospital and helped to maintain its Christian character. But it was the constant presence of the founder himself, as the father of the household, which chiefly insured its unique atmosphere. Being unmarried he was able to take up his quarters in two of the hospital rooms, and after resigning the parish in 1860, he gave himself wholly to the congenial work of a hospital chaplain, conducting the daily services for sisters, servants, and patients and lavishing his pastoral care upon the sick. The Civil War brought responsibilities

[3] *Ibid.*, 248.

even heavier than usual, for the government took over part of the hospital for wounded soldiers; and in the dreadful days of mid-July, 1863, when the draft riots rocked New York, the building came near being burnt by the mob.

When Muhlenberg reached the age of seventy he was still dreaming of new ventures. The last of these was the community of "St. Johnland." Though his school and college did not long survive the loss of their chief, his parish is still strong and his hospital stronger than ever. But his final experiment, though elements of it have survived, seems to have been prompted more by Muhlenberg the dreamer than by Muhlenberg the practical manager. The little settlement which he christened "St. Johnland" was situated on a tract of 425 acres on the north shore of Long Island about forty-five miles from New York City. Partly with the remains of his own inherited capital and partly with large gifts from friends, who were willing to support anything that their beloved Dr. Muhlenberg projected, he gradually completed a series of buildings. These were to serve as homes for such "deserving families from among the working classes" of New York as could carry on their labors on the premises. In addition to the dwelling-houses there were a home for old men, a home for crippled and destitute children, a school house, a library, a village hall, shops for baking, tailoring, and cobbling, etc., and, as the center of the community life, the "Church of the Testimony of Jesus."

St. Johnland was the child of Muhlenberg's old age and the joy of his heart. He visited it often in his declining years and was grateful to witness its growth and to receive generous donations for its support. But here for once he was not in advance of his time. He had committed himself to a scheme which future social policy was not to justify. In the course of some years the homes for workers proved to attract none. But before any real failure was visible Muhlenberg had become a semi-invalid and could take no part in the management of the enterprise. He could still bring comfort to sufferers in the hospital, and there he lived surrounded by devoted friends. In 1876, after a long illness, he died at the age of eighty and was buried at St. Johnland.[4]

Muhlenberg combined to a remarkable degree what are often accounted opposites. Physically and mentally he gave the impression of strength, yet of "indescribable benignity and tenderness." A reformer and innovator throughout his whole career, he had nevertheless a lovely disposition and he never assumed that his opponents were in league with Satan. Though a dreamer and an artist, he was seldom an impractical dreamer, and he was capable of patient drudgery. His character and his

[4] There is still a "Society of St. Johnland," which operates cottages for the aged and cottages for children at Kings Park, Long Island.

labors, said the Bishop of Long Island soon after his death, had "made him beyond, perhaps any man of his day . . . the common property of the Church throughout the land. . . . Scarcely any important movement can be named peculiar to the last forty or fifty years of our Church life, and which will be likely to tell upon the next half century of that life, that he did not originate or help others to originate. . . . His highest power was not in speech or in the pen—happy as he was in the use of both—but in personal contact, in the peculiar spiritual atmosphere that enveloped him." [5]

ALONZO POTTER

One of his associates, when they were both college professors, said of Alonzo Potter, "He was the most *efficient* man I ever knew." That efficiency, at the service of strong and genuine piety, made his episcopate a chapter of rare distinction in the history of the American Church.

Potter was born on July 6, 1800, in a small town in Dutchess County, New York, the sixth child of Joseph Potter, a farmer. Both his parents were Quakers. After preparation in a district school and at an academy in Poughkeepsie, he entered Union College, Schenectady, at the age of fifteen. Though according to a classmate he was marked at that time by "a very rustic look," he stood at the head of his class from the beginning, and before he was nineteen he had graduated with highest honors. Among his college mates had been Francis Wayland, who was to become president of Brown University, John S. Stone, the future dean of the Episcopal Theological School at Cambridge, and William H. Seward, Lincoln's Secretary of State.

On leaving college Potter went to Philadelphia to live with a brother who was a bookseller, but no such trade was to be his. Within a year he had decided to join the Episcopal Church, he had been confirmed at Christ Church by Bishop White (adding one more name to that distinguished list), and he had begun the study of theology. But before he had made much progress in this training he was called to be a tutor in Union College, and in 1821, when he had barely attained his majority, he was appointed Professor of Mathematics and Natural Philosophy. Though he found time to produce a small book on logarithms, he continued his preparation for the ministry and was ordained deacon by Bishop Hobart in 1823 and priest in the following year. It was through his influence, too, that his younger brother Horatio was led to take holy orders. After Alonzo had become Bishop of Pennsylvania Horatio became Bishop of New York, and Horatio's successor was Alonzo's son, Henry Codman Potter—a dynasty like the Tuckers and the Kinsolvings of later times.

[5] *Ibid.,* 515 ff.

At twenty-four Potter married the daughter of Eliphalet Nott, the president of Union College, adding one more to the ties which bound him to his alma mater. These were sufficiently strong to resist a call in the next year to be president of Geneva College; but when St. Paul's Church, Boston, elected him as rector in 1826 he accepted. Though the morale of this church and its finances were then at a low ebb and young Potter was only twenty-six, he proved equal to the challenge of his first parish and won a reputation not only as pastor but as preacher. As one of his laymen later testified, "His ministry gave an impetus to vital religion which is still felt."

Within a few years Potter had attained sufficient prominence in the diocese to represent it at the General Convention of 1829. There he preached a sermon before the Board of Directors of the new Domestic and Foreign Missionary Society, a warm and moving plea for foreign missions. "What for centuries," he asked his hearers, "have you been doing in pagan lands but contracting a long and fearful list of *arrears*? The influence which Christendom has sent over those lands, what is it? Her merchant ships, her vessels of war, her soldiers and her traders, what have they done for pagan morals and pagan happiness? Ah, let history answer." And to the old "charity begins at home" plea he responded, "What then? Because our brethren after the flesh have claims, does it follow that the pagan has none? Because one creditor is pressing, must the rights of another be forgotten? . . . Your charity having thus *begun at home,* let it continue and increase and advance. Its efforts are to be bounded only by your ability—by the spiritual exigencies of mankind. *The field is the world.*" [6] That was a rare type of preaching in 1829.

Potter was glad to be numbered among the Evangelicals of the more sober and balanced variety, but he had not a trace of partisanship in his make-up, and he hated party strife. By the time he had been in Boston for five years that spirit of contention was beginning to show itself in the diocese, largely owing to the initiative of the Rev. George Washington Doane who, as Dr. Manross has well observed, "seldom allowed his talents for political agitation to remain unused." Partly for this reason but chiefly because of ill-health, Potter resigned the rectorship of St. Paul's in 1831, and returned to Union College as Professor of Moral and Intellectual Philosophy and Political Economy. Here he was to remain for fourteen years, declining opportunities to join the faculty of the General Seminary and to be Assistant Bishop of Massachusetts, and advancing with every year as a power in the world of education. Especially after becoming vice-president of Union College in 1838, he became more and more active in helping to mould the educational policy of the State of New York. In

[6] M. A. DeW. Howe, *Life of Alonzo Potter,* 39, 43.

1843, the year when he received from Harvard the degree of Doctor of Divinity, he wrote with George B. Emerson of Boston a book called *The School and the Schoolmaster* in which, among other proposals, he strongly advocated normal schools for teachers, the first example of which was opened in the State in the following year. Another cause for which he felt an active concern was that of "temperance," a movement which led him to become a total abstainer, to make public addresses, and to write many articles.[7]

It seemed at this time that Potter was settled for life at Union College. His first wife, by whom he had six sons and a daughter, had died in 1839, and he had married a second time. His reputation was growing, and he had every prospect of becoming the next president of the college in succession to his father-in-law. Since in the United States professors are seldom elected to bishoprics, it came as a sharp surprise to him when he was chosen Bishop of Pennsylvania in May, 1845, and it required the most urgent persuasion to make him accept. Church parties had been quarreling in that diocese for a long time past—stimulated in recent years by the Oxford Movement—and the Convention had finally voted for Potter because he was not a partisan. The oldest priest in the diocese assured him, "You are the only man I know entirely to unite this hitherto divided diocese"; and another wrote, "You will have no party arrayed against your administration, no cliques to annoy and vex you. We will receive you to our hearts *as one man.*" And written in similar terms letters reached him from all over the Church. With such a welcome assured him and with the opportunity before him to remould a great diocese, Potter could not fail to accept; and he was consecrated in Philadelphia on September 23rd by Philander Chase and five other bishops.

The chief reason why Potter had hesitated in making his decision was that he had already promised to give, during the next few years, a long series of lectures at the Lowell Institute in Boston. But his versatility and energy proved equal to adding this burden to his episcopal duties. During the next fourteen years he gave as many as sixty lectures to large audiences in Boston; and though they were delivered with only brief pages of notes, much of the material was later written out and published after his death as *Religious Philosophy; or Nature, Man, and the Bible Witnessing to God and to Religious Truth.* Though satisfactory to many in its day, the work does not constitute its author's chief claim to fame.

As the diocese of Pennsylvania had not then been divided, and no assistant bishop was elected until 1858, Alonzo Potter was responsible for the Church in every part of the State. How his new field and his new

[7] These were the years of early prohibition legislation, beginning with the Maine law of 1846.

duties appeared to him after the first few months we may learn from a letter he wrote to a friend in Boston: "I have been at home now about ten days after an eight weeks' tour in western Pennsylvania and along the northern and eastern frontiers of the State. The weather was delightful, the country is surpassingly fine, and the inhabitants were to me all that I could have possibly asked. Our churches, however, are, many of them, very feeble; the clergy struggling to live on inadequate stipends, and great mountains of prejudice built up by ignorance without and by our own unfaithfulness and divisions within. A Diocesan of Pennsylvania must calculate at best upon great toil and sore discouragements. At present we are at peace, so far as I am concerned, and devoutly do I pray that we remain so. But I cannot be blind to the times in which we are fallen, and to the impossibility of giving satisfaction to everybody." [8]

The "great toil" was to continue to the end, but so was the peace for which he prayed. Indeed, he came as near as mortal man can come to "giving satisfaction to everybody," for to a degree not then equalled elsewhere he made Pennsylvania a tolerant and comprehensive diocese where all types of Churchmen were welcome and could feel at home. Party strife became unfashionable, and a wholesome and friendly atmosphere reflected the tone of the bishop's own character. His eagerness to allay party feeling and to maintain unity is revealed in this letter to the editor of *The Episcopal Recorder,* the hostile rival of the High Church *Banner of the Cross.* With a generosity of spirit which was more than mere diplomacy he wrote: "I am about to take a liberty which I know you will excuse and which is prompted simply by my regard for yourself and for the common cause of our Master. I allude to one principle in the management of a religious paper which, in the present state of our Church, seems to me very important. It is, that where there are two papers in the same diocese and city, representing different opinions, they shall shun as far as possible all mutual animadversion and criticism, since these will in the end almost inevitably degenerate into mutual reproach and recrimination. . . . And I should also hope that with respect to papers outside of the diocese . . . you would have as little bickering as possible. . . . As to any *right* to dictate or even *advise,* founded on my episcopal office, I disclaim it entirely. . . . I write, therefore, simply as a friend, only anxious for your success and that of the Church, and most ready to receive like suggestions from you." [9] Few bishops ever won a more complete control over their dioceses than Potter achieved in his, but he kept it without ever ceasing to maintain the temper and attitude of a Christian gentleman.

One means by which the bishop brought about closer fellowship

[8] *Ibid.,* 135.
[9] *Ibid.,* 133 f.

among his clergy and an increase of missionary activity in his diocese was by inaugurating regional convocations of clergy, especially in the rural districts. As he remarked in an address to his Convention in 1847, "Such meetings among the clergy, if connected with frequent public services, with much private prayer, and with abstinence from unprofitable and irritating controversies, must conduce to strengthen the bonds of mutual affection and confidence and to induce that spirit of general and cordial cooperation so essential to the growth of our Church and of true religion." [10] Four such convocations were organized during the next two years and brought all the advantages for which he had hoped.

As a professional teacher for nearly twenty years Potter naturally continued to maintain a marked interest in education of all grades. He became a trustee of the University of Pennsylvania. He was largely instrumental in reviving the Academy of the Protestant Episcopal Church which had been founded in the preceding century by Bishop White but had long been out of commission. To the improvement of the Sunday schools he gave constant attention, pleading for the integration of the schools with the Church and its worship and urging that they would greatly benefit "if teachers were more carefully selected and induced to prepare themselves better for the work of instruction." Having been a promoter of State Normal Schools in New York, he could not but be shocked at how lightly requirements for teaching were taken by the Church. To remedy a condition which still too widely prevails he was among the first to arrange for courses of lectures to be given to Sunday school teachers and to plan for the larger parishes to develop training schools from which many other parishes might benefit.

But it was perhaps for theological education that he felt the deepest concern, since that was more directly his own responsibility. His oversight of his candidates was as helpful as it was continuous, and being a constant student himself, he did not hesitate to recommend such study to his clergy. "A ministry," he wrote in 1860, "cannot *grow* in power and edification without *systematic* study of the Bible, of theology, and of moral philosophy. That there is so little of this study now among our ministers is one great reason why so few of them *improve* after the first few years." [11] (Words to the wise which ought still to be sufficient.)

Toward theological education his most valuable contribution was the founding of the Divinity School in Philadelphia. For several years before 1861 candidates for the ministry had been studying in that city under the Rev. George Emlen Hare; and in the fall of that year, after the war had cut off Northern students from the Virginia Seminary, instruction was

[10] *Ibid.*, 159.
[11] *Ibid.*, 281.

organized on a fuller scale with a staff of teachers. In the following winter the school received a charter from the State legislature, and with five professors and twenty students began its career as one of the great seminaries of the Church. It was during these last years of his life that Potter had not only planned its curriculum and shaped its statutes but raised a large endowment, which amounted at his death to more than $300,000. The school received permanent benefit from his successful experience as a college administrator and from his knowledge of educational problems.

In social service as well as in education Bishop Potter was a leader in the community. Early in his episcopate he organized the Churchman's Missionary Association for Seamen of the Port of Philadelphia. Soon afterward, to remedy the lawlessness among the young rowdies of the city, he took the initiative in helping to establish the Young Man's Institute, which provided libraries and reading rooms at five different centres. But the most notable of his achievements in the field of philanthropy was the large share he bore in founding the Hospital of the Protestant Episcopal Church in Philadelphia, of which the cornerstone was laid in 1860 and which was completed only a few years after St. Luke's Hospital in New York. None of these activities as a citizen, however, meant any slackening of his work as a diocesan. At the close of his first ten years in Pennsylvania he could report 8,600 confirmations, 126 ordinations, 215,000 children in the Sunday schools; and for the following decade much the same rate of progress was maintained. He was successful, too, in strengthening diocesan organization, then everywhere in a rudimentary state. And as one example of this kind of progress, in 1859 he persuaded the Convention to merge the two old independent missionary societies into one diocesan board of missions.

Before this action had been completed Potter suffered a stroke of paralysis and had to spend a year in England and Europe in an effort at recovery. During his absence the diocesan convention at last elected an assistant bishop. Though this much needed helper lived for only three years, he was replaced with little delay by the Rev. William Bacon Stevens who eventually succeeded Potter. The bishop's last four years corresponded with the dark years of the Civil War. Before their close his wife had died and he had been stricken by another seizure of paralysis. On the eve of what was to prove his last journey he married for the third time; and on April 1, 1865, he sailed with his wife on the steamship *Colorado* for a voyage to California. At the first port of call in Peru he was deeply saddened by the news of the murder of Lincoln, and by the time he reached San Francisco he was seriously ill with what was termed "Panama fever." Too weak to be moved from the ship he died on the fourth day of

July. And so great was the honor in which he was held three thousand miles from home that a committee of clergy and laity accompanied the body on its homeward voyage to New York.

"A man of noble presence, he at once impressed you as one born to rule—as a leader of men, a *jure divino* leader"—such was the verdict of Bishop Clark. Potter was by nature so calm, deliberate, and reserved that he had a reputation for being cold and austere. Yet the judgment passed upon him by the *New York Independent* shows how widely it was recognized that this coldness was only superficial: "He was the loved and trusted counsellor of his clergy. Especially did the unfortunate, the untried, and the struggling clergy find quick approach to his heart. Whether viewed closely and personally or as the great man shaping affairs, Bishop Potter never disappointed. He did more than any other man in it . . . to popularize the Episcopal Church and bring it into living, active sympathy with the surrounding community and make it felt as a recognized power and energy in all catholic movements for the general good." [12]

[12] *Ibid.*, 379. Mention of Bishop Potter in connection with the Oxford Movement in the United States and with the Muhlenberg Memorial will be found in the chapters dealing with those subjects.

Chapter XII

THE MUHLENBERG MEMORIAL

ON October 18, 1853, during the session of the General Convention in New York, Bishop Wainwright presented to the House of Bishops the Memorial which takes its name from its author and first signer. Since the document was brief and proved to be famous, it should be quoted in full:

"RIGHT REVEREND FATHERS:—The undersigned, presbyters of the Church of which you have the oversight, venture to approach your venerable body with a sentiment which their estimate of your office in relation to the times does not permit them to withhold. In so doing they have confidence in your readiness to appreciate their motives and their aims.

"The actual posture of our Church, with reference to the great moral and social necessities of the day, presents to the minds of the undersigned a subject of grave and anxious thought. Did they suppose that this was confined to themselves they would not feel warranted in submitting it to your attention; but they believe it to be participated in by many of their brethren, who may not have seen the expediency of declaring their views, or at least a mature season for such a course.

"The divided and distracted state of our American Protestant Christianity; the new and subtle forms of unbelief, adapting themselves with fatal success to the spirit of the age; the consolidated forces of Romanism, bearing with renewed skill and activity against the Protestant faith: and, as more or less the consequence of these, the utter ignorance of the Gospel among so large a portion of the lower classes of our population, making a heathen world in our midst; are among the considerations which induce your memorialists to present the inquiry whether the period has not arrived for the adoption of measures, to meet these exigencies of the times, more comprehensive than any yet provided for by our present ecclesiastical system; in other words, whether the Protestant Episcopal Church, with only her present canonical means and appliances, her fixed and invariable modes of public worship, her traditional customs and usages, is competent to the work of preaching and dispensing the Gospel to all sorts and conditions of men, and so, adequate to do the work of the Lord in this land and in this age? This question, your petitioners for their own part, and in consonance with many thoughtful minds among us, believe must be answered in the negative. Their memorial proceeds on the assumption that our Church, confined to the exercises of her present system, is not sufficient to the great purposes above mentioned; that a wider door must be opened for the admission of the Gospel ministry than that through which her candidates for holy orders are now obliged to enter. Besides such candidates among her own members, it is believed that men can be found among the other bodies of Christians around us, who would gladly receive ordination at your hands, could they obtain it without that entire surrender, which would now be required of them, of *all* the liberty in public worship to which they have been accustomed; men, who could not bring themselves to conform in all particulars to our prescriptions and customs, but yet sound in the faith, and who, having the gifts of preachers and pastors, would be able ministers of the New Testament. With deference it is asked, ought such an accession to your means in executing your high commission, 'Go into all the world, and preach the Gospel to every creature,' be refused, for the sake of conformity in matters recognized in the preface to the Book of Common Prayer as unessentials? Dare we pray the Lord of harvests to send forth laborers into the harvest, while we reject all laborers but those of one peculiar type? The extension of orders to the class of men contemplated (with whatever safeguards, not infringing on evangelical freedom, which your wisdom might deem expedient), appears to your petitioners to be a subject supremely worthy of your deliberations.

"In addition to the prospect of the immediate good which would thus be opened, an important step would be taken towards the effecting of a Church unity in the Protestant Christendom of our land. To become a central bond of union among Christians, who, though differing in name, yet hold to the one Faith, the one Lord, the one Baptism; and who need only such a bond to be drawn together in closer and more primitive fellowship, is here believed to be the peculiar province and high privilege of your venerable body as a college of *Catholic and Apostolic Bishops as such.*

"This leads your petitioners to declare the ultimate design of their memorial; which is to submit the practicability, under your auspices, of some ecclesiastical system, broader and more comprehensive than that which you now administer, surrounding and including the Protestant Episcopal Church as it now is, leaving that Church untouched, identical with that Church in all its great principles, yet providing for as much freedom in opinion, discipline, and worship, as is compatible with the essential faith and order of the Gospel. To define and act upon such a system, it is believed, must sooner or later be the work of an American Catholic Episcopate.

"In justice to themselves, on this occasion, your memorialists beg leave to remark that, although aware that the foregoing views are not confined to their own small number, they have no reason to suppose that any other parties contemplate a public expression of them, like the present. Having therefore undertaken it, they trust that they have not laid themselves open to the charge of unwarrantable intrusion. They find their warrant in the prayer now offered up by all congregations, 'that the comfortable Gospel of Christ may be truly preached, truly received, and truly followed in all places, to the breaking down the kingdom of Sin, Satan, and Death.' Convinced that, for the attainment of these blessed ends, there must be some greater concert of action among Protestant Christians than any which yet exists, and believing that with you, Right Reverend Fathers, it rests to take the first measures tending thereto, we could do no less than humbly submit this memorial to such consideration as in your wisdom you may see fit to give it.

"Assuring you, Right Reverend Fathers, of our dutiful veneration and esteem,

We are, most respectfully,

Your Brethren and Servants in the Gospel of Christ:

W. A. Muhlenberg,
Philip Berry,
G. T. Bedell,
Alex. H. Vinton,
S. H. Turner,
C. W. Andrews,
C. F. Cruse,
Edwin Harwood,
Henry Gregory,
M. A. DeWolfe Howe,
S. R. Johnson,
F. E. Lawrence,

and others.

"Concurring in the main purport of the memorial, but not able to subscribe to all its details, the following names were subscribed:

John Henry Hobart,
E. Y. Higbee,
Isaac G. Hubbard,
A. Cleveland Coxe,
Francis Vinton,
and others."

Nearly all in the first group of signers were well known leaders of the Evangelical party, six of them rectors of churches in New York, Syracuse, Boston, and Philadelphia, and two of them professors in the General Seminary. The second group, who signed with qualifications, included two High Churchmen. The list of endorsers was not intended to be long, and only a few were asked for their signatures. But the quality and standing of those whose names appeared were quite high enough to secure a respectful hearing from the House of Bishops, which appointed a committee to study the Memorial and report to the next General Convention. The fact that of the four bishops who voted against this action two were die-hard Evangelicals and two were prominent High Churchmen is enough to indicate that the Memorial was not regarded as an obviously partisan document, and the later treatment of it was never on a purely partisan basis. The committee itself, moreover, was properly balanced as to Churchmanship. Bishop Otey of Tennessee was the chairman, but Alonzo Potter of Pennsylvania was its most energetic and intelligent member.

Though the reception encountered by the Memorial in the House of Bishops was dignified and fairly sympathetic, the general reaction of the Church was not always so temperate. Muhlenberg, in fact, was pained and surprised at the number of those who called it mischievous and revolutionary. But though some were violent because alarmed and others were warm in their praise, most of those who took the trouble to read the appeal were more likely to be doubtful and confused. The fundamental reason for this prevailing state of mind was the fact that the author of the Memorial was nearly always more warm-hearted than clear-headed. There was a fine glow of right feeling and sincerity of purpose about this message to the bishops; but few outside of the signers were quite certain as to what the bishops were supposed to do about it.

Careful reading of the document, however, and close attention to the subsequent explanations offered by Muhlenberg and others make it evident that the central theme of the Memorial was a plea to the bishops for a freer and wider use of their apostolic power to ordain. As matters stood they were prepared and permitted to ordain only men who had promised to conform to the doctrine, discipline, and worship of the Episcopal Church. Muhlenberg and the group he represented urged upon them the need to bestow orders not only upon orthodox Episcopalians, but upon members of other Churches who might seek ordination with no intention of joining the Episcopal Church. As Muhlenberg later put it, "[The Memorial] proposes that, for the discharge of their office chiefly in admitting to the sacred ministry, they [the bishops] shall enlarge their borders; that they shall mark out for their action as bishops some broader and more catholic ground than that to which they are now restricted." As to the effect upon the Episcopal Church, "it puts her in no jeopardy. It need not alarm her most conservative friends. It says, Let her boundaries stand; let everything in them remain *in statu quo,* if that be desired, but let not the word of the Lord be bound. . . . Episcopal orders alone have a universal currency. Upon those, then, who have it in their power, lies the bounden duty to dispense such orders." In short, "the central idea of the movement is the emancipation of the Protestant Episcopate: upon this it all turns."[1]

It was not recommended, of course, that bishops should ordain anyone who happened to apply. Candidates must be carefully examined to make certain that they accepted the Scriptures, the Creeds, the two Sacraments, and the doctrines of grace in the Thirty-nine Articles. They must also agree to report to the bishops at stated intervals. They need not, however, be subject to all the requirements demanded of Episcopal ministers. Of this radical suggestion the motive and purpose was to further the spread of the Gospel—the supreme task of the Church—and to promote eventual unity among Protestant Churches.

Quite secondary to this central idea were other recommendations either explicit or implicit in the Memorial—the relaxation of requirements for the diaconate, the improvement of religious education, and especially the promotion of greater freedom in worship. This last aim was especially active in Muhlenberg's mind. He had long been accustomed not only to plead for more liturgical liberty but to exercise it effectively. In those days the rigidity demanded of priests was extreme. The 45th canon prescribed that "no other prayers shall be used than those prescribed by the said book"—the Prayer Book. Taken literally, this forbade all other printed prayers and all extempore prayer anywhere in the service.

In order to sound out opinion in the Church the committee on the Memorial composed a set of twenty-one questions which was sent to many bishops and other prominent leaders with the request that they express their views. The more valuable answers were later published by Bishop Potter as "Memorial Papers." If a brief analysis of these were helpful only to an understanding of the Memorial, we could hardly afford to give it space, but the replies reveal so much of contemporary ideas and conditions that they deserve quotation.

Among the various points raised by the questions asked, these six will indicate the subjects which provoked the most discussion—the religious education of the young; theological education; the quality of preaching; proposals for itinerating evangelists and for permanent deacons; liturgical changes; and the freer use by bishops of their ordaining powers.

There was general dissatisfaction with the status and the methods of Christian education, and the committee criticized the pastors of the Church for their want of attention to this phase of their duty. Suggestions for improvement, however, were neither numerous nor helpful. Bishop Doane, for instance, proposed that all Sunday schools be abolished and that the Church rely upon parochial day schools and upon the use of the Catechism. "The Catechism," he announced, "is the most wonderful

[1] *Evangelical Catholic Papers,* 1st series, 117 f., 121, 181.

manual for the religious nurture of children that ever has been produced." Fear was rightly expressed by more temperate critics that the Sunday schools were too dominated by laymen and laywomen and too much out of control by the rector.

Theological education has always been a favorite target. The more intelligent clergy are likely to be keen enough to see its real defects; the less intelligent are likely to blame it for the mediocre results which they exemplify. The faults which attracted the most comment were the failure of the schools to train the students in reading, in the devotional life, and in the practical work of the ministry. How slowly improvement in these directions has developed is suggested by the fact that these very imperfections are especially stressed today.

In the words of the committee, "The want of an impressive and devotional manner of reading the liturgy . . . is a great and crying evil." "The entire service," Bishop Upfold complained, "is read in the same tone, without discriminating between confession, supplication, thanksgiving, and the didactic portions." "Let all candidates be taught to read English," demanded Dr. Craik of Louisville. A deeper defect was the neglect of theological teachers to encourage and to train the students in personal religion. "Little attention," it was felt, "is paid by the professors to the cultivation of devotional habits in the students." But most conspicuous of all the faults listed is the lack of practical training. "Practical experience is too much divorced from study." "Professors, not themselves engaged in the active duties of the ministry, sink the minister in the scholar, and so are unfitted to send forth practical men." "No sermon written in a seminary was ever fit to be preached." Like lawyers and doctors, the men should learn by *doing*. These are some of the criticisms registered, all of which sound as if they had been written yesterday. Most up-to-date of all of them is the proposal of Dr. Paul Trapier of Charleston that in theological education the theoretical should be combined with the practical "by requiring the *vacation* in each seminary year" to be "spent in service under some parochial clergyman." The days of the Cincinnati Summer School were still far off, but here was the germ of the idea.

The poor quality of contemporary sermons was almost unanimously agreed upon. The committee testified that "the sentiment of the Church is everywhere the same, and emphatic in its expression as to the necessity of more force and directness in our preaching, and of more special adaptation to the varying circumstances of the congregations." Bishop Freeman criticized most preachers for "firing over the heads of people" and talking too exclusively to the intellectual and cultivated. "These harangues," as described by Bishop Upfold of Indiana, are "read in a dull, cold, prosy manner, and monotonous tone, and often very lengthy, with eyes bent close to the manuscript; or, if occasionally withdrawn, looking only at vacancy." Again and again the correspondents insisted that most preaching from Episcopal pulpits was "too much of the closet," "too essay-like," too theological, controversial, and didactic.

With the aim to alter the requirements for the ministry and to increase its variety, the committee submitted for comment two proposals—the use of itinerating evangelists and the development of a permanent diaconate with subnormal standards of education. In each case there was an obvious attempt to reproduce types found in the Baptist and Methodist Churches. Most of the leaders who answered the questions approved of traveling evangelists in new and unorganized territory, but pointed out that as "general missionaries" many such were already active. There was marked disapproval, however, of introducing this kind of worker into settled areas where their functions might become entangled with those of parish rectors. As for permanent deacons, few except Bishop Polk seem to have greeted them with favor.

The topic which called forth the fullest response and which appeared to interest the clergy more than any of the others was that of the need for greater liturgical variety. Yet there was a nearly unanimous reluctance to *change* any part of the Prayer Book. Throughout the Church there prevailed a morbid sensitiveness in regard to any alteration in the sacred text. Though it had been revised four times since 1549, it was treated almost as if it possessed the ultimate sanctity of the Sermon on the Mount. The bolder spirits, however, were prepared to recommend *additions* to the book, and a larger number were ready to approve changes in the customs of its *use*. Most of the additions favored have since been adopted—such as prayers for missions, for an increase in the ministry, for schools and colleges, and for State legislatures; but as interesting testimony to the rate of speed attending liturgical revision we may recall that some of these novelties were not approved until 1928—seventy-five years later. By way of desirable changes in custom, the suggestion most frequently offered was that Morning Prayer, the Litany, and the Holy Communion (or Ante-Communion) should be used as distinct services instead of being combined, as the practice then was, in one long service. Usage had made this prolonged and unliturgical combination almost obligatory, but it was gradually dawning upon many of the clergy that no rubric prescribed it. Taking account of all the proposals submitted, the committee recommended that the three familiar services should be used separately, when the minister so desired, and they offered as possible additions to the Prayer Book eight new prayers. One of these, "For the Unity of God's People," was admitted in 1892 and another, "For the Increase of the Ministry" appeared in the revision of 1928.

Though the demand for the freer use of the ordaining power of bishops was the main point of the Memorial, it received only the slightest attention in the questionnaire and even less in the replies that followed. Except for those who had endorsed the Memorial very few supported the project. One of the signers, Dr. M. A. DeWolfe Howe of Philadelphia, wrote that "the advance for unity ought to be made by the Church herself, who has something valuable to give. It might be more *just* for her to wait until they who have gone out from her return and sue for readmittance; but it would be more Christ-like, more in the genius of her mission, as the Lord's representative among men, to go out to them, and offer the gifts wherewith she is entrusted." Still more enthusiastic was Dr. Francis Vinton of New York who wrote the committee, "Give bishops, priests, and deacons to those sectarian denominations, and the schism in Christ's body is at once healed."

Arguments on the other side were naturally forcible and easy to present. Bishop Freeman probably expressed the view of the majority when he wrote: "An ordained minister of *the Church* not bound to conformity to the 'worship, discipline, etc.' of the Church! How could it have entered into the mind of man to conceive of such a thing? And to impart holy orders to one who is not *of* the Church and is *not amenable to her authority,* what is gained to the cause of truth and of Christ?" In a similar vein was the reply of Bishop Scott of Oregon and Washington: "The suggestion for uniting the Protestant denominations, or increasing our ministry, by ordaining those who at the same time decline to unite cordially with us in the general system of discipline and worship, seems to me entirely inadmissible. . . . Would there be any more of real unity than now? Would not the strife and division be rather increased, as contests within the household are always more implacable than those among strangers?" And he adds a further point not overlooked by others, "I am not aware of any desire, on the part of any considerable number of non-Episcopalians, to receive ordination at our hands." [2]

During the triennium the committee was able not only to digest the comments for which it had asked, but to profit from the widespread and animated discussion of the Memorial which agitated the Church. Especially in ecclesiastical journals and in diocesan conventions the questions raised were seriously and often hotly debated, and the trend of opinion was not difficult to gauge.

When the General Convention met again in October, 1856, it received the full and carefully drawn report of its committee. In partial

[2] The quotations from comments on the committee's questionnaire are taken from "Memorial Papers" edited by Bishop Alonzo Potter.

response to the recommendations there offered it passed the following resolutions:

"*Resolved,* as the opinion of the Bishops,

1. That the order of Morning Prayer, the Litany, and the Communion Service, being separate offices, may, as in former times, be used separately, under the advice of the Bishop of the diocese.

2. That on special occasions, or at extraordinary services, not otherwise provided for, ministers may, at their discretion, use such parts of the Book of Common Prayer, and such lesson or lessons from Holy Scripture, as shall, in their judgment, tend most to edification.

3. That the Bishops of the several Dioceses may provide such special services as in their judgment shall be required by the peculiar spiritual necessities of any class or portion of the population within said Dioceses, provided that such services shall not take the place of the services or offices of the Book of Common Prayer in congregations capable of its use.

4. That in view of the desirableness of union amongst Christians; and as a pledge of a willingness to communicate and receive information tending to that end; and in order to conference, if occasion or opportunity should occur, this House will appoint, by ballot, a committee of five Bishops as an organ of communication or conference, with such Christian bodies or individuals as may desire it, to be entitled the *Commission on Church Unity.*

5. That in making the above appointment, it is distinctly understood that the Commission is clothed with no authority to mature plans of union with other Christian bodies, or to propound expositions of doctrine and discipline."

In terms of immediate legislation the results of the Memorial were undoubtedly meager. Yet, surprisingly enough, they excited alarm in ultra-conservative quarters. Bishop DeLancey of Western New York, for example, entered a formal protest against the resolutions quoted above, and three years later the House of Deputies begged the bishops to reconsider them on the ground that they had "disturbed the minds of many in our Church"! Still, from our present point of view, "the immediate results were disappointing, but nevertheless the interest roused . . . gave a new direction to the life of the Episcopal Church. . . . Liturgical reform and Church unity have been before the Church ever since then." [3]

But it was neither surprising nor unfortunate that the plan to extend the range of episcopal ordination was rejected. Though it embodied a sound principle of the greatest value for the future of the ecumenical

[3] E. R. Hardy, Jr., "Evangelical Catholicism" in *Historical Magazine,* Sept., 1944, 188 f.

movement, as a practical project it was almost absurdly ill-contrived. That for any effective reunion there must be a ministry whose validity is acknowledged by all; that only an episcopally ordained ministry can be so recognized; and that the Episcopal Church is the body which can contribute this invaluable element—these are theses now widely accepted as a basis for action. But the action to which they may profitably lead is the *organic union* of bodies now separate. To leave these bodies separate and to scatter among them increasing numbers of episcopally ordained ministers would create more problems than it would solve.

In the first place, there was small inducement for the members of the other Churches to ask for ordination by a bishop when they were perfectly satisfied with their own orders. To accept such ordination in order to consummate a wide organic union, as in South India, there would be a strong motive; but to seek it simply as a kind of passport would appeal to few. Those who had been ordained on the terms proposed by Muhlenberg would have been out of step both with the Episcopal clergy and with the clergy of their own Churches, and would have been looked upon with distrust by both groups. In the second place, despite the fact that the plan was urged by Evangelicals, it really abandons the principle of a constitutional and controlled episcopate and implies that episcopal ordination, in and of itself, has a magical value even out of its proper context in the Church.[4] What good would such ordination do to men who disbelieved many of the Church's teachings and preferred to exercise their ministry independently of that Church? They would simply have a sacred brand put upon them and then be turned loose on the range.

Yet if Muhlenberg's own design for Church unity was condemned, at least the cause of unity was recognized as a field for discussion. But the commission on the subject appointed as a result of the Memorial had nothing of any consequence to report three years later, and though it continued to exist for another triennium, no further traces of its activity appear. Since it was denied the power to formulate plans for union, its demise was probably to be expected.

Beyond the mere gestures caused by the Memorial, the General Convention in this period was planning other approaches to unity. That the attitude toward the Roman Catholic Church remained as hostile as ever we can easily infer from a vigorous passage in the Pastoral Letter

[4] Cf. the statement in the Lambeth Conference Report (1948) of the Committee on the Unity of the Church:

"Form and manner alone are not sufficient to guarantee the character of a ministry. That can be substantiated only by the faith and practice of the Church itself. . . . We are not satisfied that what has been described as 'episcopacy *in vacuo*' would really give the non-episcopal Churches that which we or they would desire. . . . Catholicity is something which involves more than the possession of an undoubtedly valid ministry." *The Lambeth Conference, 1948,* 47, 54.

of the bishops issued in 1853—"We would hope that Romanism could not long withstand even the popular influences of our country. Besotted ignorance cannot long prevail in a land of free schools. Servile superstition must gradually decline in a land of free enquiry. Priestcraft and imposture cannot long flourish in a land of newspapers." Such language was then applauded,[5] and indeed would have been approved in Anglican circles at any time during the previous three hundred years; but we may be thankful that in the twentieth century no similar utterance could possibly emerge from the House of Bishops.

Toward the Orthodox Church, however, and toward the Church of Sweden, no such contemptuous feelings were cherished, and in the 'fifties and 'sixties attempts at closer relations with these bodies were initiated. Though they did not prove fruitful, they were earnest. The General Convention of 1856, in view of the growing extent of Swedish immigration, appointed a joint committee "to open friendly intercourse with the Church of Sweden," recognizing "that Churches believed to possess the same fundamentals of faith and discipline should be brought into closer intercourse." Three years later the committee reported various facts about the Church of Sweden, including its adherence to the Apostles' and Nicene Creeds as well as to the Lutheran Augsburg Confession. It went further to express an opinion about Swedish orders. "At the period of the Reformation," the statement reads, "the Swedish Church, thus Catholic and Protestant in faith, appears to have also preserved the order of Bishops as then recognized throughout the Christian world, and as perpetuated from the times of the Apostles; nor have your Committee cause to believe that this line of succession has ceased to be in that Church continued." Later in the session both Houses voted to continue the committee, but the bishops added a resolution declaring "that this House does not intend to commit itself to the expression of any opinion upon the subject of the orthodoxy of the Church of Sweden, or upon the succession in its episcopate." Partly because of this official reluctance to come to any decision the committee accomplished little of value. Six years later another committee on the same subject had no information to offer except that it had written a letter to the Archbishop of Upsala.

Perhaps more educative in its results was the effort to establish closer relations with the Russian Church. A joint committee for this purpose was appointed by the General Convention of 1862. Their first report in 1865 began with the announcement that a similar committee had been created by the Archbishop of Canterbury and that both committees had been in consultation. In England, moreover, there had been organized

[5] It was in this decade that the "Know-Nothing" Party chiefly flourished. Standing for 100 per cent Americanism, it was viciously anti-foreign and anti-Roman.

"The Eastern Church Association" to further mutual understanding and fellowship. Of the American committee one lay member and one clerical member had at different times visited Russia and conferred with the Metropolitans of St. Petersburg and Moscow and with other leaders. On every occasion they had met with the most friendly readiness to confer upon the question of possible intercommunion and had noted on the part of the Russians a genuine desire to learn more about the Episcopal Church. To supply the information requested they were sending much material to Russian clergy; and to give corresponding help to American Churchmen they had begun to issue a series of papers "designed to acquaint Church people with the nature and condition of the Russian Church and its affairs."

After hearing this report the Convention voted to prolong the life of the committee, but it was evidently regarded with suspicion by the Evangelicals. Rejecting a motion by Bishop Eastburn that the whole subject be dropped, a resolution was passed denying to the committee any power to correspond with the Russian and other Orthodox Churches "because such correspondence might be considered as invoking negotiation of a character for which the Church is not prepared." Since one of the most useful features of the committee's activity had been such correspondence, this new restriction severely limited its work. Yet the House of Deputies, at the same session of 1865, had adopted a resolution to the effect "that all those branches of the Apostolic Church which accept the Holy Scriptures and the Niceno-Constantinopolitan Creed, and which reject the usurpations and innovations of the Bishop of Rome, are called, by the course of events and the indications of divine Providence, to renew those primitive relations which the Roman schism has interrupted." This divine call to reunion had been answered some years before by forbidding the Commission on Church Unity "to mature any plans for reunion," and it was now to be heeded by forbidding the committee on the Russian Church to communicate with any of its leaders. Here was an early example of the refusal of General Convention to implement its own pious resolutions.

Chapter XIII

SLAVERY AND THE CIVIL WAR

SOCIAL evils were to be found in plenty throughout the America of the decades from 1835 to 1865—intemperance, for example, and the barbaric treatment of prisoners and of the insane—yet the worst of them appears almost benign compared with the malignant cancer of slavery. And however disturbing to the Church were the effects of the Oxford Movement and the issues raised by the Muhlenberg Memorial, they were only little ripples compared with the tidal wave of the Civil War. In an era when the Episcopal Church was deeply agitated by such questions as whether flowers should be placed on the altar or whether the Litany could be separated from Morning Prayer, what was the attitude of its leaders toward slavery and what was its history during the War of Secession?

For a generation or more a limited number of bishops and other clergy had taken part in philanthropic activity and lent their influence to promote various types of social reform. These days, of course, were long before the epoch of "the social gospel." No one was dreaming of "Christianizing" a "social order" which was widely believed to be nearly perfect as it stood; but where an appeal could be made to the instincts of Christian charity clerical leadership was not wanting. As a notable instance we recall that Bishop White was president, at one time or another, of the Philadelphia Dispensary, which supplied medical aid to the poor in their homes, of the Pennsylvania Institution for the Deaf and Dumb, and of the Philadelphia Society for Alleviating the Miseries of Public Prisons. White, in fact, was one of the first clergymen to preach to prisoners in jail—a venture then almost unheard of. Though the first juvenile reformatory—the House of Refuge in Boston—was founded by an Episcopal minister, the Rev. E. M. P. Wells, few of the many institutions and organizations of the day owe their origin to the Church. But the humanitarian movement was so strong at this time that clergy and laity alike came to share in its advances. Among them the Evangelicals were distinctly the more active party, especially in the fight against the evils of drink. They even succeeded, on several occasions during the 'thirties, in passing at diocesan conventions resolutions in favor of temperance reform.

Before we can justly estimate the attitude of Church leaders toward the more sinister problem of slavery we need to glance briefly at the changes in that institution since the earlier days of 1789. All the States north of Delaware and Maryland provided for immediate or gradual emancipation. The Continental Congress, in the Ordinance of 1787, prohibited slavery throughout wide areas of the West. The great Revolutionary leaders in Virginia—Washington, Madison, Monroe, and Randolph—condemned slavery. As long as he lived Jefferson pleaded for gradual emancipation combined with deportation. Patrick Henry declared, "I believe a time will come when an opportunity will be offered to abolish this lamentable evil." In 1808 the United States prohibited the importation of slaves, and in 1833 Parliament provided for the gradual extinction of slavery in all the British colonies.

In the United States, however, the situation had completely changed by 1830. The invention of the cotton gin (1792) and the development of the textile industry in England made the production of cotton enormously profitable, and its growth increased at a fabulous rate. Between 1791 and 1795, 5,200,000 pounds of cotton were produced, while between 1826 and 1830 the total was more than 307,000,000 pounds. In 1820 cotton provided only 22% of the nation's exports, but in 1860 the percentage had risen to 57. The labor of growing and preparing cotton was performed by slaves, and the more cotton was demanded the more slaves were required. Public opinion in the South therefore ceased to view slavery as temporary and came to regard it as the permanent basis of society. The million and a half slaves of 1820 increased by 1860 to nearly four million.

As if in answer to the new Southern attitude there arose in the North a new movement—abolitionism. Not only in the North but in the border States and even in the South there had long been anti-slavery societies favoring gradual emancipation. For many years it was actually a cause in which Northerners and Southerners could cooperate. But at approximately the time when the South had abandoned all thought of slavery as a transitional evil, a small group in the North began to agitate for immediate abolition. William Lloyd Garrison founded *The Liberator* in 1831, and within two years there were 300 anti-slavery societies of a new type with over 100,000 members. The main trend of Northern opinion was hostile to this extreme movement but positive in condemning slavery as evil.

With tempers rising on both sides the South proceeded in this generation to take a further step in the controversy. Its leaders advanced beyond the claim that slavery was a necessary evil to the further claim that slavery was a blessing to all concerned. They here offered a tragic example of how economic interests can color and control moral and religious thought.

In Shaw's brilliant little play, *The Man of Destiny*, Napoleon delivers a bitter diatribe against the English. "There is nothing," he declares, "so bad or so good that you will not find an Englishman doing it; but you will never find an Englishman in the wrong. He is never at a loss for an effective moral attitude. His watchword is always duty; and he never forgets that the nation which lets its duty get on the opposite side to its interest is lost." While these taunts could hardly be accepted as a fair appraisal of the British, they describe rather well the change of Southern opinion in the 'forties and 'fifties. Leaders in politics and in education believed that the economic welfare of the South depended upon the perpetuation and expansion of slavery. It was therefore important that duty should not be on the opposite side to this interest. In the face of mounting world opinion the South must not be found in the wrong. And thenceforward, it must be acknowledged, its spokesmen were "never at a loss for an effective moral attitude." The moral attitude, as declared by Professor Dew of William and Mary College, was that slavery was so beneficial both to blacks and whites that it ought to be encouraged. Or, as Governor Hammond of South Carolina put it, "God created Negroes for no other purpose than to be subordinate 'hewers of wood and drawers of water'—that is, to be the slaves of the white race."

While secular opinion was invoking God as the author and admirer of slavery and praising its promoters for spreading its blessings, what were the leaders of the Churches saying and doing? The Quakers, of course, have the cleanest record, for they were the pioneers in condemning slavery, but their numbers were too small to sway public opinion. The Methodist Church at first forbade its members to be slaveholders, but was later obliged to tolerate the practice among its laymen. As to whether its ministers might own slaves the clash of opinion grew so violent that in 1845 a convention of the Methodist churches in the South voted to separate and form a new Church. Hence arose the Methodist Church South, which doubled its membership in fifteen years and which was not reunited with its northern sister until 1939.

The Baptist churches, congregational in polity, were united only by national associations for the promotion of missions. Their Home Board and their Foreign Board, defying the Southern members, continued to deny appointments to candidates who were slave-holders. Resenting these decisions, the Baptists of eight slave-holding States met in convention in 1845 and organized "The Southern Baptist Convention for Domestic and Foreign Missions," thus inaugurating a division which has lasted to this day. A similar split in the Presbyterian Church developed more slowly, being complicated by the fact that in 1838 that Church had become divided into Old School and New School on doctrinal grounds, and the former group long endeavored to keep neutral on the slavery issue. In 1857, however, the Southern wing of the New School Presbyterians seceded from the main body, and in the summer of 1861 the Old School in the South took the same action. Before the end of the war these two Southern groups united, and their successors still form a body separate from the Northern Presbyterians.

The Episcopal Church never split on the issue of slavery because it refused to take any position on that issue. Its successful effort to retain its unity during the period of sectional agitation between 1830 and 1860 was due to various motives, some of which were undoubtedly more praiseworthy than others. Perhaps least creditable was the deep reluctance of the Church during the greater part of the century to express itself on any subject which could possibly be described as "political." It was commonly assumed that secular affairs were matters of no concern to the Church. Moral issues of a private nature, such as the sanctity of the home or the drink problem, might be discussed in ecclesiastical gatherings, but moral issues of a public nature, such as war or slavery, were taboo. The aloofness of the Church, for example, at the time of "bleeding Kansas" is indicated by the Pastoral Letter of the bishops at the General Convention of 1856. There we read that "the constituted rulers of the Church . . . are the ministry. With party politics, with sectional disputes, with earthly distinctions, with the wealth, the splendor, and the ambition of the world, they have nothing to do."

More admirable among the motives which kept the Church united were the sympathy and understanding with which many Northern members viewed their brothers in the South. Besides the ties of personal friendship there was a genuine appreciation of the distressing problems with which Southern Churchmen had to contend. The heritage of slavery had created a situation for which neither the diagnosis nor the remedy of the Abolitionist was adequate. With the best will in the world it was hard to see, even from the Christian point of view, what ought to be done with three or four million slaves in the midst of a white population. Even if all were to be emancipated over night, a baffling race problem remained—and remains. It might be true that many Church leaders in the South were simply echoing the opinions of politicians and planters, but that did not imply the inherent moral superiority of Northern Christians. Would not they act in like fashion under similar circumstances? Ought it not to be charitably acknowledged that defiant pioneers ready to challenge the overwhelming force of public opinion are rare in any age?

Strongest and perhaps worthiest of all motives to avoid pressing for a verdict upon slavery was the dread of schism in the Church. It was bad enough to watch the menacing approach of political division; it would only multiply the evils of the time if division in the Church should be added. The Church was especially strong in two of the leading Southern States—Virginia and South Carolina. In other States, though the planter aristocracy was but a small fraction of the white population, its members formed the governing class and were more likely than not to be Episcopalians. Any attempt, therefore, to adopt at a General Convention resolutions condemning slavery would have met with violent resistance. The South was then so sensitive that as far as its control extended, the subject was absolutely forbidden. If a crusading majority in either House had forced through an anti-slavery declaration, ecclesiastic secession would almost surely have followed. Those who were willing to tolerate or even to approve of slavery were just as truly members of the Episcopal Church as were those who differed from them; and a split in the Church was too high a price to pay for trying to make official the convictions of a bare majority. The governing body of the Church, then, wisely refrained from acting at all. The decision may not have been heroic, but in retrospect few will deny that it was statesmanlike.

The reluctance of Church conventions to press the issue was all the greater because even Northern opinion among Episcopalians was far from unanimous. Examples of anti-slavery leaders in the Church were not wanting. One of the vice-presidents of the American Anti-Slavery Society, for instance, was the Rev. E. M. P. Wells of Boston. A number of other clergy, moreover, during the ten or fifteen years before the war, published pamphlets denouncing slavery. Even Bishop Whittingham of Maryland declared slavery a great social evil which ought not to be extended; and Bishop Alonzo Potter replied vigorously to a book by a fellow bishop who defended human bondage. Episcopal laymen, too, were energetic in the anti-slavery cause. Very few followed the son and grandson of John Jay in becoming abolitionists, but there were many, like William H. Seward and Salmon P. Chase, who were active in the Republican party.[1] Yet it must be acknowledged that few outstanding clerical leaders made any bold public pronouncements.

[1] W. W. Manross, "The Episcopal Church and Reform," *Historical Magazine*, Dec., 1943, 349–352.

On the other hand, two of the most noted defenders of slavery were Bishop Hopkins of Vermont and Dr. Samuel Seabury of New York, who must have written *con amore* since they were certainly not subject to heavy social or political pressure. Dr. Seabury was the rector of the Church of the Annunciation at the time of his election in 1862 to be a professor at the General Seminary. In 1861, before war broke out, appeared his book *American Slavery Distinguished from the Slavery of English Theorists and Justified by the Law of Nature.* In his Preface he deplores the fact that the question of slavery should "be complicated with questions of morality, religion, and social reputation." He makes a determined effort to distinguish true slavery as condemned in England and elsewhere from the beneficent institution found in the South. Its supporters in America, he maintains, stand for order, conservatism, and Christionity; whereas its opponents are too often identified with anarchy and infidelity. The slaves must be presumed to have consented to their status, and their relation to their masters is now established by the decree of divine Providence. Not only is slavery not forbidden by the New Testament, but "the precepts of love and equity enjoined on us by our Blessed Lord have no such tendency as is supposed to impair and ultimately subvert the relation of master and slave." [2] Bishop Hopkins was equally scornful of those who denounce an institution "laid down by the Lord God of Israel for his chosen people." Even Jesus, he reminds us, "did not allude to it at all," and he adds, "How prosperous and united would our glorious republic be at this hour if the eloquent and pertinacious disclaimers against slavery had been willing to follow their Saviour's example!" Nor is slavery contrary to the command to love God and to love man, for "in the relation of master and slave we are assured by our Southern brethren that there is incomparably more mutual love than can ever be found between the employer and the hireling." Slaves, indeed, "are the happiest laborers in the world," and as for the whites, they should be encouraged to remember that "the Anglo-Saxon race is king; why should not the African race be subject?" [3]

Considering the number of its Southern members and the number of its Northern members with Southern principles, it is no wonder that the Episcopal Church was neither unanimous nor vocal on the subject of slavery. When division came it was not the result of clashing opinions within the Church but of the actual fact of secession.

It was political secession which preceded and prompted ecclesiastical secession. On December 20, 1860, South Carolina seceded from the Union. Within six weeks six more states had severed their connection

[2] S. Seabury, *American Slavery,* 2nd ed., III f., 44, 20, 145, 291.
[3] J. H. Hopkins, *Scriptural View of Slavery,* 11 f., 30, 32.

with the United States—Mississippi, Florida, Alabama, Louisiana, Georgia, and Texas. On February 4, 1861, representatives of these States met at Montgomery, Alabama, and organized the Confederate States of America. After the middle of April four more States seceded and joined the Confederacy—Virginia, North Carolina, Arkansas, and Tennessee. By official action, therefore, the inhabitants of these States declared themselves no longer citizens of the United States. According to their own view they belonged to another independent nation.

The Anglican tradition, which recognizes no central world authority for the Catholic Church, stands for national Churches. How then could citizens of the Confederate States of America continue to be loyal members of the Protestant Episcopal Church in the United States of America? That Church had become for them the Church of a foreign country, and a hostile country at that. Among Southern Churchmen, as among Southern statesmen, many deplored secession and submitted to the action with reluctance; others rejoiced in the freedom which they conceived it to bestow. One of those who recognized promptly that the Church must accommodate itself to the new situation was Bishop Leonidas Polk of Louisiana, who later served as a lieutenant-general in the Confederate Army and was killed in action. Together with Bishop Stephen Elliott of Georgia he issued as early as March 23, 1861, a call for a meeting of Southern bishops and other diocesan representatives to be held at Montgomery, Alabama, on July 3rd. At this preliminary meeting four bishops were present, together with clergy and laymen from six dioceses. The chief action taken was to agree that the organization of an independent Church was necessary and to appoint a committee of three bishops, three presbyters, and three laymen to report to an adjourned meeting a constitution and canons for the new Church.

The second preliminary meeting assembled at Columbia, South Carolina, on October 16, 1861, and continued its proceedings for eight days. At this larger gathering ten out of eleven bishops were present, in addition to nineteen clergy and fourteen laymen representing the eight dioceses of Virginia, North and South Carolina, Florida, Georgia, Tennessee, Alabama, and Mississippi. The proposed constitution was debated article by article and after amendments was adopted. This constitution of the Protestant Episcopal Church in the Confederate States of America was in all essentials the same as that of the Church in the United States, and the canons of the older body were provisionally accepted with a few alterations required by political changes. It was agreed finally that the organization of the Church should be considered as accomplished when seven or more dioceses had ratified the constitution. On September 19, 1862, three days before Lincoln issued the Emancipation Proclamation,

Bishop Elliott was able to announce that ratification was complete, and a week later he summoned a meeting of the first General Council of the Church of the Confederacy to be held in Augusta, Georgia, on November 12.

The General Council met at a period of encouraging success for the Confederacy. McClellan had just been relieved of his command, and the Union was soon to hear the news of Burnside's heavy defeat at Fredericksburg. The next few months marked the lowest point in the fortunes of the Federal Government and its armies.

Assuming undoubtedly the permanence of their new organization, seven bishops and thirty deputies from seven dioceses proceeded to take action.[4] Arkansas was admitted as a diocese and the election of its bishop (Henry C. Lay) was confirmed. Eight months earlier the Rev. Richard H. Wilmer had been consecrated as Bishop of Alabama, so that the Southern episcopate was already expanding. The Council's chief business was the adoption of a code of canons, differing but little from that of the Church in the United States, and of a Prayer Book in which the word "Confederate" took the place of the word "United" and the word "Council" replaced the word "Convention." The few alterations made in constitution, canons, and Prayer Book fully confirm the repeated assurances of Southern bishops and other leaders that the Church in the Confederate States had separated from the parent body for reasons which had no reference whatever to doctrine, discipline, or worship.

Six weeks before the General Council met at Augusta the General Convention assembled in New York. Only twenty-four bishops were present and only twenty-two dioceses were represented. In the absence of the senior bishop, Brownell of Connecticut, Bishop Hopkins presided. During the three weeks of this session debate was mainly concerned with resolutions referring to the war. There were evidently two sets of extremists—those who wanted to condemn the leaders of the Church in the South in violent terms and those who deprecated any utterance at all, on the ground that the Church was not concerned with civil affairs.[5] In the end the House of Deputies refused to denounce the bishops and other members of the Church in the Confederate States for committing "sins of rebellion, sedition, and schism." It likewise declined to be content with a weak resolution which announced that "as a legislative Council of the Church of Christ all secular and national interests are foreign to the deliberations and decisions of this Convention." The majority of the

[4] Because of war conditions not all the dioceses could be represented.

[5] Phillips Brooks (then aet. 27) must have had in mind this latter group when he wrote from New York in October, 1862, "It was ludicrous, if not sad, to see those old gentlemen sitting there for fourteen days, trying to make out whether there was a war going on or not, and whether if there was it would be safe for them to say so."

deputies, while voting against any bitter reproaches addressed to their Southern brothers, were determined that the Episcopal Church should not be the only Church in the North unwilling to proclaim its support of the Union cause. Final action therefore was embodied in the following series of firm but moderate resolutions.

"*Resolved,* By the House of Clerical and Lay Deputies of this stated Triennial Convention, That, assembling, as we have been called to do, at a period of great national peril and deplorable civil convulsion, it is meet and proper that we should call to mind, distinctly and publicly, that the Protestant Episcopal Church in the United States hath ever held and taught, in the language of one of its Articles of Religion, that 'it is the duty of all men who are professors of the Gospel to pay respectful obedience to the civil authority, regularly and legitimately constituted'; and hath accordingly incorporated into its Liturgy 'a prayer for the President of the United States and all in civil authority,' and 'a prayer for the Congress of the United States, to be used during their session'; and hath bound all orders of its ministry to the faithful and constant observance, in letter and in spirit, of these and all other parts of its prescribed ritual.

"*Resolved,* That we can not be wholly blind to the course which has been pursued, in their ecclesiastical as well as in their civil relations, since this Convention last met in perfect harmony and love, by great numbers of the ministers and members of this Church, within certain States of our Union which have arrayed themselves in open and armed resistance to the regularly constituted government of our country; and that while, in a spirit of Christian forbearance, we refrain from employing toward them any terms of condemnation or reproach, and would rather bow in humiliation before our common Father in Heaven for the sins which have brought his judgment on our land, yet we feel bound to declare our solemn sense of the deep and grievous wrong which they will have inflicted on the great Christian Communion which this Convention represents, as well as on the country within which it has been so happily and harmoniously established, should they persevere in striving to rend asunder those civil and religious bonds which have so long held together in peace, unity, and concord.

"*Resolved,* That while, as individuals and as citizens, we acknowledge our whole duty in sustaining and defending our country in the great struggle in which it is engaged, we are only at liberty, as deputies to this Council of a Church which hath ever renounced all political association and action, to pledge to the national government—as we now do—the earnest and devout prayers of us all, that its efforts may be so guided by wisdom and replenished with strength, that they may be crowned with speedy and complete success, to the glory of God and the restoration of our beloved Union." [6]

A further subject provoking hot disagreement among the bishops was the contents of their official Pastoral Letter. Bishop Hopkins, as Presiding Bishop *pro tem,* had prepared the draft of a message which included no reference whatever to the war. The House, however, chose to approve a warmly outspoken version written by Bishop McIlvaine, to which Hopkins expressed his opposition by refusing to appear in the chancel when it was read.

Of far more significance for the future of the Church than any action taken was the action which was *not* taken. No move was made to acknowledge the schism in the Church or to accept it as a completed fact. On the contrary, just as the Federal Government had taken the position that the seceded States were still members of the Union in spite of all their decrees and declarations, so the General Convention acted as though the bishops and deputies from the South were only temporarily absent. On every day of its sessions the roll of the missing dioceses was called. Their seats, so to speak, were kept waiting for them. This display of deep confidence in the Union cause and of genuine fraternity toward the Southerners made vastly easier the healing process which was soon to produce reunion.

If Bishop Hopkins had proved an obstacle to the expression of patriotism in 1862, his influence as the new Presiding Bishop at the General Convention of 1865 was a marked advantage to the cause of reconciliation. Before the Convention met at Philadelphia on October 4, six months after the fall of Richmond and the surrender of Lee, Hopkins wrote to all the Southern bishops inviting them to attend and assuring them of "a cordial welcome." His known sympathy with the South and his close friendship with the strongest and most partisan of its bishops—Elliott of Georgia—gave to his message especial weight. A further advantage accrued from the fact that the Convention was held soon after the end of the war and well before the disastrous blunders of Congressional reconstruction had embittered the South.

The Southern response to the Northern appeal of "Welcome home" was varied. Bishop Gregg of Texas and Bishop Atkinson of North Carolina, with some measure of support from their diocesan conventions, were in favor of immediate return. Bishop Davis of South Carolina was flatly opposed to reunion. Most of the other dioceses followed the leadership of Bishop Elliott in postponing their decision until the General Council of the Church in the Confederacy had met to take action. The South, then,

[6] Only a parliamentary body could have used so many words to say that they hoped the North would win.

was meagerly represented at Philadelphia. The only bishops who attended were Atkinson and Lay.[7] Yet there were also deputies from Tennessee, North Carolina, and Texas—enough, in short, to symbolize a reunion which was later to be complete.

To assure the Southern dioceses that nothing would be left undone which might make easy the return of those who were still doubtful, the members of the Convention received with friendly warmth the few deputies who had made the first venture. They soon took the further helpful step of ratifying the consecration of Dr. Wilmer as Bishop of Alabama on condition that he should sign the usual declaration of conformity. So careful, indeed, were the bishops and deputies not to wound the feelings of those who were already suffering enough from defeat, that the resolution in favor of a service of thanksgiving was modified to suit their wishes. The original motion had proposed thanks to God for (among other things) "the reestablishment of the National Government over the whole land." But Bishop Atkinson protested that while his people could not but accept the result of the war, they were not thankful for it. Here there was enough material to arouse an ugly contest, for the newspapers had seized the occasion to advertise the issue as a test of patriotism. But moderation prevailed, and the Convention voted that thanksgiving should be offered for "the restoration of peace to the country and unity to the Church." On that note all could unite.

The last chapter in the history of the Church of the Confederacy was written at its second General Council held in Augusta on November 8, 1865, a meeting attended by four bishops and eighteen clerical and lay deputies. Recognizing that the circumstances which had necessitated the formation of an independent Church had ceased to exist, the members of the Council resolved that the Southern dioceses were now free to withdraw from their present union and to unite with the Church in the United States. Before another year had elapsed all the dioceses had transferred their allegiance, and the Protestant Episcopal Church in the Confederate States of America came to an end after a career of four years.[8]

[7] During the war Lay had been elected Bishop of Arkansas. He was now allowed to resume his previous status as Missionary Bishop of Arkansas and the Southwest.

[8] For the story of the Church in the South (1861–5) see J. D. Cheshire's *The Church in the Confederate States* and the *Historical Magazine* for Dec., 1948, which is devoted to that subject.

PART IV

THE CHURCH FROM 1866 TO 1900

INTRODUCTORY

THE fifteen years which followed the Civil War witnessed what has been rightly described as "the emergence of modern America."

"In the South the whites were struggling against bitter odds to readjust their economic and social life to the conditions imposed by their defeat in the Civil War, while the Negroes, dazed by their new-found freedom, were groping their way toward a secure place in the new social organism. Beyond the Missouri a flood of population was rushing toward the last frontier, revealing to the older settled regions a new and colorful America, one built on heroic dimensions and characterized by kaleidoscopic change. In the Northeast machine-industry was rapidly asserting its supremacy, revolutionizing the older methods of carrying on business, and strongly affecting the life of all classes of society. Middle America continued to maintain its identity as a rural region, and yet, more than any other section, felt the unsettling impact of Eastern industrialism. Everywhere American life showed traces of the great struggle from which the country had so recently emerged, and public life in city, state, and nation was stricken with the moral sickness which followed the war. It was a period of striking contrasts, of contending aspirations, of new life crowding out the old." [1]

During the remaining twenty years of the century the nation was characterized by many of the same features, but above all by three movements immense in their effects and closely interdependent—the huge expansion of industrial production, the vast accumulation of national wealth, and the rapid rise of the city as the dominant influence in American life.

In the eyes of those who have lived through any large part of the twentieth century the decades from 1870 to 1900 seem almost devoid of important incidents or events, whether international or domestic. The brief Franco-Prussian War (1870--71), the little Sino-Japanese War

[1] A. M. Schlesinger and D. R. Fox in Foreword to Allan Nevins, *The Emergence of Modern America,* XVII. Copyright 1927 by The Macmillan Company and used with their permission.

(1894–95), our own Spanish War of 1898, and the war in South Africa which began in 1899 appear hardly more than skirmishes in the light of what was to follow. Once the Negroes had been emancipated and enfranchised by constitutional amendments and Reconstruction in the South was formally at an end, the United States entered upon a period of relatively small political interest but of almost incredible growth.

The darker side of the picture is perhaps the easier to see and to describe. The rough competitive confusion of industrial advance lowered the moral standards of the country, and corruption infected both business and politics. It was the era of the Tweed ring in New York City, of Jay Gould and the railroad scandals, and of bribery and peculation in the Grant administration. Cut-throat competition, later modified by trusts then uncontrolled; a ruthless exploitation of labor then inadequately equipped for defence; the devastating effects of depression after the panics of 1873 and 1893; the degrading squalor of slums in a hundred cities—these were marks of the times. And such evils seemed aggravated by the signs of the "chromo civilization" of this "gilded age," the general lack of any cultivated taste, the admiration for what was merely big and showy, and (as symbolic of much else) the unspeakable architecture of the 'seventies and 'eighties.

Yet the American people, still young in spirit and essentially healthy, found much to record on the other side. The years of prosperity far outnumbered the years of depression. If there was an increasing tendency toward standardization, it was only one sign of a growing unity. If the cities produced tenements and sweat-shops, they were no less clearly "the generating centers for social and intellectual progress." Movements that were later to advance social justice were being vigorously initiated—the campaign for woman suffrage and women's rights, the organization of labor on a national scale, and even the federal regulation of industry. As for culture, we cannot be wholly discouraged in recalling an era when experimental science was stimulating intellectual life, when universities were attaining new range and vigor, when Whistler and Sargent were known as Americans, and when Henry James and Mark Twain were at the height of their powers.

The Church in that generation had to deal with drastic changes, geographical and intellectual. It had to adapt its methods to a constituency ever less rural and ever more urban—to solve, that is, both city problems and new types of rural problems. In the same period it had to adjust its thought to the impact of modern physical and historical science upon the creeds and traditions of Christian orthodoxy.

The most notable numerical change in the Churches between 1870 and 1900 was the increase of Roman Catholics, largely due to immigration. In 1870 the Roman Church ranked fourth, outnumbered by Methodists, Baptists, and Presbyterians. In 1900 it ranked easily first. At the earlier date the Episcopal Church was sixth in order of size, but in 1900 it had to accept seventh place, being temporarily reduced in rank by the Disciples of Christ. In 1866 there were only 160,000 Episcopal communicants; in 1900 there were 720,000. Though the number of communicants had thus increased more than fourfold, the number of clergy had only been doubled. If this was a regrettable defect, there was encouragement in the fact that in 1860 the ratio of population to communicants was 209 to one, while in 1900 it was 102 to one. Not only was there a growing number of Churchmen but a growing proportion of Americans were Churchmen; and the proportion has become steadily larger ever since.

Chapter XIV

THE INCREASE AND DECLINE OF PARTY STRIFE

IN the early stages of the Oxford Movement in England the leaders were primarily interested in ideas and beliefs: they felt relatively little concern for ceremonial. As Dr. Pusey himself recorded, "The writers of the Tracts . . . always deprecated any innovation in the way of conducting the service, anything of ritualism, or especially any revival of disused vestments." It was almost inevitable, however, that the new emphasis on Catholic theology should soon express itself in Catholic forms. By 1850 Anglo-Catholics were beginning to use colored stoles and hangings and even Eucharistic vestments and to revive other practices suggestive of Rome. So widespread and violent was the opposition, voiced by a majority of the bishops, that there raged for the next thirty years "the Eucharistic Controversy" and "the Ritualistic Controversy"—two allied results of advancing Anglo-Catholicism. The English Church Union was formed to support Anglo-Catholicism, and the Church Association [1] to attack it. A series of ecclesiastical trials to test the legality of various usages sometimes led to appeals to the Judicial Committee of the Privy Council—the final court of appeal—so that what doctrines and practices were permissible in the Church of England was a question ultimately decided by laymen.

The course of events in America followed much the same lines; and though the bitterness was less extreme and there were very few formal trials, there was more than enough disturbance.

Anglo-Catholics, fully understanding and devoutly believing those doctrines of the Eucharist and of the priesthood which distinguished their group, naturally wanted to give them the outward forms with which tradition had long invested them. Others, less capable of theological

[1] Between 1868 and 1880 this Association spent nearly £40,000 in prosecuting Anglo-Catholics for ritual practices.

thought, adopted similar practices from motives merely sentimental or artistic. For one reason or another, then, as early as the 'forties ritual innovations began to appear in a growing number of parishes. The excitement produced by changes which have long since been accepted by all grades of Churchmen reveals how severely Protestant were the standards of that day.

Among the "advanced" parishes was the Church of the Advent in Boston, founded in 1844. There the Rev. William Croswell preached in his surplice, used a stone altar, and placed upon it candles and a cross. His bishop, Manton Eastburn, announced that these features caused him "inexpressible grief and pain" and refused to visit the church as long as they were visible. It was the same bishop who was preaching many years later at Grace Church in Newton, Massachusetts, when Professor Steenstra, a Low Churchman from the Theological School in Cambridge, was conducting the service. Before it was too late Eastburn observed two vases of flowers on the altar, and declared at once, "Mr. Steenstra, although I know that you make no idolatrous use of these flowers, I cannot on principle take part in a service with them on the holy table." But the Advent was not the only parish to introduce ancient usages. During the next twenty-five years many others made similar changes—St. Stephen's in Providence, Mt. Calvary in Baltimore, St. Mark's in Philadelphia, St. Mary the Virgin's in New York, and not a few more. Here were to be found not only free pews but daily matins and vespers, a weekly Eucharist, the observance of saints' days, candles, crosses, and colored stoles. In the more extreme churches, influenced by Nashotah, there was encouraged a non-communicating attendance at "Mass," a fasting communion, and even sacramental confession and absolution. No wonder that Professor Sparrow of the Virginia Seminary declared in 1866 that "ritualism seems to be spreading, sweeping over the Church."

Aware of the enthusiasm with which ritual was being introduced and of the violent criticism with which it was met, a group of the younger clergy appealed to the Presiding Bishop, John H. Hopkins of Vermont, for his views on the subject. Having recently succeeded in defending human slavery on scriptural and historical grounds, he found it relatively easy to say a good word, on similar grounds, for the revival of ceremonial practices. The result was the publication in 1866 of his little book, *The Law of Ritualism*. On this topic, instead of being behind the thought of his age, he was rather ahead of it. He expressed the sensible conviction that a wide diversity of ritual usage was permissible in the Church; he approved of such enrichment, and he prophesied quite correctly that most of what was then creating consternation would eventually be accepted as normal.

This book, nevertheless, so far from calming the agitation, proved to be only the opening chapter in a decade of heated controversy. Its appeal to laws and precedents in the Church of England was especially resented. On January 10, 1867, after a special meeting of the House of Bishops, there was issued a declaration signed by twenty-four bishops—a majority of the House. In this document the signers declared that "no Prayer Book of the Church of England . . . and no law of the Church of England have any force of law in this Church such as can be justly cited in defence of any departure from the express law of this Church." Declaring that the Episcopal Church had the right to prescribe its own ritual, the statement condemned the usages of the Anglo-Catholics, naming especially the use of candles, incense, and genuflection as expressing the Roman doctrine of the Mass. Thenceforward debate throughout the Church grew lively, and many memorials against ritualism were composed for presentation to the coming General Convention.

When the Convention met in New York in 1868 both Houses were confronted with a sheaf of resolutions, and spent many days in discussing them. It was probably fortunate, however, that no action was taken except the appointment by the Bishops (at the request of the Deputies) of a committee "to consider whether any additional provision for uniformity, by canon or otherwise, is practicable and expedient." At the next General Convention, held in Baltimore in 1871, this committee of five bishops recommended the adoption of a canon which should forbid eleven specified practices: 1. The use of incense. 2. Placing a crucifix in any part of the church. 3. Carrying a cross in procession. 4. Using lights on the holy table, except when necessary. 5. The elevation of the elements so as to offer them to the people as objects of adoration. 6. Mixing of water with wine as part of the service. 7. The washing of the priest's hands or ablution of vessels in the presence of the congregation. 8. Bowings, crossings, genuflections, prostrations, reverences, kissing the holy table, and any kneeling except as provided by rubric. 9. Celebrating or receiving the Holy Communion alone. 10. Permitting any unordained person to assist the minister in any part of the service of Holy Communion. 11. Using any prayers, collects, epistles, or gospels in the Holy Communion not provided in the Prayer Book or by canon.

Not content with urging these restrictions, the committee further recommended legislation (1) forbidding a rector to introduce a choral service without the approval of his vestry or against the prohibition of his bishop; (2) forbidding surpliced choirs except under the same conditions; (3) forbidding chancels to be so arranged as to prevent the minister from officiating at the right end of the holy table; (4) forbidding ministers to wear any vestments other than white surplices, black or white stoles, black gowns, "bands," or black cassocks not reaching below the ankles.

To prove the futility of trying by legislation to freeze ritual at any one point of development we may pause to reflect that every one of the usages forbidden by this proposed canon (except celebrating the Eucharist alone) is now familiar in all High Church parishes and at least half of them are equally customary in most Low Church parishes. Conscious no doubt of the dangers inherent in this legalism, and certainly aware that they might be better employed than in deciding how long cassocks ought to be, the members of General Convention took no action in this field except the adoption of the two following resolutions:

"*Resolved* . . . that this Convention hereby expresses its decided condemnation of all ceremonies, observances, and practices which are fitted to express a doctrine foreign to that set forth in the authorized standards of this Church.

"*Resolved,* that in the judgment of this House [of Deputies] the paternal counsel and advice of the Right Reverend Fathers, the Bishops of this Church, is deemed sufficient at this time to secure the suppression of all that is irregular and unseemly, and to promote greater uniformity in conducting the public worship of this Church, and in the administration of the Sacraments."

Though these resolutions were gentle enough, the bishops took a more definite stand in their subsequent Pastoral Letter and specifically condemned Eucharistic adoration, auricular confession, and the invocation of saints.

For the restraint and moderation manifested by this General Convention the influence of an Anglo-Catholic was in large measure responsible. The Rev. Dr. James De Koven, Warden of Racine College in Wisconsin, was not only a brilliant orator and a skillful debater but also a leader of notable charm and of the highest character. He openly proclaimed his own Catholic beliefs concerning the Eucharist and justified his right to adopt the forms which embodied those beliefs by an appeal to the *comprehensiveness* of the Anglican Communion. This fundamental principle of Anglicanism was soon to be emphasized and widely observed by many Broad Churchmen, but at this time it was offensive to Low Church Evangelicals.

The General Convention of 1874 was less wisely guided than that of 1871, for it yielded to the pressure of a series of memorials begging for canonical action on the subject of ritual. After prolonged debate, which might more profitably have been devoted to such central themes as Christian education or foreign missions, there was passed an extensive amendment to Canon 20 ("Of the Use of the Book of Common Prayer"). Since this bit of legislation constitutes the only attempt of the Church to control ritual details by canon, its main sections ought to be quoted.

"If any Bishop have reason to believe, or if complaint be made to him in writing by two or more of his Presbyters, that within his jurisdiction ceremonies or practices not ordained or authorized in the Book of Common Prayer, and setting forth or symbolizing erroneous or doubtful doctrines, have been introduced by any Minister during the celebration of the Holy Communion (such as,

"a.) The elevation of the Elements in the Holy Communion in such a manner as to expose them to the view of the people as objects toward which adoration is to be made.

"b.) Any act of adoration of or toward the Elements in the Holy Communion, such as bowings, prostrations, or genuflections; and

"c.) All other like acts not authorized by the Rubrics of the Book of Common Prayer):

"It shall be the duty of such Bishop to summon the Standing Committee as his Council of Advice, and with them to investigate the matter.

"If, after investigation, it shall appear to the Bishop and Standing Committee that ceremonies or practices not ordained or authorized as aforesaid, . . . have in fact been introduced as aforesaid, it shall be the duty of the Bishop, by instrument of writing under his hand, to admonish the Minister so offending to discontinue such practices or ceremonies; and if the Minister shall disregard such admonition, it shall be the duty of the Standing Committee to cause him to be tried for a breach of his ordination vow."

For thirty years this canon remained in force without producing any perceptible effect upon the steady advance of ritual. Apparently it resulted in only one trial, which ended in an admonition to the offender. In 1904 it was repealed by General Convention without one dissenting voice.

This canonical amendment, however, was not the only action of the Convention of 1874 which was prompted by its aversion to ritualism. The House of Deputies, entirely on the ground that he was a ritualist, refused to confirm the election of the Rev. George F. Seymour as Bishop of Illinois.[2] During the following triennium, moreover, the Standing Committees of the dioceses declined to ratify the election of Dr. De Koven as Bishop of Illinois. But this endeavor to make certain that Anglo-Catholics should never become bishops proved to be only a passing phase in the development of the Church. Within four years Seymour had become

[2] On the same principle which had postponed his own consecration to the episcopate, Bishop Seymour later exerted himself to prevent the consecration of Phillips Brooks. He disapproved of his beliefs.

Bishop of Springfield, and within fifteen years the leader of the extreme wing of Anglo-Catholics, Charles C. Grafton, had been consecrated Bishop of Fond du Lac. By 1880, in fact, the General Convention showed so few signs of party spirit and spent so much time in planning for the expansion of the Church that the historian, Bishop William Stevens Perry, calls it "the missionary Convention." The only project which always caused division along party lines was the proposal to change the name of the Church so that it should no longer include the term "Protestant." In one form or another resolutions to this effect appeared in every Convention for the rest of the century, but they were all defeated.

In this decade of the 'seventies the Anglo-Catholic group was not the only center of agitation. On the opposite wing there was also trouble. Ever since the days of organization eighty years earlier Low Churchmen had objected to the idea of baptismal "regeneration" as expressed in the Prayer Book. As theological thought was not their strong point, most of them could interpret this conception only as meaning an instantaneous moral change in the recipient of Baptism. Since they were rightly convinced that no such change took place, their consciences were disturbed by the need to use the language of the Sacrament. At times, therefore, they avoided this difficulty by omitting the words "regenerate" and "regeneration." Such deviation from the ritual of the Church was as commonly overlooked as were the deviations of High Churchmen. But in February, 1871, the Rev. Charles E. Cheney, rector of Christ Church, Chicago, was brought to trial for this offence by Bishop Whitehouse and suspended from the exercise of the ministry. When he disregarded the sentence he was tried again and deposed.

Cheney was a gifted and influential leader, and his deposition aroused indignation among many who would not have followed his example. A group of fellow-Evangelicals, including two future bishops (Jaggar and McVickar), five seminary professors, and several prominent rectors, wrote him a letter of sympathy and encouragement in which they asserted that he had a right to do what he did and that many others were in the habit of amending the Office of Baptism. To prevent further trouble by allaying the fears of Low Churchmen, the House of Bishops at the General Convention of 1871 decided to issue a declaration on the subject of baptismal regeneration. The action, of course, was not official, for the House of Bishops is not authorized to utter formal pronouncements upon doctrine. But it was none the less useful. It took the form of a statement signed by forty-eight bishops of all parties:

"We, the subscribers, Bishops of the Protestant Episcopal Church in the United States, being asked, in order to the quieting of the consciences of sundry members of the said Church, to declare our conviction as to the meaning of the word 'Regenerate' in the Offices for the Ministration of Baptism of Infants, do declare that, in our opinion, the word 'Regenerate' is not there so used as to determine that a moral change in the subject of Baptism is wrought in the Sacrament."

The Cheney trial was unfortunately only a symptom of growing discontent among certain Low Churchmen, which was too deep and varied to be dispelled by any statement about Baptism. Between the Conventions of 1871 and 1874 it was brought to a head by an actual schism led by the Rt. Rev. George D. Cummins, Assistant Bishop of Kentucky. A growing accumulation of irritants moved Bishop Cummins to lead his group out of the Church. Since his consecration in 1866 he had become increasingly disturbed by the growth of ritualism permitted by his diocesan—Bishop Benjamin Bosworth Smith, who became Presiding Bishop in 1868. He deplored the failure of General Convention to legislate against the Anglo-Catholics. The deposition of Cheney added to his resentment, and the last straw was contributed by an incident in New York which occurred in October, 1873. At that time, as part of the program of an international gathering of the Evangelical Alliance, Cummins participated in the celebration of the Lord's Supper in a Presbyterian Church. In protest against this action the English Bishop of Zanzibar, who was then in New York, took it upon himself to write a letter of protest to Bishop Horatio Potter; but, though others joined in condemning Cummins, no official steps were taken against him.

In spite of the fact that no one was trying to remove him from the Episcopal Church, Bishop Cummins decided that for him, and presumably for many others, the Episcopal Church was no longer a fit home. On November 10, 1873, he wrote to Bishop Smith announcing his "purpose of transferring his work and office to another sphere." Three weeks later he met in New York with eight clergy and nineteen laymen and took the actions necessary to inaugurate a separate Church. The name agreed upon was "The Reformed Episcopal Church" and the Prayer Book adopted was the "Proposed Book" of 1785. Cummins was elected Presiding Bishop and later consecrated Dr. Cheney as bishop. But whatever the reformers may have expected, there was no general exodus from the mother Church.[3] Cummins was brought to trial and deposed from his office and from the ministry in June, 1874, and the action was later ratified by the House of Bishops at their meeting in the following October. Even among the Evangelicals he received little sympathy. Liberals like Phillips Brooks and Low

[3] By 1890, when the Episcopal Church had about half a million communicants, the Reformed Episcopal Church had 8,500, distributed in 84 churches in 12 States. In 1926, after 53 years of existence, it had 69 churches and 8,651 communicants in the U.S. There were also 25 congregations in England.

Churchmen like Stephen Tyng deplored his action as certain to accomplish no good.

Not being true Anglicans in spirit, Cummins and his followers could not endure the tension which characterizes a comprehensive Church. Essentially sectarian in their conception of the Church, they could be satisfied with nothing short of uniformity. They departed not because their own convictions had been declared heretical but because they thought the Church was not energetic enough in suppressing convictions which they opposed. The Declaration of Principles which they issued gives prominence to the positive statement that "this Church [i.e. the Reformed Episcopal Church] recognizes and adheres to Episcopacy, not as of divine right but as a very ancient and desirable form of church polity." But its negative character appears in the list of doctrines which are condemned. These include the teaching "(1) that the Church of Christ exists only in one order or form of ecclesiastical polity; (2) that Christian ministers are 'priests' in another sense than that in which all believers are 'a royal priesthood'; (3) that the Lord's Table is an altar on which the oblation of the Body and Blood of Christ is offered anew to the Father; (4) that the presence of Christ in the Lord's Supper is a presence in the elements of Bread and Wine; (5) that Regeneration is inseparably connected with Baptism."

These are doctrines all of which were then condemned by all Low Churchmen and some of which were disapproved by some High Churchmen. Yet the seceders were not content that their beliefs should be shared by so many. They could breathe freely only in a body where there were none to disagree.

Aided rather than otherwise by this unnecessary schism, the Catholic movement continued to grow in range and influence. Vestments and usages once regarded as objectionably Roman became widely accepted before 1900 in all but the most conservative Low Church areas. Meantime ever new advances were made, introducing such forms of worship as the invocation of saints and the service of Benediction. To promote the spread of Catholic teaching *The Living Church* was established in 1878, and nine years later appeared the first branches of "The Clerical Union for the Maintenance and Defense of Catholic Principles," commonly known as "The Catholic Club." Its stated objects were the defence of the Church against latitudinarianism and rationalistic assaults, the defence of the Catholic claims of the Anglican Communion against Roman denials, and an increased emphasis upon Eucharistic worship.

To Catholic influence we may attribute the development of cathedrals during this period. In no narrow sense were they ever a party project, and their growth has been furthered by many who were far from being Anglo-Catholics. Yet in promoting the dignity and influence of bishops and enhancing the beauty of worship they may be held to emphasize the Catholic rather than the Protestant aspect of Anglicanism. Among the earliest to be founded were those in the dioceses of Chicago, Minnesota, and Iowa. Later came the cathedrals in Garden City, Long Island, and in Albany. In 1892 there was laid the cornerstone of the great cathedral of St. John the Divine in New York City and in 1907 that of the cathedral in Washington. American cathedrals, it is true, often lacked the marks of a real cathedral and ignored many Anglican traditions. Most of them were simply parish churches with a few labels changed. But in course of time some have emerged to proclaim by example the unique contribution which a cathedral can make as an active diocesan centre freed of parochial obligations, and as "a house of prayer for all people."

Entirely Catholic both in origin and in influence were the monastic orders for men and women which arose during the second half of the century. The earliest permanent order for men was the Society of St. John the Evangelist in the founding of which an American was associated. In 1865, a young priest, Charles C. Grafton, who had been brought up in the Church of the Advent in Boston, went to England to seek help and guidance in founding a religious order. An Eton tutor whom he met, the Rev. S. W. O'Neill, joined him in asking the Rev. R. M. Benson to act as their Superior in establishing a community at Cowley, near Oxford. After living together for about a year the three men took the monastic vows of poverty, celibacy, and obedience, and the "Cowley Fathers" began their history. During the next few years a number of Englishmen and several Americans joined the Order. Upon the invitation of the Parish of the Advent in Boston, Grafton became rector of the church in 1872 and headed the Society's work in this country. Four years later Father Oliver Prescott, another American, assumed the rectorship of St. Clement's Church in Philadelphia where he was assisted by other members of the Society.

In the course of time tension developed between American and English members of the Order. As Superior, Father Benson demanded absolute obedience, but the American Fathers recognized that this occasionally conflicted with the obedience which they owed to the bishops in the United States. Impatient, moreover, at the postponement of the granting of autonomy, they secured release from the Society in 1882. As a result of this controversy the growth and reputation of the Society in this country suffered injury. Not until 1914 did an American Congregation come into existence, and it was another ten years before an American became its Superior. Since then the Society has developed its works from its Mother

House in Cambridge, Massachusetts, and has nurtured a Province in Japan and an autonomous Congregation in Canada—signs of the renewed vitality of the Order.

Wholly indigenous in origin is the other leading monastic order in the Episcopal Church—the Order of the Holy Cross, founded by the Rev. James O. S. Huntington, son of Bishop Frederic D. Huntington of Central New York. In the autumn of 1881, with two other priests who had lived for some time at Cowley, Huntington was at work in the Holy Cross Mission in New York City, living in the slums of the East Side. He was an ardent social reformer, and the original aim of the future Order was to practice the social gospel among the underprivileged. Not yet prepared to take vows, the three men began their novitiate in what they already called the Order of the Holy Cross. Within three years his two companions had withdrawn, but Huntington in November, 1884, took the three-fold vow before Bishop Henry C. Potter of New York. For participating in this ceremony Potter encountered a storm of criticism. The heaviest attack was delivered by the Presiding Bishop, Alfred Lee of Delaware, who expressed "astonishment and distress" and who referred to sacerdotal celibacy as having "a history of shame, suffering and sin." Much to his assailant's surprise, Potter defended himself vigorously on the ground, among other reasons, that he did not regard the Reformation as the last word in Christian development, and that poverty, celibacy, and obedience were not inconsistent with the Christian life. So rapidly, however, does Church opinion sometimes change that only thirteen years later the Lambeth Conference passed a resolution in which the bishops recognized "with thankfulness the revival alike of Brotherhoods and Sisterhoods, . . . in our branch of the Church."

For two years Huntington was the only member of the Order, and when in 1892 he moved to a little monastery in Maryland, he had only one companion. Thenceforward, however, the numbers gradually increased. In 1904 the present monastery at West Park on the Hudson was occupied, and within two years Father Sill had founded the Kent School in Connecticut and Father Allen St. Andrew's School in the mountains of eastern Tennessee. In 1922, in their first adventure overseas, the Holy Cross fathers established what is now the thriving mission at Bolahun in Liberia.

Sisterhoods began in England twenty years before there was a religious order for men. In 1845 a little group of women formed a sisterhood in London for work among the poor, and another group with the same purpose established at Devonport in 1848 the Society of the Sisters of Mercy. Both were under the patronage and guidance of Dr. Pusey. Neither community, however, demanded lifelong vows, nor did either of them prove permanent. But within a few years full-fledged sisterhoods appeared, of which the earliest were the Community of St. Mary the Virgin at Wantage and the Sisterhood of St. Margaret at East Grinstead.

Since we may count the group of "sisters" in Muhlenberg's church and hospital as more like deaconesses than nuns, the first monastic community of women in the American Church was the Sisterhood of St. Mary founded in New York in 1865, an order which now has its center at Peekskill, New York. In its eastern and western provinces the sisters conduct schools for girls and hospitals for children; and Sagada in the Philippines owes much to their ministry. Affiliated with the English Societies of the same name are the Society of St. Margaret established in Boston in 1873 and the Community of St. John Baptist (1881) whose mother-house is at Ralston, New Jersey. The Sisterhood of the Holy Nativity was founded by Grafton in 1882. Though its center is in Fond du Lac its members are at work in seven States. Of more recent origin are the Community of the Transfiguration (1898)—the first sisterhood to send nuns to the foreign field—and the Order of St. Anne (1910).

Small associations of women workers who might be described as deaconesses had been formed in New York, Philadelphia, and Mobile, Alabama, in earlier years; but no official notice was taken of this Order until 1871, when, upon motion of Dr. W. R. Huntington of New York, a joint committee was appointed by General Convention to investigate and report on "the expediency of reviving in this Church the primitive order of deaconesses." The course of legislative progress was so slow, chiefly owing to the doubts and fears of Evangelicals, that no canon was adopted until eighteen years later by the Convention of 1889. As expanded and improved on subsequent occasions, this canon now supplies, in its first two sections, an excellent summary of what deaconesses are and what they do.

"A woman of devout character and proved fitness, unmarried or widowed, may be appointed Deaconess by any Bishop of this Church, subject to the provisions of this canon. Such appointment shall be vacated by marriage.

"The duty of a Deaconess is to assist in the work of the Parish, Mission, or institution to which she may be appointed, under the direction of the Rector or Priest in charge. . . .

"The following are the chief functions which may be entrusted to a Deaconess:

1.) To care for the sick, the afflicted, and the poor;

2.) To give instruction in the Christian faith;

3.) Under the Rector or the Priest in charge, to prepare candidates for Baptism and for Confirmation;

4.) To assist at the administration of Holy Baptism and in the absence of the Priest or Deacon to baptize infants;

5.) Under the Rector or Priest in charge to organize, superintend, and carry out the Church's work among women and children;

6.) With the approval of the Bishop and the incumbent, to read Morning and Evening Prayer (except such portions as are reserved for the Priest) and the Litany in Church or Chapel in the absence of the Minister; and when licensed by the Bishop to give instruction or deliver addresses at such services;

7.) To organize and carry on social work; and in colleges and schools to have a responsible part in the education of women and children, and to promote the welfare of women students."

So reluctant was the Church to make any canonical provision for monastic orders (and thereby to recognize their legitimate existence) that it was not until 1913 that General Convention adopted the canon dealing with "Religious Communities" of men and women. Its provisions are chiefly concerned with making certain that such communities shall recognize the doctrine, discipline, and worship of the Church as of supreme authority, that they shall not be established in any diocese without the consent of the bishop, and that the bishop shall be given extensive powers of supervision.

Chapter XV

THE CHURCH AND EDUCATION

IN the 'sixties and 'seventies of the nineteenth century there was little educational progress in the United States, but the next two decades saw a veritable educational renaissance.[1] "Despite all setbacks and shortcomings the educational advance during the 1880's and 1890's was astonishing. All parts of the country and all classes of society were affected. Through the spread of schools, bookstores, libraries, magazines, and newspapers America had become . . . 'the land of the general reader,' the home of the greatest reading public known in the history of the world." [2]

The progress of the Church in promoting Christian education was slow, and its ineffective measures were unequal to the expanding opportunities of the age. Not until the very end of the century did the national Church or the dioceses take energetic steps to bring the Church abreast of the rising educational standards in secular life.

The official contribution of the national Church was meager enough. It consisted of a report presented every three years by a Committee on Christian Education appointed by General Convention. The time consumed in preparing these reports was limited to the days when the Convention was in session. Partly for this reason and partly because few of the members of these committees were experts in education, the reports were not often valuable. They consisted of nine parts of handsome language and one part of oft repeated recommendations. They generally dwelt fervently upon such truths as that "Christian education must begin at home" and that "the first educator is the parent." Beyond the home the chief remedy proposed in the four Conventions which followed the close

[1] To cite only three results, in 1878 there were less than 800 high schools; in 1898 there were 5,500. Between 1880 and 1900 the percentage of illiteracy dropped from 17 to 11. By 1900 there were 9,000 public libraries.

[2] A. M. Schlesinger, *The Rise of the City,* 201.

of the war was to multiply Church institutions. Let there be more parochial grammar-schools, more Church boarding-schools, more Church colleges. Parents are reproached for not sending their sons to Church institutions and are urged to give liberally to no others. By 1877 the Committee had decided that there was less need for increasing the number of Church schools and colleges than for improving their quality. Yet as late as 1880 the main theme of exhortation was that the Church "must surround and guard her children in *all* their training with the instruction and influence of religion." They must be *protected* from infancy to manhood from the evil influences of purely secular education. The fact that few parents were willing to adopt this protection theory of education could only be deplored.

Conscious perhaps that for some time past there had been much talk and little action, the General Convention of 1886 adopted a resolution instructing the standing committees on Christian Education of both Houses, acting as a joint committee, "to devise and report to this General Convention such ways and means as may seem to them most effective for giving practical force to some or all of the recommendations and suggestions touching this great interest which have been reported to the General Convention at sundry times during the past twenty years." But this combined wisdom proved equal to no more than the proposal that the endowments of Church schools and colleges should be increased and that their heads should meet at intervals for joint action. Three years later the next Convention established "The Church University Board of Regents," the aim of which was to promote education under the auspices of the Church and to receive and distribute benefactions to that end. After nine years (1898) this Board was dissolved, having accomplished little more than the provision of money for a few scholarships.

Between 1866 and 1900 the number of Sunday school scholars increased from 158,000 to 430,000, and the number of teachers from 18,000 to 46,000, a rate of progress much slower than that which marked the growth in communicant membership. The advance of these schools, however, both in quantity and in quality, was due almost wholly to parochial initiative and energy, for in this age neither the national Church nor the dioceses provided any aid or guidance beyond occasional words of criticism or counsel. The Committee on Christian Education of General Convention voiced in 1865 the familiar complaint of the lack of trained teachers, together with the much needed advice that the Sunday school should be kept subordinate to the Church and that the rector should assume full responsibility. Even at this early date the Committee made the original suggestion that the Protestant ministers in any locality should arrange with school authorities for children to be released for one or two hours a week to receive religious instruction from their pastors—a plan which was to bear fruit in the next century.

In default of any adequate organization, national or diocesan, there was organized in 1884 the American Church Sunday School Institute, of which branches were later formed in many dioceses. The general purpose of the Institute was to stimulate and inspire rather than to administer, and its aims were stated to be: "to form a bond of union between the 350,000 children in our Sunday schools and the 22,000 teachers"; to create enthusiasm for Sunday school work; and to "find appliances for the work of the Sunday school teacher." As an official organ there soon appeared *The American Church Sunday School Magazine.*

As late as 1892 and 1895 the Committee on Christian Education, declaring that most Sunday schools were poor and most teachers unfitted, could still only plead that the Catechism should be used more frequently and that more parochial schools and boarding-schools should be established. The one novel, forward-looking suggestion offered was that a Normal Department for teacher training should be created in at least one of the Church colleges. It was not to General Convention, then, that we owe the initial impulse to the intelligent enthusiasm which has marked the Church's reform of its education in the twentieth century. It was in the dioceses that this modern movement began, with New York in the lead.

Bishop Henry C. Potter appointed in 1898 a diocesan Sunday School Commission to recommend improvements in religious education. Its first chairman and foremost leader was the Rev. Pascal Harrower. The guiding principle which it adopted was that since the Sunday school is primarily a *school,* it must use modern methods of education and organization already approved in secular schools. To train teachers was the commission's first and most valuable undertaking. Courses of lectures for them were offered not only in such subjects as the Bible and the Prayer Book but also in child study and pedagogy. In the course of the next few years, by means of extension classes in various churches, as many as three hundred teachers were equipped with new ideals and new methods. A standard curriculum was composed and more than twenty manuals were prepared to implement it. So widely recognized were the successful operations of this New York group that other dioceses soon followed its example by the action either of bishops or of diocesan conventions. Within six years twenty-one dioceses, beginning with Long Island, Connecticut, and Michigan, had formed active commissions.

The need for more and better Church boarding-schools for boys and girls, often voiced at General Conventions, was so generally felt that during the years between the Civil War and the end of the century many such schools were founded. At least fifty of them are still active in various sections of the country. As only a few examples among the better known and more influential institutions for boys we may cite St. Mark's (1865) and Groton (1884) in Massachusetts, and for girls St. Agnes' (1870) in Albany, New York, Chatham Hall (1894) in Virginia, and the National Cathedral School in Washington (1900). The achievements of the Church schools in relation to Christian education and to the growth and welfare of the Church is difficult to estimate. On the whole, most of them have been more distinguished, at their best, for maintaining high moral standards and a fine spirit than for inculcating permanent devotion to the Church. Their chief contribution has been to stand for the truth, by teaching and by example, that education which leaves out God is not only defective but ultimately sterile.

During the last thirty-five years of the nineteenth century there was a phenomenal growth in the field of higher education.[3] Not only did the number of colleges increase rapidly with every decade but college after college expanded to university proportions. In many cases the educational world was none the better for the multiplication of little denominational colleges, especially in the South and Middle West. It was, indeed, only a very local patriot who proudly declared that "there are two universities in England, four in France, ten in Prussia, and thirty-seven in Ohio." But in this generation arose such great institutions as the Massachusetts Institute of Technology (1865), Johns Hopkins in Baltimore (1876), Leland Stanford in California (1885), and the University of Chicago (1892). It was the period, too, of the remarkable expansion of State universities, of which those in California, Michigan, Illinois, Minnesota, and Wisconsin have remained foremost. By the end of the century four out of every five colleges and universities admitted women; and Smith, Bryn Mawr, Vassar, and other colleges were offering to women the highest quality of training.

That the colleges identified with the Episcopal Church should be able to maintain high rank in the face of this intense competition was more than could be expected. Compared with the best universities or even with the best small colleges, their *academic* standing (according to varying circumstances) was anywhere from second-rate to fifth-rate. Racine College in Wisconsin (founded in 1852) was of collegiate grade for only a brief time. Kenyon, through internal strife and lack of support, never regained prosperity until the turn of the century. St. Stephen's College at Annandale-on-the-Hudson was founded in 1860, under the leadership of Bishop Horatio Potter, by the liberality of John Bard. Its primary aim

[3] In the twenty years between 1878 and 1898 colleges and universities in the U.S. increased in number from 350 to 500 and their students from 58,000 to 100,000.

was to prepare men for entrance to theological schools, preferably for the General Seminary. It added to the number, without greatly enhancing the reputation of Church colleges. Of Hobart, Trinity, and the University of the South at Sewanee, the three stronger institutions, we may say what a committee of General Convention said in 1898 of the Church colleges in the North: "They are good colleges, but they are not good enough for this Church." Yet they were to show renewed vitality and rising standards in the generation to come.

Though at this time the official remedy for keeping young men attached to the Church was to send them to Church institutions, there are occasional signs that the Church's duty toward the thousands of youths who had to brave the supposed perils of secular colleges was not forgotten. We can note here and there the earliest stirrings of those plans and purposes which have since matured in what we now call "college work." As far back as 1877 the committee which we have often quoted declared that "we should endeavor in every collegiate town to secure for pastor the man who is best fitted by nature and acquirements to reach and influence the fresh young life around him. . . . [The Church] should have a strong post in every seat of learning in this country." Twenty-one years later in more specific terms it was pointed out that "it is of strategic importance to the Church that the altar, the pulpit, and the parish house of the academic town shall be attractive and profitable to the students." Such parishes should be endowed, because "the clergyman must be a man of such character and scholarship as shall commend him to the respect and regard of the community." It was to be another thirty and more years before this wise advice was carried into action on an effective scale.

The adoption in 1889 of the canon on deaconesses added to the educational responsibilities of the Church. It had been decreed that deaconesses must be adequately prepared for their vocation, and it therefore became necessary to provide for their training. To satisfy this new requirement there were established in 1891 two schools which have since contributed hundreds of women to the parochial and missionary work of the Church: St. Faith's—the Training School for Deaconesses in New York—and the Church Training and Deaconess House in Philadelphia. In 1908 the Deaconess Training School of the Pacific (St. Margaret's House) was organized at Berkeley, California. As in course of time a larger number of women sought professional training for the service of the Church without becoming deaconesses, these schools have enlarged their scope and membership to meet this demand.

In the epoch we are reviewing, the theological schools presented a highly variegated pattern in size, wealth, standards, atmosphere, and reputation. During the 'sixties and 'seventies the General Seminary encountered such heavy financial difficulties that it barely succeeded in surviving, and its academic standards were almost as low as its income. But with the coming in 1879 of the Rev. Eugene A. Hoffman as dean the seminary began to be prosperous. Largely owing to his efficiency and to the generosity of the Hoffman family, the endowment had reached a million and a quarter dollars by 1900, and the building program had so far advanced that the plant had assumed very nearly its present form. Yet not until the twentieth century brought new leadership did intellectual progress keep pace with material growth.

The Virginia Seminary, after recovering from the effects of the war, continued to supply the Church with most of its foreign missionaries, inspired by the ardent evangelical spirit of the institution. Here, too, theological development was not encouraged. It was in 1876, for example, that the Trustees requested the Professor of Systematic Divinity to require his students to commit to memory the Thirty-nine Articles and all the proof texts in Knapp's handbook of theology. At the other end of the scale Nashotah had outgrown its status as a merely diocesan seminary and under the influence of Grafton, Seymour, and other bishops stood out clearly as the representative of the most advanced Anglo-Catholicism. Bexley Hall was no stronger than its parent Kenyon, and the Seabury Divinity School, though active especially in training valuable men for diocesan and domestic missions, lacked the means for further development. The school in Philadelphia moved into new buildings and added more than one distinguished scholar to its staff. The Berkeley Divinity School had been founded at Middletown, Connecticut, by Bishop John Williams in 1854, and remained in safe-keeping with the bishop as dean for the rest of the century. To an ever growing degree it served the Church outside its own diocese.

Four new seminaries were created during the first three decades after the war. The Episcopal Theological School at Cambridge, beginning in 1867, long enjoyed what many regarded as the doubtful distinction of being the only school to welcome modern biblical scholarship and to teach its results freely. The School of Theology in the University of the South opened its doors in 1878 and soon shared with the Virginia Seminary in the training of clergy chiefly for the Southern dioceses by which it was owned and controlled. In 1885 the Western Theological Seminary was inaugurated in Chicago by Bishop William E. McLaren. As a dominating and intractable dean he followed so closely the bad example of Bishop Chase in early days at Gambier that the school had nearly disintegrated by the time of his death in 1905. Skillful leadership has since raised it to high rank. Youngest of the seminaries is the Church Divinity School of the Pacific organized in 1893 by Bishop William Ford Nichols of California. In 1900 its past was brief, but to the eye of faith its future was promising.

Though there were more than enough schools for educating men before ordination, the agencies for educating them thereafter were few, since in those days there were no Summer Conferences or College of Preachers. The most valuable institution for stimulating and guiding thought was the Church Congress. This organ of opinion was formed, chiefly by a group of Broad Churchmen, in the year 1874 when party feeling was inflamed. It was dedicated to the proposition that the Episcopal Church was comprehensive enough to include highly divergent types and that intellectual liberty and freedom of discussion should be encouraged and provided for by practical organization. The first meeting in New York, at which Bishop Whipple of Minnesota presided, included representatives of all groups and parties and proved highly rewarding. The chance to meet unofficially and to confer and debate with no thought of voting proved welcome to all concerned. Among the topics at this first session were: The Limits of Legislation as to Doctrine and Ritual, The Relation of the Church to other Christian Bodies, and the Mutual Obligations of Capital and Labor. The committee which directed the Church Congress during the next twenty-five years remained alert to the changing needs of the times and never failed to afford succeeding Congresses (generally annual) the opportunity to debate questions that were currently acute—The Ministrations of the Church to the Working Classes, Socialism, The Interpretation of the Bible in relation to the Present Condition of Learning and Science, The Positive Gains in Biblical Criticism, and The Use and Abuse of Ritual. From that day to this the papers and addresses of each meeting have been published as valuable aids to education in their time and useful sources for future historians.

In the production of religious literature of permanent value the Episcopal Church was weak. Its clergy lacked the leisure and the rich academic background which their brothers in England put to such good use. Then, as now, thoughtful readers often turned to British writers for nourishment. Yet there were a few books of which the influence, and even the sales, lasted for more than a generation—books such as William Reed Huntington's *The Church Idea* (1870) and Phillips Brooks's *Lectures on Preaching* (1878). In the field of scholarship the deficiency of the Church was even more marked, for it can be said in all fairness that there were hardly more than two of its scholars whose work was known and valued abroad. When Alexander V. G. Allen of the Theological School in Cambridge wrote *The Continuity of Christian Thought* (1884) it was hailed in England as "the most significant book on theology so far written by an American." And William Porcher Du Bose at Sewanee, who wrote *The Soteriology of the New Testament* (1892) was described by the Oxford scholar Sanday as "the wisest Anglican writer on both sides of the Atlantic."

If the Church had not yet reached that stage of maturity when the ripe scholarship characteristic of the Church of England should no longer be rare, it had at least one advantage over the Mother Church. Not being dependent upon the vote of Parliamentary majorities, it could revise its Prayer Book at will. Before that attempt was made, however, General Convention had taken several steps in the easier process of revising the Hymnal. Both series of actions may properly be counted as part of the educational progress of the time.

For some years before the war the music of the Church had been tending to get out of control. An English observer in the 'forties remarked that "the love of variety creates a constant change in the selection of chants, anthems, and meter psalm tunes, in which a correct ecclesiastical taste is more the exception than the rule." Some ten years later a Pastoral Letter of the House of Bishops included these words of warning: "We cannot . . . regard it as anything short of a most grievous and dangerous inconsistency when the house of prayer is desecrated by a choice of music and a style of performance which are rather suited to the Opera than to the Church." Again, resolutions of the House of Bishops in 1859 record the conviction that rectors should control the music of the services and do all in their power to produce a spirit of devotion and to promote congregational singing. Finally, at a time when artistic taste of every kind was at its lowest, the General Convention of 1874 passed a canon, "Of the Music of the Church," which is substantially that now in force. It protected the clergy from over-ambitious organists and choirs by these clear provisions: "It shall be the duty of every Minister of this Church, with such assistance as he may see fit to employ from persons skilled in music, to give order concerning the tunes to be sung at any time in his Church, and especially it shall be his duty to suppress all light and unseemly music, and all indecency and irreverence in the performance. . . ."

Meantime changes which served to expand the Hymnal had been adopted. The General Convention of 1865 set forth sixty additional hymns for use in public worship, and the Convention of 1871 approved the first hymnal which can be called strictly official, since it banned all others. It was likewise the first thorough revision in half a century, retaining only 135 out of the original 212, keeping two-thirds of the "additional hymns," and adding 241 wholly new ones—to produce a total of 496. Unlike the twentieth century Hymnals this version contained no tunes, so that various musical editions were soon in circulation. The last revision of the century, approved by the Convention of 1892, was destined to last for the next twenty-four years.

There could scarcely be a more valuable contribution to religious literature than a wise and temperate revision of the *Book of Common Prayer*. Such a revision, though very slight in extent, was initiated at the General Convention of 1880 by the Rev. William R. Huntington, who offered a resolution calling for a joint committee to consider Prayer Book revision "in the direction of liturgical enrichment and increased flexibility." The language was diplomatically chosen to avoid opposition from many who still believed that it was to remain forever impossible to *change* the book. Thenceforward the revision owed more to the tact, learning, and patience of Dr. Huntington than to any other leader; but during the next twelve years all the proposals were widely discussed, and many shared in the process. The Convention of 1883 received from the committee the "Book Annexed," that is, a Prayer Book embodying all the changes recommended. These had been controlled by two guiding principles—that there should be no amendments prompted by doctrine and no alterations in the liturgy of the Holy Communion. Partly because of these conservative restrictions, most of the committee's proposals were adopted. Three years later, however, many of them were rejected, and even in 1889 no final action was taken. At length in the Convention of 1892 the new Prayer Book was approved, and it remained the Church's standard for the next thirty-six years.

The revision had been completed, in the most gratifying fashion, without arousing partisan animosity, nor was the cleavage of opinion along party lines. In fact, the only opposition to changing the book at all was voiced by a small group composed about equally of extreme High Churchmen and extreme Low Churchmen. Relatively few as were the changes authorized, they contributed both flexibility and enrichment.[4] Among examples of the former was the permission to omit on weekdays the Exhortation in Morning Prayer and the prayers after the third collect—liberties which might be taken with Evening Prayer even on Sundays. Additions which clearly served to enrich the book were the Penitential Office, the prayers For Missions and For the Unity of God's People, and the inclusion of the full *Benedictus*. Best of all was the restoration in Evening Prayer of the *Magnificat* and the *Nunc Dimittis,* of which the Church had unnecessarily deprived itself for a hundred years. And the Feast of the Transfiguration was now numbered among the holy days of the Church. In the collect for that day, composed by Dr. Huntington, we have a prayer unexcelled in beauty since the days of Cranmer.

[4] Two of the proposals failing in 1892 but adopted in 1928 were the short Absolution in Evening Prayer and the *Benedictus Es* in Morning Prayer.

"O God, who on the mount didst reveal to chosen witnesses thine only-begotten Son wonderfully transfigured, in raiment white and glistering; Mercifully grant that we, being delivered from the disquietude of this world, may be permitted to behold the King in his beauty, who with thee, O Father, and thee, O Holy Ghost, liveth and reigneth, one God, world without end."

Chapter XVI

MISSIONS: DOMESTIC AND FOREIGN

DURING the first half-century of its existence the Domestic and Foreign Missionary Society was not regulated by any canon, though its constitution had been approved by General Convention. At the Convention of 1871, however, a canon was enacted dealing with the Board of Missions, and in 1877 the canon was not only amended but expanded to include the constitution of the Society, so that the official missionary organization became solidly embedded in the legal structure of the Church. At that time the Board of Missions consisted of all the bishops of the Church and all the members for the time being of General Convention. In other words, once in three years General Convention met and acted in its capacity as the Board of Missions. To conduct operations between Conventions there was a Board of Managers; but even this reduced body included all the bishops in addition to fifteen presbyters and fifteen laymen elected triennially. This Board, as before, continued to administer its affairs through a Committee of Domestic Missions and a Committee of Foreign Missions, each with its executive secretary and treasurer. It was by these committees that most of the business was transacted.

The organization for conducting missionary activities was clumsy because it had been created when there were few bishops and few dioceses and all could be easily represented on the Board. To produce an executive body small enough for effective action was the motive of the constant tinkering with this canon which continued for the next forty years until the formation of the National Council. The most important change within the period before 1900 (brought about by actions in 1886 and 1892) resulted in three organs, named in order of diminishing size—the Board of Missions, the Missionary Council (meeting annually), and the Board of Managers. This last body, consisting of only forty-six voting members meeting every month, assumed the powers of the old Domestic and Foreign Committees.

More significant than any of these phases of reorganization was the founding of the Woman's Auxiliary to the Board of Missions. During the first fifty years after the establishment of the Missionary Society there had grown up a crop of little miscellaneous women's societies, each contributing to a particular branch of missionary endeavor—groups such as the Indians' Hope Committee of Philadelphia or the Ladies' Domestic Mission Relief Association of New York. To unify these scattered efforts and to create one strong body to represent all the women of the Church the Board of Missions in October, 1871 organized the Woman's Auxiliary. As reported by the Board in 1874, "The Woman's Auxiliary, a new department of the Board of Missions, aids the work of the different departments of the Board by means of parochial, city, and diocesan associations of ladies, formed for the purpose of raising money, forwarding boxes, and otherwise helping the mission of the Church." Twenty-one years later the bishops' Pastoral Letter declared, "We note with grateful commendation the constantly growing work of that efficient and generous helper of the Church's Missions, the Woman's Auxiliary." Throughout these first decades the wise and energetic leadership of Miss Mary A. Emery and Miss Julia C. Emery, who came from the diocese of Massachusetts, was a determining factor in the success of the movement.

To increase the opportunities and motives for giving to missions the Woman's Auxiliary established the United Thank Offering, with parochial and diocesan treasurers, a plan which eventually enlisted the efforts of so many thousands of women that by unnumbered small gifts the first triennial total of $2,188, presented to the General Convention of 1889, had grown to $107,000 in the Convention year of 1901. To expand the educative influence of the Auxiliary its leaders formed in 1889 a Junior Department, which aimed to unite many existing minor societies and to enlist the interest of both boys and girls of all ages. During its thirty years of existence it was mainly effective among girls. The other chief organizations for girls during this era were the Girls' Friendly Society (1877) and the Daughters of the King (1885). Though service to the Church and the advancement of Christ's Kingdom were their general aims, their most distinctive contribution was not directed toward the aid of domestic and foreign missions.

For men there was nothing corresponding to the Woman's Auxiliary. No doubt they supplied most of the money which financed the Church's missions. They may even have earned some of the cash that was dropped into the little blue boxes of the United Thank Offering. But they had no nation-wide organization that existed solely to serve as auxiliary to the Board of Missions. The largest and most widely known society for men was the Brotherhood of St. Andrew, first established at St. James's Church,

Chicago, in 1883. Its primary purpose has been to engage in personal work within the local parish—a good point for evangelism to begin; but even where its chapters have been most evidently alive, its influence upon missions at home or overseas has been only indirect.

Chiefly because so small a proportion of the men of the Church had any knowledge of missions or any interest in them, the contributions to the Board between 1868 and 1898 were not generous. Even in 1898 they amounted to no more than fifty-five cents per year per communicant. Those who continue to dream of a golden age in the past when giving to missions was widespread and lavish ought to read some of the Pastoral Letters of the House of Bishops. In 1883 the bishops asked, "Must there not be some illusion to account for the shameful selfishness and the wicked disobedience which in hundreds of whole parishes and tens of thousands of baptized persons hold back offerings from Christ, for the conversion of those for whom he died? The reproach of it is guilty enough to make men wonder that God does not remove the flameless candlestick out of its place." Nor was the situation any better three years later. "In spite of all our stupendous accumulations of wealth," ran the Letter of that year, "the impoverished missionary treasury of the Church threatens a reduction of the already meagre stipends of the pioneers of the Cross. . . . During the past triennium of our Church's life the action of this missionary spirit has not been so powerful or so constant, so regular or so vigorous, as to keep the wheels ever in motion and to justify larger enterprise of Missions." Again, in 1898 we read of "the painful evidences of wide indifference and of inadequate support." If the money was hard to get, so were the men. According to the bishops, writing in 1895, "It is the fault of much of our training for the ministry that it fails to produce the kind and number of clergy demanded by the Church for its missionary work at home and abroad. . . . To call for such men, and to call in vain, is the bitterest experience that can befall the Church."

It was, then, as the servant of a Church only half-awakened to the meaning of its divine commission that the Board of Missions directed with what resources it could command the Church's advance in America and overseas.

DOMESTIC

The West was still wild when the Civil War ended, and over wide areas it so remained for several decades. Throughout this immense area development was rapid. In the eight great Territories of Dakota, Montana, Wyoming, Idaho, Washington, Utah, New Mexico, and Indian Territory agriculture was coming more and more to rival mining and cattle ranching as the occupation of the steadily increasing inhabitants. By 1890 five of these eight territories had been admitted as States and their population had risen to 1,500,000 whites, drawn largely from the Middle West. "The census of 1890 officially recorded the passing of the frontier. Thenceforth there was to be no fringe of settlement in the United States, for the whole country belonged in the 'settled area,' though in some parts the settlement was still thin . . . [but] much of the West remained a frontier region for the Church long after it had ceased to be a frontier for population." [1]

Thanks to the initiative of General Convention, much prompter than in earlier years, and thanks still more to the leadership of several intrepid bishops, the Western record of the Church in this period calls less for apology than for applause. Typical of such initiative and leadership was the career of Daniel Sylvester Tuttle whose episcopate lasted for fifty-six years. In October, 1866, the House of Bishops chose him, when he was rector of Zion Church at Morris, New York, to be "Missionary Bishop of Montana with jurisdiction in Idaho and Utah." As he was still under thirty, his consecration could not take place until May 1, 1867. A few weeks later he set forth to explore his new district, which covered 340,000 square miles inhabited by no more than 155,000 souls.

Since the young missionary had never been west of Niagara the journey itself was an adventure. It was all the more exciting because beyond Nebraska there was then no railroad, and he had to proceed to Denver by stage. From there on June 14th he wrote to his wife, "How long we are to stay here I don't know. Under God's Providence it depends, first, on the Indians; second, on Wells Fargo & Co. The Indians have been stealing a hundred horses and murdering a dozen men between here and Salt Lake. At present Wells Fargo & Co. will not send stages." After two weeks delay he left for Salt Lake and reported on his arrival on July 3rd, "We rode day and night until Friday noon, having for more than a hundred and fifty miles through the hostile country an escort of three cavalrymen."

Utah had been organized as a Territory in 1850 and was not to be a State until 1896. At that time nine-tenths of its 100,000 inhabitans were Mormons, a circumstance which could not fail to retard the progress of the Church. Nor had the bishop any foundation on which to build, for the two missionaries who met him there had been in Salt Lake only six weeks. After making their acquaintance he paid a visit to the Mormon chief Brigham Young, who chatted with him courteously, conscious no doubt that there was nothing this young man could do to lessen the pros-

[1] W. W. Manross, *History of the American Episcopal Church,* 332 f. (Morehouse-Gorham Co., Copyright 1950.)

perity of the Latter Day Saints. "He is so powerful a man in everything here," wrote Tuttle, "and so unscrupulous a man, I fear, in most things, that my policy will be to have as little as possible to do with him."

Though Utah offered endless opportunities for work, Tuttle was Bishop of Montana, and it was not long before he set off for that northern area, a Territory which then had a population of only 30,000, a large fraction of it in the tough mining towns of Helena and Virginia City. "A mining community," so he declared, "is eminently excitable, unruly, defiant, without fear of God or man." When he reached Virginia City on July 19th he encountered a raw town only four years old, built mostly of logs. Every other business building was a saloon. He soon met a Roman Catholic priest and a Methodist preacher, but there were no Baptists or Presbyterians. By this time the Church could be proud of the fact that its bishops were genuine pioneers, for it had not always been true that they could be found several stages ahead of the Baptists.

After a trip to Helena and a longer visit in the autumn to Idaho City and Boise City in Idaho, Tuttle returned to Virginia City to spend the winter. "I was quartered in No. 6 in the 'Planters' House,' " he reported, "a corner bedroom seven feet by nine, without any stove. For these accommodations and board I paid $25 a week. . . . I was uneasy over personal expenses. I did not feel it right to spend $25 a week on my own living. Soon I found a log cabin to go into. It was empty and seemed abandoned, but I hunted up the person with whom the key had been left and I got the use of the cabin for nothing." That dreary dwelling might well symbolize the hardships of winter in Montana. When the worst months were over he acknowledged, "It is terribly dull here. People are woefully blue . . . I have just come home from service. We had full services, singing and all, but without the Holy Communion. . . . Five men and five women were present. The mud is deep and the air is cold." "In eight months of uninterrupted work," he confessed, "I did not find one single person to be confirmed." But he had succeeded in forming a Sunday school with four teachers and twenty-seven scholars. In the midst of these trials, on June 1, 1868, he received word of his election as Bishop of Missouri. Considering his prospects and surroundings in the Far West, it must have cost him a struggle to resist the call, but he gallantly declined it and settled down to eighteen more years in his wide domain. Henceforth, however, he was not to live alone. After a year and a half of separation he was overjoyed in the autumn of 1868 to be united once again with his wife and child, and the family spent the ensuing winter in Helena.

In a later account of these first years in the Northwest the *Portland Oregonian* gave an admirable account of the man and his work. "The good bishop might well have been appalled at the first view of his diocese.

It was an empire in extent, but it barely afforded him a single congregation. Afterwards, when he had planted the Church in a few of the chief centers of population, he had congregations a thousand miles apart, requiring weeks of painful and dangerous travel to reach them, for the hostile savages held sway on the plains, while bandits, more daring than the savages, and no less bloodthirsty, infested every mountain pass through which the lines of travel led. But never was a man better fitted by nature and grace for his high mission. Of heroic stature, in every physical sense a man among men, he had a heart for every fate and a courage and resolution equal to any demand. He entered into the lives of the people and made their troubles his own, and when the rude mountaineers, as they presently did, came to know this strong, brave, and gentle man, his fame went through the mountains and he became the beloved bishop." [2] He had the faculty, useful in Montana, of being beloved even by desperadoes, one of whom gave notice at this time to the populace of Helena—"He's full jewelled, and eighteen karats fine. He's a better man than Joe Floweree [a leading gambler]; he's the biggest and best bishop that ever wore a black gown, and the whitest man in these mountains. Whenever he chooses to go on a brimstone raid among the sinners in this gulch, he can do it, and I'll back him with my pile. He is the best bishop, and you can hear me howl." [3]

In the course of the year 1869 the bishop succeeded in establishing clergy at Helena and Virginia City, and the Tuttles then moved to Salt Lake City, which remained their home for the next sixteen years. The town was five times larger than any other in his jurisdiction, and the Mormon problem made it a center of difficulty as well as of population. His policy was to preach the Gospel with vigor but not to attack Mormonism. As one of his successors put it, "This Church aims not to convert Mormons but Mormonism," or, in the words of Bishop Edward L. Parsons, "to bring to bear upon the Mormon community those influences which would slowly eat away its peculiar tenets and bring it little by little closer to normal Christianity." By way of starting this slow process of education, Tuttle founded two institutions which are still flourishing—St. Mark's Hospital and Rowland Hall, a boarding and day school for girls. And Mormons not only used the hospital but even sent children to the school.

How cordial were the relations which he maintained with the Latter Day Saints, without yielding a single conviction, is witnessed not only by his own testimony but also by theirs. In later life he wrote of his days in Utah, "As bishop and missionary I asked no favors of the Mormon

[2] D. S. Tuttle, *Reminiscences,* 233 f.
[3] *Ibid.,* 236 f.

hierarchy and gave none. As neighbor and friend I strove to be neighborly and friendly. And there does not dwell in my memory today the recollection of one unkind personal action from them to me or from me to them."[4] When the bishop left Salt Lake the official Mormon newspaper had this to say: "Kind, courteous, and urbane, yet dignified and firm in his demeanor, he has made friends among people of various shades of opinion. Although very pronounced in his opposition to the 'Mormon' faith, he has not acted as an enemy to the 'Mormon' people. . . . He has not, like many of his cloth, used his ecclesiastical influence towards the oppression and spoliation of the Latter Day Saints, but has on many occasions borne testimony to their good qualities in public and in private. We respect a consistent antagonist."[5]

After Bishop Tuttle had had oversight of Montana for fourteen years the House of Bishops set it apart in 1880 as a separate missionary jurisdiction. During his episcopate he had held services in fifty-one places, and, as he said, had "wandered over the Territory widely, and never for a single mile upon a railroad." "The people of Montana seemed especially near and dear to me; I knew them nearly all by name and face." Bishop Leigh Richmond Brewer, his successor, then began a fruitful career of thirty-six years, and by 1900 the clergy had more than tripled and the number of communicants had increased sevenfold.

After another six years there came to Tuttle in 1886 a second call to the diocese of Missouri, and this time his decision was to accept. He knew how much was still left to accomplish, yet he could not but realize the results of twenty years' labor. When he came to Utah and Idaho the Church there had barely begun to exist; when he left those districts there were two parishes and thirteen organized missions, with twelve clergy and nearly a thousand communicants. And a message from Idaho spoke also for his devoted friends in Utah—"Your name is written upon the hearts and indelibly impressed upon the annals of the Church in Idaho." His episcopate in Missouri was to last for thirty-seven years, and for the last twenty years of that time he was, by seniority, Presiding Bishop.

A like story of courageous pioneering, of discouraging obstacles, of slow growth, but of ultimate achievement might be related of all the other western and southwestern districts. Though the scenery varied, and the types of population, the problems were much the same. Of Bishop Hare in the Dakotas we shall learn in another chapter; but there were others, too, whom the Church remembers with gratitude—bishops such as John M. Kendrick in Arizona and New Mexico, John F. Spalding in Colorado, and Ethelbert Talbot in Wyoming. Of the accelerating growth

[4] *Ibid.,* 251.
[5] *Ibid.,* 356.

in this region before the end of the century we may form some idea by noting that in eight western Territories and States [6] in 1880 the forces of the Church numbered 67 clergy and 3,800 communicants. In the same area in 1898 there were to be counted 174 clergy and 17,000 communicants.[7]

A vast area of nearly 600,000 square miles was added to the domain of the United States by the purchase of Alaska from Russia in 1867. Before that date the Russian Church had been active in the territory and thereafter a few English and Canadian missionaries became the earliest Protestant pioneers. As a missionary district Alaska may be roughly divided into three parts—the southern coast towns where the work is largely with Americans, the immense interior, especially the valleys of the Yukon and Tanana Rivers, where the Church can reach the Indians and a few Eskimos, and the more distant North beyond the Arctic Circle where the Eskimo villages and camps are scattered. But the divisions overlap, for far inland, as at Fort Yukon and Fairbanks there are settlements of our own people.

It was not until 1887 that the first Episcopal missionary, the Rev. John W. Chapman, began work among the Indians at Anvik, three hundred miles up the Yukon River. With sawmill and school and church he spent there a lifetime of selfless and arduous service. Three years later Dr. John B. Driggs launched an even more difficult mission among the Eskimos on the northwest coast at Point Hope; and in 1891 Tanana on the Yukon in central Alaska became the third center. At the General Convention of 1892 Alaska was constituted a missionary district but not until the next Convention did the House of Bishops elect as bishop the Rev. Peter Trimble Rowe. Long inured to missionary labor in northern Michigan, Rowe entered upon an episcopate of forty-seven years, during which his winning simplicity and stalwart heroism helped to make Alaska perhaps the most popular of all the missionary areas of the Church. After his first five years as leader, which included the famous gold rush to the Klondike, there were seven clergy and ten white lay-readers in the district, and the stations had grown in number to thirteen, including churches at Nome, Sitka, and Juneau.[8]

In the field of domestic missions no opportunity was greater and

[6] Montana, Utah, Idaho, Colorado, Wyoming, Oregon, Washington, and Nevada.

[7] The missionary jurisdictions were frequently regrouped by the House of Bishops, a series of changes not profitable to relate. Nor is it necessary in this book to note the numerous subdivisions of dioceses in this period, such as the separation of East Carolina from North Carolina in 1883. As part of the story of missions, however, it is well to record the stages by which missionary jurisdictions became dioceses: in 1868 Nebraska, in 1871 Arkansas, in 1887 Colorado, in 1889 Oregon; and in 1895 what was then the missionary jurisdiction of Northern Texas became the diocese of Dallas.

[8] Fifty years later there were only seventeen stations, including eight of these thirteen, but the communicants had increased from four or five hundred to more than two thousand.

none beset with more perplexing difficulties than work with the Negroes. When the Civil War brought an end to slavery it left in its place a race problem still unsolved. In 1880, after Reconstruction had ended, there were 6,000,000 Negroes in the former slave States and in 1900 these had increased to 8,000,000. In several States, in fact, they outnumbered the whites. One result of a situation so novel and abnormal was the disfranchisement of the colored man; another was the unchecked growth of the practice of lynching which between 1882 and 1898 resulted in sixteen hundred deaths. While laws and constitutions were being thus defied, there were evident at the same time increasing efforts to educate the Negro and to teach him to help himself. In this enterprise the highest achievements were those of Hampton Institute in Virginia, established in 1870 by General Samuel C. Armstrong, and Tuskegee Institute in Alabama founded and guided for thirty-four years by a former slave, Booker T. Washington. Thanks to these and other endeavors, by the end of the century one Negro in five owned his own home and the percentage of illiteracy recorded in 1880 had been almost cut in half.

From the point of view of all the Churches the most obvious phenomenon of these years was the rapid and heavy loss of Negro membership and the formation of many Negro churches, the immense majority being Baptist and Methodist. Few Negroes were Episcopalians, but these few never attempted to form a separate body. Parishes for colored people there were, but no Negro organization on a diocesan or national scale.

Work for and with the Negro, seldom pursued with vigor and always feebly supported, was largely carried on by the Southern dioceses and is part of diocesan history. The contribution of the national Church, which has only slowly increased in energy and intelligence, began in 1865 with the formation by General Convention, acting through the Board of Missions, of a "Commission of Home Missions to Colored People, to whom shall be committed the religious and other instruction of the freedmen," a body equipped with its own general agent and treasurer. Within a year its funds had made possible the opening of elementary schools for Negroes in five towns in Virginia and at five other points in the South, and by 1875 the number of these schools had risen to thirty-one. In 1898 the Commission on Work among the Colored People (which had become the successor of the earlier body) reported that out of an annual income of $55,000 it was giving aid to seventy-five colored clergy in thirty-four dioceses. Its slim resources—small indeed as representing the 700,000 communicants of the Church—were sufficient only to offer partial support to men and women in the field, but not enough to supply help to institutions. Yet even without such help private philanthropy, with diocesan assistance, was operating several valuable secondary schools for Negroes, of which the largest and most prosperous were St. Augustine's School at Raleigh, North Carolina, and St. Paul's School at Lawrenceville, Virginia. For the training of Negro clergy the trustees of the Virginia Seminary chartered in 1884 the Bishop Payne Divinity School at Petersburg, Virginia, which three years later began to offer instruction on a small scale. Yet between 1866 and 1880 only twenty-seven colored men had been ordained, of whom only seventeen were in the South.

FOREIGN

In its work in Latin America the Church is concerned with a population nominally Christian. Yet the need for what the Protestant and Anglican forces can give has been widespread and obvious. The Roman Catholic Church has long been the chief representative of religion in Latin America and has certain noble achievements to its credit. But throughout Central and South America and the West Indies that Church, to put it mildly, is not at its best. The dense ignorance of masses of the population and the indifference or hostility to religion of the greater part of the educated classes indicate that Christianity, as there known, has not proved an enlightening and vitalizing force. To the Episcopal Church, therefore, this call long since became clear, for in all its mission work it has aimed not only to appeal to the educated but to reach and train the untaught. To make Christianity real and living within large groups which have been either neglected or alienated has been a worthy purpose measurably accomplished.

After Mexico received in 1857 a new and liberal constitution separating Church and State and giving freedom of worship, opportunity opened for Protestants and Anglicans to supplement a Church which was showing every sign of degeneracy. Until 1877 the activity of the Episcopal Church was exercised through auxiliary agencies, like the American Church Missionary Society and the Mexican Missionary Society. Its contribution consisted in aiding several large reformed bodies which had begun to flourish under such titles as "The Mexican Catholic Apostolic Society." In 1875 the House of Bishops made a covenant with the largest of these groups, "The Church of Jesus," which then accepted the name "The Mexican Branch of the Catholic Church" and agreed to terms by which bishops might be consecrated. After another two years the Board of Missions decided to support the enterprise, and in 1879 the Rev. Henry C. Riley, who had long been a leader in the reform movement, was consecrated bishop by seven bishops of the Episcopal Church. At this time the Church to which he ministered had fifty organized congregations and 3,500 communicants. Riley, however, after five years of incompetent administration, was obliged to resign, and for the remaining years of the century the Church was represented in Mexico City only by a priest acting as "resident."

Lying between Cuba and Puerto Rico is the large island of which one-third is Haiti and two-thirds the Dominican Republic. In Haiti the population is mainly composed of descendants of Negro slaves speaking in a debased form the French of their former masters, living in villages of thatched huts, and drawing a bare subsistence from the soil. Above this level there is the small governing class of mixed stock living in the coastal cities. It was in 1861 that there sailed for Haiti a company of Negro emigrants under the care of an American Negro priest of the Episcopal Church—James T. Holly. First with the support of the American Church Missionary Society and then of the Board of Missions, Holly established the Church of the Holy Trinity at Port au Prince. After a thorough inspection of this growing work by Bishop Arthur Coxe in 1871, the House of Bishops in 1874 approved a covenant with "The Orthodox Apostolic Church of Haiti" and pledged assistance to this new independent Church. Holly was consecrated in New York as its first bishop; and in spite of frequent political and social upheavals, which might well have extinguished a leader less dauntless, he served with success until his death in 1911.

As in Mexico, Haiti, and Brazil, Episcopalians began work in Cuba on the initiative of private agencies, without authorization by General Convention or even by the Board of Missions. Charitable impulse, uninfluenced by any strategic planning on the part of an official body, launched all these enterprises in Latin America. It was the Female Bible Society of Philadelphia which began to circulate Bibles in Cuba in 1882; and when one of its colporteurs began to organize congregations and became ordained, he was supported by the Ladies' Cuban Guild of Philadelphia and later by the American Church Missionary Society. But these Cubans who had withdrawn from the Roman Church were not without episcopal care, for the Bishop of Florida made several visits to administer Confirmation. By 1900 there were four clergy and six congregations, for whom no higher authority was responsible.

Meantime in 1898 our brief war with Spain had ended the long ages of Spanish misrule in Cuba and Puerto Rico and in the Philippine Islands. Conscious of the opportunities which had been opened, General Convention appointed a Committee on the Increased Responsibilities of the Church, and as a result of its actions two missionaries were sent to Puerto Rico and one to the Philippines; but no districts were organized or bishops elected until the opening of the next century.

Appointed by the American Church Missionary Society in 1889, the

Rev. James W. Morris and the Rev. Lucien Lee Kinsolving, classmates just graduated from the Virginia Seminary, sailed in the summer of that year for southern Brazil, and soon began to study Portuguese at Sao Paulo. Within a year they moved to Porto Alegre, capital of the province of Rio Grande do Sul, and there they held their first service in the parlor of a rented house. Reinforced by the later arrival of three other clergy and by the aid of Brazilian fellow-workers, they succeeded within ten years in establishing missions and schools at five stations. Since occasional episcopal visitations were not adequate to the needs of this growing Church, the House of Bishops took advantage of its constitutional right to provide bishops for foreign Churches and elected Kinsolving, who was consecrated on January 6, 1899.

During the period we are reviewing the Church in Liberia suffered a number of relapses followed by substantial recovery. When Bishop Payne, after twenty years of service, resigned in 1871 on account of ill-health, he could point to mission stations at twenty-two points in addition to nine organized churches and two schools for training boys and young men. His successor as bishop, John G. Auer, the only white man left on the staff, lived for only a few months after his consecration. It was three years more before the next bishop reached the field, during which the mission barely survived the long interval without episcopal oversight. When Bishop Charles C. Penick arrived from the United States in February, 1877, he wrote to the Board of "confusion worse confounded." "The work here," he explained, "has been so long without any head that the disorder is very very great . . . no educational system, not the first move toward self-support." And it was not the last time that the Church was to permit a similar deplorable lapse. Penick, however, restored some measure of order, and when illness caused by the climate forced him to retire after five years he left eleven clergy and more than five hundred communicants. Again there followed three years of partial disintegration before the remarkable episcopate of Samuel D. Ferguson. This "Missionary Bishop of Cape Palmas and Parts Adjacent" had been the foremost Negro priest in Liberia, and for thirty-one years to come he provided the firm and prolonged leadership for which the Church had been waiting. The development of Cuttington College and the growth of the institutions at Cape Mount were only two signs among many of an advance increasingly secure.

Bishop Channing Moore Williams arrived in Japan in 1868, just after the outbreak of the revolution which resulted in the restoration of the Emperor to power, the end of the Shogunate, and the beginning of the amazing new era which was to witness the rise of Japan as a westernized world power. By 1873 the government had decided to ignore the ancient edicts against Christianity, and everywhere missionaries began to take advantage of this long awaited event. Williams moved to Tokyo, the new capital, where there was soon opened a Divinity School and the school which was later to become St. Paul's University. This prompt founding of schools was an indication of what was to be the permanent policy of the mission. The Japanese most open to Christian approach were the "samurai," or the knightly class, a middle group between the nobles and the common people; and from the beginning of the revolution they proved intensely eager to understand and to adopt Western learning. Education, therefore, was heavily stressed as a missionary method, and most of the converts were above the average in intelligence and ability. Under these circumstances, early in the 'eighties, the attitude of the Japanese toward Western civilization, and toward Christianity as a part of that culture, became so warmly favorable that for some six or eight years the growth of all the Churches was surprisingly rapid, and there was even talk that Christianity would soon become the state religion.

Though the Anglican group in 1882 included only two hundred communicants out of 38,000 Christians, it was soon so enlarged that a movement was begun to form an autonomous national Church. In Japan, as in China, the English Societies were slower than the American Church in sending bishops; but by 1887 a new English bishop was able to join with Bishop Williams and with clergy and laity of the British and American missions in a Synod which adopted the constitution of the Nippon Sei Ko Kwai, or Holy Catholic Church of Japan. Into the foundation of the new structure were built the Scriptures, the Nicene Creed, the two Sacraments, and the three Orders of the ministry; and the Anglican Prayer Book and the Thirty-nine Articles were retained for the time being. Both foreigners and Japanese were members of the Sei Ko Kwai on an equal footing; but the autonomy of the Church was at first more apparent than real, as the only bishops were foreigners and to a high degree the work was dependent on foreign money. Nevertheless the framework had been constructed within which independence became more genuine with every decade.

Seven years later another Synod set up six dioceses, two of them connected with the Church in America. By that time a nationalistic reaction had set in, and the advance of Christianity was everywhere retarded. Yet Anglican progress was not seriously checked. John Cole McKim, who succeeded Williams in 1893, brought vigorous leadership, and by 1900 institutions were flourishing, and nearly all the larger centers in the American missionary districts of Tokyo and Kyoto had been occupied.

In 1868 Bishop Williams gave up trying to be bishop of China and

Japan and wisely set himself to meet the crisis which was developing in the smaller country. But he was not officially relieved of his Chinese see for another six years, nor was his successor consecrated until 1877. In other words, the Church made the mistake of leaving China without an active bishop for nearly ten years. And the new bishop, Samuel Isaac Joseph Schereschewsky, was miscast for his exacting role. A brilliant linguist, he had been spending thirteen years in Peking in the translation of the Bible, a task which years later he nobly fulfilled.[9] Though he was not meant for administrative labors, he sustained them manfully until a stroke of paralysis led to his resignation in 1881. During his short episcopate he made the wisest contribution to the future prosperity of the Chinese Church which at that time could have been made—the purchase of large property just outside of Shanghai and the founding there of St. John's School, which was to expand under the leadership of F. L. Hawks Pott into the famous St. John's University. In his address at the laying of the school's cornerstone Schereschewsky declared, "We want an institution in which to train youth for the service of Christ. I believe the true apostles of China must be natives." And the development of a clergy highly trained to be leaders of an indigenous Church has since been a far-sighted aim steadfastly pursued.

Long before this time the mission had opened new stations six hundred miles up the Yangtze River at the vital industrial and educational center of Hankow and Wuchang. Evangelistic work began; a small hospital was set up; and the Boone Memorial School (1871) became the nucleus of the future Boone College. St. Mary's School (situated next to St. John's) and St. Luke's Hospital in Shanghai were further developments at the older station—institutions still active on a vastly enlarged scale.

Schereschewsky's successor, William J. Boone (son of the first Bishop Boone), lived for only seven years after his consecration. At the time of his death, half a century after his father had entered Shanghai, he left four centers where missionaries were in permanent residence—Shanghai, Hankow, Wuchang, and Ichang. There were, in addition, lesser stations near Shanghai and others recently initiated in the river ports of Shasi and Wuhu. Boone was followed by a missionary of long experience, Frederick Rogers Graves, who proved during the next forty-five years to be a firm ruler and a constructive statesman. It was he who in 1897 brought together for their first conference the bishops of the Anglican Communion in China, the earliest step in a process of union which was to be consummated fifteen years later.

[9] For a fascinating record of his heroic labors the reader is referred to J. A. Muller's biography, *Apostle of China* (1937).

But this event, interesting enough to the Church historian, was noticed by only a handful of observers in a huge country then in the midst of troubles which have since varied in character but have never come to an end. In 1894 and 1895 a war with Japan brought defeat and disgrace to China; the foreign Powers began to demand territory; an abortive movement of reform came to grief; and conservative anti-foreign reaction, led by the masterful Empress Dowager, vented itself in the Boxer Rebellion of 1900. The century closed with the humiliation of China's last dynasty and the temporary dominance of the Western Powers.[10]

[10] Deserving no less and no more than a footnote in a section devoted to foreign affairs are the six Episcopal churches in Europe which before the end of the century had been organized at various times at Paris, Nice, Rome, Florence, Geneva, and Dresden. They had been founded by American Episcopalians resident in these cities and, with their rectors and vestries, were self-supporting. They were visited regularly or irregularly by bishops appointed for that duty by the Presiding Bishop.

Chapter XVII

THE NEW SCIENCE AND THE LIBERALS

BEFORE the nineteenth century was well advanced a series of apparently hostile forces began to converge upon Christian orthodoxy with striking results. Foremost among them were German philosophy and theology, German biblical criticism, and European and British physical science.

Hegel's was the dominant philosophy in Germany during the 'twenties and 'thirties, and though his immense structure embodied idealism and not materialism, it could be reconciled with traditional Christianity only by revising one or the other. Moreover, it had a bad effect on the biblical critics, leading Baur and others of "the Tübingen School" to make the New Testament conform to Hegel's doctrines instead of studying it on the basis of purely historical evidence. Other critics, too, by methods more scientific, were likewise treating the Bible like any other literature. The resulting novel conclusions about books and authors and dates would have been disturbing enough if they had not been outdone by Strauss's *Life of Jesus* published in 1835 and later translated into English. For the Hegelian Strauss, Jesus was a real person, but the Christ of the Gospels was largely a mythical creation of the Church. The French Renan's *Life of Jesus,* appearing in 1863, though more artistic than Strauss's, was not much more reassuring. By that time this movement in philosophy and biblical study, which was then called "rationalism" in England and America, seemed a devastating Continental disease which must not be allowed to spread. The situation appeared to be helped but little by the efforts of Schleiermacher in Germany and Coleridge in England to absorb and adapt the new thought without abandoning the essence of Christianity, for these thinkers were themselves regarded by the orthodox as dangerous radicals. The "Higher Criticism" [1] had thus made notable advances on the Continent and its conclusions were already widely known in England by the middle of the nineteenth century. To the vast majority of English clergy, and to such laymen as took any interest in these matters, it was shocking to learn that scholars in Germany, and perhaps a few in the bosom of the Church of England itself, held that Moses did not write the Pentateuch, doubted the authenticity of some of St. Paul's Epistles, and worst of all, were ready to deny the infallibility of Scripture and to treat the Bible by the same methods that they would use in the study of Homer or the Sanskrit Vedas. The average pious man (then as now) viewed all features intimately *associated* with his religion as vitally *essential* to his religion.[2] For in the minds of most orthodox persons Christianity is a monolithic structure. It must be totally accepted, with all the factors generally agreed upon in any given age, or else, once shattered by any intrusive novelty, it must be totally abandoned. Yet even a sophomore's study of Church history would reveal the fact that from the time of its founding the Christian Church has been a flexible and growing organism with almost unequalled capacity for adjusting itself to all kinds of truth and for absorbing whatever in the long run will serve to nourish and expand its divine life.

But even in the England of that era there were those who agreed with John Milton in his famous plea for freedom of thought. "Truth is compared in Scripture to a streaming fountain; if her waters flow not in a perpetual progression, they sicken into a muddy pool of conformity and tradition. . . . Give me the liberty to know, to utter, to argue freely according to conscience, above all liberties. . . . And though all the winds of doctrine were let loose to play upon the earth, so truth be in the field, we do injuriously by licensing and prohibiting to misdoubt her strength. Let her and falsehood grapple; who ever knew truth put to the worse, in a free and open encounter?" [3] A group of those who were inspired with this confidence produced in 1860 a book entitled *Essays and Reviews.*

This volume of essays by seven men (all but one ordained) provoked such violent resistance and resentment on both sides of the Atlantic that it deserves examination by all who value historical evidence that truth is

[1] The term "Higher Criticism" caused serious misunderstanding among many who took it to mean that such criticism regarded itself as superior to other kinds. It is simply, however, a technical term meaning "literary criticism," i.e., the investigation of the sources, authors, dates, etc., of biblical literature. It is thus distinguished from the "Lower Criticism," or textual criticism, which concerns itself only with producing an accurate text.

[2] Such are those who have held that to give up Jonah and the whale is to undermine Christianity; to abandon the fall of Adam is to discard the Atonement; to doubt that the heathen are going to hell is "to cut the nerve of foreign missions," etc.

[3] John Milton, *Areopagitica,* Bohn ed., London, 1848, 85, 95 f.

mighty and will prevail, and that the loud lamentations of Churchmen do not always prove that Christianity is in danger. Unlike future collections of theological papers, such as *Lux Mundi* or the productions of the groups led by Streeter, *Essays and Reviews* was not the product of group thinking. Except in the book the authors had never come together, and indeed each was unaware of what the others were writing. Though this lack of co-operation reduced the value of the work, there was still a genuine unity in its contents, for all the writers were facing the same set of problems, chiefly those created by scientific criticism. The general tone of the essays was so cautious and reverent and their theses are so generally accepted today that it is hard to recreate in imagination the angry opposition they excited. It is not difficult, however, to identify the kind of passages that caused alarm.

Frederick Temple (then Headmaster of Rugby), writing on "The Education of the World," when he treats of the Patristic period, says, "Many of the doctrinal statements are plainly unfitted for permanent use. . . . We can acknowledge the great value of the forms in which the first ages of the Church defined the truth, and yet refuse to be bound by them. . . . He is guilty of high treason against the faith who fears the result of any investigation, whether philosophical, or scientific, or historical." [4] Rowland Williams, writing on "Bunsen's Biblical Researches," reminds his readers that "we cannot encourage a remorseless criticism of Gentile historians and escape its contagion when we approach Hebrew annals"; and he dares to add, "Even with those in our universities who no longer repeat the required shibboleths, the explicitness of truth is rare." [5] Baden Powell, Professor of Geometry at Oxford, writing "On the Study of the Evidences of Christianity," remarks that "if miracles were in the estimation of a former age among the chief *supports* of Christianity, they are at present among the main difficulties and hindrances to its acceptance." [6] Henry B. Wilson, writing on "The National Church," declares that "the freedom of opinion which belongs to the English citizen should be conceded to the English Churchman." [7] C. W. Goodwin, writing on "Mosaic Cosmogony," with an eye to the stories of creation, makes the bold comment, "It would have been well if theologians had made up their minds to accept frankly the principle that those things for the discovery of which man has faculties specially provided, are not fit subjects of a divine revelation." [8]

The best written essay, and perhaps the most disturbing, was by

[4] *Essays and Reviews*, 3rd ed., 41, 44, 47.
[5] *Ibid.*, 51 ff.
[6] *Ibid.*, 140.
[7] *Ibid.*, 180.
[8] *Ibid.*, 209.

Benjamin Jowett, Regius Professor of Greek at Oxford and future translator of Plato. "On the Interpretation of Scripture" he has this to say: "Any true doctrine of inspiration must conform to all well-ascertained facts of history and of science. . . . The same fact cannot be true in religion when seen by the light of faith and untrue in science when looked at through the medium of evidence or experiment." And toward the close of his brilliant paper he allows himself a flash of indignation. "It is a mischief that critical observations which any intelligent man can make for himself, should be ascribed to atheism or unbelief. It would be a strange and almost incredible thing that the Gospel, which at first made war only on the vices of mankind, should now be opposed to one of the highest and rarest of human virtues—the love of truth." [9]

Once this outspoken book had been launched into the England of 1860 the Anglican hierarchy reacted promptly. In February, 1861, the archbishops and bishops met in London and agreed to publish a circular letter. Drafted by Bishop Wilberforce of Oxford, this document denounced the *Essays and Reviews* and reflected seriously upon the honesty of the authors as beneficed priests. Three years later the book was condemned by the Convocation of Canterbury. Meantime Rowland Williams had been brought to trial before an ecclesiastical court and found guilty of heretical beliefs about the inspiration of the Bible. The verdict, however, was set aside by the highest court of appeal—the Judicial Committee of the Privy Council—which affirmed that the Church of England, while maintaining the inspiration of Scripture, insisted on no particular theory of inspiration.[10] Nor was any effort made to carry out Bishop Wilberforce's proposal that all the essayists should be compelled to withdraw from the ministry. In fact, the first of them, Frederick Temple, eventually became Archbishop of Canterbury, father of a still more noted Archbishop Temple.

Balked by a court of laymen, the bishops were further disconcerted to discover that they were dealing not with a single book, which could be metaphorically burned, but with a growing movement. In the midst of the agitation over *Essays and Reviews* a new bomb was thrown into the camp by John William Colenso. A brilliant Cambridge scholar, combative and impulsive, he had become Bishop of Natal in South Africa in 1853. Between 1861 and 1863 he published a commentary on the Epistle to the Romans and two volumes on the Pentateuch and the book of Joshua which caused even more pain than the *Essays*. To his destructive conclusions about Moses and Joshua he added statements denying supernatural knowledge to Jesus and repudiating eternal punishment and the

[9] *Ibid.*, 348, 374.

[10] H. B. Wilson was condemned for denying eternal punishment and was similarly acquitted by the Judicial Committee.

substitutionary theory of the Atonement. This *cause célèbre* is part of the history of our sister Church; but the details of the long legal fight to oust Colenso, which resulted in a schism of fourteen years in the Church in South Africa, were well-known to clerical leaders in the United States and furnished ammunition for the fight against "rationalism."

The American Church had long been awake to the dangers of the new Higher Criticism, for as early as 1844, when a committee of bishops was investigating the General Seminary, they asked the professors, "Has it been publicly or privately taught in the Seminary that any portion of the sacred narrative in the book of Genesis is in the nature of myth or is merely or principally allegorical?" But it took *Essays and Reviews* to produce widespread indignation. In 1865 the House of Bishops voted approval of the excommunication of Bishop Colenso and authorized the publication of a letter written by Bishop McIlvaine "To the Clergy and Candidates for Orders of the Protestant Episcopal Church." This epistle dealt in severe terms both with the authors of the *Essays* and with Colenso, and accused them all of "infidelity" and of denying truths "precious to the sinner's hope of salvation." Other bishops (including Whitehouse of Illinois and Upfold of Indiana) were addressing their people in much the same strain, warning them against the "licentious and rationalistic tendency" of these English heretics and pleading for a firm adherence to the plenary inspiration of the Scriptures.

The guardians of dogma did not realize that the worst was yet to come. Unorthodox beliefs about the Bible and its writers and the infiltration of dubious German theology were bad enough; but they affected only a relatively small number of thoughtful people and certainly did not strike at the root of all religion. It was otherwise, however, with the advance of physical science and its rapid popularization. The appearance in 1859 of Darwin's *Origin of Species* was by no means the earliest shock administered by scientists, but it serves as a convenient point from which to date a powerful movement of thought which challenged Christianity at every point. Unlike the scientific men of a former age—such as Boyle and Newton—Spencer, Darwin, Huxley, and Tyndall were openly agnostic, and other writers, under scientific influence, like Mill and Buckle, made no secret of their rejection of Christianity.

If the conclusions of scientists and philosophers had been accepted only in learned circles, the effect would have been small. But their beliefs were quickly spread and readily absorbed, especially by the younger and more intelligent liberal elements in the country. Again, if scientific pronouncements had been only of technical interest, they would have had few repercussions. As a matter of fact, however, they appeared to deny a series of fundamental Christian beliefs. This irresistible new knowledge, promoted by high-minded seekers after truth, proclaimed the theory of natural selection and the reign of law throughout the universe. It proved that the earth was millions of years old and that all forms of life had taken untold ages to evolve. Its spokesmen not only denied miracles and life after death but eliminated a personal God. As ultimate reality they recognized Matter or the Unknowable, or else they retired into a reverent agnosticism. Scepticism, in consequence, seemed to many to be the only reasonable attitude for educated men and women.

During the 'sixties and 'seventies the men of science, and those who interpreted their findings as fatal to religion, appeared to grow in power and influence. Tyndall and Huxley were lecturing in the United States, and on both sides of the Atlantic the imposing works of Herbert Spencer were easily mistaken for profound wisdom of permanent value. The reaction of the Churches was mainly that of violent denial. Occasionally there was a pathetic attempt at reconciliation, such as the assertion that geology and Genesis were in harmony because "days" meant aeons and not hours. On the whole, however, indignant resistance was the usual response of religious leaders. Professor Noah Porter of Yale taught courses in which Spencer was refuted; scientists were occasionally expelled from minor colleges and higher critics from seminaries; and as late as 1886 the Pastoral Letter of the House of Bishops referred to "this flood of infidelity which is sweeping over our land."

In contrast with conservatives, whether Evangelical or Anglo-Catholic, there gradually arose, to meet the new situation, a growing group commonly referred to as "Broad Churchmen." Since the issues which stimulated them and the views which marked them were not chiefly concerned with Churchmanship, they might better be termed Liberals. This early Liberalism "was essentially a reconstructive movement of Christian ideas which were losing their hold on contemporary minds. . . . The real struggle was no longer, as in the preceding decade, between Pope and Protestantism, but between atheism and Christ." [11] Using "apologist" in its ancient and best sense, the Liberals were the nineteenth-century apologists for Christianity: that is, they defended Christianity by restating its fundamental truths in the light of current thought. They were characterized by an open-minded readiness to accept truth wherever found. Unwilling to deny the findings of science, they were equally unwilling to let the scientists do all the thinking. They were resolved that the effect of science upon Christianity should be interpreted by *Christians*, and they were prepared to do the interpreting. As an American Liberal who lived and wrote in this generation has expressed it: "They were fearless men unterrified by the discoveries of science or the results of

[11] John Tulloch, *Movements of Religious Thought*, 279.

Biblical criticism. They had not shared in the panic caused by the famous *Essays and Reviews*; they refused to join in the cry that 'the Church is in danger!' Rather did they see a larger opening for true religion in the fruits of an awakened intellectual activity. They held with Hooker and Bishop Butler that the human reason was the God-given faculty for verifying the divine revelation. . . . In a word, they were the new generation of Christian thinkers." [12]

The Liberal movement began in England, and with its earlier years are usually associated the names of Frederick Denison Maurice (1805–1872), Frederick William Robertson (1816–1853), the gifted preacher who died young, and Charles Kingsley (1819–1875). Though Maurice lost his chair at King's College, London, because he denied the doctrines of eternal punishment and substitutionary Atonement, he was far from being a Liberal, and he repudiated the title "Broad Churchman." Yet he seems to have been the cause of Liberalism in others, for Kingsley looked to him as master and he produced a strong effect upon American Liberals. Kingsley, though not important as a theologian, was a bracing personality, a valued friend of scientists, exerting a tonic influence on the younger generation through his courageous confidence in times of doubt and hesitation. Another influential Liberal was his contemporary Arthur Stanley, Dean of Westminster. And somewhat younger were the great Cambridge scholars, Westcott, Hort, and Lightfoot, men deeply religious but wholeheartedly devoted to the modern scientific study of the New Testament.

The Church in the United States, subject to the same disturbing forces, duplicated the varied reactions observable in England. The only American theologian of high rank who wrote in this period was the Congregationalist Horace Bushnell of Hartford, a conservative Liberal whose works were widely influential outside of his own communion. In contrast to the evangelist Dwight Moody, who fiercely assailed all conclusions of the new thought, Henry Ward Beecher and Washington Gladden in their pulpits accepted evolution and sought to reconcile religion and science. The Episcopal Church, too, was not slow to produce Liberals who were unafraid of discoveries and who did not regard the faith as a "deposit" kept under glass. As early as the Church Congress of 1875 Dr. W. R. Huntington of Worcester was expressing his conviction that "the theologians must learn to look upon the naturalists as their allies rather than their antagonists. . . . Truth is truth, however and whencesoever obtained, and we can never have occasion to be either afraid of it or unthankful for it." And at the Congress three years later Professor Frederick Gardiner of the Berkeley Divinity School was prepared to affirm that "the present and future condition of natural science, however

[12] A. V. G. Allen, *Phillips Brooks,* I, 447 f.

far it may advance, must be of service to the interpretation of the Bible, for it must tend to increase the knowledge of truth." Others there were, too—Henry C. Potter and Edward A. Washburn of New York, and Bishop Clark of Rhode Island. But for personal eminence Phillips Brooks was the outstanding Liberal of the Church for twenty years and more. He declared, "The world will never go back again to the old ideas of verbal inspiration"; but when he confessed, "The new theology in all its great general characteristics I love with all my heart, I rejoice to preach it," he meant a message completely positive.

In view of the diluted quality of later Liberalism and its twentieth-century decadence, it is important to remember that the genuine Liberalism of this earlier generation was vigorous and served to perpetuate the essential doctrines of Christianity. It accepted the principle of *development* in theology, but so did the Fathers and the best Scholastics. The same breadth of view and wideness of sympathy which led Liberals to try to understand and assimilate the discoveries of science led them also to a wide sympathy with Christians of Protestant communions. Their Churchmanship was therefore more congenial to Low Churchmen than to High. Their theology, however, was an open reaction against the Calvinistic tendencies of narrow Evangelicalism. Its characteristic themes were an emphasis on the immanence of God, on law as God's method of working, on the historic Jesus and His character, and (to an increasing degree) on the social aspect of the Gospel. For some twenty years they were the only Churchmen in the country who were contributing anything new to scholarship or to Christian thought.

Thus the Broad Churchmen, running the risks and taking the punishment of pioneers, gradually taught their more or less reluctant brothers in other groups not to be afraid of scientific truth or of theological restatement. One of the first signs that this lesson had been learned by the more intellectual Anglo-Catholics was the publication in 1889 of a volume of twelve essays entitled *Lux Mundi,* edited by Charles Gore, then Principal of Pusey House at Oxford, and written by him and ten other priests. Its stated aim was "to put the Catholic faith into its right relation to modern intellectual and moral problems . . . to present positively the central ideas and principles of religion in the light of contemporary thought and current problems."

The authors of *Lux Mundi* were theologians not only thoroughly competent but distinctly conservative. Yet they were prepared to publish statements not unlike many which had drawn fire upon the writers of *Essays and Reviews* thirty years earlier. Henry Scott Holland, later Regius Professor of Divinity at Oxford, avows his belief that "[faith's] eternal task lies in rapid readjustment to each fresh situation which the motion of time may disclose to it. It has that in it which can apply to all, and learn from all."[13] Aubrey Moore writes, "It seems as if, in the providence of God, the mission of modern science was to bring home to our unmetaphysical ways of thinking the great truth of the Divine immanence in creation, which is not less essential to the Christian idea of God than to a philosophical view of nature."[14] J. R. Illingworth is ready to maintain that the popular outcry against the evolutionary origin of man "was largely due to sentiment not altogether untinged by human pride."[15] The cautious Charles Gore reminds his readers that "the Church is not restrained . . . by having committed herself to any dogmatic definitions of the meaning of inspiration." He adds that "the recorders of Israel's history were subject to the ordinary laws in the estimate of evidence," and he even goes so far as to say that Jesus showed no signs of transcending either the science or the history of his age.[16] There is some justification for Phillips Brooks's comment that these essayists "are asking not simply what is absolutely true, but what can be reconciled to certain pre-established standards of unity outside of which they must not go."[17] But that they had not waited till it was "prosperous to be just" is proved by the fact that even their sober and temperate contribution met with denial and abuse. Nevertheless their thoughtful studies registered genuine progress and prevented the attitude toward science and toward the reconstruction of theology from becoming a party issue.

For more than forty years harsh criticism and occasional persecution were the lot of Liberals in several Protestant Churches. Professors were particularly subject to attacks, for their effect upon the young made them dangerous. In 1886, for example, five members of the faculty of the Andover Theological Seminary were tried for heresy, and one was found guilty. The most famous of such cases was that of the Rev. Dr. Charles A. Briggs, Professor of Biblical Theology at Union Theological Seminary in New York, who was deposed from the Presbyterian ministry for his teaching as a pioneer in the Higher Criticism. In 1899 he applied for ordination in the Episcopal Church, and in the face of vigorous protest Bishop Henry Potter ordained him. In Episcopal seminaries no such radical scholars were to be found except in the Episcopal Theological School in Cambridge which for about twenty-five years was the only Church institution which frankly accepted the new Higher Criticism and taught it freely. Though none of its faculty was brought to trial, most bishops declined to submit their candidates to such instruction.

[13] *Lux Mundi,* 2nd ed., 1890, 37.
[14] *Ibid.,* 100.
[15] *Ibid.,* 195.
[16] *Ibid.,* 353, 360.
[17] Allen, *Phillips Brooks,* II, 489.

By the closing years of the century the modern scientific literary criticism of the Bible had become respectable in the Episcopal Church; and while not all its conclusions were generally endorsed, its methods were accepted. Encouraging proof of this change may be found in the Encyclical Letter issued by the Lambeth Conference of 1897, which offers an instructive contrast to the prosecution of Bishop Colenso which had absorbed the attention of the Conference of 1867. In their admirable statement the bishops announced to all members of the Anglican Communion: "The critical study of the Bible by competent scholars is essential to the maintenance in the Church of a healthy faith. That faith is always in serious danger which refuses to face questions that may be raised either on the authority or the genuineness of any part of the Scriptures. . . . Such refusal creates painful suspicion in the minds of many whom we have to teach, and will weaken the strength of our conviction of the truth that God has revealed to us. A faith which is always or often attended by a secret fear that we dare not inquire lest inquiry should lead us to results inconsistent with what we believe, is already infected with a disease which may soon destroy it. But all inquiry is attended with a danger on the other side unless it be protected by the guard of reverence, confidence, and patience."

Liberals, or Broad Churchmen, had been engaged during a whole generation not only in admitting the ideals and methods of science into biblical study but also in reconstructing theology in the light of modern philosophy. They had been active in dealing not only with Christian literature but with Christian thought. And their influence as preachers and teachers of Christian doctrine was far more widely known and far more subject to hostile criticism than any views they might hold about the Synoptic problem or the number of Isaiahs to be identified. It was the theological beliefs of certain Liberals which called forth an episcopal message in October, 1894.

After the adjournment of a special session of the House of Bishops the bishops met "in council" and authorized six of their number to issue a "Pastoral Letter." Only forty-seven bishops out of seventy-nine were present, and even this quorum never passed upon the Letter. It therefore lacked the authority of a true Pastoral approved by the House, and its authors were rightly blamed for calling it a "Pastoral Letter." But its contents were reaffirmed at the next meeting of the House and undoubtedly expressed the views of the majority of bishops. The Letter was written by Bishop Williams of Connecticut, then seventy-seven years old, and was endorsed by his five colleagues, having an average age of sixty-seven. Its treatment of the subjects with which it dealt was therefore not likely to be qualified by any very full understanding of the problems with which the younger generation was wrestling or by any imaginative sympathy with opinions not obviously orthodox.

Two "novelties . . . subversive of the fundamental verities of Christ's religion," which had "disturbed and distressed" many clergy and laity, were cited and attacked. These were doubts about the Incarnation shown by denying or ignoring the Virgin Birth and doubt about the Resurrection of Christ shown by affirming that the Resurrection was "spiritual" and not bodily. Any interpretation of the Incarnation which failed to make the Virgin Birth absolutely essential was condemned, and any interpretation of the Resurrection which did not include the revivification of flesh and bones was branded as heresy. It was not difficult, of course, to prove that in taking this position the bishops were supported by traditional orthodoxy. This fact was probably recognized not only by those who agreed with them but also by those who disagreed.

Not content, however, with these declarations, the bishops went further to commit themselves to the proposition that "fixedness of interpretation is of the essence of the Creeds." And this thesis they applied not only to the *facts* recorded in the Creeds but to the *doctrines*. Here was a claim that doctrinal statements (such as "for us men and for our salvation he came" and "very God of very God") can never have but one true interpretation. It was an assertion which could have been prompted only by a regrettable ignorance of the past and a somewhat optimistic view of the future. This clause, indeed, stuck in the throats of many who did not share the views of advanced Liberals. Partly for this reason and partly because of its unauthentic character the Letter caused much excitement. But the lapse of half a century has been enough to remind the Church that theological development, whether in a conservative or a radical direction, cannot be limited or controlled by official pronouncements.[18]

[18] A kind of dying echo of this Pastoral Letter controversy was heard as late as 1923 in the publication of another Pastoral Letter approved by the House of Bishops meeting at Dallas. This message likewise described itself as instigated by "widespread distress and disturbance of mind among many earnest Church people, both clerical and lay, caused by several recent utterances concerning the Creeds." (Chief of these utterances, it was well known, was an address by Bishop William Lawrence of Massachusetts published under the title *Fifty Years.*) The Letter, like its predecessor in 1894, was written especially to condemn those whose teaching might cast doubts upon the Virgin Birth and the physical Resurrection and to reflect upon their loyalty and honesty. Its contents were effectively dealt with in a book later written by members of the faculty of the Episcopal Theological School in Cambridge and entitled *Creeds and Loyalty*—a small volume worth reading but read by few.

Chapter XVIII

TYPES OF LEADERSHIP: WILLIAM HOBART HARE AND PHILLIPS BROOKS

WILLIAM HOBART HARE

"SANCTITY and chivalry were so inherent in the nature of William Hobart Hare that 'Saint' and 'Knight' stand in the first rank of the generic terms by which he may be characterized. More specifically he was also an 'apostle' and a 'pioneer.'"[1]

Hare was born in Princeton, New Jersey, on May 17, 1838. On both sides his parentage was favorable to a career of distinction in the Church. His father was the Rev. Dr. George Emlen Hare, whom we have noted as the first dean of the Divinity School in Philadelphia. His mother was Elizabeth Catharine Hobart, a daughter of Bishop Hobart of New York. Though the sons of ministers, and even of bishops, are not always remarkable for sanctity, William was one of those who took every advantage of a rich inheritance.

After seven years of schooling at the Episcopal Academy in Philadelphia Hare joined the Sophomore class of the University of Pennsylvania; but ill-health, of which eye trouble was a symptom, obliged him to leave college at the end of his Junior year. It was not long, however, before he was able to return to study; and by that time, having decided for the ministry, he entered the Divinity School in Philadelphia. In 1859, just after his twenty-first birthday, he was ordained deacon and spent the next two years as assistant to the Rev. Dr. M. A. DeWolfe Howe at St. Luke's Church. Before another two years had passed he had married Dr. Howe's daughter and had accepted the rectorship of St. Paul's Church in the Philadelphia suburb of Chestnut Hill.

[1] M. A. DeW. Howe, *Life and Labors of Bishop Hare,* 3. An admirable life of Hare, presented largely in the bishop's own words.

But his new work and his new happiness were soon interrupted by his wife's failing health. To give her the benefit of a more bracing climate he resigned his parish and took her and his infant son for a long visit to Minnesota. There he made his first acquaintance with the Indians and saw at first hand the evil that white men had wrought among them and the little that the Church had then accomplished on their behalf. Returning to Philadelphia in the following year, he served once more for a time at St. Luke's, and in 1867, just after he had been stricken by his wife's death, he became rector of the Church of the Ascension. Four years later his missionary career began with his appointment as Secretary and General Agent of the Foreign Committee of the Board of Missions. But he was not long to serve as an executive at the home base, for in 1872 the House of Bishops created the Missionary Jurisdiction of Niobrara and elected Hare as its bishop.

Niobrara, as described by Hare, "was the name of a river running along the border line between Nebraska and Dakota, and had been chosen as a convenient term in ecclesiastical nomenclature for the large tract of country of which then little was known, save that it stretched northward from the river Niobrara and was roamed over by the Poncas and different tribes of Sioux or Dakota Indians." [2] The call to leadership in this wide and wild area was not easy to accept. Hare had just begun to serve in a missionary office, and his deep interest in the foreign field was already aroused. In the end, however, he reached the firm conviction that "a man who seems to shrink from hard places weakens men's faith in the reality of Christian character," and that "it would be quixotic to work for heathen far off unless we are grappling also with the heathen question at home." His decision made, Hare was consecrated bishop on January 9, 1873, at the age of thirty-four—the one hundredth bishop in the line of the American Episcopate.

Few sharper contrasts could be experienced than that between life in the Philadelphia of the 'seventies among friends and relatives in a settled and comfortable society with a rich cultural background, and life in the Dakotas beyond the edge of civilization in cold and lonely country where Indians in a state of barbarism far outnumbered the whites. But Hare was to become one proof among many that it does not take a tough man to succeed in a tough job. It was a sensitive and sweet-natured and highly cultivated bishop who was to face the rigors of Dakota life for the next thirty years and to win the devotion of Indian tribes.

When Hare entered his field in April, 1873, he found not only that work had been begun by Roman Catholics and by Presbyterians and Congregationalists but that the Episcopal Church was active in the suc-

[2] *Ibid.*, 29.

cessful Santee mission and at several other points. Yet so few and small were the missionary centers that the vast territory could almost be said to be unoccupied. Of these earliest days the bishop's own account shows us what he encountered, and reminds us how the "before" of 1873 compared with the "after" of 1909.

"From Yankton I passed up the Missouri River along which the main body of the missionary enterprise of our Church among the Indians was then located. I found that missionary work had been established on the Santee, Yankton, and Ponca Reserves, and three brave young deacons, fresh from the Berkeley Divinity School, had, the previous fall, pressed up the river and begun the task of opening the way for missionary effort among the Indians of the Lower Brulé, the Crow Creek, and Cheyenne River Reserves. All together there were, besides three natives, five white clergymen and five ministering women. . . . The scenes grew wilder as I pushed farther on. A service held at the Cheyenne River Agency in the open air left a deep impression on my mind. It was a strange scene. In front of us, forty or fifty feet distant, rolled the Missouri River. Nearer at hand, grouped in a semi-circle, fringed with a few curious soldiers and employees of the Agency, sat the Indians; many bedecked with paint and feathers and carrying guns and tomahawks; some in a soberer guise, betokening that they were inclining to the white man's ways; while all gazed, apparently half-amused, half awe-struck, at the vested missionary of the station as he sang hymns and offered the prayers of the Church, and then at the Indian deacon and me as we spoke the words of Life." [3]

Though Hare had few precedents to guide him and few men with whom he could consult, it was not long before he had begun to formulate plans and policies. "I soon saw," he continues, "that my work was not to be that of a settled pastor in daily contact with his flock; but that of a general superintendent whose duty it would be to reach the people through their pastors; not so much to do local work as to make local work possible and easy for others. The whole field was therefore mapped out into divisions, these divisions being ordinarily the territory connected with a United States Indian Agency. The special care of each of them was entrusted to one experienced preacher, and around him were grouped the Indian ministers and catechists and others who were engaged in evangelistic work within his division." [4] "My study of the Indian problem," he recorded, "convinced me quite early that the Boarding School ought to be one of the most prominent features of our missionary work. . . . I also proposed to establish a central boarding-school of higher grade, at the place of the bishop's residence. . . . This plan was carried out, and thus

[3] *Ibid.*, 47, 49 f.
[4] *Ibid.*, 50 f.

grew up the St. Paul's, St. Mary's, St. John's, and Hope Indian boarding-schools which, under their respective heads, have won a deservedly high reputation."[5]

As to his general views on the Indian question we have his word that he "soon came to look upon everything as provisional . . . which, if permanently maintained, would tend to make Indian life something separate from the common life of the country: a solid foreign mass indigestible by our common civilization. . . . All *reservations,* whether the *reserving* of land from the ordinary laws of settlement, or the *reserving* of the Indian nationality from absorption into ours, or the *reserving* of old tribal superstitions and notions and habits from the natural process of decadence, or the *reserving* of the Indian language from extinction, are only necessary evils or but temporary expedients. . . . The Indians are not an insulated people. . . . From the first, therefore, I struggled against the notion that we were missionaries to Indians alone and not missionaries to all men."[6]

What life was like after three months in Dakota is vividly related by Hare in a letter to his mother-in-law dated July 30, 1873. In this frank narrative we read of his nights in the log huts of ranches where the food was loathsome, the vermin various, and the company often inclusive of drunken desperadoes. Comfortable by comparison were the government stations or Agencies, for "at each Agency there is besides the agent, a head farmer, head blacksmith, head miller, etc., so that there is a little gathering of white people besides the Mission family. The Yankton reservation stretches along the Missouri River which is bounded by beautiful bluffs on the other side; a fair share of the conveniences of life can be enjoyed there; and, except that all I love are far away, there is no reason why I should not be happy there. Indeed, I believe I am happier than most as things now are. I have made already many friends at the various military posts along the river, am received with a cordiality which is an inexpressible balm, and have had the joy of seeing a deep religious interest spring up among officers and others who have been, to say the least, indifferent to religion."[7]

It was not only raw discomfort that the bishop had to encounter during the first ten years of his service. It was among the Sioux that the famous Custer massacre occurred in June, 1876; Indian warfare was not yet an affair of the past; and Hare's life was in danger on more than one occasion. Such adventures, of course, were extremely rare; but the wearing routine of missionary labor (with here and there encouraging moments) was constant. Looking back on these years, another fellow worker

[5] *Ibid.,* 51 f.
[6] *Ibid.,* 54 f.
[7] *Ibid.,* 65 f.

wrote in 1893: "Who in any small measure can enter into the burden of it? The anxious thought and care, the weary explorations in the almost pathless wilds to prepare the way of the Lord, the hardships of the pilgrimages, the conferences with wild men often opposed to the white man's way and utterly misunderstanding motives and needing to be dealt with with so much tact and self-restraint to make them see their own best interests, and to save them from themselves; the disappointments and desolating sins of some workers in the field; the lack of sympathy of some, apathy and failure in others to enter heartily into his plans. And again, there is the financial burden—enough in itself to crush any ordinary mortal—for the bishop very soon discovered that it was left largely to him to raise the funds, and he must go before the churchmen and churchwomen and plead. . . . The vexations of seeing golden opportunities passing by, or the impossibility of enlargement of important work, and sometimes the curtailing or abandonment because the funds were insufficient. . . . And then there is the correspondence, the incessant writing in the cars, in camps, in the few minutes caught here and there while waiting, as well as in hours stolen from much needed rest and sleep. And all this, and much more, in a body often tortured by weakness and serious ailments, craving rest and recuperation." [8]

So seriously impaired had Bishop Hare's health become that the House of Bishops passed a resolution urging him to take a long vacation. Since resignation seemed the only alternative, he agreed to the proposal, and between December, 1875, and September, 1876, he enjoyed the refreshment of travel in England, France, and Italy. Though he nearly died of fever in Venice, the trip as a whole restored him to a fair degree of vigor, and for another fifteen years he was never so long absent from his field.

To follow his journeyings during this period and to relate his achievements in each one of his increasing centers of work would be neither interesting nor profitable. To view him at his labors after another decade will be quite as revealing of the man and his methods. And by that time there will be results to record.

In 1883 the House of Bishops changed the limits of Hare's jurisdiction to make them correspond almost exactly to the limits of the present State of South Dakota, and the name of the State became the name of his district. One reason for this step was the flood of white immigration which was beginning to populate more thickly the territory which, within six years, was to become the States of North and South Dakota. These enterprising and energetic Americans and Canadians often brought the bishop the encouragement of enthusiastic response, and it was for the daughters

[8] *Ibid.,* 136–138.

of these newcomers and of his own missionaries that he succeeded in opening All Saints School for girls at Sioux Falls in September, 1885. There he made his own home, and there he could return for refuge and rest from many journeys and from the care of all the churches. For primitive conditions still kept progress slow among the Indians, as we may learn from the bishop's account of one of his visitations in 1884.

"Early Monday we started out upon our trip up the river. Our party consisted of five selected Indians, the Rev. Mr. Swift, and myself. Our destination was the Standing Rock Agency, where there is a large body of Indians as yet unreached by educational and missionary effort, some of whom have again and again sent us requests that we would come and do for them the work which we had done for other Indians. Mr. Swift's Christian Indians have taken up their plea and pressed it upon us with great earnestness, No Heart, a Christian chief, and others volunteering to accompany us and smooth our way. A good deal of smoothing is sometimes necessary, for Indian life is a tangle of intrigue and diverse parties and clashing plans and interests through which the benevolent, however clever, may find it hard to make his way.

"We reached the Agency in two days without mishap. . . . We busied ourselves for two days, while our Indian colleagues moved among the Indians and quietly arranged for an interview. . . . At the appointed time we met a large council of the Indians composed of men of all kinds, and all kinds of speeches were delivered; one chief saying that 'he blamed our grandfathers and his grandfathers. He blamed ours because they killed the Son of God, and he blamed his because they had not taught their children better ways!' Some intimated that they would be more favorably disposed to listen to us were the Indians who had listened to us better off! Some said they were glad to see us if we had come to bring them more beef and sugar and coffee. After this fusillade of speeches made for effect, the representatives of the Indians who had again and again invoked our help rose and sententiously remarked that their minds were not changed, that they wanted our Mission, that they had said this several times before, and now said it again.

"The mental and spiritual destitution of these poor people is appalling. Their call to us to come to their deliverance is distinct and emphatic. The work which the Church has done for their neighbors has provoked it. Somehow or other we must respond to it." [9] And in course of time they did.

As the result of ten years of unresting initiative and unremitting effort the Mission could show definite advance. "In place of the three native and five white clergy, and five women helpers whom he had found

[9] *Ibid.*, 203–205.

in Niobrara, there were under Bishop Hare in 1884, five native clergy, five native candidates for the ministry, and twelve native catechists; seventeen white clergy and four white catechists; and twelve women helpers. In the four Indian boarding-schools he could report in 1884 an average attendance of forty pupils at St. Paul's, of thirty-four at St. Mary's, of thirty-four at St. John's, and of twenty-three at Hope School. By this time, moreover, many pupils had carried the teachings and influence of each of those schools back into their native surroundings, and some of them had gone on to the Indian schools in the East. . . . Still another token of the new order dawning for the Indians came in 1891, when the daughter of the celebrated Standing Rock chief, Gall, leader of the Indians in the Custer fight, presented, at the annual Indian Convocation over which Bishop Hare presided, an offering of eight hundred dollars on behalf of the Niobrara branch of the Woman's Auxiliary, made up of Indian women. On the fourth of the next July, Chief Gall was baptized in the Episcopal Church." [10]

In view of this measure of success, a verdict upon Bishop Hare expressed in 1887 seems no overstatement of the truth. It comes from a book on Indian Reservations written by J. B. Harrison. "I know of no man," he wrote, "who has accomplished more for the civilization of the Indians of Dakota . . . than Bishop Hare. Some religious workers on the frontier are successful by means of mere rude strength or physical vigor. . . . But here is a man made up of all gentle and pure qualities; at home in 'the still air of delightful studies'; who would be a leader among the best anywhere; who unites to a soldier's fearlessness and invincible devotion a spirituality so lofty and tender that one shrinks from characterizing it while he is still in the flesh, who is laying the foundations of Christian civilization on broad and far-reaching lines in a region large enough to be a mighty empire." [11]

After eighteen years in the Dakotas Hare's work was interrupted by two journeys to the Far East. At the urgent request of the House of Bishops he visited Japan between March and August, 1891, and both Japan and China between January and April, 1892. At that time the missionary districts in both countries had been deprived of their bishops by death, and their successors had not been elected. The coming of Bishop Hare brought encouragement and guidance at a critical moment in the history of the missions, and his counsel in the field and his later reports to the Board at home proved of high value.

Within a few years of his return to South Dakota he began more plainly than ever to feel the results of an organic defect of the heart from

[10] *Ibid.,* 228 f., 231.
[11] *Ibid.,* 243 f.

which to some extent he had suffered for twenty years. During the autumn of 1895 and the winter and summer of the following year he obeyed the doctor's orders to find complete rest in the East and in Europe. Though he never enjoyed again his former vigor, he could report in November, 1897, that he had preached twenty times in twenty days and travelled over a thousand miles by wagon and rail—proof that he was still not quite frail. And for five or six years longer he was equal to the wear and tear of life in the Indian field, where progress was steady and enheartening but the strain of effort never much diminished.

By 1903, however, Hare had begun to suffer from a facial cancer, and now in the grip of two diseases, he could work only at intervals during the remaining six years of his life. The Rev. Frederick Foote Johnson was elected as his coadjutor, so that the burden of responsibility might be lightened. In 1907, after many months of acute pain, his right eye was removed by a skilful New York surgeon. Yet a year later he found strength to deliver the Convocation address to the thousands gathered at Sioux Falls. "No complaining," Bishop Tuttle wrote of him. "No letting up of work. No pitying of self. No relaxing of duty or devotion." But with the return of the malignant growth he had to confess in a letter to a kinsman written in March, 1909, "My suffering is intense and constant." After another seven months death finally released him from pain.

Just before he died the bishop said, "I have lived in South Dakota and have been one of its people for thirty-six years. I wish to rest in its soil, and in their midst." And how the people of South Dakota felt about him he had learned (surely not for the first time) only six months before, when the mayor and aldermen of Sioux Falls sent him this message: "We wish to extend to you our deepest sympathy in your great affliction and to indicate the universal love, respect, and admiration with which you are regarded, not only by your personal friends and neighbors, but also by every citizen of Sioux Falls and South Dakota, and to express to you our sincerest congratulations upon your approaching seventy-first birthday, and the earnest hope that your health may be restored and that you may long be spared to continue the great work in this State to which you have given your life. The work which you have done will live long after you have passed away. The civilization of our western Indians is due more largely to you than to any other man. Your life and labors have made the world better. You are one of the great missionaries of America, and it is a source of pride to every citizen of Sioux Falls and South Dakota that you decided to cast your life among us."[12]

[12] *Ibid.*, 399 f.

When the Church came to reckon in figures the fruits of the work of Bishop Hare it proved a surprise to many that, in round numbers, out of the twenty thousand Indians in South Dakota, ten thousand were baptized members of the Episcopal Church. Yet they would not have been surprised if only they could have seen what few had ever seen—the assembly of the Indians at one of the great annual Convocations of the Niobrara Deanery. Once an occasion for the meeting of a few hundred, it had grown through the years to be a mighty gathering of three thousand and more Indian men and women from all parts of the State. They travelled for many hours and often for days by train and wagon until they met at the chosen mission station and set up their hundreds of tents and tepees and prepared for the great processions with banners and for the open-air services of preaching and of the Holy Communion and made ready the offerings which they had been laying aside through months of self-denial. Everywhere perfect order prevailed, and dignity and devotion. And what Christ and His Church had come to mean to those Indians none could fail to realize who had once heard them raise their voices in the hymn of praise to the God "from whom all blessings flow," and, like the men of Cromwell's army, "roll it strong and great against the sky."

PHILLIPS BROOKS

Phillips Brooks was not an ecclesiastical statesman, an energetic executive, or an adventurous missionary. He led no movement; he wrought no reforms; and except for sermons and lectures he wrote no books. Yet he was the greatest preacher and the most impressive personality which the Episcopal Church has yet produced. Through nearly a whole generation his name and influence stood out above all others. But the effect he produced as a preacher and as a man is exceptionally difficult to transmit in biography. The engineer, the architect, the poet, and the founder of institutions can be known and judged by their works. The actor, the orator, and the teacher, however, while their immediate effect can be tremendous, survive only by reputation; and with each passing decade the echoes of their fame become fainter.

Just so it is with the man whose claim to a place in history rests upon the glory of his preaching and the power of his personality. If you have never heard him or met him, you have missed what is essential. Whoever would write of Phillips Brooks, moreover, has not even an eventful life to record. He was educated; he was the rector of two parishes in Philadelphia and of one in Boston; he spent the last year of his life as a bishop; and from time to time he travelled abroad under comfortable circumstances. It was the kind of career that could be duplicated a hundred-fold. It is not a story to rouse posterity. Yet to hear Brooks was to experience a thrill never to be forgotten, and upon countless lives, as pastor and friend, the impression he made was life-long. To make such a man seem real today will be to treat lightly of mere events, and to try to restore, through his own words and the words of those who knew him, what may still prove only a shadow of the effect he produced.

William Gray Brooks and Mary Ann Phillips, the father and mother of Phillips Brooks, came of thoroughly New England ancestry, and while their son was far from what his countrymen would call a typical New Englander, he inherited the best traits that Massachusetts blood can transmit. Phillips was born on December 13, 1835, the second of six sons. A genuinely religious family, the Brookses were members of a Congregational church already tending toward conservative Unitarianism; but the piety of Mrs. Brooks was of a more intense and traditional type, and through her influence, when Phillips was only four years old, they transferred their allegiance to the Episcopal Church.

The Boston Latin School prepared Phillips for Harvard by the time he was fifteen, and he had only to cross the Charles River to enter that small college of three hundred members. But if the undergraduates were few, the teachers included such noted figures as Longfellow and Agassiz. Inactive in athletics, sociable and likeable enough to be elected to several well-known clubs, Brooks was successful as a student, especially in the classics. The most brilliant phase of his record was as a writer, for the power of vigorous, lucid, and graceful self-expression he acquired early and never ceased to develop. His future as a man and as a scholar appeared so promising that on graduation he was asked to be a teacher at the Boston Latin School, and there he began to work in September, 1855. Within a few weeks it was evident that he had every qualification for a schoolmaster except the power to maintain discipline. Here his defects were so complete and disastrous that after four months he resigned; and until the following summer he passed through a period of gloom and depression. With every advantage of birth and education he found himself at twenty a failure.

Though he confessed then and later that at that time he had not been inwardly converted and his determination to enter the ministry was not firm or final, he decided to study at the Theological Seminary at Alexandria, Virginia. Yet more than he acknowledged—perhaps more than he realized—he was not without the sustaining sense of divine guidance. For when he left Boston he wrote these words: "As we pass from some experience to some experiment, from a tried to an untried scene of life, it is as when we turn to a new page in a book we have never read before, but whose author we know and love and trust to give us on every page words of counsel and purity and strengthening virtue."

Striking in personal appearance, with his six feet four inches of height, his large and handsome head, and his dark deep-set eyes, Phillips Brooks was both reserved and sensitive. His abundant capacity both for fun and for friendship needed time to be manifest; and for months in his strange surroundings he was homesick. He found the Seminary at first "the most shiftless, slipshod place I ever saw," and Professor Sparrow "the only real live man we have here." But like all who have come to know that family community at Alexandria he grew to love it and to express his gratitude for the rich experiences of the next three years.

If we find it hard not to devote an undue amount of space to these earlier years, it is because Brooks was right, at least about himself, when he said, "It is the five years after college which are the most decisive in a man's career. . . . The years which come before are too fluid. The years which come after are too solid." It was in Virginia, then, to a surprising extent that the future Phillips Brooks was formed and nourished by a process that was largely self-education. It was there that he began the practice of filling note-book after note-book with the fruit of his thought, of his imagination, and of his extraordinarily wide and varied reading, so that even of this youth of twenty-two his biographer could say, "He was still destined to grow and to expand, but every germ and principle of the later expansion is here revealed." And the growth he experienced was not only intellectual. By the slow process that was natural for a "once-born" soul his conversion to the service of Christ and the vocation of the ministry became complete and profound. He was confirmed in 1857, and in June, 1859, he was ordained deacon.

The day after his ordination Brooks preached at Fredericksburg, Virginia, a sermon of which the rector wrote long after, "I have heard him often since, and the impression is always the same . . . a singular absence of self-consciousness, a spontaneity of beautiful thinking, clothed in pure English words, a joy in his own thoughts, and a victorious mastery of the truth he was telling, combined with humility and reverence and love for the congregation." [1] On the following Sunday he began his ministry at the Church of the Advent in Philadelphia, where for three years he filled the church to overflowing, declining each year a series of calls to points as far separated as New York and San Francisco.

In 1862, when he was still only twenty-six, Brooks became the rector of Holy Trinity Church, Philadelphia, one of the largest parishes in the country. His popularity was growing, and the adulation he received was

[1] W. Lawrence, *Phillips Brooks,* 44 f. (Harpers).

so widespread and obvious that his loving and watchful parents were moved to write him at different times always to keep humble and not to let his head be turned by flattery. But as Bishop Lawrence once wrote, "Brooks is popularly known as a great preacher, and such he was. But in all my relations with him I could never discover that he thought he was." Unlike many other "stars" he loved to visit his people and was continually active in parish calling. "I would like to do nothing but make pastoral calls," he said. "Indeed if I didn't I could not preach." Yet, after all, it was as a preacher that he was famous, and even in these first Philadelphia years reporters came from New York to hear him. As one of them recorded of "the clerical prodigy of our Church," "In appearance he is tall and commanding, but not over-graceful; his style of elocution is rapid, even to discomfort, many of his glowing periods being lost through the quickness of their utterance. His composition is marked by striking originality and comprehensiveness. A rich vein of Gospel truth runs through his discourses." [2]

Phillips Brooks's first three years at Holy Trinity were years of civil war, an experience into which he entered fully with no doubt as to his convictions. He had always been eager for the abolition of slavery, and he welcomed the Emancipation Proclamation with joy. Though in Philadelphia there were many Southern sympathizers and not a few Copperheads, he preached his beliefs without fear, and in his support of Lincoln and the Republican administration he never wavered. He was constantly active in the service of the soldiers in and near Philadelphia, cooperating with the Sanitary Commission and visiting the camps and hospitals; and after Gettysburg he spent a week in the battle area among the wounded and the prisoners of war. When the conflict had ended he became an active member of the Freedman's Relief Association and championed the cause of Negro suffrage.

It was two months after the surrender of Lee that a huge gathering met at Harvard in honor of the alumni who had died in the war. On that occasion poems were read by Emerson and Holmes, and Lowell delivered his famous Ode. A brief prayer was offered by Phillips Brooks—"his great head thrown back," as Dr. Huntington remembered that moment, "his face looking as if it might be Stephen's, while there went forth from his lips a fiery stream of thanksgiving and supplication the like of which I never knew." And Eliot—soon to be President of Harvard—said, "It was the most impressive utterance of a proud and happy day. Even Lowell's Commemoration Ode did not at the moment so touch the hearts of his hearers; that one spontaneous and intimate expression of Brooks's noble

[2] A. V. G. Allen, *Phillips Brooks,* I, 398.

spirit convinced all Harvard men that a young prophet had risen up in Israel." [3]

Three weeks later Phillips Brooks sailed for Europe to enjoy a year of holidays which his generous and devouted parishioners had given him. The year after his return they came near losing him when the new Episcopal Theological School in Cambridge asked him to be its dean. Calls to parishes he had refused in great numbers, but this opportunity was more attractive. He declined it, however, and denied also a most urgent summons in 1868 to be rector of Trinity Church in Boston. But when the vestry of Trinity tried again the next year he was persuaded to say yes. After ten years in Philadelphia he began in October, 1869, the great ministry of twenty-two years in that Boston church where his presence still seems real.

In terms of events there is little to record of these two decades. Within three years the downtown church of the ancient Trinity parish was burned in the great Boston fire, and the genius of Henry H. Richardson created in the new Back Bay the noble Romanesque Trinity Church of today. Long before it was consecrated in 1877 the general pattern of Brooks's life had taken shape. Three times a week he preached—twice on Sundays and again on Wednesday evenings. In pastoral ministration he was ceaselessly active, for the *parish,* rather than social causes or civic or ecclesiastical affairs, was the center of his interest. To Harvard, however, he gave much attention as overseer, preacher, and friend of students. Yet when he was asked in 1881 to be Preacher to the University (a call urgently supported by a huge mass meeting of students), his decision was not to leave Trinity. Every other summer he was accustomed to spend in travel abroad. Once he voyaged as far as Japan, and once to India, when a whole year's leave was given him. But in England his welcome was warmest, and there he preached often in Westminster Abbey and, on many a visit, in one or another cathedral.

His growing power as a preacher seemed inexhaustible, and there is a wealth of testimony to the impression he made upon listeners. "He is exceedingly portly," one wrote, "and also very tall; in bearing one of the most commanding men of his day. He has a fine well-proportioned head, covered with a short growth of thick dark hair. . . . A certain throwing of his head up and a little to one side is his most prominent gesture. . . . There is nothing in his voice, bearing, or look which can explain his almost unexampled popularity. For popular he is almost beyond precedent." [5]

[3] *Ibid.,* I, 552.
[4] This prolonged tour, the first of many, included Ireland, Scotland, England, Belgium, Germany, Austria, Turkey, Syria, Palestine, Egypt, Greece, Italy, and France.
[5] A. V. G. Allen, II, 18.

But it was not Bostonians alone who left records of Phillips Brooks in the pulpit. James Bryce had this to say of him, "There was no sign of art about his preaching, no touch of self-consciousness. He spoke to his audience as a man might speak to his friend, pouring forth with swift, yet quiet and seldom impassioned earnestness the thoughts and feelings of his singularly pure and lofty spirit. The listeners never thought of style or manner, but only of the substance of the thoughts. They were entranced and carried out of themselves by the strength and sweetness and beauty of the aspects of religious truth and its helpfulness to weak human nature which he presented. There was a wealth of keen observation, fine reflection, and insight both subtle and imaginative, all touched with warmth and tenderness which seemed to transfuse and irradiate the thought itself."[6] And John Tulloch, the famous Scottish theologian, wrote to his wife in 1874, "I have just heard the most remarkable sermon I ever heard in my life from Mr. Phillips Brooks, an Episcopal clergyman here: equal to the best of Frederick Robertson's sermons, with a vigor and force of thought which he has not always. I never heard preaching like it, and you know how slow I am to praise preachers. So much thought and so much life combined; such a reach of mind, and such a depth and insight of soul. I was electrified. I could have got up and shouted."[7]

Behind the preaching of Brooks there lay not only creative power and personal charm but the unsparing toil of the thinker and the artist. Day in and day out whatever in his experience could be put to use in his sermons was recorded in memory or in writing. The sermon of any given week would begin with a brief hint in his note-book. On Monday and Tuesday mornings he would assemble in the book the thoughts and illustrations which were to provide his material; and the following morning he would produce a plan of the entire composition, noting how many pages each paragraph was to occupy. Finally, on the mornings of Thursday and Friday he would write out the sermon in full. Thus when he stood in the pulpit his people reaped the benefit not only of his genius and character but of his labor.

The convictions about preaching which the experience of Brooks had brought him were expressed in memorable form in the *Lectures on Preaching* delivered at Yale in 1877 and later published and widely read. These addresses, in which he never mentions himself, reveal on almost every page what his vocation meant to him and why so many thousands looked to him to sustain what was best in their lives. "Preaching is the bringing of truth through personality. . . . There must be a man behind every sermon." "To be dead in earnest is to be eloquent." "The personal

[6] W. Lawrence, *Phillips Brooks,* 107 f. (Harpers).
[7] A. V. G. Allen, II, 121.

interest of the preacher is the buoyant air that fills the mass and lifts it." "Say nothing which you do not believe to be true because you think it may be helpful." "Pray for and work for fulness of life above everything; full red blood in the body; full honesty and truth in the mind; and the fulness of a grateful love for the Saviour in your heart."

The content of his sermons was richly varied and always positive. In spite of the fact that the years of his ministry coincided with the era of scientific advance and religious doubt and the discrediting of dogmas, his preaching was never controversial. He followed those homely pieces of advice to ministers—"Burn your own smoke" and "Don't preach your processes: preach your results." Though receptive of the thought of the day and endowed with mental powers capable of reconstructing theology, he thought the pulpit no fit place for threshing out problems. He never argued or debated. As his gifted Congregationalist neighbor, the Rev. George A. Gordon, expressed it, "He chose, as indispensable for his calling, to let the artist in him prevail, to do all his thinking through the forms of the imagination and to give truth a body corresponding, as far as possible, to its own ineffable beauty." [8] He might have taken as his guide the counsel to ministers of a later age given by Bishop Brent—"Melt your theology into poetry. But note that you must have a theology before you can melt it."

Contrary to later ideas of what it means to be a "liberal," the attitude of Phillips Brooks toward the essential elements of Christianity was conservative and orthodox. Deriding the contemporary scorn of theology, he maintained with fervor the fundamental tenets of the Christian faith. Though a passionate defender of the right to individual freedom of thought, he never used the liberty he claimed to spread doubt or to encourage denials. That is why his effect upon the youth of the period was so tonic and bracing. Here was a man, they found, with his eyes wide open, who knew everything that was going on, and who yet radiated confidence. For the central principles of his theology and of his life and the leading motif of all his utterances was the Incarnation of God in Christ. The Immanence of God, the Fatherhood of God, the glory of the Christian life—all were interpreted in the light of the Deity of the Living Christ. It was no formal compliment when the Regius Professor of Divinity at Oxford, on that day in 1885 when Brooks received the honorary degree of Doctor of Divinity, hailed him as "a defender of the Catholic faith."

As Phillips Brooks himself said, "There must be a man behind every sermon." What, then, was the man behind these sermons? To any ob-

[8] *Ibid.*, II, 781 f.

server there was evident in him both physical robustness and a completely normal sanity devoid of eccentricity. Even to those who did not know him well there was obvious his "exuberance and buoyancy," "his talent for nonsense in little things," "his boundless vitality." He gave the impression of being "the happiest of men, a happiness whose foundation was deep and inexhaustible, as though he drank from sources more rich and full than others, and to most men inaccessible." Yet this joyous quality was not inconsistent with a sense of loneliness of which he rarely spoke.

But there were many other traits in a nature as manifold as his; and perhaps they have never been expressed with more discerning care than by one who was both his biographer and his close friend. In Brooks he found "a fineness and delicacy unsurpassed in women, but utter freedom from any remotest approach to sentimentality; the powerful rugged will that, when roused, was like the whirlwind; scorn for whatever was base and unworthy written all over him; the love of the beautiful, which entered into his religion and his life, making it an end to do always whatever should seem beautiful to all, showing itself also in little things, the minutiae of life and manner; what was rarest of all, perfect simplicity and naturalness, with total absence of anything like affectation or hint of self-consciousness, as though he never gave himself a thought; and utter transparency, until the nature within was revealed in the voice and look. . . . He gave his capacious, loving heart full scope for its exercise, yet concentrated his energies upon one supreme purpose, going forth to meet every soul with the same boundless affection and earnest, impassioned longing for its salvation." [9]

That "going forth to meet every soul"—that pastoral eagerness—always overcame every temptation to seclude himself or to spare himself. Of the kind of call he was always ready to answer, his successor, Dr. Donald, gives a touching example. "A workingman, living in one of the suburbs of Boston, was told at the hospital that he must undergo a dangerous surgical operation; that he could not live unless it were performed; that it was doubtful even then if his life could be saved, but there might be a chance. He returned with the information to his home and his wife. The operation was to take place the next day. They had the evening before them, and they proposed to spend it in a call on Phillips Brooks whom neither of them knew, or had the slightest claim on his interest or attention. Only, as they faced the crisis, it seemed as if a call on Phillips Brooks was adequate to its portentousness for them both. Mr. Brooks received them as they had expected he must, talked with them and soothed them, and promised to be with them at the hospital on the following day.

[9] *Ibid.*, II, 593 f.

All which their imagination had conceived of what he might be to them in their emergency was fulfilled to the letter."[10] That the laborer and his wife should feel that Phillips Brooks belonged to them and that in trouble they should seek him first of all, offers a surer testimony to sainthood than huge congregations and honorary degrees.

But pastoral work was soon to be curtailed by the last great event in Brooks's life—his election as Bishop of Massachusetts in May, 1891, when he was fifty-five years old. His consecration followed in October, and for the next fifteen months he set himself to answering fully all the exacting demands of a diocese which then included the whole of Massachusetts. Signs of weariness and of a decline in health had been noticed even before his consecration, but now they began to multiply. Yet there was no thought of serious danger even when a severe throat infection seized him; and the shock of his death within a few days, on January 23, 1893, was profound. An entire city in mourning bore witness to his life; and when the funeral service at Trinity was ended, another service was held outside for the silent thousands who had gathered in Copley Square. "In my long life," said Dr. Andrew Peabody of Harvard, "I have not known an instance in which . . . so many men and women have had the sense of severe public bereavement."

What was the secret of that life whose power and joy had been shared by so many? It was a question which was asked him reverently by one of his younger clergy during the last months of his life. And his answer was uniquely self-revealing. ". . . These last years have had a peace and fulness which there did not use to be. . . . I am sure that it is a deeper knowledge and truer love of Christ. . . . All experience comes to be but more and more of pressure of His life on ours. It cannot come by one flash of light, or one great convulsive event. It comes without haste and without rest in this perpetual living of our life with Him. And all the history, of outer or inner life, of the changes of circumstances, or the changes of thought, gets its meaning and value from this constantly growing relation to Christ. I cannot tell you how personal this grows to me. He is here. He knows me and I know Him. It is no figure of speech. It is the reallest thing in the world. And every day makes it realler. And one wonders with delight what it will grow to as the years go on. . . . Less and less, I think, grows the consciousness of seeking God. Greater and greater grows the certainty that He is seeking us and giving Himself to us to the complete measure of our present capacity. That is Love,—not that we loved Him, but that He loved us."[11]

[10] *Ibid.*, II, 674.
[11] *Ibid.*, II, 871.

Chapter XIX

APPROACHES TO CHURCH UNITY

INCREASING readiness to cooperate and to explore the possibilities of reunion marked the temper and attitude of most of the non-Roman Churches in America during the last third of the nineteenth century. The movement which was to achieve so much in the next century had already begun to gather momentum. In this process the activity of the Episcopal Church, while not daring, was thoughtful and steady.

The easiest and most natural form of cooperation was to promote closer relations with other branches of the Anglican Communion. The first impulse to this end came in 1865 from a Synod of the Church of England in Canada which sent a message to the Archbishop of Canterbury recommending that he should arrange for a conference of all the bishops of the Anglican Communion. With remarkable promptness Archbishop Longley responded favorably to this proposal and sent invitations to one hundred and forty-four bishops, noting in his call that "such a meeting would not be competent to make declarations or lay down definitions on points of doctrine." As a result of this friendly summons seventy-six bishops met at Lambeth Palace in London for five days in September, 1867, nineteen of them from the United States. The meeting, however, was not a success, partly because an absurdly small time had been allowed for proper consideration of the many reports submitted, and partly because at that time nobody could think of anything but the Colenso controversy, a celebrated case which we have treated in an earlier chapter, and which succeeded in edging its way into the Conference.

Eleven years later, with Archbishop Tait presiding, a second Lambeth Conference was attended by a hundred bishops, of whom nineteen represented the Episcopal Church. Their meetings lasted for twenty-five days and were accounted so profitable that, except for interruptions caused by wars, Lambeth Conferences every ten years have become an honored tradition in the Anglican Communion. At these sessions varied topics have been discussed, including temperance, divorce, socialism, war, Christian education, and many more. Always, however, it has been borne in mind that the function of the Conference is advisory and not legislative. Its resolutions and findings are only opinions. Yet so great is its prestige that its beneficent influence has grown in power. As a factor in the movement toward Church union it has acted along two lines: it has furthered cooperation and an increasing sense of unity within the Anglican Communion, and it has provided a forum for the discussion of union with other bodies and for the utterance of pronouncements which carry weight.

Among these discussions and pronouncements one was the chief feature of the Conference of 1888—"The Lambeth Quadrilateral." It was the outcome of thought and of initiative in the American Church. Eighteen years earlier the Rev. William R. Huntington, then rector of All Saints' Church in Worcester, Massachusetts, had written a book called *The Church-Idea, an Essay towards Unity.* In the last chapter, entitled "Reconciliation," he presented the Episcopal Church as the best hope for promoting Church unity in the United States. Disavowing any intention of urging upon all others the full Anglican system, he offered as a basis what he declared to be the Anglican *principles.* "The true Anglican position," he wrote, "like the city of God in the Apocalypse, may be said to be foursquare. Honestly to accept that position is to accept—

1. The Holy Scriptures as the Word of God.
2. The Primitive Creeds as the Rule of Faith.
   [i.e., the Apostles' and Nicene Creeds]
3. The Two Sacraments Ordained by Christ Himself.
4. The Episcopate as the key-stone of Governmental Unity."

Proposing these four fundamentals as a ground-work for possible unity, he concluded with an ardent plea as well warranted now as then: "If our whole ambition as Anglicans in America be to continue as a small but eminently respectable body of Christians, and to offer a refuge to people of refinement and sensibility, who are shocked by the irreverences they are apt to encounter elsewhere; in a word, if we care to be only a countercheck and not a force in society; then let us say as much in plain terms, and frankly renounce any and all claim to Catholicity. We have only in such a case, to wrap the robe of our dignity about us, and walk quietly along in a seclusion no one will take much trouble to disturb. Thus may we be a Church in name and a sect in deed. But if we aim at something nobler than this, if we would have our Communion become national in very truth,—in other words, if we would bring the Church of Christ into the closest possible sympathy with the throbbing, sorrowing, sinning, repenting, aspiring heart of this great people—then let us press our reasonable claims to be the reconciler of a divided household, not in a spirit of arrogance . . . but with affectionate earnestness and an intelligent zeal."[1]

At that time (1870), as Huntington later remarked, "Acquiescence in sectarianism [was] the almost universal state of mind in the United States," and another sixteen years elapsed before the Church took any responsive action. At the General Convention of 1886, held at Chicago, the House of Bishops received a memorial dealing with the subject of Church unity and signed by more than eleven hundred clergy and three thousand laymen. A committee appointed at once to consider "the matter of the reunion of Christendom" recommended a Declaration concerning Unity which was later adopted by the House of Bishops. Since it is the most important statement on the subject ever officially published by the Episcopal Church, its main paragraphs should be quoted in full.

Addressing "all whom it may concern, and especially our fellow-Christians of the different communions in our land, who, in their several spheres, have contended for the religion of Christ," the bishops declared:

"1. Our earnest desire that the Saviour's prayer that we all may be one may, in its deepest and truest sense, be speedily fulfilled;

"2. That we believe that all who have been duly baptized with water in the name of the Father, and of the Son, and of the Holy Ghost, are members of the Holy Catholic Church;

"3. That in all things of human ordering or human choice relating to modes of worship and discipline, or to traditional customs, this Church is ready, in the spirit of love and humility, to forego all preferences of her own;

"4. That this Church does not seek to absorb other communions, but rather, cooperating with them on the basis of a common faith and order, to discountenance schism, to heal the wounds of the body of Christ, and to promote the charity which is the chief of Christian graces and the visible manifestation of Christ to the world:

"But furthermore, we do hereby affirm that the Christian unity now so earnestly desired by the memorialists can be restored only by the principles of unity exemplified by the undivided Catholic Church during the first ages of its existence, which principles we believe to be the substantial deposit of Christian faith and order committed by Christ and His Apostles to the Church unto the end of the world, and therefore incapable of compromise or surrender by those who have been ordained to be its stewards and trustees for the common and equal benefit of all men.

[1] W. R. Huntington, *Church-Idea,* 4th ed., 169 f.

"As inherent parts of this sacred deposit, and therefore as essential to the restoration of unity among the divided branches of Christendom, we account the following, to wit:

"I. The Holy Scriptures of the Old and New Testaments, as the revealed Word of God;

"II. The Nicene Creed, as the sufficient statement of the Christian faith;

"III. The two sacraments, Baptism and the Supper of the Lord, ministered with unfailing use of Christ's words of institution, and of the elements ordained by Him;

"IV. The Historic Episcopate, locally adapted in the methods of its administration to the varying needs of the nations and peoples called of God into the unity of His Church.

"Furthermore, deeply grieved by the sad divisions which afflict the Christian Church in our own land, we hereby declare our desire and readiness, so soon as there shall be any authorized response to this Declaration, to enter into brotherly conference with all or any Christian bodies seeking the restoration of the organic unity of the Church, with a view to the earnest study of the conditions under which so priceless a blessing might happily be brought to pass."

Upon the receipt of this Declaration the House of Deputies asked for a Joint Commission on Church Unity, which was soon appointed and directed to communicate the Declaration to all Protestant Churches in the country and to hold themselves in readiness to confer with any bodies seeking union.

Two years after this "Chicago Quadrilateral" had been issued, a hundred and forty-five bishops (including twenty-nine from the United States) assembled for the third Lambeth Conference in July, 1888. The opening sermon was preached by Bishop Whipple of Minnesota, who avowed his conviction that "no one branch of the Church is absolutely by itself alone the Catholic Church; all branches need reunion in order to the completeness of the Church." "We all know," he pleaded, "that this divided Christianity cannot conquer the world. At a time when every form of error and sin is banded together to oppose the Kingdom of Christ the world needs the witness of a united Church." Then followed a series of meetings lasting four weeks, devoted to many problems besides those of Church unity. And before the sessions ended all the bishops present voted for a Declaration nearly identical with that set forth at Chicago. The third and fourth pillars of Anglicanism were not even reworded. The first and second were slightly amended to read—

"(a) The Holy Scriptures of the Old and New Testaments, as

'containing all things necessary to salvation,' and as being the rule and ultimate standard of faith;

"(b) The Apostles' Creed, as the Baptismal Symbol; and the Nicene Creed, as the sufficient statement of the Christian faith."

This Lambeth Quadrilateral has been interpreted from time to time, especially as to the meaning of its fourth section; but it still expresses the official position of the Church in relation to projects for union with Protestant bodies. Its authority was further strengthened in 1892 when the House of Deputies voted approval of the four principles. By that time the Commission on Church Unity had transmitted the Declaration to eighteen Protestant communions in the hope that it would prompt them to replies which might lead to negotiation, and it had been conferring for several years with the Presbyterians and Lutherans. These negotiations, though friendly, were extremely cautious. Most of them, in fact, took the form of the exchange of carefully worded letters, lest meeting face to face might (it was said) provoke to debate.

Progress with the Presbyterian commission was encouraging at first. The General Assembly which appointed it accepted the Quadrilateral as a basis for negotiation, and the commission declared that organic union should be the ultimate goal. But as the two groups seldom communicated more than once in six months and sometimes at intervals of two years, the advantages of informal discussion were not enjoyed. All differences of opinion, of course, centered around Point Four, the episcopate. The Episcopal representatives interpreted it to permit a *constitutional* episcopate, like their own, limiting the authority of bishops and assigning extensive powers to presbyters. But the Presbyterians were not satisfied with this explanation, nor would they abandon their traditional teaching that all presbyters are bishops and that therefore bishops do not constitute a higher order. They affirmed, too, the further belief that all bodies "professing the true religion" are branches of the visible Church of Christ regardless of their Church polity and that their ministries and sacraments are valid. This being the case, they insisted that the first step toward unity was "mutual recognition and reciprocity," by which they evidently meant intercommunion.

In 1894, eight years after negotiation had begun, the Presbyterian General Assembly directed its commission to suspend further correspondence until General Convention should have instructed its own commission to accept and act upon this doctrine of "mutual recognition and reciprocity." This decision, which ended further conference, was really a change of front on the part of the Presbyterians. Having first accepted the Quadrilateral as the basis of negotiation, they later demanded as a new basis the adoption of a principle which cancelled Point Four of the Quadrilateral. Intercommunion regardless of polities is no doubt worthy of discussion, but it assumes that the episcopate is not a factor essential to union with the Episcopal Church. Regrettable as was the failure of this early approach, it served to register the important fact that in dealing with the Presbyterian Church the sensitive point will always be not doctrine but polity.

Of quite another sort was the experience of the Commission in their intercourse with the Lutherans. Though the Evangelical Lutheran Church appointed a commission and correspondence with them lasted for a year or two, their Synod passed resolutions declaring that they did not consider organic union at present to be either desirable or practical, and that they did not agree that the Nicene Creed is "a sufficient statement of the Christian faith," for (among other defects) it is silent on the subject of the Sacraments. In place of the Quadrilateral they proposed as a basis for cooperation the Augsburg Confession of 1530. Even less content with the famous Four Points was the Evangelical Lutheran Church of the South, which found the Nicene Creed inadequate because it failed to mention the total depravity of man. The two statements dealing with the Sacraments and the episcopate they found "too uncertain and capable of too many constructions to be approved by us." Quite clearly, then, discussion with the Lutherans did not prove fruitful. But even a brief interchange of notes illustrated the well-known fact that in dealing with this Church the sensitive point is not polity but doctrine.

It was only with Presbyterians and Lutherans that the Commission reached the talking or writing stage. The Methodists sent no official response to the original message; and the Baptists, as might have been expected, explained that their congregational polity prevented the appointment of any commission to speak for the whole body of Baptist churches. Thus ten years after the promulgation of the Quadrilateral one Church had accepted it as a basis for an approach to reunion; one had explicitly rejected it; and all the others had let it pass. It was quite plain that the method of hanging out a sign, as it were, did not produce a psychological effect sufficiently warm. Conscious perhaps of this fact, the Lambeth Conference of 1897, for which nearly two hundred bishops gathered, approved a resolution to the effect that "the time has now arrived in which the constituted authorities of the various branches of our Communion should not merely make it known that they hold themselves in readiness to enter into brotherly conference with representatives of other Christian communities in the English-speaking races, but should themselves *originate such conferences and especially arrange for representative meetings for united humiliation and intercession.*"

Of quite a different order was the exchange of salutations and information with certain foreign Churches. This was not the function of the Joint Commission on Church Unity but of several other committees, such as the Joint Committee on Ecclesiastical Relations and Religious Reform. The Churches to which these bodies gave most attention were the Old Catholic Church,[2] the Church of Sweden, and the Russian Church. The General Convention of 1874 regarded the Old Catholics as "preparing the way for a return to Apostolic truth and primitive order," and the House of Bishops adopted resolutions voicing sympathy with their leaders. Moreover, they appointed a commission of three bishops "to keep up fraternal correspondence with the Bishop and Synod, for exchange of information and consideration of overtures for reconciliation and intercommunion between sundered Churches." At succeeding Conventions reports were submitted giving long accounts of the nature and development of the Old Catholic movement. No more appears to have been attempted than the expression of friendly greetings and the transmission of facts.

It was the Convention of 1892 which appointed a Joint Commission "to confer on the regularity and validity of the orders of the Church of Sweden." The report of this body in 1895 conceded "a very strong probability that in the Established Church of Sweden a tactual ministerial succession has been continued since the period of the Lutheran Reformation." But the mode of ordination and the rejection of the diaconate were cited as adverse circumstances. The commission in conclusion offered a resolution which, though declining to pass judgment on the validity of Swedish orders, recommended that no minister of that Church be allowed to officiate in any Episcopal Church. Consideration of the report, however, was indefinitely postponed. Yet even this failure to act caused sufficient alarm to produce in 1898 a memorial presented to the House of Bishops and signed by ten bishops, which stated that "there is at least the gravest doubt as to the validity of Swedish orders." The signers included not only certain well-known High Churchmen but also the Bishops of Southern Virginia, Washington, and Maryland, whose Churchmanship made it clear that the document was not partisan. The net result of these researches into legitimacy was certainly not to promote more cordial relations between the two Churches.

The General Convention of 1868 restored to the Joint Committee on the Russo-Greek Church the right "to correspond with the authorities

[2] The Old Catholic Church was organized by former Roman Catholics in Germany, Austria, and Switzerland who had been alienated by the action of the Vatican Council of 1870, which set forth the dogma of Papal Infallibility. The schism was a protest against this decision and against the extreme Ultramontanism which produced it. Their first formal Synod was held in 1874.

of the Russian and other branches of the Oriental Church," but only "for the acquisition of further authentic information." Six years later the committee asked to be relieved from further duty on the ground that only a committee of bishops could effectively engage in correspondence with the hierarchy of the Eastern Churches. A committee of three bishops was therefore appointed, and the following two resolutions were passed, which indicate the general purpose and attitude of the Episcopal Church.

"*Resolved,* that we regard the establishment of full and free reciprocal relations of Christian brotherhood between the great Eastern Churches and our own Communion as daily growing in importance and in hopefulness, and heartily pray the great Head of the Church that His Spirit may so rule in all our councils as to remove all hindrances which the pride, prejudice, or error of human frailty may present to impede its consummation.

"*Resolved,* that we desire the continuance and increased frequency of friendly correspondence with our brethren of the Holy Eastern Churches in the assured confidence that on either part there will be the fullest recognition of all feelings and rights which might be imperilled by undue or inconsiderate interference."

In spite of the earnest hopes expressed in these resolutions no one in the Eastern Orthodox Churches or in the Episcopal Church was empowered to conduct anything that could be called negotiation. Indeed, no proposals of any kind were discussed. The chief obstacle on the other side was of course the fact that the Orthodox Church was not prepared to affirm the validity of Anglican orders. The chief obstacle on this side was the watchful suspicion of Evangelicals, who regarded these Eastern Churches as but little better than the Church of Rome. Thus hampered by restrictions explicit and implicit, the committee could scarcely do more than continue correspondence, in the usual stately fashion, with patriarchs in Russia, Constantinople, and elsewhere. The letters which were received and reported consisted largely of messages of thanks for the receipt of the journals of General Conventions. This may seem a small point to record; but anyone who can write a letter, reading almost like an apostolic epistle, full of gratitude for anything so painfully uninteresting as a journal of General Convention deserves honorable mention in the pages of history.

While the Episcopal Church, with an eye to the far future, was initiating the earliest approaches to organic union at home and abroad, Protestant Churches in the United States were taking important steps toward federation for immediately practical purposes. In 1886, for example, the Student Volunteer Movement was organized at Northfield, and under the irresistible leadership of John R. Mott began its amazingly successful career as a recruiting force for missionary service—"international, interdenominational, and intercollegiate." Though the Church treated this organization with coolness, it often profited from its activities. Likewise prompted by the needs of missions was the Foreign Missions Conference of North America organized in 1893 to represent, as a cooperative group, the Boards of Missions of nearly all the leading non-Roman communions. Operating through its Committee of Reference and Counsel, it has proved more and more valuable in enabling Boards to act in concert on matters of vital moment; and ever since its origin the Episcopal Church has been a valued member.

Chapter XX

"THE SOCIAL GOSPEL"

CHRISTIAN *philanthropy,* such as charity to the sick and needy, has been familiar enough in all periods of the Church's history, and it was a phase in the activity of the American Churches from their earliest days. Even campaigns of *reform* in the name of Christianity were promoted by American Churches in the first half of the nineteenth century—efforts, for example, toward the improvement of prisons and the abatement of the liquor traffic. The anti-slavery contest was of course the greatest crusade of all. Of much slower growth were the movements for social *reconstruction* in accordance with the principles of Christ, for these were not prominent until the last decade or two of the century.

These three phases of social Christianity are often hard to distinguish and gradually shade into each other. Philanthropy, unless it is content to keep on treating symptoms, is almost certain to lead to reform, and as soon as reform becomes radical and begins to question the whole social structure, it finds itself committed to reconstruction. With each stage the number of Christians who can be counted upon for support grows smaller, for each stage demands ever higher ideals and an increasing discontent with things as they are. There can hardly be found a decent citizen who will not give a dime to provide milk for a sick baby; and on a larger scale philanthropic benefactions have always stood to the credit of even the most reactionary Christians. Reform, however, is another matter. The average Church member is likely to conclude that it is "none of his business." Yet the temperance movement, the peace movement, and the movements on behalf of prisoners and the insane have enlisted hundreds of thousands of professing Christians. Such work, indeed, is only a far-sighted kind of philanthropy. But to conclude that the social system as a whole is faulty and that the hardest problems which reform is trying to solve can find their solution only through a radical reconstruction of the social fabric—that is a further step which few take.

Because the Church and its leaders are characteristically conservative (and nearly always have been) it is an advance which has so far enlisted only a handful of Church members.

In this chapter we shall be little concerned with philanthropy in the narrower sense, but rather with the Church's activity in social reform, and with the few signs of a novel zeal for social reconstruction.

In the era with which we are dealing conditions calling for reform in every department of American life were openly shocking. The opportunity and the stimulus for remedial action could hardly have been greater. The treatment of the pauper insane was horrible. The suffering caused by child labor and by sweat-shops was taken for granted. Public health control was so feeble that devastating epidemics of small-pox, typhus, and yellow fever were of frequent occurrence. The densely crowded city slums bred vice and disease. Political corruption was at its maximum. In the 1880's over $200,000,000 was invested in the liquor business. And labor was only slowly learning how to defend its rights and to improve conditions of life which we should now regard as intolerable.

In few cases, if any, did the Churches officially pioneer in reform; but at this time so large a number of humanitarian leaders were active Church members that in a real sense the initiative was Christian in origin and in spirit. Nor is this distinction to the discredit of the Church, for the Church as such cannot be expected to establish Boards of Health or to manage county jails. If it can inspire its members to launch remedial projects, it has performed one of its vital functions. And so it was in the United States from 1865 onward.

Prompted by sound social motives, usually traceable to Christian convictions, steady progress was registered in field after field. In 1866, for instance, New York established the first municipal Board of Health. In 1870 there was organized the National Prison Association. Four years later the Woman's Christian Temperance Union began its campaigning. Buffalo formed in 1877 its Charity Organization Society, and in twenty-five years there were nearly a hundred and fifty others. The American Red Cross Society was established in 1881. It was in New York City in 1886 that the first social settlement was opened, to be followed within a decade by fifty others. Labor, moreover, was learning through organization increasingly effective and through the more frequent use of strikes to raise its standard of living and to win rights hitherto denied.

The slow reaction of the Churches to the evils calling for such efforts at reform was gradually quickened during the last two decades of the century chiefly by two phenomena of the time—the rapidly growing cities and the intensity of strife between capital and labor. These two dominating factors in the life of the nation forced themselves upon the attention of Christian leaders, prompting some to attempts at reform, others to plans for social reconstruction.

Typical of organizations to ameliorate some of the evils of city life were the Young Men's Christian Association, which was well established in America by the end of the war, and the Salvation Army, which eventually added social service to evangelism. Campaigns against corruption and commercialized vice were another contribution made at intervals by influential pastors, such as the Presbyterian preacher Charles H. Parkhurst, who stirred New York to good effect in the 'nineties. Most characteristic of the period was "the institutional parish"—a city church organized to provide not only worship and instruction but an expanding array of social services. Among these were the People's Temple (Congregational) of Denver and the Baptist Temple in Philadelphia, including a school since grown to Temple University. The Episcopal Church had long before supplied leadership in Dr. Muhlenberg's Church of the Holy Communion; but in this later era the most notable examples were Grace Church, New York (first under Henry C. Potter and then under William R. Huntington), and St. George's Church, New York, under William S. Rainsford.

In 1883 St. George's Church was almost empty. Most of the rich people had moved away, and few of the poor had ventured to take their place. A wise vestry, headed by J. Pierpont Morgan, called from Canada a powerful young Englishman, William S. Rainsford. He demanded that all the sittings in the church should be made free; that all committees except the vestry be abolished; and that $10,000 a year be set aside for use at his discretion. Thanks to the abounding energy of Rainsford's personality, the unwavering support of his vestry, and the exceptional quality of the curates whose loyalty he enlisted through many years, St. George's was completely transformed into a giant hive of Christian activity. There crowds were drawn not only by vigorous preaching but by nearly every variety of social service. Under the leadership of the rector, his four assistants, three deaconesses, and numerous lay helpers, there flourished various organizations for boys and girls—the Boys' Club, the Trade School, the Cadet Battalion, the Girls' Friendly Society, and the Daughters of the King. The interests of men were cared for by a Men's Club and a gymnasium. Married women met in a society especially for them, and young men and young women were attracted in large numbers by the Sunday Afternoon Club and by dramatic and literary societies. To offer varied kinds of relief there was a series of organizations—a general Poor Fund, a Grocery Department, a Women's Industrial Exchange, and a house in the country for those in need of "fresh air." In addition, a visiting trained nurse was in constant attendance upon the sick.

Even more than the appealing needs of the great cities the mounting conflict between capital and labor stirred Churchmen to participation in movements of reform and eventually to sponsoring programs for economic reorganization. It was the industrial revolution and all that flowed from it which constituted the strongest single factor in the rise and spread of "the Social Gospel."

During the generation before the Civil War "organized Protestantism supported the dominant economic beliefs and institutions even more unanimously than it accepted the existing form of government. . . . Support for the moral, political, and economic *status quo* was ingrained in American Protestantism." [1] The future bishop Alonzo Potter in his *Political Economy,* published in 1840, asserted that trade unions were bound to injure the interests of their members because they disregarded the laws of nature "which are nothing less than the laws of God." A similar conviction was expressed in 1866 by *The Congregationalist* in the statement, "The laws of political economy . . . are part of God's providence in the world." In fact it may be observed, curiously enough, that until nearly the last decade of the century pious people refused to believe any facts reported by scientists when they contradicted Christian tradition; but they were only too ready to accept as gospel truth anything whatever that economists told them. To these "laws" of economics all Christian principles were supposed to bow in subjection. And the economics of that epoch were of course of the classical type, proving the divine right of individualism, competition, and laissez-faire.

One of the most vicious features of the current political economy was its assumption that labor was a commodity; that neither laws nor bargains could change the rate of wages, which were determined by supply and demand; and that poverty was chiefly due to vice and could never be eliminated. All these dogmas were consoling to the prosperous and were echoed by ministers and by Church journals. To the rich nothing more disturbing was preached during the 'sixties and 'seventies than the stewardship which accompanied wealth. Henry Ward Beecher condemned the eight-hour day and denounced labor unions during the strikes of 1877. Typical, too, was the paper of W. D. Wilson read before the Episcopal Church Congress in 1874 which advised the poor: "Be content with your wages; work for what you can get, but work. . . . Deserve more, and in the Lord's good time you will get more. . . . Whatever you suffer here from the injustice of others will turn to your account hereafter." [2]

It is from the early 'eighties that we may date the first manifest

[1] H. F. May, *Protestant Churches and Industrial America,* 6, 13.
[2] *Report of Church Congress,* 1874, 53 f.

signs in America of a new attitude toward social problems on the part of certain leaders in the Churches. Labor conflicts, especially acute in 1877 and 1886, served to disturb complacent satisfaction with the *status quo*. Orthodox economics began to be modified by younger thinkers under European influence; and Henry George—more radical than these—had published in 1879 his famous *Progress and Poverty,* widely read among clergy as well as laymen.

While these influences from outside the Churches were operating upon thoughtful Christians, their conception of the meaning and function of Christianity in society was being affected by the Liberal theology which was laying even greater stress not upon traditional dogmas but upon the personality and the ethical teaching of the historical Jesus. As Visser 't Hooft has observed, "There is a remarkable coincidence in time between the scientific and the social movement. Both begin in the later decades of the nineteenth century. Both come to full fruition in the first decades of the twentieth. . . . The first advocates of an adjustment of theology to the new views of science and those who seek a more socially interested religion are often the same men." [3] But Liberals in theology were by no means always social Liberals, and in England the Anglo-Catholics were foremost in social Christianity before the century had ended.

Responsive to all these elements in the life and thought of the times, there gradually became effective what was later known as "the Social Gospel." It was a conscious movement to apply the Christian ethic to the solution of social problems, or, in other words to interpret the meaning of Christianity and the function of the Church in social terms directly related to the needs of contemporary society. A generation earlier this development had begun in England (where the industrial revolution was already an old story), with the "Christian Socialism" of Maurice and Kingsley.

Though John M. Ludlow, a lawyer, was the real founder of Christian Socialism, which flourished between 1850 and 1854, Frederick D. Maurice "was its seer and prophet and Charles Kingsley its most brilliant interpreter and spokesman." [4] It had been stimulated by the cooperative movement of Robert Owen, by the Chartist agitation, and by the revolutions of 1848 in Europe. Its avowed aim was "to reach the unsocial Christians and the un-Christian socialists." The leaders of this group published *The Christian Socialist* and organized a Society for the Promoting of Workingmen's Associations. They exerted themselves to develop co-

[3] W. A. Visser 't Hooft, *Background of the Social Gospel,* 147. Kingsley in England, Washington Gladden and Lyman Abbott among Protestants in America, and Bishop Potter among Episcopalians are obvious examples.

[4] S. Miller and J. F. Fletcher, *The Church and Industry,* 9.

operative associations and founded a Workingman's College in London. Both Maurice and Kingsley were intensely earnest in their efforts to better the living conditions of the laboring man, but neither of them understood the meaning of socialism or of democracy. Aristocratic in temper, they believed that society should be organized in classes and that the gentleman should lead the lower classes along the ways of peace and prosperity.[5] Indeed, "Christian Socialism was on the tiniest scale:—a few thousand tracts sold, a couple of unsuccessful weekly journals, a few hundred pounds subscribed—just a little eddy in the midst of the great turmoil of London and of England. . . . Its notoriety was largely created by its enemies." [6] Yet as pioneers in an adventure that called for hardihood Maurice and Kingsley are rightly honored a hundred years later.

Thirty years after the activities of Christian Socialism in England had ceased, the movement in America to Christianize the economic order began to be evident. Its most prominent leader for twenty years was the Rev. Washington Gladden, who began his pastorate in Columbus, Ohio, in 1882. Episcopalians know him as the author of the hymn, "O Master, let me walk with thee," but he was famous in his day as a champion in the cause of labor. Though he opposed political socialism, he was radical enough for his time in his declaration, "When the wage system rests on competition as its sole basis, it is anti-social and anti-Christian," and "The doctrine which bases all the relations of employer and employed upon self-interest is a doctrine of the pit; it has been bringing hell to earth in large installments for a good many years." [7] Other representatives of Protestant Churches, moreover, such as the editor Lyman Abbott and Professor Francis G. Peabody of Harvard, were active in this decade in the cause of Christian social ethics and its application.

But despite the reputation of the Episcopal Church for dignified conservatism, it is the opinion of impartial historians that the leaders of that Church were foremost in their advocacy of a Christian social order. One of them asserts that "undoubtedly the Protestant Episcopal Church was the first major denomination to receive the new doctrines with any general welcome"; [8] and another speaks of "the deep concern in social problems that has characterized its significant contribution to the growth of American social Christianity." [9]

Forgetting some of their prejudices of 1874, the Church Congress in 1884 invited Henry George to address them on the subject, "Is our civilization just to workingmen?" Though another speaker on the same

[5] G. F. Masterman, *F. D. Maurice,* 110.
[6] *Ibid.,* 109.
[7] H. F. May, *Protestant Churches and Industrial America,* 173.
[8] *Ibid.,* 182.
[9] C. H. Hopkins, *Rise of the Social Gospel,* 38.

occasion pronounced George's single tax theories to be absurd, and affirmed that legal interference with wages was robbery, George himself called our civilization "glaringly, bitterly, and increasingly unjust." Seven years later another Congress held a symposium on Socialism in which Christian socialists and single-taxers spoke. Bishops, too, were not afraid to take unpopular stands. Henry C. Potter of New York was not only energetic in civic reform, attacking the evils of slums, sweat-shops, and child labor, but ventured in 1886 to issue a Pastoral Letter in which he opposed the familiar dogma that labor and the laborer are commodities "to be bought and sold as the market shall decree." In the same year Bishop Frederick D. Huntington of Central New York demanded a Christian solution of labor problems and stated that "a system in which men and women of the wage-earning class are subjected to the control and caprice of their paymasters is not one that consistent Americans or intelligent Christians can contemplate with complacency."[10] And perhaps next to Gladden in prominence among the pastors who preached the social gospel was the Episcopalian R. Heber Newton of New York, who wrote books on labor problems in which he favored a gradual approach to a cooperative society.

Not content with individual utterances, those who were deeply committed to the cause went further to form organizations. In 1887 a group of clergy in New York founded "The Church Association for the Advancement of the Interests of Labor," which soon came to be known by its initials as CAIL. The leader was the young social radical James O. S. Huntington, founder of the Order of the Holy Cross; and his father, the Bishop of Central New York, became its president for the next seventeen years. Potter was an active member, and in spite of disapproval from many quarters, the new association soon had forty-seven bishops as honorary vice-presidents. Chapters were formed in other cities, especially in the East, and by 1890 CAIL was becoming widely known to unions as a friend and supporter of labor. It had special committees on sweat-shops and slum tenements, and it was active in promoting remedial legislation and in arbitrating strikes.[11]

A more advanced group, led by the Rev. W. D. P. Bliss, organized in Boston in 1889 the Society of Christian Socialists—"to awaken members of the Christian Churches to the fact that the teachings of Jesus Christ lead directly to some specific form or forms of Socialism." The Society sometimes played a part in local labor contests, but its main work was educational. As preacher and organizer Bliss was aided by the

[10] May, 180 f.

[11] For an excellent account of this organization and of the Christian Social Union I am indebted to S. Miller and J. F. Fletcher's book *The Church and Industry*.

Rev. Philo W. Sprague, who wrote a book on Christian Socialism in which he contended that the existing economic system was incompatible with Christianity. Though led by men who were both able and devoted, the Society was limited in influence. It had few members outside of Boston and made no strong appeal to representatives of labor.

More conservative and wholly educational in its purposes and methods was the Christian Social Union established in New York in 1891. The Union was modelled after the British society of the same name, which had been recently formed under the leadership of Scott Holland. Its first president was Bishop Huntington, and the noted economist, Richard T. Ely, of Johns Hopkins University, served as its secretary. Its aim was to promote the study and discussion of social problems from the Christian point of view. Through annual meetings, furthered by its chapters in a dozen cities, and through numerous carefully written pamphlets, the Union kept vital subjects before the Church public and set people to thinking. By 1897 it had enrolled seven hundred members.

Official bodies were of course far slower than these advance guards to give expression to social Christianity. No extended reference to industrial conditions can be found in any Pastoral Letters of the House of Bishops until 1889. In that year the bishops wrote that "the existing industrial system is subjected . . . to vehement criticism," though they themselves did not criticize it. They warned labor against "unreasonable" demands concerning hours and wages, though they did not indicate who was to decide what was unreasonable. One important statement, however, put their message abreast of the times: "It is a fallacy in social economics, as well as in Christian thinking, to look upon the labor of men and women and children as a mere commercial commodity to be bought and sold as an inanimate and irresponsible thing."

The year before this message to the Church was issued the Lambeth Conference had received from its Committee on Socialism a report which disapproved of any form of state ownership but recommended the development of cooperative societies. The Encyclical Letter which summed up the convictions of the assembled bishops proclaimed that "no more important problems can well occupy the attention—whether of clergy or laity—than such as are connected with what is popularly called Socialism. To study schemes proposed for redressing the social balance, to welcome the good which may be found in the aims or operations of any, and to devise methods, whether by legislation or by social combinations, or in any other way, for a peaceful solution of the problems without violence or injustice, is one of the noblest pursuits which can engage the thoughts of those who strive to follow in the footsteps of Christ." It was not until the Conference of 1897, however, that its Committee on Industrial Problems expressed the conviction that "Christian opinion . . . ought to condemn the belief that economic conditions are to be left to the action of material causes and mechanical laws, uncontrolled by any moral responsibility. . . . It can speak plainly of evils which attach to the economic system under which we live."

After a brief summary of the social problems of the day we have reviewed the work of those who were trying to further their solution by applying the principles of Christ. At the end of the century, after some twenty years of such efforts, what results could be noted? By the year 1900 what had been the consequences of the Social Gospel?

The main result had been the enlightenment of a small but increasing proportion of middle-class Church members. Books and articles on the social aspects of Christianity were becoming numerous and their thought was penetrating the life of most of the denominations. Hundreds of clergy had awakened to social issues and not a few of them were preaching the Gospel in social terms. Yet only a slim minority of the Christian community had been even partly converted to the cause of Christianizing the economic order. Most of its members were either too indifferent or too conservative to respond. Nor was there any marked change in the attitude of labor toward the Churches. Their record in the past had been spread too broadly on the pages of history to be cancelled by the recent enthusiasm of an unofficial minority. Wage-earners were not being drawn into the Churches by any new movement, and direct cooperative contacts between labor leaders and representatives of the Churches were few.

Yet progress between 1865 and 1900, while slow and irregular, had been immensely encouraging when we consider the dead weight of resistance. It was a hopeful and wholesome circumstance that preaching like that of George Hodges in the Pittsburgh of 1890 was not only possible but widely popular, there and elsewhere. Where could there have been heard in earlier decades any such bold message as his sermon on "The Heresy of Cain": "Christianity is interested in everything which is meant to make earth more like heaven,—in the progress of education and its universal extension; in the improvement of machinery; in the discoveries of the men of science; in the researches of the scholars; in political reform and social betterment; in the houses that men and women live in, and the clothes they wear, and the dinners they eat, and the wages they get, and the amount of pleasure and of opportunity that enters into their lives. . . . What is the matter with society? That is what the new philanthropy desires to learn. . . . That owners of unsanitary tenements should be able to sit comfortably cushioned in the house of God and listen serenely and somnolently to the preacher's sermon, Sunday after Sunday, shows that the preacher is making a mistake as to the meaning and application of the Christian religion. . . . The Church . . . is concerned indeed with what is commonly called religion . . . but just as much with society and just as much with politics." [12]

[12] G. Hodges, *Heresy of Cain,* 15 f, 20, 67, 95.

PART V

THE CHURCH FROM 1901 TO 1931

INTRODUCTORY

JUST before the twentieth century opened, the United States had begun to play the novel role of a world power. The defeat of Spain in 1898 was followed by the acquisition of Puerto Rico and the Philippines, and the country embarked upon colonial administration and the education of subject peoples. An American Secretary of State led in the formation and adoption of the Open Door policy in a China which till then had seemed about to disintegrate. An American president, Theodore Roosevelt, served as mediator to bring to an end the Russo-Japanese War of 1904–5. The same president had recognized the new Republic of Panama in the previous year, and had started to "make the dirt fly" in digging the Panama Canal. But it was not until the first World War of 1914–18 that America became the foremost world power, with a destiny and a mission which it was not fully prepared to face and to discharge. After two years and a half of neutrality the United States declared war on Germany in April, 1917, and made toward victory the heavy contribution of two million soldiers in France. So powerful, however, was the postwar reaction against participation in the affairs of Europe that the Senate refused to ratify a peace treaty which involved membership in the League of Nations, and in 1920 the country withdrew into a sterile isolation which proved one contributing cause of the second World War.

In domestic affairs, no less than in foreign relations and adventures, the first thirty years of the century were crowded with events and with achievements. In terms of population it was a period of vast increase in the number of city-dwellers and of huge immigration, sometimes amounting to as many as a million a year, mostly from southern Europe. Except for a short financial panic in 1907, it was an era of unprecedented prosperity and industrial expansion, which witnessed not only the growth of great trusts but also steady advance in the organization of labor.

Unlike several previous epochs of prosperity the earlier years of the century were fortunately marked by an ever-growing agitation for economic and political reform. "The quest for social justice" was the outstanding characteristic of American life from the beginning of Theodore Roosevelt's administration in 1901 to the outbreak of the war under Wilson in 1917. As one observer put it, it took the form of "a Hamiltonian exertion of governmental power, necessary in order to restore Jeffersonian conditions of equal opportunity." The expanding strength of organized labor and the rise of the Socialist Party, which cast nearly a million votes in 1912, were but two of many factors which served to stimulate the reforming energies of municipal, state, and national leaders. These were the days of campaigns to purge city governments of corruption and to restore popular control in the administration of States. In these years, too, social legislation of the widest variety was achieved—the federal income tax, minimum wage laws, laws against child labor, employers' liability acts, and programs for the conservation of natural resources. In 1919 there was ratified the constitutional amendment authorizing the national prohibition of liquor, and in 1920 Woman Suffrage became part of the Constitution.

The end of the war brought reaction in every sphere—not only a dread of foreign entanglements but extreme political conservatism of the "back to normalcy" type, an unreasoning fear of red Bolshevism, and a narrow "America First" nationalism. In social life there came the usual post-war slackening of moral standards aided by widespread efforts to nullify Prohibition. And finally, beginning about 1920, there followed nine years of economic overexpansion, feverish speculation, and mounting extravagance which ended in 1929 in the Great Depression.

The characteristic features of these three decades were those most likely to affect the Churches. The continued draining of rural districts led to the abandonment of many country churches and to the rethinking of rural policies. The flood of foreign immigration benefited chiefly the Roman Catholic Church, but by increasing congestion in the cities it posed problems for other Christian bodies. Into the campaigns for social reform the Churches entered actively by measures which we shall later review, and to the World War they gave whole-hearted support. Throughout this period, moreover, the contest with secularism was heightened in intensity by the number of interests which competed with the Church. In ever growing areas the Church ceased to be the social center of life. It had to maintain its position in the face not only of multiplying amusements but of satisfaction with things material and of overconfidence in the claims and achievements of science.

The power and range of influence of the Churches may be estimated by the government statistics published after the religious census of 1926. This revealed that in the United States there were then 213 denominations with a membership of 54,600,000 and an annual expenditure of $814,300,000. By far the largest group was the Roman Catholic Church with 18,600,000 members; and sixth in numbers—after the Baptists, Methodists, Lutherans, and Presbyterians—was the Episcopal Church.

In 1901 the Episcopal Church had 751,000 communicants, 5,067 clergy, and 442,000 pupils in its Sunday schools, and its total contributions to all Church causes were $14,856,000. Thirty years later there were 1,312,000 communicants, 6,323 clergy, and 501,000 pupils in Sunday schools, and the contributions were $44,241,000. Its giving had trebled in amount, its communicant strength had not quite doubled, but its clergy had increased only 24 per cent. The membership of the Church continued to be prevailingly urban and eastern. In 1900 the ratio of communicants to the whole population was one to 102, whereas in 1930 it was one to 97. For the fact that this advance was so slight there were many less tangible reasons, but the part played in the increase of population by a type of heavy immigration from which the Church did not profit was a leading cause. Even with this handicap the Church was growing at a speedier rate than the population. But it is not because of any census figures that these decades are of high significance in the life of the Church. They are memorable because in the generation which they embrace the Church set itself with greater wisdom and zeal than ever before to the accomplishment of its essential tasks—in missionary expansion, in religious education, in the Christianizing of social relations, and in measurable progress toward the reunion of Christendom.

Chapter XXI

CHANGES IN ORGANIZATION

DESCRIPTIONS of machinery are never very interesting either for the writer or for the reader. Yet during the first twenty years of the present century the changes in the organization of the Episcopal Church were so extensive that their significance must be noted. These new developments were not merely formal; they wrought a marked increase in the efficiency of the Church and enriched its contribution to the causes to which it was committed.

One of the less important changes was the readjustment of the status of assistant bishops. As far back as the first year of the nineteenth century assistant bishops had been elected, but not until 1829 was a canon enacted which dealt with them. It was provided therein that a bishop could ask for an assistant on the ground of old age or of "permanent cause of infirmity," and that the assistant should always have the right of succession. In 1871 the extent of a bishop's diocese was added by amendment to the reasons for an assistant. In 1889 a further clause required that the bishop should state in advance the duties to be assigned to his assistant. It was in 1895 that the title "assistant bishop" was altered to "bishop coadjutor," and nine years later "extent of diocesan *work*" was admitted as a legitimate reason for a coadjutor. It has thus been possible ever since for a bishop to request a coadjutor for almost any sound reason; but either General Convention or the majority of the bishops and standing committees of the dioceses must consent to the proposal.

The canon of 1829 forbade the election of assistant bishops without the right of succession, and in spite of many subsequent attempts to legalize them, such "suffragans" were banned until 1904. Not for another six years, however, was the constitution amended to authorize dioceses to elect suffragan bishops. A canon at the same time provided that there should never be more than two in a diocese and that none should be chosen except on the initiative of the diocesan. It was further declared by later enactments that suffragans might be elected as bishops, bishops coadjutor, or missionary bishops. In the House of Bishops they were denied votes until 1946.

Until the beginning of this century the position and authority of the Presiding Bishop depended entirely on a rule of the House of Bishops which stated that the senior bishop, in point of consecration, should be the presiding officer of the House. In 1901, however, a constitutional amendment was enacted which made the senior bishop having jurisdiction in the United States to be the Presiding Bishop. In this same year, too, began a series of efforts to make the office elective; but it was not until 1919 that another constitutional amendment was passed which provided that the Presiding Bishop should be elected by the House of Bishops and his election confirmed by the House of Deputies. His term of office was limited to six years (with no obstacle to re-election), and he was obliged to retain his diocesan jurisdiction.[1]

This wholesome change was long overdue, and it was accomplished in the nick of time. The custom of having the bishop first consecrated preside at meetings of the bishops was natural enough when there were only a small number of bishops and when there were few duties for him to perform between sessions of the House other than arranging for consecrations. In course of time, however, as the responsibilities laid upon the Presiding Bishop increased, advanced age ceased to be the best qualification for their proper discharge. This fact had long been recognized in the practice of electing a younger man to serve as Chairman of the House of Bishops. The reluctance to make any more radical change may be partly explained by the extraordinary vitality and popularity of Bishop Tuttle, who held the office of Presiding Bishop for twenty years. But in 1919, as we shall see, the National Council was organized, a new plan which made the Presiding Bishop the President of the Council and assigned to him heavy administrative duties. Only a man in full vigor of body and mind could perform the functions which the office now involved.

Bishop Tuttle died in April, 1923, and before General Convention could meet, two more bishops served as Presiding Bishop on the basis of seniority. At the Convention of 1925 John Gardner Murray, Bishop of Maryland, was chosen as the first elected Presiding Bishop, an able executive from whose leadership the new National Council promptly benefited. Within four years, however, his death made necessary another

[1] This original arrangement may be contrasted with the present law by which the Presiding Bishop's term is limited only by age and by which he is *required* to *resign* his diocesan jurisdiction.

election. His successor, Charles P. Anderson, Bishop of Chicago, died after less than three months in office. The House of Bishops filled his place at a special meeting in March, 1930, by electing as Presiding Bishop James DeWolf Perry, Bishop of Rhode Island, a choice confirmed by General Convention in the following year.

In the apparently endless process of rearranging the missionary organization of the Church there was adopted at the General Convention of 1904 a revised constitution of the Domestic and Foreign Missionary Society. For the former Board of Managers there was substituted a Board of Missions of forty-six members, with the Presiding Bishop as President. For the first time this effective group was to be hampered by no larger body. At the end of another six years an amendment provided that the President of the Board of Missions should be elected by General Convention, and Arthur S. Lloyd was chosen to fill the office.

Lloyd, who had been consecrated as Bishop Coadjutor of Virginia only a year before, had served from 1899 to 1909 as general secretary of the Board of Missions and was to be its president for another nine years. This period of nearly twenty years at the Church Missions House was an era of unprecedented missionary expansion in terms of men and money and of heightened interest throughout the Church. No man contributed more to this advance than Arthur Lloyd. Though not a born executive, he had nearly every other qualification for missionary leadership. He was no less a saint for being exceptionally charming. His contagious enthusiasm, sustained by a deep piety, "turned 281 Fourth Avenue from a counting-house into a power-house."

By the side of Lloyd as chief of staff for nearly twenty years and as his successor in the post of executive secretary for another twenty, stood a layman, John Wilson Wood. In 1925 General Convention recognized with gratitude his years of labor and passed the following resolution in recognition of a term of service which had still fifteen years to run: "Whereas, John Wilson Wood, D.C.L., has served the missionary cause of this Church for a quarter of a century with great personal sacrifice, but to the great satisfaction of the men, women, and children of the Church, therefore be it *Resolved,* that the General Convention . . . extends to Dr. Wood its hearty appreciation of his labors and its sincere gratitude for the earnest and devoted way in which he has promoted the missionary work of this Church during his twenty-five years of service; and we hope and pray that in continuing his labors for the Church he may enjoy that rich reward which comes to all those who serve their Master with love and devotion."

As we shall note in succeeding chapters, the Church found itself by the year 1910 equipped not only with a Board of Missions but also with a General Board of Religious Education and a Joint Commission on Social Service. Each of these bodies was responsible to General Convention but otherwise independent. Each had its own members and its own executive secretary and treasurer, and each was appealing to the Church for a degree of financial support difficult to obtain. Realizing, after some years, the need for coordinating and integrating the different branches of the work of the national Church, representatives of the three organizations concerned met often during the year 1919 with the Committee on Canons of the House of Deputies. The result of these skilful negotiations was agreement upon a new canon, the virtues of which were so obvious that it was enacted by General Convention in October of that year.

The canon created a central organization known as "The Presiding Bishop and Council" to "administer and carry on the missionary, educational, and social work of the Church, of which work the Presiding Bishop shall be the executive head." This body not only took over the functions of the General Board of Religious Education and the Joint Commission on Social Service but also replaced the Board of Missions as the organ of the Domestic and Foreign Missionary Society. The Council was to be composed of four bishops, four presbyters, and eight laymen to be elected by General Convention and eight members to be elected by the eight provinces. A treasurer was to be chosen by the Convention and likewise a president, until the office of Presiding Bishop should become elective. Thomas F. Gailor, Bishop of Tennessee, who had seen service on the Board of Missions, was elected President of the Council.

The new Council was directed to organize the following departments: 1. Missions and Church Extension. 2. Religious Education. 3. Christian Social Service. 4. Finance. 5. Publicity. The membership of these departments was to consist of members of the Council together with additional members chosen from outside, and each department was to have its executive secretary. The canon further ordered that the Presiding Bishop and Council should submit to each General Convention a budget for the ensuing triennium and should present annual reports both to the Convention and to the Church public. It was to hold at least four meetings every year. As a profound student of the Church's laws has written, this canon "undoubtedly marks a greater change in the polity of the American Church than any other canon ever enacted by General Convention, and is one of the greatest pieces of constructive legislation, if not the greatest, ever enacted by that body since the first General Convention of 1789." [2] It endowed the Church with what it had never had before—a strong central executive authority with the power to initiate and develop new work.

[2] E. A. White, *Constitution and Canons,* 958.

The newly elected Council officially assumed control of its affairs on January 1, 1920, and held its first formal meeting a week later. It elected as secretary the Rev. Franklin J. Clark, who served in that capacity for the next twenty-seven years during which his accuracy and patience won admiration from successive Councils. Already General Convention had elected as treasurer of the Council Lewis B. Franklin. In a fortunate hour for the Church Bishop Lloyd had persuaded Franklin to resign his position as vice-president of a leading New York bank and to devote his talents as a financier to the service of the Church. During nearly thirty years as treasurer he proved to be equally valuable as a missionary statesman and an ardent promoter of the missionary cause.

After three years the next Convention proceeded to make a few changes in the agency it had recently created. Its rather awkward title was changed to "The National Council," and arrangements were made for so distributing the terms of its members that only one-half should be chosen at each Convention and everyone in future should serve for six years. A Vice-President was added to the officers, and a sixth department was called for—the Field Department. The Department of Publicity confined itself wholly to publications, such as *The Spirit of Missions* and *The Church at Work,* whereas the Field Department assumed responsibility for the many other forms of promotion. To the existing duties of the Council was added the task of computing the missionary "quotas" assigned to the dioceses according to plans approved by General Convention. No further alterations were made in the machinery of the Council until 1931, when amendments to the canon divided the Department of Missions and Church Extension into two departments—Domestic Missions and Foreign Missions. And to lighten the administrative duties of the Presiding Bishop the departments were grouped into two divisions, each under a Vice-President—the first comprising Domestic Missions, Foreign Missions, Religious Education, and Social Service, and the second comprising the Finance, Publicity, and Field Departments.

Never did a subject excite in General Convention so much discussion and produce so little action as the subject of provinces. The topic was first broached in 1850. In 1865 there was defeated in the House of Deputies a canon providing for the subdivision of the Church into six provinces, in each of which there should be a synod and a presiding Bishop having in his province the same powers as the Presiding Bishop in the national Church. But it was to be nearly half a century before any such plan was put into operation. In fifteen subsequent Conventions there was further argument (and occasionally incompleted action) dealing both with the provincial system and with a similar proposal for "Federate Councils," each Council to include all the dioceses within a single

State. In 1901 an amendment to the constitution *authorizing* the organization of provinces was enacted, but no steps were then taken to implement it. Still hesitating on the brink of a provincial organization, the General Convention of 1907 adopted an amendment to the canon which contained the constitution of the Missionary Society. This amendment divided the Church into eight "Missionary Departments," each with its Missionary Council.

After six years of trial these Missionary Councils proved ineffective. Unable to legislate or to discuss subjects other than missionary, they came to be recognized as not very interesting debating societies. To replace them with an organization at once more traditional and more efficient the General Convention of 1913 adopted a canon on provinces. Subsequent amendment and revision resulted in the canon of 1922 which was practically identical with that in force in 1950.

Instead of declaring that the national Church shall be *divided* into provinces—a negative description suggesting dangers to be feared—the canon states that the dioceses and missionary districts shall be *united* into provinces—a positive description implying advantages to be gained.[3] In each of the eight provinces there was a Synod of two houses, a House of Bishops composed of the bishops of the province and a House of Deputies composed of four presbyters and four laymen from each diocese and two presbyters and two laymen from each missionary district. The Presiding Bishop of the province was elected by the Synod.

Few legislative powers were granted to the provinces, but quite enough to enable them to undertake important projects. They were authorized to create Provincial Councils with departments corresponding to those of the National Council; and, in more general terms, they were empowered "to deal with all matters within the province; *provided,* however, that no Provincial Synod shall have power to regulate or control the internal policy or affairs of any constituent diocese or missionary district, and *provided,* further, that all actions and proceedings of the Synod

[3] The First Province consisted of the dioceses within the States of Maine, New Hampshire, Vermont, Massachusetts, Rhode Island, and Connecticut. The Second Province consisted of the dioceses within the States of New York and New Jersey plus the missionary district of Puerto Rico. (The Canal Zone was later added, and also Haiti, at its own request.) The Third Province consisted of the dioceses within the States of Pennsylvania, Delaware, Maryland, Virginia, West Virginia, and the District of Columbia. The Fourth Province consisted of the dioceses within the States of North Carolina, South Carolina, Georgia, Florida, Alabama, Mississippi, Louisiana, Tennessee, and Kentucky. The Fifth Province consisted of the dioceses within the States of Ohio, Indiana, Illinois, Michigan, and Wisconsin. The Sixth Province consisted of the dioceses and missionary districts within the States of Minnesota, Iowa, North Dakota, South Dakota, Nebraska, Montana, Wyoming, and Colorado. The Seventh Province consisted of the dioceses and missionary districts within the States of Missouri, Arkansas, Texas, Kansas, Oklahoma, and New Mexico. The Eighth Province consisted of the dioceses and missionary districts within the States of Idaho, Utah, Washington, Oregon, Nevada, California, Arizona, and the Territories of Alaska and Hawaii, plus the missionary district of the Philippine Islands.

shall be subject to and in conformity with the provisions of the constitution and canons for the government of this Church."

As might be expected from the variegated composition of the provinces and from the fact that they were practically turned loose to sink or swim, their records between 1913 and 1931 were diverse and irregular. With no precedents to guide them, with little or no money upon which to count, and with everything depending on the initiative of leadership as yet undeveloped, it is surprising that they achieved as much as they did. In no long time all the provinces organized Provincial Councils with departments of missions, religious education, and social service, but the work of these departments was very uneven in quantity and quality. For some years the National Council supplied a certain amount of financial aid to the provinces, but after 1926 they had to depend on what they could obtain from the dioceses, usually in amounts that were small and unreliable.[4] Except in the First Province no one person was responsible for formulating and executing plans, because only in that area was there a full-time paid executive secretary. In New England the Rev. Malcolm Taylor for twenty-one years came as near as one man could do to exhibiting in action what a province can accomplish.

It had been expected that such tasks as the provinces might undertake would be handed down to them from above in the form of assignments from the National Council. Though this step was taken in many instances, perhaps more frequent were the cases in which the weaker dioceses looked up to the province to give leadership and guidance which they found themselves unable to supply. It was especially in all the phases of religious education that both processes were active, and it was distinctly in that field that nearly all the provinces were most successful. Few dioceses could afford to have full-time directors of religious education or of work with young people, and few were able to support summer conferences of their own; but all could make some contribution toward officers or enterprises centering in the province. In 1931, for example, the Fourth Province employed three part-time leaders in religious education and conducted an annual summer conference at Sewanee; the Seventh Province had a secretary for young people's work; and the First Province, besides founding a Church boarding-school for boys, was carrying on the most active college work in the Church. There was good reason in that year for a commission to report to General Convention that "there has been a steady and wholesome growth in provincial activities."

Another enterprise which took fifty years to find itself, but came to rich fruition in the early years of the century was the Church Pension

[4] To cite one of the more favorable examples, in 1931 the First Province spen about $7,000, more than half of this amount coming from Massachusetts and Con necticut.

Fund. The General Convention of 1853 passed a resolution authorizing the incorporation of a Fund for the relief of aged, infirm, and disabled clergymen and of the widows and orphans of deceased clergymen. Two years later the elected trustees secured the incorporation of this Fund. Partly because of the Civil War, however, but chiefly because of general indifference to the cause, almost nothing was accomplished for another twenty-one years. By 1874 the Fund was distributing $2,300 a year to twenty-six persons, and most of the money came from royalties on the Church hymnal. Though a few dioceses had funds of a similar character, this trivial total was not to the credit of a Church which numbered a quarter of a million communicants, with over three thousand clergy.

In the course of another fifteen years the Fund had increased its income to $32,000 a year, and it was offering aid to 178 beneficiaries, at the average annual rate of about $180 to each. In that year (1889) the Committee on the State of the Church reported to General Convention that it was "convinced that a Clergy Pension Fund is one of the great needs of the Church." "Experience," they added, "proves that every clergyman reaching a certain age should receive as a *right,* and not as a *charity,* some provision for his support. The workings of the 'Aged and Infirm Clergy Funds' in our dioceses are always inadequate and often humiliating." These statements were fully justified, for the Church pension system still depended upon unsuccessful pleas for pity.[5] Yet it was another twenty-eight years before a sound plan was in operation.

As if to prove that the cause was hopeless, a Joint Commission appointed in 1907 to raise $5,000,000 for the General Clergy Relief Fund reported to General Convention three years later that only $118,000 had been received! But the cause was not hopeless; it simply had not been seriously undertaken by any leader of ability. It was William Lawrence, Bishop of Massachusetts, who began in 1910 the campaign which eventually provided the Church with a system of pensions unexcelled by any other in the country.

"In 1910," according to Bishop Lawrence, "there were about fifty separate societies, national, state, and diocesan [for clergy relief], with discordant rules or no rules at all, often overlapping each other in their gifts and bewildering the laity with their variety of appeals. About $230,000 a year was spent in aid; giving from fifty to four hundred dollars to beneficiaries according to their supposed need, though no one could judge the relative merit of the cases." "No body of persons dependent upon charity," the bishop declared, "can long retain their self-respect.

[5] In 1895 the Pastoral Letter of the bishops was still striking the sentimental note: "The unfilled treasury of this hallowed Fund puts forth through us not only a pathetic appeal but a righteous demand for large and constant gifts."

. . . The more I thought and studied the situation, the clearer I became that the whole system of charity for the clergy and their families must go by the board if the ministry must hold its own self-respect and the respect of the people." [6] Moved by these strong convictions Bishop Lawrence sponsored a resolution at the Convention of 1910 which appointed a Joint Commission "to consider the whole question of the support of the clergy, including salaries, sustentation, insurance, annuities, and pensions." Most of its work was done by Lawrence, its chairman, who produced, with the aid of Monell Sayre, an actuarial expert, a report to the next Convention of 1913. This radical document declared in favor of a sound business system offering pensions as a right to be claimed and not as a charity to be begged. Its proposals, carefully prepared and convincingly presented, were adopted by the Convention as the permanent policy of the Church. The basic principles were: (1) That it must be the only pension system of the whole Church; (2) that the assessments or annual premiums it demanded must be scientifically calculated so as to balance its liabilities, and (3) that as a first step an amount of money must be raised sufficient to meet the "accrued liabilities," that is, to supply the money needed for the clergy who would retire before the complete system was in operation.

Needless to say, it was William Lawrence who was mainly responsible for raising the $5,000,000 for accrued liabilities, the largest sum of money ever raised at one time by a Church for a single cause through voluntary contributions. Anticipating many of the methods later used in war "drives," the bishop and the thousands who cooperated with him carried on for three years a brilliant campaign of education which brought home the need to every Church member. Not only was the necessary sum in hand at the time required—March 1, 1917—but by the following September the amount was so generously overpaid that $8,750,000 had accumulated. Meantime the Church Pension Fund had been incorporated and authorized to administer the system approved by General Convention. From first to last, of course, it was to be entirely on a voluntary basis.

This system, as described by Bishop Lawrence, demanded that "every parish should year by year pay as assessments a certain added percentage of their rector's salary, which, forwarded to the Church Pension Fund, would be put at interest, and on the basis of our actuarial tables be sufficient to see him and his widow through to the end of their lives: in other words, it was part of his life salary; but a deferred salary, held for later years, when it would be paid out to him in proportion to the salaries of his life: those who had received larger salaries would have

[6] Lawrence, *Memories of a Happy Life,* 348 f.

larger pensions."[7] The rate of assessment was seven and one-half per cent (later ten and fifteen) of the salary, calculated to give a clergyman at sixty-eight an annual amount roughly equal to half his average salary, or to his widow half that amount. For a full generation now this Fund has brought to retired ministers a degree of comfort previously unknown.

During the same period in which provinces and the Pension Fund were being organized the Church was engaged in revising the *Hymnal* and the *Book of Common Prayer,* revisions both more radical and more beneficial than any in the American past. A Joint Commission appointed by General Convention in 1910 presented in 1916 a new *Hymnal,* which was then approved and remained the standard until 1940. For the first time music as well as words was authorized; as much consideration was given to the one as to the other; and the presence on the commission of such distinguished musicians as Winfred Douglas and T. Tertius Noble guaranteed that the canons of good taste would be maintained. It was an era when the prevailing standards both in music and in poetry were far superior to those which guided any earlier *Hymnals,* and the final product deserved the applause which it ultimately received. So many old hymns were discarded that though many new were added, the total was one hundred and eighteen less than the *Hymnal* of 1892 contained.

The number of sentimental and "evangelical" hymns was reduced, and their places were taken by sturdier compositions from the Middle Ages, like "Hail, festal day," or from later centuries, like Luther's "A mighty fortress" and Bunyan's "He who would valiant be," or from the best of modern religious poetry, such as Whittier's "Dear Lord and Father of mankind," Matheson's "O Love that wilt not let me go," and Kipling's "Recessional." And among the new tunes which replaced many Victorian pieces were to be found examples of medieval music, German chorales, and very recent productions of dignity and worth.

The third revision of the Prayer Book required fifteen years of study and legislation, from the appointment of a Joint Commission in 1913 to the final authorization of the new book in 1928. The members of the commission were carefully chosen to include those whose learning and talent fitted them for an exacting task. Their enterprise called not only for the scholarship, artistic sense, and rich pastoral and liturgical experience needed to produce a revision. It demanded also on the part of their leaders that capacity for patient and persuasive exposition required to win the approval of conservative Conventions. Foremost among these leaders in liturgical lore and in parliamentary appeal were Bishop Edward L. Parsons, Bishop Charles L. Slattery, the Rev. John W. Suter, and the Rev. H. B. St. George. Since the personnel of the commission was not only

[7] *Ibid.,* 356.

gifted but also well balanced from the point of view of Churchmanship, revision never became a party issue, and its results were a tribute not to the strength of any party but to the comprehensiveness of the Church.

Though the commission had been directed to report "no proposition involving the Faith or Doctrine of the Church," there was a gentlemen's agreement to overlook this restriction when such propositions were neither fundamental nor partisan. It cannot be denied, for example, that modification in doctrine was implied when prayers were altered to eliminate the notion that God sends disease and bad weather as a direct punishment for sins. And orthodox Protestant dogma was plainly defied when prayer for the departed was approved. Yet the Church was all the better for both changes.

Most of the new features in the Prayer Book of 1928 were additions serving to enrich the liturgy; and they were so numerous that only a few more important instances can be listed here. Among them were a new canticle in Morning Prayer (the *Benedictus Es*), a short Absolution in Evening Prayer, a large increase in the number of Occasional Prayers, including prayers For Our Country, For the Church, For Religious Education, For Christian Service, For Social Justice, and others. Three Offices of Baptism were consolidated into one. "Offices of Instruction" made the use of the Catechism more helpfully intelligent, and the Order for use At the Burial of a Child added an office of deeply moving beauty.

For the first time since 1789 the Liturgy of the Holy Communion underwent revision. Several new Collects, Epistles, and Gospels were introduced, such as those for A Saint's Day and for Independence Day. Three new Proper Prefaces appeared. A clause interceding for the departed was included in the Prayer for the Whole State of Christ's Church; and the Lord's Prayer and the Prayer of Humble Access were placed after the Prayer of Consecration and before the administration of the elements.

The same Convention which authorized the Prayer Book of 1928 established a permanent Liturgical Commission which was charged to study the liturgical needs of the Church, to receive and appraise proposals for change, and to prepare offices for special occasions. As Bishop Parsons has remarked, "Its chief value is that its appointment is recognition of the fact that worship is an ever-growing, ever-changing thing. Further revision is inevitable."

Chapter XXII

EVENTS AND MOVEMENTS OF THE TIME

THE first World War and its aftermath threw into the shadow all other events of the time. It brought the most devastating years in the history of Europe since the Thirty Years' War three centuries earlier. Yet the effect upon the United States, while highly stimulating for a season, was not profound. It did not change fundamentally the mode of thought or the way of life of the people; and except for a certain relaxation of morale and morality in limited circles, its influence upon American Christianity was not marked.

The movement for world peace had been increasing in strength before 1914. It was in 1910 that the World Peace Foundation was established by Edwin Ginn, and in the very year that the conflict began Carnegie endowed the Church Peace Union. By that time there were at least eighty peace societies in the United States. But pacifism flourishes most readily in times of peace, and only its more persistent adherents maintain their faith under the stress of war. Dissidents, in fact, were in a tiny minority when the Churches of America openly supported the fight against Germany.

Cordial sympathy with the cause of the Allies in their struggle against the Central Powers was the almost universal sentiment of the members of the Episcopal Church and their representatives in Convention. Two years after the declarations of war and a year and a half before the United States entered the contest, the Pastoral Letter of the House of Bishops issued at the General Convention of 1916 expressed not only the convictions of its author, Bishop Brent, but also the beliefs of his colleagues and of a large proportion of their people. "No self-isolation on our part is possible," it declared. "The fortunes of the nations of the world are interwoven as the threads of a tapestry. . . . God hates a Godless and empty peace as much as he hates unrighteous war. . . . If America comes out of this day of world disorder richer in purse and poorer in manhood, she will invite and bring upon herself the penalty of a debased national life or even of losing her very soul." These were words of scornful warning directed not against pacifism—for which in its purer forms Christians can only feel a puzzled but profound respect—but against isolationism, which in that day and age (and still more in this) was politically stupid and morally contemptible.

Once the United States became an Associated Power and threw its strength into the balance, Church opinion, reflecting public opinion, became practically unanimous. At a special meeting held in Chicago in October, 1917, the House of Bishops adopted a resolution affirming that "this House of Bishops assures the President of the United States and his cabinet of our patriotic support of the Government, pledging ourselves to cooperate in every possible way to aid, sustain, and protect the brave soldiers and sailors of this great Christian nation in the heroic efforts to destroy the oppression, tyranny, and brutality now threatening the world, and to establish justice, righteousness, and liberty among all nations." The Pastoral Letter published at the same time not only supported the cause in general terms but encouraged participation in the most practical fashion. "We hate war," the bishops wrote, "and shrink from its horrors, but we who enjoy the privileges of civil liberty won by the blood of our fathers must, when they are endangered, defend them at the cost of our blood. . . . Loyalty demands of every citizen unconditional consecration to the service of the nation. . . . To express this, we must not only work for the Red Cross and give generously in money and comforts; we must also be ready to pay heavy taxes cheerfully and to buy Liberty Bonds."

At this same October meeting the bishops were called upon not only to express the enthusiasm of the vast majority, which they genuinely shared, but also to do justice to an inharmonious minority. They received a memorial from the Council of Advice of the missionary district of Utah denouncing the pacifist opinions of their bishop, Paul Jones, accusing him of disloyalty to his country, and petitioning for his removal. The House, in response, passed a resolution requesting Bishop Jones to take a leave of absence pending an investigation of the case, and appointed a committee to consider the matter and report. When the House of Bishops met again in April, 1918, and received a report, they adopted three resolutions. In the first the bishops declared that the war was both righteous and inevitable. In the second they acknowledged that every bishop was entitled to freedom of speech but that he should be guided by "a deep sense of the responsibility which rests upon one who occupies a representative position." In the third they stated clearly that they were "unwilling to accept the resignation of any bishop in deference to an excited state of public opinion," and therefore declined to accept the resignation of the Bishop of Utah for the reasons he had assigned in presenting it. Jones then offered his resignation without giving any reasons for it; and seizing the opportunity for face-saving thus generously extended to them, the House accepted the resignation, while repeating their affirmation about freedom of speech. They could not resist the chance to enjoy the credit of a verbal defiance of public opinion and at the same time the credit of bringing peace and satisfaction to the missionary district of Utah. Only those who have not lived through a war will find it easy to blame them.

In August, 1917, Bishop Tuttle, as Presiding Bishop, appointed an able War Commission with Lawrence as chairman, and through this body the Church gave far-sighted and constructive aid to its chaplains and brought material and spiritual comfort to unnumbered soldiers and sailors. The sum of $500,000—later increased by another $300,000—was raised to defray the expenses of the commission. It was spent upon a growing array of goods and services gratefully accepted. A small war-time Prayer Book was published in large quantities. Chaplains were supplied with such equipment as typewriters, portable altars, and diminutive organs, and with discretionary funds for use among their men to the amount of $50 a month in this country and $100 a month abroad. Tours in France by several of its members kept the commission in touch with needs and opportunities. It was concerned, however, not merely with material goods. It saw the necessity in the many camps and cantonments for the service of civilian chaplains who could supplement the work of those in uniform. These were enlisted to the number of nearly one hundred and given equipment like their military and naval brothers. And chaplains of all types were not merely supplied and forgotten. They were expected to report to the commission at frequent intervals, and an extensive correspondence kept the home staff in touch with the field. Everywhere the men who represented the Church in Army and Navy felt the Church to be active and interested in their support.

Other agencies made further contributions in service to the armed forces or toward the winning of the war. The Joint Commission on Army and Navy Chaplains, which had been in existence for many years, performed the important function of collecting material concerning the applicants for the office and was responsible for recommending clergy for commissions. It bore a part, too, in the agitation required to move Congress to increase the number of chaplains to one for every 1,200 men. In response to this growing demand 187 Episcopal priests served as chaplains in the Army and 25 in the Navy. The needs of soldiers and sailors were not forgotten by the Church Periodical Club, which was busy in furnishing not only Prayer Books, Hymnals, and Bibles, but books and magazines in mounting quantities; and the Brotherhood of St. Andrew, through its Army and Navy Department, spent $150,000 in both religious and secular activities. The Joint Commission on Social Service, moreover, issued a useful series of war bulletins dealing with such matters of general concern as war relief, training camp programs, food conservation, and labor problems in war time. The diocesan social service commissions, too, were often energetic in organizing parishes for war service and in co-operating with secular agencies.

At the General Convention of 1919, held three months after the signing of the Treaty of Versailles, the War Commission was discharged, and in its place there was appointed a permanent Army and Navy Commission, whose efficiency was to prove indispensable in the second World War. The Convention passed a resolution in favor of the League of Nations and another which urged "discriminating executive clemency" on behalf of imprisoned conscientious objectors and other political prisoners. But creditable as were these expressions of opinion, they cost no more than the casting of votes. The action taken in 1919 which was to stir the Church from end to end was the inauguration of the Nation-wide Campaign.

Episcopalians, like all other Americans, had learned during the war what results could be brought about by intense united effort and far-flung organization. It was rightly concluded that since the country had produced achievements of which no one had thought it capable, so could the Church. With the aim to arouse the Church to new life and to unprecedented activity the Convention launched a movement described as "The Nation-wide Campaign," "designed to bring the spiritual and material resources of the Church to bear most effectively and adequately upon her whole task as witness to the Master." A Joint Commission was appointed to carry out an ambitious program of "information, education, and inspiration." Bishop Lloyd of the Board of Missions and scores of other leaders were hearty in their support of the plan; diocesan conventions endorsed it; but the chief engineer was the Rev. Robert W. Patton of Virginia, to whose gifts as an enthusiastic campaigner the Church was greatly in debt. The enterprise may have appeared to the average observer as merely a money-raising "drive"; but it involved such a careful survey of the Church's needs, such deliberate formulation of plans, and such widespread enlightenment of the people as to the nature and meaning of the Church's program that its success was quite as clearly educational as financial. It was the first time that the Church had embarked with energy upon skilful "promotion" on a national scale; and the results astonished even the promoters.

After three years of the campaign the House of Bishops, meeting at the Convention held in Portland, reported that "when the movement began, it revealed the lack of corporate consciousness within the Church itself. We were a congeries of parishes and a too loosely united collection of dioceses and missionary districts. The campaign brought us together in a remarkable way." "Its outstanding feature," they believed, was "the awakening of the whole Church to its opportunity and obligation." These conclusions were certainly justified by the facts and figures. Some of the deeper consequences were imponderable and could not be assessed. But during the triennium 187 missionaries had been sent out. Pupils in Sunday schools had increased by 24,000 and teachers by 1,700. And the financial results were vastly encouraging. Money given annually to the general Church increased 117 per cent and diocesan revenues 300 per cent, while at the same time parishes were contributing much more than ever to their own support. To name but one consequence of this enlarged income, the Department of Missions was able to supply so much additional money to the domestic missionary bishops that thenceforth they were no longer required (or even permitted) to engage in the wearisome practice of travelling about the country trying to collect funds to keep their work alive. The official seal of approval was set upon the Nation-wide Campaign in 1920 by making it a department of the Presiding Bishop and Council, responsible, along with the Department of Publicity, for the promotion of the Church's program.

Though the early twentieth century produced no events comparable to the first World War, it witnessed in America the development of various movements, some of which were directly religious, while others were capable of religious application. Within the limited space which such a history as this can afford, only a few can be named, and those few must be treated with less fulness than they deserve. Easily the greatest movement of the time was the fight for the federal prohibition of alcoholic liquors, a long struggle involving political, moral, and religious factors. But the Episcopal Church—in contrast, for example, with the Methodist—never took much interest in Prohibition. Though large numbers of its members disapproved of the eighteenth constitutional amendment, the Church never officially exerted itself either for or against this gigantic effort to produce temperance by law. It was relatively narrower and less conspicuous trends of the day which made an impression on the life of the Church. Among these were the evangelistic movement commonly known as "Buchmanism"; the development of psychology and psychotherapeutics which led to the use of religious forces in mental healing; and the rise of the Barthian school of theology. Within the Episcopal Church itself, moreover, there came new tendencies in the thought of groups and parties of which the emergence of Liberal Catholicism and Liberal Evangelicalism were the most interesting.

Frank N. D. Buchman was a Lutheran minister in Pennsylvania, born in 1878, who became in middle life the leader of an evangelistic movement which for lack of a better name was widely known as "Buchmanism." Its activity and influence were strongest in England and the United States, though its adherents, at one time or another, were at work in several European countries, in Canada and South Africa, and in the Far East. For a time its leaders wished to be known as "A First Century Christian Fellowship," but its successes at Oxford led to the more permanent term "The Oxford Groups," a borrowed plume, the use of which was not relished by the university authorities. Since the historian W. W. Sweet, writing of religion in America, is probably right in stating that "their principal influence has been exerted among Episcopalians," a brief estimate of their virtues and defects is appropriate in a history of the Church.

The *essential* features of the movement are essential features in the Christian religion—the longing (conscious or unconscious) for salvation, repentance, surrender to God in Christ, a new life controlled by God through prayer, and the readiness to win others by sharing that life. The *special* features of the Groups that gave them individuality were their connection with certain leaders, of whom Buchman was chief, their emphasis on direct work with individuals (as contrasted with preaching to masses), their distinctive method of meeting in three-or-four-day "houseparties," their development of a fellowship of converts who gave aid and comfort to one another by sharing experience, and their peculiar stress upon daily "guidance." Even most of these special characteristics were to be found in early Christianity and in many subsequent religious revivals. So far as the movement was in honorable line of descent from such predecessors as the Franciscan, the Pietist, and the Wesleyan movements, it may be credited with some measure of their creative achievements. In cases beyond enumeration it remade broken and hopeless lives; it brought blessings to families; and it produced in group after group a corporate religious life of evident vitality, judged by the true test of vitality—the capacity to reproduce itself. Especially between 1921 and 1938 the fellowship of these groups, both as a whole and in its local phases, was genuine, alive, and growing. It was particularly successful among prosperous men and women whose religion had been rather formal and objective. That was why it won so many Episcopalians.

Yet in scope and lasting value the Oxford Group Movement cannot be ranked with the greater revivals of earlier centuries. And for the limitations which place it in a lesser category there are not a few reasons. Though it ostensibly encouraged Church affiliations, it tended to be a substitute for the Church and seldom had the net effect of reinforcing the Church. Several of its foremost spokesmen, who made the Church central and worked within the Church, broke with the official leadership. Furthermore, it was far too much a one-class affair. Though exceptions were widely advertised, it was distinctly a group of well-to-do folk who could afford house-parties and hotels. No doubt these needed God as much as any and often were found of Him; but the high-class tone limited the range of evangelism and suggested a sharp contrast with Franciscanism and Wesleyanism. Moreover, the interpretation of "guidance" had the effect of encouraging a spasmodic mode of life which found routine drudgery and regular obligations unwelcome; a narrow conception of Christian vocation ignored the richness and variety of the callings to which God summons His children; and (with less excuse than early Christians had) there was too self-conscious a distinction between the Elect and the Outsiders.[1]

The religious group especially concerned with healing disease is of course Christian Science. This American sect, initiated by Mary Baker Eddy, began as a distinct organized body in 1879, with the founding of "The Church of Christ, Scientist" in Boston, and fifty years later there were nearly two thousand Christian Science congregations in the country. Contemporary with the progress of this radical movement went the development, in genuinely scientific circles, of the study of psychology and psychiatry. It brought discoveries of the nature and treatment of the subconscious mind; it evolved various methods of psychotherapeutics; and it culminated, for this generation, in the work of Freud, Jung, and others through which psychoanalysis came to be widely practised.

These trends in religion and science were not without their effect on the Episcopal Church; and it is certainly not accidental that the first and most successful modern attempt within the Church to combine religion and medicine should have been made at Emmanuel Church, Boston, in a center where Christian Science had its headquarters and neuropathology was a subject of study in famous hospitals and medical schools. Deeply convinced of the contribution which religion could make to mental healing, the Rev. Elwood Worcester, rector of Emmanuel Church, who had earned a German doctorate in philosophy and psychology, opened a clinic

[1] Beginning in 1938 the top leadership of the movement, carrying many with it, shifted its emphasis from a type of personal evangelism which practically ignored social problems to a new goal known as "Moral Rearmament," the purpose of which was to change the course of history and the destiny of nations by the application of Christian principles through the conversion of "key men" in all the nations. Favorable results have undoubtedly ensued, but they are difficult to estimate because of far too pretentious claims.

at his church in 1906. With him was associated the Rev. Samuel McComb, his assistant, and cooperating with his project were several psychiatrists and other physicians in the city. In the next twenty-three years, until Dr. Worcester's resignation in 1929, he and his fellow-workers conducted what the whole Church came to know as the Emmanuel Movement.

This successful venture in psychotherapeutics was based on the belief in the power of mind over body, in the efficacy of faith and of prayer as healing powers, and in the limitless divine resources upon which man can draw. Its system was sound and practical. The ministers confined themselves to the treatment of functional nervous disorders such as hysteria, hypochondria, and neurasthenia, not omitting alcoholism and the drug habit. They accepted as patients only those who had been carefully examined by a doctor. They kept careful records and took no pay. Their chief method was the use of mental suggestion, operating upon the subconscious mind, usually in the waking state but occasionally involving hypnosis; and in later years psychoanalysis was employed. These forms of treatment were supplemented by moral and spiritual re-education conducted in part through the Emmanuel Class whose regular meetings included the use of intercessory prayer.[2]

The methods used at Emmanuel were copied in a number of other churches, and the responsibility of the Church for sharing in the work of healing the sick came to be widely recognized at this time. Where clergymen undertook to attempt this ministry it usually took the form of intercessory prayer and sometimes of the laying on of hands or of anointing with oil. The movement went so far as to produce in General Convention several committees on the subject. Their reports, submitted between 1922 and 1931, are of much the same conservative tenor. They note with gratitude the revival of the ministry of healing and clearly affirm that this ministry is "an integral element of the Gospel" and "normal in the life of the Church." But in dealing with the means of healing they lay particular stress upon prayer—especially corporate intercessory prayer—and discourage the use of sensational methods by those who may believe themselves to have "the gift of healing." The embodiment in the Prayer Book of 1928 of prayers for the unction of the sick meant official recognition of this neglected phase of pastoral care.

In the field of theological thought by far the most significant movement in Protestantism which has so far emerged in the twentieth century is that associated with the names of Karl Barth, Emil Brunner, and their followers. It has been known as "the theology of crisis" and less accurately

[2] The first two years of the work at Emmanuel are fully described in a book written by Worcester, McComb, and Dr. Coriat and entitled *Religion and Medicine* (1908).

as "neo-orthodoxy." Of these two Swiss theologians the former taught chiefly in Germany until Hitler's coming, the latter for the most part in his native land. Negatively defined, their thought appears as a violent reaction to the complacent liberalism of pre-war days which in some quarters was fading into a humanism lacking all religious fibre. Positively defined, they represent an attempt to restate, in the light of historical criticism, some of what might be called the "creative insights" of the great Reformers. Though rejecting Fundamentalism and its infallible Bible, they are essentially *biblical* theologians, fervently reminding the men of their time that the Bible is the source (and perhaps the only source) of revelation. In this intense emphasis Barth may deserve the comment of an English critic that he is "more biblical than the Bible and more Hebraic than the Old Testament." He and his theological kin are defective not only in their characteristically German obscurity, in their want of the sanity and balance found in Catholic theology, but also in their total blindness to the value of the mystical element in religion and to the *social* meaning and message of Christianity. Yet they have infused into this generation of Protestant thinking an earnest vigor needed and welcomed by many.

Any full treatment of this theology, however, would draw us into a later period than that with which we are dealing. The earliest of Barth's famous books, his *Commentary on the Epistle to the Romans,* was not translated into English until 1933. Before 1931, therefore, his influence in the Church of England was slight and in the Episcopal Church practically negligible. Even in later years this school has never made the impact upon Anglicanism which it has elsewhere achieved, because Anglicans do not have to be saved from choosing between a diluted Liberalism and a fundamentalist type of Protestant orthodoxy. They find in thinkers like William Temple and even in Roman Catholics like von Hügel an interpretation of Christianity more congenial (and some would say less warped) than these descendants of Luther and Calvin can offer.

For many years following 1910 there was hot controversy within several Protestant Churches, especially the Presbyterian and the Baptist. The two extreme contending groups were known as Fundamentalists and Modernists. The former declared that certain beliefs which recent theology had questioned were essential pillars of Christianity. These included a verbally infallible Bible, the physical resurrection of Christ, His imminent bodily Second Coming, and the substitutionary theory of the Atonement. The Modernists, who sometimes doubted or denied these dogmas, were Liberals of various types ranging from nearly orthodox conservatives to left-wing humanists. No division quite comparable to this disturbed the peace of the Episcopal Church, for Anglicanism was not peculiarly sensitive on these particular doctrinal points, and as to its own sensitive points, it had long ago become accustomed to marked differences of opinion. In England, it is true, there arose a Modern Churchmen's Union which held conferences and published an interesting journal voicing liberal thought. But the attempt to give life to a similar Union in the United States was not successful. The temper of the English group was too intellectual to suit the talents or interests of American clergy, and the whole enterprise was too negative and defensive in its attitude to enlist any widely cordial support.

The decades during which tension was being heightened within other bodies fortunately saw a relaxation of party stress within the Episcopal Church. Between differing types of Churchmen a closer approach to fellowship developed, in happy contrast to the misunderstanding and ill-will of earlier days; and the life of the Church was thereby enriched. For this improvement in atmosphere we may credit especially the movements known as Liberal Evangelicalism and Liberal Catholicism. That each deserved the same adjective and that each was prepared to learn from the other were good omens. This more rational and less hostile relation between Evangelicals and Catholics may be attributed in part to a more enlightened and objective interpretation of Church history and doctrine, but it was surely due in some measure to the contemporary efforts to understand the beliefs and practices of other Churches. If the values exemplified by relatively alien bodies called for sympathetic appreciation, it was not too much to expect that Churchmen of different varieties should grow to know each other better and to regard their special emphases as contributions of which all were indispensable to a comprehensive Church.

As in the case of earlier trends of thought, both these movements originated in England and there found their most articulate expression. From the beginning of the century a group of younger Evangelical leaders in Britain were active in the attempt to put new life into the Evangelical party by rethinking their creed and by appropriating some of the values to be found among the High Churchmen and the Liberals. After the first World War they formed the Anglican Evangelical Group Movement, to which six hundred clergy belonged in 1925. Two years earlier their position and program had been stated in a volume of essays written by twelve clergymen and entitled *Liberal Evangelicalism*. The preface to these essays explains the nature of the movement not only in England but in the United States.

The term "Liberal Evangelicals" the authors heartily approve because "it suggests that the 'heredity' of their movement is rooted in the great Evangelical Revival, and that the 'environment' in which they are at home is the modern world with its historical method, its philosophy of personality, and its scientific view of the universe. The Evangelical Revival, with its renewed emphasis on the soul's direct relationship to God, on the freedom of the Spirit, the authority of the Bible, the centrality of the Cross, and the need of conversion, has been a dynamic force within the Church of England. . . . Restatement, however, has become essential. . . . It must be made clear that the emphasis spoken of is not tied to a particular point, but can shift freely along the line of the Spirit's guidance from age to age." [3] Though the authority of the Bible, for example, still stands in its unique position, it "is seen to center in its relation to the revelation of God in Christ. It is the mind of Christ, not the letter of Holy Scripture, which is authoritative." [4] Again, with reference to the Atonement, "The modern Evangelical finds salvation for himself and for society at the Cross of Jesus. This is as central to his religious experience as it was for St. Paul. . . . But the doctrine is no longer related in his mind to a primeval Fall of Man, nor need it find expression in forensic terms. The modern Evangelical is dissatisfied with some of the older and cruder penal and substitutionary theories of the Atonement." [5] In short, modern Evangelicals seek "to adjust themselves to the clearer light, deeper knowledge, and wider charity of today." [6]

During the late 'twenties there emerged in the Church in America the "Liberal Evangelicals," [7] a group with the same principles and program as their British counterpart, aiming to modernize the old fundamentalist type of Evangelicalism and at the same time to retain a religious fervor and a depth of conviction not always to be found in "Modernism." Both in England and on this side of the Atlantic these newer Evangelicals have shown a specially keen interest both in reunion with non-episcopal Churches and in the Christian solution of social problems.

During these same years the Anglo-Catholics abroad and at home were active both in organization and in intellectual output, with the Church of England as usual in the lead. One wing of the party continued to be definitely pro-Roman, Anglican neither in spirit nor in liturgical practices, and contributing little or nothing to thought. The opposite wing was described in this country as "Liberal Catholics." Their position was given admirable expression in *Essays, Catholic and Critical, by Members of the Anglican Communion,* a volume published in England in 1926 and

[3] *Liberal Evangelicalism,* V f.
[4] *Ibid.,* VI.
[5] *Ibid.,* VI f.
[6] *Ibid.,* 27. For Anglican Evangelicalism in general see A. C. Zabriskie's *Anglican Evangelicalism.*
[7] Now known as the Episcopal Evangelical Fellowship.

written by thirteen British scholars. Among them were A. E. J. Rawlinson, A. E. Taylor, J. K. Mozley, Kenneth E. Kirk, and Will Spens—an array which reminds us that in England in this era there was far more theological talent among Liberal Catholics than among Liberal Evangelicals. In an introduction the writers of these essays announce that "they have been drawn together by a common desire to attempt a fresh exposition and defence of the Catholic faith. . . . They have been compelled, both for themselves and for others, to think out afresh the content and the grounds of their religion. This book is the result of their endeavor. Among precursors in the same field, the essayists owe preeminent acknowledgment to the authors of *Lux Mundi,* a book which exercised upon many of them a formative influence and still has a living message." [8] And preparing the reader to profit from the ensuing essays on such subjects as the Incarnation and the Eucharist, the preface explains that "the two terms 'Catholic' and 'critical' represent principles, habits, and tempers of the religious mind which only reach their maturity in combination." [9]

Eight years after this book was published in England a group of American priests issued a similar volume of essays called *Liberal Catholicism and the Modern World* (1934). They were consciously carrying out the aims pursued by *Lux Mundi* and *Essays, Catholic and Critical,* to whose authors they refer with admiration. Among their number were Frederick C. Grant, then Dean of Seabury-Western Theological Seminary, Wilbur M. Urban, Professor of Philosophy at Yale, Father Granville M. Williams of the Society of St. John the Evangelist, and Cuthbert A. Simpson, Professor of Old Testament Literature at the General Seminary. But the editor and guiding spirit both of the book and of the movement was Frank Gavin, then Professor of Ecclesiastical History at the General Seminary, whose untimely death was a severe loss to the cause he represented. In the Introduction which he wrote he explained that "if one could set off in a few words the quality of progressive Anglo-Catholicism today, the result might be stated succinctly: to preserve the best of the past in the light of the best of the present so as to build for the best future." [10] "The word 'Liberal,' " he continued, "is a good term. It connotes freedom, adventure, independence, and that dignified quality of the human spirit by which it affirms its hostility to all enslavements, tyrannies, blindnesses, errors, and falsehoods. . . . The claims of the Anglo-Catholic to it are justifiable. . . ." [11] "It is our peculiar privilege as Anglicans to set forward and bear witness to a Catholicism that is not imperialistic but free; and to a liberalism that has its living roots in the

[8] *Essays, Catholic and Critical,* p. V.
[9] *Ibid.,* VI.
[10] *Liberal Catholicism,* p. VI.
[11] *Ibid.,* VII f.

congenial atmosphere of a vital tradition. The least inadequate way to describe the ideal adumbrated, nay, proclaimed by the fact of our position is by these two words: Liberal Catholic." [12]

This attitude and these convictions are characteristic of the essays which follow. "Liberal Catholics," in the words of Dr. Simpson, "accept and welcome the results of literary and historical criticism." [13] "We are Catholics," wrote Father Williams, "but we are also modern men and women. We believe utterly the truths of our holy religion, and because we so believe we are unafraid of any truth." [14] Dr. Grant was prepared to declare that "what is positive and fruitful in Protestantism will contribute eventually and is already contributing now, to the enrichment and strengthening of the Catholic Church. . . . What is false in the interpretations and emphases of the historic Catholic Churches will be done away; only what is true will survive." [15] And it was in this same year that there was published an address delivered in New York by Will Spens of Corpus Christi College, Cambridge, in which the speaker, reporting on the Catholic movement in England, noted an increasing respect for Reformation theology and affirmed his belief that "truth must be sought in a liberalized Catholicism."

In view of such tendencies and utterances as these it is no wonder that an acute foreign observer, writing in 1933 of "Evangelicalism and the Oxford Movement" should have expressed this conclusion: "Today, an observer of the two movements . . . must be struck by the fact of their mutual interpenetration. . . . The contributions of Evangelicalism to the Anglo-Catholic worship and piety is perhaps more important than is sometimes assumed. An analysis of *Essays, Catholic and Critical* on the one hand and *Liberal Evangelicalism* on the other, could certainly show how much the teaching of both schools had been influenced by each other. Neither can be understood if the contributions from the other side are ignored. Their friendly competition, their fruitful interaction is essential for the life of the Anglican Church and the fulfilling of its task in the Church Universal." [16]

[12] *Ibid.*, XI.
[13] *Ibid.*, 25.
[14] *Ibid.*, 93.
[15] *Ibid.*, 48.
[16] Y. T. Brilioth, *Evangelicalism and the Oxford Movement*, 53.

Chapter XXIII

"CHRISTIANIZING THE SOCIAL ORDER"

AT the opening of the twentieth century the preaching of "the social Gospel" was increasing in power and range of application, and until the outbreak of the first World War in 1914 the social movement in the Churches made optimistic progress. As we have earlier recorded, it was a period in the nation's history marked by the campaign for social justice. William Jennings Bryan as orator and recurrent candidate, Theodore Roosevelt as President from 1901 to 1909, and Woodrow Wilson after 1912 were only the three most noted leaders, among scores less prominent, to concentrate their energies upon programs of economic and political reform. What has been called "the progressive climate of the day," manifest in zeal for social betterment in nation, State, and city, could not fail to stimulate the life of the Churches. But it has been remarked, not without reason, that "generally speaking, the Church floated on the current of a great popular tide, participating prominently at times, but neither initiating nor directing the movement." [1]

Yet the activity of the Churches was no mere reflection of the spirit and the enterprises of the secular world. However much they may have been stirred by their environment, they had their own contribution to make. They could invigorate the forces working for a juster social order by preaching a message and by appealing to motives which drew their inspiration from the historical Jesus. It was, in fact, the discovery of the social teachings of Jesus which gave both enthusiasm and authority to the Churches' social program. Later New Testament research and the subsequent experience of two world wars have modified the version of the social Gospel then adopted and acclaimed. In an age of hopeful confidence in inevitable progress the Kingdom of God was often interpreted as little more than a regenerated society—"a religious version of evolu-

[1] H. U. Faulkner, *The Quest for Social Justice,* 218.

tion." No post-war reaction, however, can permanently affect the essential truth that the Christian is called by God to apply the fundamental principles of Jesus in the life of society, and that when they are fearlessly put into practice we shall have a new and nobler social order. That summons and the promise which attends it are not at the mercy of the shifting phases of New Testament criticism nor of the psychological effects of international strife.

Typical of the age and widely influential among liberal-minded Christians were such books as Francis G. Peabody's *Jesus Christ and the Social Question* (1900), Charles R. Brown's *The Social Message of the Modern Pulpit* (1906), and Shailer Mathews' *The Church and the Changing Order* (1907). But by far the most effective and popular exponent of social Christianity was Walter Rauschenbusch, professor in the Baptist Theological Seminary at Rochester, New York. In 1907 appeared his *Christianity and the Social Crisis,* three years later came his *Christianizing the Social Order,* and in 1917 he delivered at Yale the lectures which were published as *A Theology of the Social Gospel.*

These books, eventually translated into eight languages, found thousands of enthusiastic readers in many of the Churches. Their central theme was the interpretation of Jesus' teaching in terms of the Kingdom of God and the interpretation of the Kingdom of God as "humanity organized according to the will of God." Like other contemporary writers in the same field Rauschenbusch laid constant stress upon the supreme value of human personality in the eyes of God, and upon the highest development and enrichment of personality as the aim of a just social order and the test of its Christian quality. He taught that the process of Christianizing society was the process of extending into the harsh competitive realms of business and industry the fraternal and cooperative principles already active and accepted in the family, the church, and the school. He pleaded for industrial democracy, since "political democracy without economic democracy is an uncashed promissory note." Natural monopolies must become public property, and capitalism must be freed from its complete reliance upon the profit motive. Yet though he championed what was still called "Christian Socialism," he repudiated the materialism of orthodox Socialism.

Not only books but official pronouncements served both to express and to promote the growing concern of the Churches for social welfare. Perhaps the most effective of these was "A Social Creed" set forth in 1912 by the recently organized Federal Council of the Churches of Christ. It took the shape of a platform stating the principles and the measures which the Churches ought to stand for. Among the fifteen projects of social reform which it enumerated were the abolition of child labor, the protection of women from the hazards of industry, the abatement of poverty, the conservation of health, and the adoption of a living wage as a minimum. It concluded with the statement of a sixteenth article: "A new emphasis upon the application of Christian principles to the acquisition and use of property, and for the most equitable division of the product of industry that can ultimately be devised."

Not content with utterances in books and creeds, the Churches were proceeding at the same time to form agencies to put social convictions into actual operation. The first of these bodies to employ a full-time paid secretary and to engage in an efficient campaign was established by the Presbyterian Church (North) in its Department of Church and Labor, which the Rev. Charles Stelzle endowed with vitality. By the year 1912 most of the larger denominations had created official social service commissions.

The Episcopal Church was represented in all three fields of activity—in the production of books, in the publication of pronouncements, and in the formation of effective agencies. To cite but two examples of writings by Churchmen, Professor Henry S. Nash in his *Genesis of the Social Conscience* (1897) gave a searching and scholarly treatment of origins, and Bishop Charles D. Williams of Michigan popularized the social message in his book *A Valid Christianity for Today* (1909). The resolutions of General Convention offer several admirable examples of the Christian attitude toward social problems. They set a standard to which it has not always proved easy for Church members to conform.

In the course of thirty years there were many special resolutions dealing with particular causes and conditions. The Convention, for instance, condemned child labor, mob violence, and the opium traffic, and commended the League of Nations, the Washington Conference, the Near East Relief, and the Cooperative Movement. Of more permanent significance were the broader resolutions adopted by the Conventions of 1913, 1916, and 1919. They registered the high-water mark of the response of the Church to the Christian social thought of the time; and since they are just as sound now as they were then they deserve full quotation.

1913. "*Resolved,* that we the members of General Convention of the Protestant Episcopal Church do hereby affirm that the Church stands for the ideal of social justice, and that it demands the achievement of a social order in which the social cause of poverty and the gross human waste of the present order shall be eliminated, and in which every worker shall have a just return for that which he produces, a free opportunity for self-development, and a fair share in all the gains of progress. . . . The Church calls upon every communicant, clerical and lay, so to act that the present prejudice and injustice may be supplanted by mutual understanding, sympathy, and just dealings, and the ideal of thorough-going democracy may be finally realized in our land."

1916. "Resolved, that the service of the community and the welfare of the workers, not primarily private profit, should be the aim of every industry and its justification; and that the Church should seek to keep this aim constantly before the mind of the public; and that Christians as individuals are under the solemn obligation on the one hand conscientiously to scrutinize the sources of their income, and on the other hand to give moral support and prayer to every just effort to secure fair conditions and regular employment for wage-earners, and the extension of true democracy to industrial matters." [2]

1919. "Resolved, that this Convention urges upon capital and labor alike the acceptance of 'the principle of partnership as the business aspect of brotherhood,' the submission of all industrial differences to competent boards of arbitration and the recognition of service to the community as a whole, rather than individual gain, as the primary motive in every kind of work."

The Christian convictions which prompted these official statements received their most widely heralded expression at the Lambeth Conference of 1920. There words were spoken and solemnly ratified which lent vigorous encouragement to all who were striving to Christianize the social order. The Encyclical Letter of the bishops gave a forceful reply to all who sought refuge from Christian obligation in the familiar plea—"Economic and social questions are no business of the Church." "Whenever," it declared, "in the working out of economic or political theory moral issues are directly involved, the Church has a duty to see that the requirements of righteousness are faced and fairly met."

And among the resolutions of the Conference there will long be remembered this outspoken affirmation: "An outstanding and pressing duty of the Church is to convince its members of the necessity of nothing less than a fundamental change in the spirit and working of our economic life. This change can only be effected by accepting as the basis of industrial relations the principle of cooperation in service for the common good in place of unrestricted competition for private or sectional advantage. All Christian people ought to take an active part in bringing about this change, by which alone we can hope to remove class dissensions and resolve industrial discords.

"Even in matters of economic and political controversy the Church

[2] This resolution was proposed to the House of Bishops by the Society of the Companions of the Holy Cross.

is bound to give its positive and active corporate witness to the Christian principles of justice, brotherhood, and the equal and infinite value of every human personality."

Long before these manifestoes were issued at home and abroad the Episcopal Church had taken steps to implement its declared beliefs and to provide machinery for putting its social program into action. The first step, however, was limited and tentative. In 1901 General Convention appointed a Joint Commission on the Relations of Capital and Labor which was charged "to study carefully the aims and purposes of the labor organizations of our country; in particular to investigate the causes of industrial disturbances as these may arise; and to hold themselves in readiness to act as arbitrators, should their services be desired, between the men and their employers, with a view to bring about mutual conciliation and harmony in the spirit of the Prince of Peace."

Though this commission included such distinguished figures as Bishop Henry Potter, Bishop William Lawrence, Dean Hodges, Jacob Riis, and Seth Low, several of whom were noted for their sympathy with labor, it is perhaps not surprising that they had to announce in 1904 that their services as arbitrators had not been requested. Their report, however, was wholesome medicine for their fellow Churchmen. It gave notice that at last the Church was supporting the cause of union labor. "We are convinced," wrote the Commission, "that the organization of labor is essential to the well-being of the working people." (As Hodges elsewhere put it, "the union is as inevitable as the weather.") Moreover, "while we condemn the tyranny and turbulence of the Labor Union . . . we deprecate the hasty temper which, in condemning the errors of the Unions, condemns at the same time the whole movement with which they are connected. The offences of the Union are as distinct from the cause for which the organization of labor stands as the Inquisition is distinct from the Gospel." Here indeed could be heard a tone of voice scarcely audible twenty years earlier.

Six years later, in 1910, General Convention discharged this commission; and to enlarge the functions which it had efficiently performed, appointed a Joint Commission on Social Service. Its purpose was "to study and report upon social and industrial conditions; to coordinate the activities of the various organizations existing in the Church in the interests of social service; to cooperate with similar bodies in other communions; to encourage sympathetic relations between capital and labor; and to deal according to their discretion with these and kindred matters." For the next nine years this commission of five bishops, five presbyters, and five laymen constituted the chief national authority of the Church serving the cause of Christian social relations. It was able to perform its functions more effectively than any earlier group because it soon employed an energetic field secretary, the Rev. Frank M. Crouch, with several assistants and an office at the Church Missions House in New York.

By the time this agency had been established in 1912, sixty dioceses and missionary districts, beginning with Long Island, had adopted some form of social service organization, and within another four years twenty-one more had taken similar action. These bodies varied greatly in character and value. In a few dioceses there were able commissions with paid secretaries. Elsewhere there might be only a part-time volunteer worker or a group which seldom met and still less often acted. But the spirit and purpose which they represented were highly encouraging; and their activities included the investigation of social conditions, cooperation with denominational and secular agencies in promoting measures of social reform, and working for the support and improvement of municipal and State institutions. To increase and develop these diocesan groups and through them to enlarge the number of similar parochial committees were among the chief aims of the Joint Commission of General Convention.

Since direct action was not often feasible, the slow process of educating the membership of the Church was one of the valuable functions of the Commission. Sermons and addresses and study classes, courses in Sunday schools and theological schools, the publication of many pamphlets, and conferences held at intervals in different parts of the country—all helped to arouse the indifferent to the Church's obligations and opportunities. On a smaller scale the same methods were in use wherever diocesan or parochial groups were active.

Among the societies which reinforced the work of the Commission and with which it cooperated was the Church Mission of Help. This organization—the only national case-working agency under the auspices of the Church—was founded in New York in 1911 by Father James Huntington, Mr. and Mrs. John M. Glenn, and others. Its purpose was to give help to adolescent youth, especially to girls, faced with serious difficulties. Eight years later it had formed a National Council and had received recognition by General Convention. In 1927 its branches were to be found in seventeen dioceses. Its expanding activity and its permanent value are well expressed in its present title—"Episcopal Service for Youth, Inc."

When the National Council of the Church was organized in 1919 the Joint Commission on Social Service was succeeded by the new Department of Christian Social Service. The Rev. Charles N. Lathrop served for the next ten years as its executive secretary, and during that time its functions were gradually enlarged and its influence extended.

Like the body which preceded it, its settled policy was to spread the activity of social service and to decentralize its control by promoting and stimulating provincial, diocesan, and parochial agencies, and at the same time to coordinate their efforts and to give them the guidance they usually needed. Frequent surveys of Church institutions and the production of educative literature continued as regular functions of the Department. Among the newer developments of proved value were the inauguration in 1921 of the annual National Conference of Social Service Workers of the Episcopal Church, the effective use made of summer conferences, and the increased attention given to labor and industry.

In the multiplying number of summer conferences, of one or two weeks' duration, which were then reporting increased attendance in all parts of the country, courses on social service were often provided, sometimes with leaders especially trained to teach them. One of these schools, offering a strenuous curriculum of six weeks or more, was the Cincinnati Summer School founded and led by Dr. William Keller, a physician with social enthusiasm. Beginning in 1923 with support from the diocese of Southern Ohio and the Department of Christian Social Service, Dr. Keller developed a course of training in social and institutional work offered to theological students. Within five years twenty-five students from twelve seminaries were in attendance, and most of the members of its growing body of alumni became zealous converts to the cause of Christianizing the social order.

The Department of Christian Social Service could trace its origin to a Commission on the Relations of Capital and Labor, but it was not until 1926 that it created a Division of Industrial Relations, which began its work early in the following year, with Spencer Miller, Jr. as consultant and the Rev. Joseph F. Fletcher as research assistant. Though their varied program embraced many other features, such as the investigation of labor disputes and the conduct of field studies in industrial centers, perhaps their contribution of most enduring value was the publication in 1930 of a substantial volume called *The Church and Industry,* which gave a survey of the relations of the Church of England and the Church in America to the problems of capital and labor during the previous sixty years. The progress it recorded, though not inspiring, was distinctly cheering.

In one field of human relations the Church could directly intervene by legislative action—in marriage and divorce. The divorce problem had been growing steadily more serious for a generation past. Between 1867 and 1900 the number of divorces in every 100,000 of the population had risen from 27 to 73. Conditions grew worse in the twentieth century, for in 1914 the annual ratio of divorces to marriages was one to ten and in 1928 it was one to six. Here was a situation in which the Church could act not only through the training of its members (which had evidently been none too effective) but also through its attitude toward remarriage.

As early as 1808 General Convention passed a resolution declaring it contrary to the law of God for a minister to remarry any divorced person, with the exception of the innocent party in a divorce on the ground of adultery. Since it was subsequently decided that resolutions had no binding legal force, the same prohibition with the same exception was enacted as a canon in 1868. Nine years later this law was replaced by a fuller canon which included the words "No minister . . . shall solemnize the marriage of any person who has a divorced husband or wife still living, if such husband or wife has been put away *for any cause arising after marriage*"; and there follows once again the exception of the innocent party. Here we have the first suggestion of pre-marital causes which was later to develop into ample arrangements for annulments. The new canon further provided for all cases of remarriage to be referred to the bishop for full enquiry.

For the next twenty-seven years no changes were made in this canon, though on several occasions the House of Bishops tried to remove the one exception allowed. To make that exception more difficult to exploit, the Convention of 1904 added certain safeguards—the requirements that remarriage must be at least one year after divorce and that the bishop could give permission only after taking legal advice based upon court records. It was further enacted—in deference to the consciences of many —that no minister was obliged to perform the marriage ceremony for any divorced person. To these prohibitions the Convention of 1922 added a clause making it unlawful for a member of the Church to be a party to any marriage which it was unlawful for a minister to solemnize. In other words, the law now not only restrained Episcopal ministers but directly touched any divorced member who remarried.

Thus the canon stood until 1931, when General Convention added a series of new features to the legislation of Holy Matrimony. The purpose of several of these was to introduce a positive and constructive note into a law which had been mainly negative in character. Ministers were now to be required to give public and private instruction on the nature and responsibilities of matrimony, and persons whose marriage was threatened with disaster were bidden to lay their troubles before a minister with the intent that he might serve to reconcile them. Encouragement was thus given to take educative and preventive measures.

Another section of the canon provided that any person whose former marriage had been annulled, or who had been divorced, might apply to the bishop or to the ecclesiastic court to have the marriage declared null and void by reason of any one or more of nine impediments existing before marriage. Among those listed were lack of free consent, insanity, and venereal disease. If the bishop or ecclesiastical court declared the marriage in question to be null, the person might be married. Here at length was a measure which made possible the marriage of a divorced person who was not the innocent party in a divorce for adultery. Strictly speaking, however, this would not be *re*-marriage, since permission could be given only after it had been declared that the original marriage was not a marriage at all. We may account for the form which this new amendment took by remembering that those who believe that all Christian marriages are indissoluble are likely to adjust themselves to the facts of life by making increasing use of the practice of annulment.

As we have recalled in a previous chapter, no account of the Church's concern for the social order would be complete without mention of the unofficial groups dedicated to practising the social Gospel. In every generation they serve as skirmishers sent out in advance of the principal forces. They are in more direct contact with the enemy and run more risk of opposition and abuse than the slower and solider main body. They have, moreover, a special interest for the historian, because their principles and programs are often adopted in the course of time by those who once rejected them as dangerous.

Two such organizations in the Church we found to be active in the last decade of the nineteenth century—the Christian Social Union (C.S.U.) and the Church Association for the Advancement of the Interests of Labor (CAIL). The C.S.U. continued until 1912 its educational campaign by publishing monographs and by arranging for discussion groups and for conferences with representatives of labor. After the Joint Commission on Social Service had begun operations, the members of the C.S.U., finding an official body now engaged in much the same work, decided to dissolve their Union. Though CAIL maintained its work for a longer time, especially in its efforts to support constructive labor legislation, the national and diocesan departments of social service came more and more to duplicate its activities and to diminish their range. Finally, when the national Department formed its Division of Industrial Relations in 1926 the need for CAIL appeared to have passed, and the organization was disbanded. The fact that other groups were fulfilling its purposes may rightly be counted as proof of its success.

The Church Socialist League was established in 1911. Though it was sponsored by several bishops, it attracted few members and did not long survive the first World War. Far more prosperous has been the career of the Church League for Industrial Democracy.[3] It originated at a meet-

[3] Now known as the Episcopal League for Social Action.

ing of clergy and laity held in May, 1919, in New York. Within a few months it was holding conferences and mass meetings at the General Convention in Detroit. Bishop Charles D. Williams was elected President and Professor Vida D. Scudder of Wellesley College chairman of the executive committee. In its original statement of principles the League made this declaration: "We face a world in revolution. Some regret the fact; some thank God for it. Regret and gratitude are in a sense irrelevant; the Church is called to act, and the contemporary situation furnishes her with a challenge and an opportunity unsurpassed since Pentecost. We affirm our belief that only that social order can properly be called Christian which substitutes fraternal cooperation for mastership in industry and life."

In the course of another six months more than three hundred had joined the League, and active chapters had been formed in Philadelphia, Baltimore, New York, and Boston. In 1924 the Rev. William B. Spofford was elected executive secretary. For more than twenty years thereafter his fearless and sympathetic leadership was a prime factor in maintaining the League's vitality. By 1931 there were over one thousand regular members, most of them in the East and Middle West. To keep the conscience of the Church alive to social evils and to social issues, especially in the sphere of industry, and to stimulate social action where action was called for, were the central aims of the League. Its program was necessarily educational. The publication of a quarterly, the organization of public meetings and of conferences on social problems (sometimes including employers), and the formation of student groups both in colleges and for summer work in industries—these were a few of the methods employed to interpret the meaning and to advance the cause of industrial democracy.

Chapter XXIV

PROGRESS IN CHRISTIAN EDUCATION

THE first thirty years of the twentieth century were a period of unprecedented educational expansion in the United States. The number of high school and college students increased to such a degree that the proportion of the young enjoying higher education resembled the proportion which had once enjoyed secondary education; and high schools were as populous as grammar schools had once been. At the same time the quality of teaching showed marked improvement. New methods were widely developed, and new theories (some more valuable than others) kept large sections of the educational world in a state of interesting ferment. In this same era the Church gave really effective evidence of advance in Christian education.

The report of the Joint Committee on Christian Education to the General Convention of 1904 noted the fact that pedagogy had become a science based on the findings of psychology and that the purpose of teaching had ceased to be merely the instruction of the mind and had come to emphasize the training of the will and the development of character. "Happily our Church is awake," it declared, "in applying the principles of the most scientific pedagogy to the child, as the child's nature and the laws governing it are revealed by modern psychology. The American Church Sunday School Institute, with its diocesan auxiliaries, and the Sunday school commissions in several dioceses, have contributed to further development and improvement of religious education within the Church to a degree difficult to estimate." Three years later, however, the same committee felt bound to confess that many Church schools had not learned to adapt themselves to the newer methods. And they added, "In some institutions instruction in the Catechism and Church doctrine is so dull that the pupils get little, if anything, that is valuable from it, and lose interest in the subject; while in others the teaching is vague and unsystematic." But in 1910 the Joint Committee on Sunday School Instruction (established in 1904) encouraged the Convention with the news that the principle of graded lessons was becoming more and more accepted, that progress in missionary education was hopeful, and that several seminaries were beginning to teach religious education.

The notable educational event of 1910 was the adoption of a canon constituting a General Board of Religious Education, the purpose of which was "the unification and development of the Church's work of religious instruction . . . especially through the Sunday school." The Board was to be composed of the Presiding Bishop, seven other bishops, seven presbyters, and seven laymen, together with two members from each of the eight "missionary departments" in which the Church was then divided, units soon to be superseded by the provinces. The duties of the Board were to be carried out by a general secretary, by department secretaries, and by Sunday school conventions in each department. At the next General Convention the scope of the Board's responsibilities was wisely enlarged by charging it with "the unification and development of the educational work of the Church"—a range that was all-embracing.

For fifteen years the General Board, and its counterpart in the National Council, profited from the initiative and the experienced wisdom of its first general secretary, the Rev. William E. Gardner, who was succeeded in 1925 by a gifted expert, the Rev. John W. Suter, Jr. Though the new organization had to subsist for its first three years on less than $14,000 in contributions per year, after two trienniums Dr. Gardner could report the kind of progress for which the Church had been waiting for a century. At last a central body with authority was carrying out definite plans. The Board had set up four departments—for parochial education, secondary education, collegiate education, and theological education. Though most of its work was concerned with parochial education, the acceptance of the other fields as part of the Church's responsibility was significant. Practical measures already well advanced included a correspondence school reaching some five hundred teachers and the publication for trial use of *The Christian Nurture Series* of text-books. This material for pupils and teachers, as its name implies, conceived religious education as "Christian nurture," a process far richer and more varied than mere biblical instruction. "Informational" matter was therefore only part of what was offered, and there was valuable emphasis upon the development of Church loyalty, training in the devotional life, and stimulus to active service. The series was easily the best then available.

By the year 1920 the General Board had ceased to be, and its functions were thenceforth performed by the Department of Religious Education of the National Council, with leadership and purposes unchanged. Over 200,000 teachers and pupils were then using the Christian Nurture Series, which was being frequently revised; teacher training manuals were in preparation; eighteen summer schools and conferences were growing in popularity; diocesan normal schools and institutes were helping to improve instruction; and diocesan boards of religious education were operating in more than half the dioceses. Nor was missionary education forgotten, since in 1923 it was part of the activity of four departments. In that year week-day religious instruction in cooperation with public schools was in operation in 125 cities. The following year saw the inauguration of the National Accredited Teachers Association based upon the awarding by the Department of certificates to teachers who had passed the required examinations. In the course of the next seven years the Department had provided 502 teachers with full diplomas and had listed 900 others as "recognized instructors." It was gratefully evident to all observers that the Church's standards of education were rapidly rising.

During the later years we are reviewing other forward steps were taken. An indication of the widespread concern for education was the encouraging fact that in the year 1929 parishes, dioceses, and provinces were employing as many as a hundred trained directors of religious education, though a generation earlier it would have been hard to find more than half a dozen. There had come to be as many as seventy summer conferences—regional, provincial, and diocesan—with a capacity for training lay leaders which grew more effective with every year. To exploit this field more fully there had already been formed a Commission on Adult Education, and in 1927 an Adult Division of the Department was organized.

What had been achieved in the Church's work for youth and for college students was part of Christian education in the broader sense. "Youth," as defined by the national Church, included boys and girls between the ages of fourteen or fifteen and twenty-one. The effort to win and hold these young people had long taken the form of organizations to attract and educate them, such as several already mentioned—the Girls' Friendly Society (1877), the Brotherhood of St. Andrew (1883), with its Junior Chapters, the Daughters of the King (1896), the Order of Sir Galahad (1896), and the Order of the Fleur de Lis (1914). But never was more than a very small proportion of the youth enrolled in these associations; and it was not primarily from their activity that the Youth Movement of today was derived.

It was in 1915 and 1916 that there arose in Michigan and in Massachusetts the earliest "Young People's Fellowships," informal groups of older boys and girls, in several parishes, who conducted their own meetings and services with a minimum of oversight from their rectors. The need met by these fellowships was so urgent and their initial success so apparent that their numbers multiplied rapidly, and in 1924 a national convention of young people was held at Racine, Wisconsin. At this meeting, which included representatives from half the dioceses, there was organized what came to be known as the National Federation of Episcopal Young People. It was a loose union of diocesan groups bound together by a triennial convention and an interim national commission composed of eight young people and four adults. This event was reported to the next General Convention in the following year, and a committee of the House of Bishops noted "the rapid and wide development of Young People's Fellowships and the remarkable response made to them." Up to that point their activity had been wholly independent of the National Council and under no recognized Church authority. Beginning in 1925, however, the Department of Religious Education employed a part-time director of Youth work and attempted, as far as lack of funds permitted, to provide some measure of leadership. Its contribution increased in value with the appointment in 1931 of an associate secretary for young people's work, but the era of rising prosperity for the Youth Movement did not begin until the formation of the Division of Youth in 1940.

Since it lacked any organ through which to operate, the national Church produced little effect on the life of secular colleges until the formation of the National Council in 1920. The Department of Religious Education then appointed a Commission on College and University Work which began at once a correspondence with some two hundred and fifty clergy whose duties brought them into touch with students. To make this surveying process more effective and to initiate "sample" work, several young priests were engaged as "student enquirers" and for the next few years conducted in the colleges where they were placed not only a general investigation of conditions but also direct work with students. Their subsequent extensive report proved valuable in later planning. There had already been formed in 1918 the National Student Council. It took shape as the result of several conferences called by the Board of Religious Education at which there met representatives of the Board, clergy and professors from college towns, and bishops. The new body provided in its constitution for student representation, and its purpose was to be the accepted agency through which matters of policy were to be communicated to college workers and to students. It recognized and promoted groups of Episcopal students on campuses as "units," so far as they agreed to carry out an active program of worship and varied service. Within six years seventy-four such units became affiliated with the Council.

Until 1926, it must be acknowledged, the National Council had contributed to college work chiefly information and good advice. A new era of direct action opened with the arrival in 1926 of the Rev. C. Leslie Glenn, who served as secretary for College Work for the next four years. His missionary ardor was infectious and soon made the Church "college-conscious." It was brought home to Episcopalians that though the baptized members of the Church in 1928 were only 1.6 per cent of the population, Church members constituted 5.5 per cent of the total enrollment in colleges and universities. Here was a huge field. That it was largely neglected was shown by the fact that out of 300 clergy in or near college communities only 125 gave any time whatever to students and only 27 gave more than half-time. To find and place the right men and women in the parishes of college cities and towns became the immediate aim of the National Council. It was necessarily a slow process, but by 1930 the Department was placing twenty or more men and women a year in full-time or part-time positions, and five provinces had associate secretaries giving part time to college work. In 1939 the enterprise had reached a point which justified the National Council in establishing a separate Division of College Work and Youth, which became two separate Divisions in 1940.

The Church colleges were improving in quality as the twentieth century progressed. Except for the smaller St. Stephen's, they were nearly equal in size, with their students numbering between two and three hundred. William Smith College for women began in 1908 to share with Hobart the same campus, trustees, and faculty. Kenyon benefited in 1912 from a thorough reorganization, and Trinity showed signs of new vigor for twenty-four years during the presidency of the Rev. Remsen B. Ogilby. An association of Church college presidents was formed in 1922, and for several years in that wealthy period following the Nation-wide Campaign the National Council gave $10,000 a year to each of the five colleges. They continued to inspire loyalty among their alumni and to combine a wholesome spirit with intellectual mediocrity.

Between 1901 and 1931 theological education made highly encouraging progress. Perhaps its most significant feature was the extent to which academic attitudes and methods came to be more and more alike in the different seminaries. The scientific study of the Bible and of Church history won its way to general acceptance; there were no longer the sharp contrasts of earlier decades between orthodox and liberal schools. Even the treatment of theology as material for thought rather than for memorization was increasingly familiar. Anglo-Catholics in small numbers began to feel at home in Alexandria and Cambridge, and standards of scholarship tended slowly toward approximation. In this era, too, General

Convention began to manifest a more helpful interest in divinity schools. In 1910 it established a Commission on Theological Education. So far as may be judged by occasional amendments to the canons, there was a growing inclination to broaden the curriculum and to encourage the modernizing of practical theology. Passing examinations in the principles and methods of religious education and the history and methods of Christian missions became requirements for ordination.

Under Hughell Fosbroke as dean for thirty-one years (1916–1947) the General Seminary attained a degree of scholarship in faculty and students never before experienced. Professors of the international standing of Burton S. Easton and Leonard Hodgson gave dignity and weight to instruction. A tutorial system introduced in 1926 kept the students more alert, and the teaching of pastoral care was successfully combined with supervised parochial work. At Cambridge, too, another type of tutorial system, in preparation for general examinations, proved a stimulating supplement to courses and lectures. A close affiliation with Harvard University enlarged the opportunities open to members of the school, who were granted many free electives. While pure scholarship on the faculty was represented only by William H. P. Hatch in the chair of the New Testament, the theological teaching of Edward S. Drown and the biographical presentation of Church history by Dean Henry B. Washburn made two central subjects vital for a generation of students.

The Berkeley Divinity School, under Dean William P. Ladd, moved from Middletown to New Haven in 1927, preferring society to isolation; and an affiliation with Yale brought an academic enrichment to which many visiting English lecturers also contributed. The Philadelphia Divinity School continued to profit from the prestige of such scholars as James A. Montgomery. Moving to a better area of the city, it erected new buildings of admirable design. The Western Theological Seminary, by uniting in 1933 with Seabury Divinity School, entered upon a period of growth and prosperity, with Frederick C. Grant as first president of the double institution. The Virginia Seminary discovered that evangelical religion was not to be forever identified with biblical fundamentalism or with any fixed type of theology. The school became as popular with Northerners as with Southerners, for its very atmosphere was Christian, and teachers of theology like W. Cosby Bell had a message for the times. On the other side of the country the Church Divinity School of the Pacific ceased to be of merely diocesan value. It was transferred in 1911 from San Mateo to San Francisco and, under the leadership of Dean H. H. Powell, made its final move to Berkeley in 1930. There the University of California and the Pacific School of Religion could supplement what the seminary offered. And at the same time the number of its students and the standing of its faculty began to justify its ambition to be the strong western center for theological education.

Neither in the last decades of the nineteenth century nor in the first of the twentieth did bishops and theological faculties have much reason to be encouraged about the number of candidates for the ministry. They were not increasing in proportion to the number of Church members. In 1856 one deacon was ordained for every 1,481 communicants; in 1886 one for every 3,701 communicants; and in 1926 one for every 6,288 communicants. In spite of growing Church membership the record reported 412 candidates for orders in 1871, 391 in 1881, 375 in 1891, and 343 in 1921.[1] Though there were intervening years when the showing was better, it was clear enough that in relation to its task the Episcopal ministry was dwindling in size.

Whatever remedies may have been attempted by individuals, no corporate official effort was made to recruit for the ministry until the Department of Religious Education appointed a Commission on the Ministry in 1920. Five years later the Department reported to General Convention some significant facts about the clergy who had been ordained between October, 1922, and September, 1925. On the basis of an enquiry to which 77 per cent of the men replied, it appeared that only 69 per cent had been brought up in the Anglican Communion, and of those brought up elsewhere the Methodists supplied nearly one-third. Only 77 per cent had attended any college and only 58 per cent had a bachelor's degree. Though 80 per cent had attended some seminary only 45 per cent had a B.D. degree. It thus became plain that but little more than two-thirds of the very small number of candidates was being furnished by families in the Episcopal Church or in other branches of the Anglican Communion; and it was quite as evident that the standards of education were too low for the twentieth century.

To present the ministry to young men of high quality the Commission helped to initiate a series of conferences at which college men could meet with chosen leaders among the clergy. One of the first and largest of these gatherings was a conference at St. Paul's School, Concord, New Hampshire, in 1922, organized by the rector, the Rev. Samuel S. Drury, where 400 men from 19 states were assembled. Further meetings of this type both there and at other points in the country, together with the less concentrated but more continuous efforts of college workers, were partly responsible for the larger number of candidates between 1930 and 1934. Yet no heavy increase was to come until after the second World War.

Summer conferences continued to make an ever more valuable con-

[1] These statistics are taken from the *Living Church Annual* for 1949, published by the Morehouse-Gorham Co.

tribution to adult education. To name but three of the larger and better known, Wellesley in Massachusetts, Kanuga in North Carolina, and Sewanee in Tennessee grew in numbers and in variety of curriculum. A few of them, including Kanuga and the Albany Summer School, offered special courses for clergy. But the great "School of the Prophets," which began in this period to provide post-graduate training for the clergy, was the College of Preachers in Washington. The conception of such a college had originated in the mind of Henry W. Satterlee, Bishop of Washington from 1896 to 1908, and had been developed to the point of action by Bishop James E. Freeman. The work of the school began informally in 1924 with conferences and discussion groups held in the Washington Cathedral, chiefly under Philip M. Rhinelander, who had resigned as Bishop of Pennsylvania the year before. A gift of $1,500,000 from Alexander S. Cochran of Yonkers, New York, made possible the erection of a group of buildings at once ample and beautiful, situated close to the cathedral. These were dedicated in 1929, and with Bishop Rhinelander as warden the college began its unique career. Since then it has served some three thousand clergy, all of whom have attended by invitation, most of them for sessions lasting a week, a few for much longer periods. Assembling in groups of fifteen or twenty, the men have met with carefully selected leaders to write and deliver sermons and not only to receive homiletical training but to profit from a regular devotional life and from lectures and discussions on the Bible, on Christian doctrine, and on various aspects of the Church's practical work. By encouraging the belief that a minister's education ought never to come to an end and by offering the means to enrich it, the College of Preachers has rendered to the Church distinguished service.

Chapter XXV

THE EXPANDING CHURCH: AT HOME AND ABROAD

DURING the first twenty years of the twentieth century the number of communicants in the Church increased fifty per cent. Within the same period the annual amount contributed to the domestic and foreign missionary work of the national Church and the number of missionaries sent out increased more than five hundred per cent.[1] This brilliant advance was due to two causes—the inauguration of the Apportionment System in 1901 and the Nation-wide Campaign in 1919.

The General Convention of 1901 instructed the Board of Managers of the Missionary Society to put in operation a plan for formulating an annual budget and distributing the amount needed among the dioceses and missionary districts in the form of apportionments or quotas. It was then to be the duty of the dioceses and districts to continue the distribution by notifying parishes and missions of their quotas. Thus for the first time in the history of the Church every unit was officially informed of its proper share in the total sum required to carry on the Church's mission. As a result of this stimulus during the next three years the money contributed increased about fifty per cent, and better still, the number of

[1] In 1901 eleven missionaries were appointed; in 1920 sixty-four. Exclusive of legacies and of gifts for special purposes (such as buildings and equipment) the amount given in 1900 was $440,000. The amount in 1920 was $2,969,000. From this, however, should be subtracted the relatively small sum of $81,000 appropriated for the Departments of Religious Education and Christian Social Service, since there were no such items in the General Church Budget for 1900. Neglecting the inclusion of these minor items after 1919 (as they scarcely affect the figures) we may note these significant facts. The giving to General Missions per communicant per year was as follows:

1880—$0.80
1890— 0.63
1900— 0.61
1910— 1.04
1920—$2.73
1930— 2.25
1940— 0.96

The lapse after 1930 was mainly due to the depression, but the Church has so far never returned to its earlier maximum.

congregations which sent offerings almost doubled. Even before the Nation-wide Campaign the per capita giving had more than doubled between 1900 and 1919. Yet as late as 1913 it was officially reported that ovee 1,200 parishes were giving nothing to the national Church.

After the war came the Nation-wide Campaign, which has been described in a preceding chapter. In one year, as we have noted, the money given for the Church's mission was doubled, rising from $1,473,000 to $2,969,000. For the next five years this annual sum was never greatly diminished, and in 1926 it rose to more than $3,000,000, which still remains the largest total ever achieved in one year. By this time, however, expenditure had so far outrun even these receipts that at the General Convention of 1925 the treasurer of the National Council had to announce a rapidly growing deficit of over $1,000,000. To remedy the situation two moves were made. The bishops and deputies proceeded to pledge such large contributions from their dioceses to clear the deficit that most of the debt was paid off by the end of the year. More than that, the Convention adopted what came to be known as "the pay-as-you-go policy": it directed the National Council to trim its budget each year to fit the amount which the dioceses declared that they *expected* to pay instead of to fit the amount which they were *asked* to pay. As a result, budgets have had to be cut nearly every year, but no debts accumulate. To warm-hearted enthusiasts for the cause of missions this new plan appeared to be cold-blooded and faithless. Nevertheless most responsible persons came to realize that there was no moral glory to be won by piling up debts and that it was wholesome for delinquent dioceses to remember that if they failed in their payments, someone was bound to suffer.

In the process of financing the missionary enterprise an ever-increasing share was taken by the Woman's Auxiliary through its United Thank Offering. From the little sum of $2,188 in 1889 this offering grew to $107,000 in 1901 and $243,000 in 1910, and in 1931 it went beyond the million mark.[2] Yet it would be a mistake to think of the Woman's Auxiliary simply as a money-raising society, though it happens to be more successful as such than any other agency in the Church. That success, however, is really a natural by-product of all its other activities. And those activities expanded during the thirty years we are surveying. After the National Council was organized the Woman's Auxiliary to the Board of Missions became the Woman's Auxiliary to the National Council, and its purpose was broadly defined in these official terms: "The Woman's Auxiliary to the National Council is an international, interracial fellow-

[2] Though of course reduced during the depression after 1930, the offering recovered its momentum much quicker than the general giving of the Church. It was almost $2,000,000 in 1949.

ship of the women of the Church, organized for service to the Church in every phase of its life and all fields of its activity." Since the work of the National Council is mainly concerned with missions, so likewise is the work of the Woman's Auxiliary, through study and giving and prayer. But in social service and in Christian education it has enlisted a growing number of women by means of its carefully planned programs, and in missionary education its success has been particularly notable. From 1916 to 1940 the Auxiliary owed much to the quiet leadership of Miss Grace Lindley, one of those rare characters who combine sanctity, efficiency, and charm.

AT HOME

In reviewing the advance of domestic missions during earlier periods the story could be told most easily in terms of enlarging territory and of pioneer personalities. But once we reach the twentieth century the frontiers are no longer geographical, and circumstances do not call for the same type of adventurous leadership. The expansion of the Church, instead, can be more readily recorded in terms of racial groups and types of work. The activities of the Church in rural areas and on behalf of Indians and Negroes are the movements that deserve attention.

Even after 1900, it is true, there were tokens of progress which can be described only by reference to geography—the growth of missionary districts into dioceses and the creation of new missionary districts. Between 1904 and 1922 six missionary districts became dioceses—Montana, Olympia, Sacramento, Southern Florida, West Texas, and Asheville (now Western North Carolina).[3] While these areas were thus showing signs of maturity, new regions had been organized as missionary districts—Eastern Oregon, North Texas, Salina (Kansas) and San Joaquin (California).[4] Here, then, was evidence not only of growth but of determination to go forward.

In the rural field—or, to use the current term, "town and country"—the Church was slow in displaying interest and still slower in action. Indeed, it was only after 1941 that any remarkable advances were made, and before that date only hopeful signs of awakening could be observed. In 1922 General Convention adopted a resolution asking the National Council "to consider the conditions of the rural districts in their relation to the Church and to make such recommendations as may lead to the reconstruction of the country church so that it may reassume its province

[3] In 1901 the canons were amended to substitute the term "missionary district" for "missionary jurisdiction."

[4] In addition to new missionary districts, eight new dioceses were organized between 1901 and 1931 by setting apart portions of existing dioceses.

of ministry to the whole of rural life." As one response to this request the National Council held a conference at Philadelphia in February, 1923, composed of representatives from five dioceses, a meeting at which a practical rural program was approved and later published. In the following year the important step was taken of organizing a Division of Rural Work, and a secretary was appointed, supported by the cooperation of the Department of Missions and the Department of Christian Social Service. The division, as interpreted by its first chief—the Rev. F. D. Goodwin of Virginia—aimed "to bring the Church to a realization of the great rural problem . . . and to enlist her whole-hearted support in the furtherance of the Church's rural work." Its methods were to include the publication of pamphlets and articles, the holding of national, regional, and diocesan conferences, and the development of instruction in rural work by theological seminaries.

These designs were carried out with varying degrees of success during the next seven years. Among the first moves was the organization of the Rural Workers' Fellowship in 1924, with *The Rural Messenger* as its organ. Several seminaries responded to the appeal for rural study in their curricula; the Woman's Auxiliary provided scholarships for students who were planning to prepare for the rural ministry; and clergy began to attend the rural schools offered by a number of colleges and universities. In 1926 the National Council produced the study-book *Beyond City Limits,* which helped to educate more than fifteen thousand readers in the needs of the field. But it was probably through the conferences, large and small, and the summer schools for rural clergy that slow but definite progress was best insured. They formed the basis for provincial and diocesan programs which could stimulate and guide any further advance. What had already been accomplished was recognized by the General Convention of 1928, which gave aid to the cause by appointing a Joint Commission on Rural Work "for fostering of the Church's work in village and country life." To the next Convention this Commission reported a growing interest in the rural field and submitted a valuable "National Program of Village and Country Work" covering not only education and research but definite plans to meet such practical needs as adequate salaries and necessary equipment.

Three years after these encouraging events the effects of the economic depression began to be so evident that the National Council, in severely reducing its budget in 1934, decided to abolish the Division of Rural Work. Many of its activities, however, were loyally sustained during a difficult interval of seven years by the executive secretary of the Department of Christian Social Service.

One phase of rural enterprise of which the Church has not been neglectful is that among the mountain people in the Appalachian region of the South. In that extensive territory may be found three or four million descendants of early American pioneers, most of them living in poverty and more or less cut off from the cultural influences that surround them. Work with the mountaineers has been undertaken chiefly by the dioceses in which they live, especially in Virginia, West Virginia, Tennessee, and North Carolina. But since aid from the Board of Missions and later from the National Council has long helped these missions to prosper, they demand a word in any record of domestic missions. Strongest of all these centers has been the Archdeaconry of the Blue Ridge in Virginia, inaugurated in 1888. By 1931 it had developed into an organization with thirty mission stations, twelve day-schools, an industrial boarding-school, and a tuberculosis preventorium. Schools are of course an essential feature of any mountain mission, institutions like the boarding-schools in the diocese of Western North Carolina. But often these schools form centers for evangelistic expansion through associate missions, as at St. Andrew's School for boys near Sewanee, Tennessee, and at the Valle Crucis School for girls in North Carolina.

In rural evangelism a new agency began in 1927 to prove itself of growing value—the Church Army. It was in 1925, at the invitation of several bishops, that a team of twenty-five members of the English Church Army (founded in 1882) came to this country and gave a three months' demonstration of their work. Two years later the Church Army was organized in the United States, with an Advisory Board of bishops, priests, and laymen. The first article of the constitution then adopted stated that the purposes of the Army were "to win souls for Jesus Christ by providing the clergy with trained Church Army evangelists and mission sisters, who shall assist them in developing the evangelizing powers of the laity; to preach the need of real conversion, holiness of heart and life, and loyal and intelligent Churchmanship; the work to be conducted free from party spirit, solely on Church lines and under diocesan supervision." It is a society of lay workers who have been carefully trained for their difficult duties at the Army's center in New York, and who are supported by voluntary gifts to their organization. At the end of their first four years of service they numbered twenty-six captains and one mission sister, and they had already been employed in thirty-two dioceses. In lumber camps and prisons, in neglected rural areas, and as leaders of preaching missions both in parishes and in the countryside, their success had won from the House of Bishops a tribute of hearty commendation.

In 1931 there were about 350,000 Indians in the United States, of whom 200,000 were wards of the government. Their political status had been changed in 1924 when they were officially declared to be citizens. Yet most of them continued to dwell in the two hundred reservations and communities cared for by the government through its Bureau of Indian Affairs.

Among the Indians the strongest and most extensive work of the Church continued to be with the tribes in South Dakota, the development of which has been described in recording the life of Bishop Hare. Twenty years after his death in 1909, in the episcopate of Bishop Hugh L. Burleson, there were nearly a hundred little churches and chapels served by a score of Indian clergy and three times that number of Indian lay helpers. But this success had been at the cost of two generations of devoted labor. Those who came after Hare in his field had not forgotten his warning that "the Indian work will probably be less romantic and eventful in the future, but not less important nor less difficult." Except in regard to size it was just as important and difficult in ten other dioceses and missionary districts.[5] In four reservations in the diocese of Duluth the Church ministered to the Chippewa (Ojibway) Indians at seventeen missions under an archdeacon. Among the Oneidas at Green Bay, Wisconsin, the Church of the Holy Apostles—a center for a thousand baptized members—testified to the permanence of the earliest endeavors a century before. The Arapahoes of Wyoming had been served by the Church since 1873, and at St. Michael's Mission at Ethete (begun in 1912) the work found a focus in a model community. Of no less value were the Church's stations among the Navajos of Arizona and New Mexico and the Utes of Utah.

During the first thirty years of this century the status of the Negroes and their opportunities began steadily to improve. Lynchings, which numbered 214 in the two years 1900 and 1901, grew less and less frequent. The percentage of illiteracy dropped with every year and the number of farms owned by Negroes increased. The organization in 1910 of the National Association for the Advancement of Colored People testified to the power of Negro leadership; and the eagerness of the colored race for education was shown by the fact that between 1917 and 1927 the institutions for the higher education of the Negro doubled in number and their enrollment multiplied six-fold.

In the course of these decades the concern of the national Church for the welfare of the Negro began to be more effective. It was expressed in three forms—by financial aid to southern dioceses, by missions directly responsible to the Board of Missions (and later to the National Council),

[5] Fond du Lac, Duluth (now part of Minnesota), North Dakota, Utah, Arizona, New Mexico, Nevada, Idaho, Wyoming, and Sacramento. In Oklahoma the large Indian population was so widely distributed among the white majority that no special mission was required to meet their needs.

but chiefly by the organization and support of the American Church Institute for Negroes.

In 1904 the Commission on Work among Colored People was discontinued and its functions were wisely transferred to the Board of Missions in recognition of the fact that the Negro was perhaps the most important factor in domestic missions. Thenceforward the Board, and its successor the Council, became responsible for the subsidies which helped to invigorate diocesan enterprises as well as for Negro work of its own. It was well for the future of these endeavors, and ultimately for the benefit of the race, that General Convention consistently rejected proposals put forward between 1907 and 1916 for the creation of missionary districts "upon racial lines," for a racial episcopate of inferior status, and even for a practically independent African Episcopal Church. Though these projects were repeatedly urged both by white and colored leaders, the wisdom of the Negroes' best friends was opposed to segregation on such a fatally large scale. One of the reasons, however, for authorizing in 1910 the election of suffragan bishops was to provide for Negro bishops in the South. Though it was another eight years before any such were elected, the Church benefited for twenty-one years from the devoted services of Bishop Edward T. Demby as suffragan in Arkansas and for a shorter time from the work of Bishop Henry B. Delaney in North Carolina. Of all the evangelistic endeavors among the Negroes the small result by 1930 was a communicant roll of 40,000 in 310 congregations, ministered to by 158 clergy; and most of the Church members were in the North. Energetic planning and wise guidance were not markedly in evidence until the appointment by the National Council of a Secretary for Negro Work in 1942.

In the Negro field the enterprise upon which the Church most clearly deserves congratulation is the American Church Institute for Negroes. The Institute was created by the Board of Missions in 1906 for the purpose of promoting the cause of education under Church auspices. It is an incorporated body with a Board of Trustees, a treasurer, and a director. Adopting from the outset the method of aiding and guiding institutions already established, it has selected certain schools for recognition and assistance and has devoted its energies to raising their standards and heightening their efficiency. Having at first only very small funds, the Institute began by sponsoring only those schools which we have noticed in a former chapter—St. Paul's Normal and Industrial School at Lawrenceville, Virginia, St. Augustine's School at Raleigh, North Carolina, and the Bishop Payne Divinity School at Petersburg, Virginia. In the course of the next twenty-five years, during most of which the Rev. Robert W. Patton served with effective enthusiasm as director, the income of the Institute rose to $600,000 a year (including a subsidy from the National Council), and five more schools were taken under its wing, among which were the Voorhees Normal and Industrial School at Denmark, South Carolina, and the Fort Valley School at Fort Valley, Georgia.

The success of the Institute not only in providing funds but in improving the quality of education, with special emphasis upon training teachers, farmers, and artisans, won from all the southern bishops and dioceses an ever-growing degree of cordial support. That intelligent approval was not confined to Church circles is shown by the fact that the General Education Board of the Rockefeller Foundation, the Rosenwald Foundation, and the Carnegie Corporation made generous donations. In 1932 Bishop Creighton was justified in writing of the Institute, "Its success has been phenomenal in developing the minds and broadening the lives of countless boys and girls, changing the character of communities and sometimes of entire counties. It is today the largest educational organization in existence maintained exclusively for Negroes."

To use the term adopted by the National Council, the Church has four "extra-continental" missionary districts—districts, that is, which are outside the forty-eight States and yet in territory under the American flag. These four jurisdictions are Alaska, Honolulu, the Panama Canal Zone, and Puerto Rico. Throughout the thirty years we are reviewing the Philippine Islands constituted a fifth.

Alaska, combining a very small population with a huge area, was certain to limit the Church to slow growth; but the first decades of the century saw the founding of several new stations and the opening of new institutions. To name but a few, Fairbanks, in central Alaska, as the terminus of a railroad and the seat of a university offered opportunities which were effectively exploited. Nenana, on the Tenana River, was chosen as the center for a boarding-school for Indian boys and girls. And at Fort Yukon the Hudson Stuck Memorial Hospital, founded in 1916, perpetuated the memory of Archdeacon Stuck, that versatile, picturesque, and fearless missionary who traveled 15,000 miles by dogsled and another 30,000 in the mission boat. The vigor of Bishop Rowe lasted into old age, and not until the veteran was seventy-five did Bishop John B. Bentley become his suffragan and twelve years later his successor.

The Hawaiian Islands in the northern Pacific two thousand miles from the nearest mainland, were annexed by the United States in August, 1898, and were organized as a territory in 1900. At that time the population was 154,000, only one-quarter of which was Hawaiian. During the next forty years the figures rose to more than half a million, with the native stock an ever-diminishing factor and with immigrants from Japan, China, and the Philippines increasing in number. It is thus a land not only of American churches and schools but of Buddhist and Shinto temples; and the Church there has been working not only with white citizens from the States but with non-Christian Orientals.

The Islands had been a missionary jurisdiction of the Church of England for forty years when authority was transferred to the American Church in 1902, and Henry B. Restarick was elected bishop, beginning an active episcopate of eighteen years. By 1931 the communicants he first found had quadrupled in number. In the city of Honolulu, on Oahu Island, St. Andrew's Cathedral was the missionary center, with two organized congregations, Hawaiian and Anglo-American. Close by was St. Andrew's Priory, a boarding- and day-school for girls, of whom nine-tenths were then of native Hawaiian blood. More interesting in their racial variety were the three hundred boys in Iolani School, where eight nationalities were represented. St. Luke's Mission ministered to the Koreans, St. Peter's to the Chinese, and Trinity to the Japanese—each with a school attached to the church. On three of the other islands, Kauai, Maui, and Hawaii, were small churches which cared for the employees of the great sugar plantations. Honolulu offered—what it still affords—an opportunity of strategic importance, for from that point influences extend to all the countries of the Far East.

In 1903 the United States recognized the new Republic of Panama and soon acquired ownership of the Canal Zone, preparatory to the gigantic engineering feat which ended with the opening of the canal in 1914. It was in 1906 that the Church of England ceded to the Church in America jurisdictions over the area later organized (1919) as the Missionary District of the Panama Canal Zone, which included not only the Zone itself but also the Republic of Panama south and east of the canal together with parts of Colombia. In this region the development of the Church was retarded by failure to send any missionary bishop until 1920, when James Craik Morris was consecrated. During his episcopate of ten years the Church maintained with slowly advancing success a ministry chiefly to the American military and civil population and to the thousands of West Indian Negroes whose traditional allegiance was to the Church of England. So limited had been the resources supplied to a devoted leader that at the bishop's death there were only five clergy in the district and 3,000 communicants.

In 1898 at the close of the Spanish War the United States found itself in possession of Puerto Rico, an island of only 3,600 square miles, in which the population had grown by 1930 to a dense total of a million and a half. Thanks to the system of government education, illiteracy had been reduced from 85 per cent to 60 per cent, and there had been genuine progress in road-building, sanitation, and hygiene. But much remained (and remains) to be done among a people overcrowded, close to the poverty line, and weakened by the prevalence of such diseases as hookworm and tuberculosis.

In 1901 Puerto Rico was constituted a missionary district of the Episcopal Church, and in the following year James H. Van Buren took office as bishop. He was right in declaring that "the adherence of the vast majority of the people to any vestige of the Christian faith is purely nominal," and he set himself to interpret the mission of the Church as an endeavor to present "a religion which adds to faith virtue, and measures the fruits of the Spirit in terms of conduct and character as well as in splendor of worship." During the ten years of his episcopate, and after 1912 under his successor Bishop Charles B. Colmore, the communicants grew in number from a point near zero to a total in 1931 of 5,500, half of whom were in the near-by Virgin Islands. In the large commercial centers on the coast were the leading institutions—at Ponce St. Luke's Hospital with its Nurses' Training School, at San Juan St. Catherine's School for training women workers, and at Mayaguez St. Andrew's Parochial and Industrial School. But it was in the mountains and valleys of the interior, among the sugar and tobacco plantations and the fruit orchards that the opportunities were even more urgent. In one of these mountainous districts, Quebrada Limon, the Church combined with a strong congregation an experimental farm to train the people to make better use of their land. After a generation of effort the most hopeful fact about the district was the success of Bishop Colmore and his assistants in developing a Puerto Rican clergy. With Manuel Ferrando as suffragan (1923–1934) and a staff of eight native priests, all products of the mission, a strong nucleus for an independent Church had been created.

Attached to the Missionary District of Puerto Rico after 1918 were the Virgin Islands, which had been purchased from Denmark the year before. From the Church of England, which had long ministered to their people, Bishop Colmore inherited three large congregations with more than 2,800 communicants, chiefly West Indian Negroes. The poverty of most of them, under existing economic conditions, reduced their capacity to produce a self-supporting Church.

Ten thousand miles from the United States lie the Philippine Islands. This small empire of three thousand islands and islets five hundred miles off the coast of China belonged to Spain until it passed under our flag at the end of the Spanish War. Spain had long before Christianized nine-tenths of the inhabitants—the tribes that we know as Filipinos, who numbered in 1930 more than ten millions. The Philippines therefore constituted a country mainly Christian. But the Spaniards had left untouched the 400,000 Igorots who live in the northern mountains of the main island, and the 435,000 warlike Mohammedan Malays (the Moros) who inhabit some of the southern islands.

The share of the Church in the developing life of the Philippines was made notable for sixteen years by the leadership of Bishop Charles Henry Brent, who labored in the islands from 1902 to 1918. The Church adopted his policy of concentrating its small forces on two main groups, the Americans who went out to serve in the government, in the Army, and in business, and the inhabitants who had not yet been Christianized. These included not only the Igorot tribes in the north and the Moslem Moros in the south but also the Chinese in the capital, Manila. By 1908 work had begun in all these areas, and in 1931 it was advancing under the guidance of Brent's successor, Bishop Mosher.

In Manila was the Cathedral of St. Mary and St. John, a religious center "for all people," and St. Luke's Hospital, the first modern civilian hospital in the capital, which treated over 12,000 free patients a year, most of them Filipinos. In Manila, too, was St. Stephen's Mission for Chinese, the only exclusively Chinese Christian work in the Islands. Far up in the mountains of Luzon were the flourishing churches and schools among the pagan Igorots—Bontoc with its All Saints' School for boys and its seven smaller out-stations, and Sagada with its thousand communicants, a center for eight other missions in the area round about. Six hundred and fifty miles to the south, at Zamboanga, were to be found the Brent Hospital and a school for Moro boys and girls. What Bishop Brent wrote of these first courageous efforts to reach the hostile Moslems might have been written of all the work in the Philippines: "None knows, except those of us on the spot, through what travail our little enterprises were born. In themselves they are not commanding. But by their influence an indelible mark is being made on the life of the Islands."

ABROAD

Cuba was organized as a missionary district in 1904, with Albion W. Knight as its first bishop. There he found a population approaching two million, most of whom were native-born Spanish-speaking Cubans, about one-third of them Negroes. Though relatively few in number, there were two other groups for whom the Church was especially responsible—the Americans and the English-speaking Negroes from Jamaica and other islands. When Bishop Knight arrived there were only five clergy under him and 150 communicants. When his successor, Hiram R. Hulse (after sixteen years in office) reported to the National Council in 1931 he could tell of twenty active clergy, all but three of whom were Cuban, and 2,300 communicants. Sixty stations, large and small, the bishop visited by motor, on horseback, and on foot, holding services in private houses or in huts on the sugar plantations, in little wooden chapels, and in churches in a few of the larger towns. Holy Trinity Cathedral at Havana was of statelier proportions. He had acted with energy for many years upon his conviction that education was the Church's most immediately vital need. As a result there were a dozen parochial schools throughout the island and several large institutions of outstanding quality—such as the Cathedral School for girls in Havana and All Saints' School at Guantanamo.

Since the origin and general nature of the Church's activity in Mexico, Haiti, Brazil, and Liberia have been already described, later progress in these areas may be noted more briefly.

The missionary district of Mexico was organized in 1904, and Henry D. Aves was consecrated as its first bishop, charged only with the oversight of the churches for the Americans and English. Two years later, however, the Mexican Church, after thirty-seven years of independent existence, was incorporated into the district at its own request, and the bishop's ministrations became primarily to Mexicans. Within five years a long period of revolutions began from which the masses of the people eventually benefited but which meantime kept the country in turmoil and severely restricted the extent to which foreigners could serve the Church. Bishop Creighton, who followed Aves in 1926, loyally observed these legal limitations, residing after 1930 in the United States. When he resigned in 1933 his successor was a Mexican, Efrain Salinas y Velasco.[6]

In 1912, the year after Bishop Holly of Haiti died, the National Convocation of the Orthodox Apostolic Church of Haiti petitioned the House of Bishops to be admitted as a foreign missionary district of the Church in the United States. At its session in 1913 the House of Bishops took the requested action, and for the next ten years entrusted Haiti to the care of various neighboring bishops. Not until 1923 was Harry Roberts Carson consecrated as its first white bishop. At the close of his first eight years of work all but one of his eighteen clergy were Haitians, most of them trained at the Seminary at Port au Prince; but their number was inadequate to care for nearly 5,000 communicants.

By resolution of the House of Bishops the future Church in the Dominican Republic (on the same island with Haiti) was placed under the care of the Bishop of Puerto Rico, but no work was begun there for another five years. In 1928 the Bishop of Haiti was given jurisdiction. In this Spanish-speaking country five times the size of Puerto Rico, the

[6] In 1931 the district of Mexico, with a population of 14,000,000, had 21 clergy and 1,680 communicants. Its best known schools were the Hooker Memorial School at Mexico City and St. Andrew's Industrial School at Guadalajara. The work with the Americans and English was at Mexico City and three other cities.

chances of development were promising, but the Church supplied the district with such meager funds and so few men that even in 1931 there were but four clergy to serve ten mission stations.

The Episcopal Church in Brazil presented to the General Convention of 1907 an earnest request for admission as a missionary district, a petition which was cordially granted.[7] Bishop Kinsolving, having resigned as Bishop of the Brazilian Church, was elected Missionary Bishop of Southern Brazil. Though his see was no longer independent, it continued to move at an undiminished rate toward self-support. When William M. M. Thomas became bishop in 1928, the prosperous Southern Cross School at Porto Alegre had long been self-sustaining, independent parishes were growing in number, and all but four of the clergy were Brazilians—a sound proportion for which large credit was due to the Theological School, of which W. Cabell Brown and Thomas had been deans.[8]

When Bishop Ferguson of Liberia,[9] after an episcopate of thirty-one years, died in 1916, the House of Bishops sent no successor to the field until late in 1919. Bishop Walter H. Overs then assumed the trying task of recovery and repair. Under his administration a native suffragan, Theophilus Momolu Gardiner, began his twenty years of service; the new St. Timothy's Hospital at Cape Mount was developed; and the fathers of the Order of the Holy Cross opened their station in the far interior. It was time that such an enterprise should be initiated; for too much of the Church's work was with the fifty thousand English-speaking Negroes living near the coast, to the neglect of a million and a half tribesmen in the hinterland. After less than six years in office Bishop Overs was forced by ill-health to resign, and Robert E. Campbell of the Order of the Holy Cross became Missionary Bishop of Liberia. In the middle of his ten years' episcopate the work in Liberia had to suffer not only from its chronic disadvantages—climate and constant changes in personnel—but after 1930 from drastic reduction in financial support from the home Church. It was not to enjoy the feeling of prosperous advance until 1946.[10]

Hardly large enough to be mentioned in this array of missionary districts was the Church's contribution to Palestine and to India. In these

[7] By that time responsibility for financial support had been transferred from the American Church Missionary Society to the Board of Missions. In the same year (1905) the A.C.M.S. transferred its work in Cuba to the Board. In 1930, after seventy years of existence, the A.C.M.S. was dissolved and the National Council took over its assets.

[8] In 1899, when Kinsolving first became bishop, there were seven clergy (of whom four were Brazilian) and 365 communicants. In 1931 there were 32 clergy (of whom 28 were Brazilian) and 3,400 communicants.

[9] The title of the district was changed to "Liberia" in 1913.

[10] Between 1901 and 1931 the number of clergy doubled and the number of communicants tripled. Though in 1948 both totals had diminished, they were more than usually reliable and furnished firmer ground for growth.

regions, where the Church of England was so predominant, the Church in America has recently made what might be called "token" offerings. Since 1925 the Church has supported on the staff of the bishop's cathedral at Jerusalem a representative as "American Chaplain in the Holy Land," who has been constantly helpful in work with the various Oriental Churches. In 1931, in response to repeated requests from the Church of England, General Convention authorized the National Council (as a project outside the budget) to send missionaries to the diocese of Dornakal in south India. But only one was sent in 1933 and very few thereafter. This failure to expand in a huge country was due to a fact often forgotten—that a Church as small as the Episcopal Church, with missionary funds no larger than it annually provides, cannot successfully undertake work everywhere at once. Yet someone can always be counted upon to rise and propose a new missionary district.

The first thirty years of the present century were crowded with events and movements in the life of Japan. Her alliance with Great Britain in 1902 and her victory in the war with Russia (1904–5) strengthened her position as a first-class world power, and encouraged her military leaders to plan aggressive action in China. Yet in these same decades there was also developing an immense commercial expansion and a steady growth of democracy. Chauvinistic nationalism and a democratic policy of peace and prosperity were competing for the future of Japan. Not until the invasion of Manchuria in 1931 was the die cast.

By the year 1923 the evangelistic work in the missionary districts aided by the Church in America was being extended in range and progressing toward self-support. St. Paul's College, Tokyo, had been established in 1907 with H. St. George Tucker as its first president, and under his successor, Charles S. Reifsnider, had moved into new buildings in the suburbs and had received recognition by the government as a university. St. Agnes' School in Kyoto and St. Margaret's in Tokyo were flourishing under Japanese control. Just at this encouraging point, in the late summer of 1923, Tokyo and Yokohama, its port, were devastated by earthquake and fire. The great city of Yokohama was laid flat and the larger part of Tokyo destroyed. Prompt and generous aid flowed in at once from the United States, and it seemed for a time that America was to be Japan's best friend. In the loss and in the aid supplied the Church bore its share. "All is lost save faith in God," cabled Bishop McKim, and his report was not far wrong. Except for the new buildings of St. Paul's every structure of importance which served the Church in Tokyo had been demolished, a total value of $1,780,000. But in reply to the disaster an emergency fund of over $500,000 was raised, and in course of time far more than that amount was invested in reconstruction. Within fifteen years the Church was better supplied with buildings and equipment than ever before.

In the midst of all the horror and confusion of that year a significant event took place in the Japanese Church. Two independent dioceses were formed and two Japanese bishops consecrated—Tokyo under J. S. Motoda and Osaka under J. Y. Naide. A Japanese episcopate had begun, and autonomy was becoming a reality. In 1887 the Nippon Sei Ko Kwai had no Japanese priests, only three deacons, and less than 500 communicants. In 1930 there were 213 Japanese clergy and 24,000 baptized Christians; and the share of the American Church in this Anglican total was not far from one-third. By that time a new missionary district had been added—Tohoku, under Bishop Norman S. Binsted. And in institutional progress the outstanding factor was the rise to eminence of St. Luke's International Medical Center in Tokyo—a tribute to its dynamic director, Dr. Rudolph B. Teusler, and to both Japanese and American generosity amply dispensed. But whatever optimism may have been justified, it had need to be modified by the thought of what had not yet been accomplished. A sober statement to that effect was offered in 1938 by Bishop Tucker, who had been Bishop of Kyoto and was then Presiding Bishop. "Up to the present," he wrote, "Christianity in Japan has been like a plant raised in a hothouse. It has flourished in what one might call the foreignized side of Japanese life, but it has not yet taken firm root and proved its capacity to live in the native soil, producing from the Yamato-damashii (Spirit of Japan) the fruits of the Christian spirit. The time has come when this transplanting must be attempted through the agency of the Japanese Church." [11]

For eleven years after the failure of the Boxer uprising (1900) to eject the foreigner from China, the country enjoyed unity and peace. During that brief time the imperial authorities abandoned the ancient Confucian system of education and proceeded to copy Western models. But the Manchu dynasty had repented too late, and the Revolution of 1911–12 brought about the abdication of the last emperor and the creation of a Republic. It was Western-educated—and usually mission-educated—Chinese who led this movement of drastic reformation; and the articulate classes in China remained enthusiastically pro-Western for another ten or fifteen years. The period from 1901 to 1927—and more particularly from 1911 to 1925—was a time of prosperity for the Christian movement, especially for its popular educational institutions. By 1925, however, the Nationalist Movement was strongly in evidence. Chaotic military rule and protracted civil war had produced a longing for peace

[11] Tucker, *Episcopal Church in Japan,* 187.

and a reaction against foreign influence. The Nationalist army under Chiang Kai-shek won control for the Nationalist government. After passing through a phase of Russian Communist guidance, the government established itself at the new capital Nanking in 1928, and was acknowledged and obeyed over the greater part of China when the Japanese invasion of Manchuria in 1931 began a process of combined military disaster and political degeneration.

While these four hundred million people were thus undergoing a series of political revolutions, they were passing at the same time through four other kinds of revolution—more than enough to disturb even a phlegmatic race. They were experiencing simultaneously a cultural, an educational, an industrial, and a religious revolution. Since Christianity had no serious rival (except scientific materialism) in the nation-wide endeavor to find answers to these insistent problems, the need for the Church was increasingly obvious, though the difficulties with which it was confronted were multiplying. A degree of unity among the Christian forces hitherto unknown was achieved in 1922 when a National Christian Conference of 1,100 delegates (one-half Chinese) inaugurated the National Christian Council, federating two-thirds of the non-Roman missions, including the American Episcopal. Ten years earlier, however, the Anglican Communion, after a series of conferences held by the missionary bishops of the Church of England and the Church in America, had been established in China as the Chung Hua Sheng Kung Hui, or Holy Catholic Church in China. In 1930 this autonomous Church, with a constitution much like that of the Sei Ko Kwai in Japan, comprised eleven dioceses, with seven English bishops, four American, and one Canadian, who were aided by five Chinese assistant bishops.

But as we are engaged upon a history not of China nor of Christianity in China, we must conclude with a brief summary of what the American Episcopal Church had been accomplishing. During these three decades its huge jurisdiction had been twice divided. It was first (1901) split into the district of Shanghai, near the coast, and that of Hankow, comprising all the rest of the Yang-tse valley; and in 1910 Hankow was reduced in size by the formation of the district of Anking. David T. Huntington became Bishop of Anking; and for thirty-three years Logan H. Roots was Bishop of Hankow, perhaps the most beloved and widely known American Christian in China. In 1915, three years after the Chinese Church had been formally organized, it established its own Board of Missions, and in the following year, at its own charge, began work in the northern province of Shensi. Within each diocese, too, evangelistic expansion was marked by the opening of new stations, as at Wusih, Soochow, and Nanking in the district of Shanghai.

The advance of Christian medical service resulted in a Church General Hospital at Wuchang, new buildings and new doctors at St. Luke's, Shanghai, and younger hospitals, including St. Elizabeth's at Shanghai and the institutions at Anking and Wusih. To keep pace with the times and to offer western learning under Christian influence the schools and colleges were taxed to capacity. To name only the colleges, St. John's at Shanghai and Boone at Wuchang became universities, and in numbers and in property enjoyed healthy expansion. In cordial agreement with recommendations of an international Christian Educational Commission, Boone united in 1924 with four other smaller colleges to form Central China College (now Huachung University), of which Francis C. M. Wei became the distinguished president. The choice of a Chinese for so important a post was indicative of the increasing subordination of foreign leadership to Chinese. In 1930 the Chinese clergy outnumbered the American three to one. The Sheng Kung Hui elected its own bishops whenever these were Chinese, and it was on Chinese nomination that the American House of Bishops elected the few Americans who were still to govern dioceses in the future. The Chinese Church and its leaders were already prepared for the victorious endurance of the afflictions with which the coming years were to visit them.

Chapter XXVI

TYPES OF LEADERSHIP: WILLIAM LAWRENCE AND CHARLES HENRY BRENT

WILLIAM LAWRENCE

WILLIAM LAWRENCE, in succession to Phillips Brooks, was Bishop of Massachusetts from 1893 to 1927. In the course of thirty-four years he led in the development of a model diocese; he served a great community of which he eventually became the foremost citizen; and to his unfaltering leadership the national Church owes the abundant success of its first War Commission and its Church Pension Fund. For the better part of ninety years Lawrence exhibited the rare combination of simple piety and cool efficiency. He illustrated the encouraging fact that you do not have to be absent-minded and unsystematic in order to be widely beloved.

William Lawrence was born in Boston on May 30, 1850. His ancestors on both sides—Lawrences and Appletons—were of Massachusetts stock. His father, Amos Adams Lawrence, made a fortune in the textile industry and transmitted ample means to his many descendants. He became famous, when William was a small boy, for his generous share in supporting the cause of freedom in "bleeding Kansas," and for him the town of Lawrence, Kansas, is named. At the age of seventeen the boy entered Harvard two years before Charles William Eliot became president, and the principles which Eliot then first declared were not forgotten in after years when Lawrence was one of the university's governing body: "A University must be indigenous: it must be rich, but above all it must be free. The winnowing breeze of freedom must blow through all its chambers." But during these college years a deeper influence than Eliot's was the sway exerted upon his life and character by Phillips Brooks. "What first turned my thoughts to the ministry I do not know," he wrote in his old age, "probably the life and preaching of Phillips Brooks. . . . Friends and parents were good enough to let me alone in my doubts and questionings. My only adviser was Phillips Brooks, who, entirely open-minded as to my future, in response to my questions put clearly the opportunity as well as the romance of the ministry." [1]

It was for the ministry that he soon decided; and in preparation he spent three years at the Andover Seminary, adding a fourth year divided between the Philadelphia Divinity School and the new Theological School in Cambridge. On June 20, 1875, he was ordained deacon by Bishop Paddock, and a few months later he became assistant at Grace Church, Lawrence, Massachusetts, a city of mills named after his own kin. A year earlier he had been married to Julia Cunningham, the beginning of a marriage of unbroken happiness which lasted for fifty-three years. Seven children were born to them, five daughters and two sons, and both the boys entered the ministry.

After the first year at Grace Church the rector died, and Lawrence was elected to succeed him. For another seven years he found in his parish an ample field for varied work that enriched his life with pastoral experience. It was the only parish he ever had, and it taught him much. But in 1884 he was drawn from a parochial career by a call to become professor of homiletics and pastoral care at the Episcopal Theological School in Cambridge; and at the end of four years, upon the death of Dean Gray, Lawrence was elected dean. It might have seemed as if academic life had claimed him for good, since, though he was not a scholar, his talent for administration was already notable. It was soon, however, to be given wider scope when four months after the death of Phillips Brooks he was chosen Bishop of Massachusetts, and on October 5, 1893, he was consecrated.

Though especially gifted as an executive, Lawrence, through all his episcopate, never ceased to be a pastor. "A true bishop," he wrote, "will never allow himself to be so overwhelmed with administration as to cut himself off from occasional ministrations among the lowliest of the people; only thus can he understand the patience, faith, and cheer with which his clergy are carrying through that work week in and week out." [2] And of his first years in office he recalled: "Instead of finding a bishop's duties monotonous or narrow, I was increasingly amazed—indeed my amazement still continues—at the wonderful variety of interests and subjects coming before him. Each day brings fresh personalities, new problems, broader interests, religious, social, commercial, political, personal. I can think of a hundred paths of service which I should like to have followed

[1] Lawrence, *Memories of a Happy Life,* 30.
[2] *Ibid.,* 92.

through to the end: and the various callings of doctor, prison reformer, financier, publicity writer, social worker, detective, and plumber have beckoned to me. But life, even though it be very full of activity, is too short to fulfil in a very imperfect way even one calling, one so great and inspiring as that of a bishop." [3]

Characteristic of Lawrence's episcopate was its creative quality. He was never content merely to make his visitations and keep the necessary appointments and turn the work of a bishop into a kind of treadmill. He was always looking ahead to fresh opportunities and planning well in advance for new developments which would invigorate the diocese or expand its activities. In every case he proceeded with an almost irresistible combination of firmness, caution, and diplomacy. One of the first needs which he met successfully was the division of the diocese. By the end of the century the whole State of Massachusetts was an area far too populous to be under the care of one man. To persuade the half of his see which was weaker in numbers and in wealth that the welfare of the Church demanded a division was no easy task; but by the quiet and steady pressure of an appeal to facts and to reason in the course of three years he succeeded in winning, with perfect good feeling, a unanimous approval. When Western Massachusetts elected its first bishop in 1902, Lawrence little thought that his fourteen-year-old son would later become its third bishop.

No sooner was this achievement on record than Bishop Lawrence began to meditate a new design for enlivening the diocese. "Moving about the Diocese," he wrote, "in trolley-car, carriage, and railroad, with valise in hand, I soon found that each parish and mission was a unit in itself; and while the people recognized the Bishop as the head, they were, to a large degree, Congregationalists." [4] One step toward greater cohesion would be the development of a cathedral, but most American cathedrals were never designed for such a unifying function. Lawrence, however, had advanced and definite views as to what the right kind of cathedral could do for a diocese. In an address to his convention in 1904 he said: "The unit of the Church is the Diocese—the Bishop, clergy, and laity. The Cathedral is simply the expression in architectural form of the Diocese, its constituents and spiritual purpose. The Cathedral may be as noble as that of Durham or as humble as the chapel of a missionary Bishop. Its essential features are that it be the official seat of the Bishop and his spiritual home; that through its officers or chapter of clergy and laity it represent the whole Diocese; that it be recognized as the center of diocesan worship, work, teaching, and preaching, as the church belong-

[3] *Ibid.*, 89.
[4] *Ibid.*, 311.

ing, not to the Bishop, but to the whole Diocese; and that all the people, coming from the various parishes for counsel and mutual inspiration, find that here also is their spiritual home." [5]

By a series of slow steps carefully designed and persuasively presented, the cathedral was incorporated in 1908; its charter was organized in 1909; and after St. Paul's Church, Boston, had been gradually prepared for its coming promotion, its rector in 1912 became dean of the Cathedral Church of St. Paul. Under Edmund S. Rousmaniere the diocese soon began to profit from just the kind of vital center for which the bishop had so long labored. He was right in saying that "for practical spiritual purposes it has been unique in the history of cathedrals."

Of equal value in the long run was another enterprise which helped to weld an unusually compact diocese into a consciously active whole. Early in his episcopate Lawrence enlisted the Rev. Edward T. Sullivan, a priest who had had newspaper experience, to serve as editor in the creation and publication of *The Church Militant*—"the only diocesan paper at the time which limited its circulation to paying subscribers" and which felt under obligation to be interesting.

Always meticulous in attention to detail and inheriting the conscience of honorable business men, Lawrence was often irked and sometimes scandalized by the slipshod methods of parochial finance. He believed that "the moment that a dime drops from the hand of a working woman into the contribution plate, the Church becomes its trustee, bound to see that it is used for the purpose given in the most prompt and efficient way. Multiply that contribution by a thousand and everybody will recognize the obligation. . . . The very fact that the dime is of insignificant value makes the danger of its loss or misuse all the greater. There are more careless than dishonest people." [6] Thanks to the bishop's energetic initiative his diocesan convention in 1912 took definite steps to require a better financial system and auditing, and the following year General Convention appointed a committee of which he was chairman to promote sounder financial methods in the Church. Thus through the canons and commissions of dioceses and of the national Church "the Church is now approaching in her financial and statistical methods the best nation-wide organizations, secular or religious."

Of relatively minor achievements the last twenty-five years of Lawrence's episcopate were full—the entertainment of the General Convention in 1904, with Randall Davidson, Archbishop of Canterbury, as its guest; the establishment of prison chaplains for State and city institutions; the restoration to beauty and usefulness of the Old North Church of

[5] *Ibid.*, 315.
[6] *Ibid.*, 173.

Paul Revere fame; and the opening at Swansea of the Rest House for clergy. To these we must add two further moves which can hardly be called minor, so prosperous has been their career—the organization of a board of religious education and a commission on social service.

In 1913, when Bishop Lawrence was sixty-three, he requested and received a suffragan as assistant. Nine years later, with his own retirement in mind, he welcomed Charles Lewis Slattery as bishop coadjutor. In 1925 Lawrence resigned from all active responsibility in the diocese, retaining only the title of bishop; and on May 4, 1927, his resignation became complete. At the end of his diary for that day, after a record of action in the convention and at a great farewell dinner, are these words: "A most happy day in the gratitude which the people seem to feel and their regret at my resignation. It is, I am sure, right and wise, and I hope will set an example to other old bishops to clear the way for younger men." [7]

Even so compressed and reduced a recital of what William Lawrence accomplished for his diocese might easily give the impression that he had no time to be anything but a bishop. As a matter of fact, however, he found opportunity for trips abroad at fairly frequent intervals and for almost continuous activity in the service of Harvard University and of the national Church. His executive ability was so widely recognized, and as a man he was attractive to so many that his range of influence could never be confined to local church circles. Though he was a devout Christian and a loyal Churchman, he was distinctly not an ecclesiastic, and one would never have described him as a "prelate." For in the very best sense of the term he was "a man of the world"—that is to say, he was at ease in dealing with all kinds of groups and as deeply respected in a committee of business men or an audience of "doughboys" or a garden party in England as in his own Diocesan House. His high breeding, his complete lack of self-consciousness, his quiet self-possession, his disarming (if occasionally alarming) frankness, his candor, and his perfect sense of humor made him a welcome companion wherever he was called to be a fellow-worker or a leader.

Outside of the Church it was Harvard University that made the heaviest demand upon his loyalty. For two terms of three years each he was a Preacher to the University. From 1894 to 1906 and again from 1907 to 1913 he was on the Board of Overseers, and in 1913 he was elected a member of "The President and Fellows" of Harvard, the small Corporation which controls the University. On that body he served for the next eighteen years. Before he had joined it, however, his responsibilities as President of the Alumni Association had led him to play the leading

[7] H. K. Sherrill, *William Lawrence*, 3 (Harvard University Press).

part in raising an endowment of $2,500,000 for the purpose of increasing the salaries of professors. In 1924, at the age of seventy-three, he undertook to find three times that amount, to give Harvard a new chemical laboratory, a new Art Museum, and all the buildings of the School of Business Administration. By this time Lawrence was as skilled in the raising of money for great causes as any man in the country, and only those who did not know his capacity were surprised at his prompt success. But Harvard and the Episcopal Theological School, its near neighbor, never thought of him primarily as one who could satisfy their financial needs. It was his steadiness, open-mindedness, and ripe wisdom from which they benefited gratefully for so many years.

In spite of his abundant activities in Massachusetts, no man of his generation contributed more to the welfare of the national Church than William Lawrence. From 1903 to 1913 he was a valuable member of the Board of Missions and later served on the National Council. During all that time he not only supported the cause of missions by his counsel and his votes—a relatively easy process—but transmitted to his well-organized diocese such a serious concern for missions that its quotas were regularly paid.

How and why the Church decided to establish a Pension Fund and what were the striking results of the campaign to launch it we have already described in a previous chapter. At that time, as we noted, the Church had recently tried to raise $5,000,000 for pensions and had accumulated $218,000 in three years. In far less time than that, with Lawrence as leader, the Church gave $8,750,000. Others might have done as well, but it was to him that the task was committed. "From a distance I hated the job," he later confessed, "and shrank from it with dread," for "up to this time there had been no campaign like it. . . . There were no professional campaign firms, and but little skilled publicity. There were no precedents for the organization of our work, which covered the Church throughout the country and in the mission field. . . . I was sixty-six years old, ten years too old for such a job. At first I thought the work might kill me. What if it did?—the cause was more than worth it. As the months passed, my dread was that I might break before March 1, 1917. After that I didn't care." But he added, "The consciousness that one has a big and ennobling job ahead, and that upon him depends the success is stimulating: the unexpected successes make one leap, and the failures call up a determination and courage even finer and more buoyant." [8]

Establishing his office in New York, Bishop Lawrence said good-bye to his diocese for the time being and set to work. "My duty," he tells us

[8] Lawrence, *Memories of a Happy Life,* 365 ff.

in his memoirs, "besides that of general oversight and suggestion, was that of starting organizations in the leading cities, and especially of reaching those who might give in substantial sums. In this line of duty came the exhilaration, sometimes the depression, of a good sportsman. . . . For weeks, however, the campaign would not move. As I talked in offices and at downtown lunches, then as I went uptown day after day, I felt as if my shoulder were against a heavy motor truck that would not budge. I recall with gratitude a response from a friend, 'Keep at it, Bishop; some day the old thing will move and begin to run.' Sure enough, it did." [9]

Within two months Lawrence was able to announce that the first million had been pledged, and after another two months the second million was in hand. From week to week the figures mounted until the total was reached and far surpassed. It was a campaign in which the entire Church participated and which won the support of men, women, and children in every economic group. One line in the bishop's diary is enough to show how wide was the appeal and how extreme the contrasts in the gifts that reached him. "Received from a little girl a card in which she had cut a hole and placed one cent. Four brothers gave $100,000." Before the end was reached its outcome was so certain that Lawrence was cheered upon his way by a resolution of the House of Bishops at the General Convention of 1916: "*Resolved,* that the House of Bishops desires to record its grateful appreciation of the extraordinary service which the Bishop of Massachusetts has rendered to the Church as President of the Church Pension Fund. His conspicuous ability and his unselfish devotion to the welfare of his brethren have won for him the admiration and affection of the whole Church."

Within a month after the Church Pension Fund had announced its first $5,000,000 the United States declared war on imperial Germany. But even before the President's war message had been delivered Bishop Lawrence began the preparation of a war Prayer Book and was conferring with John R. Mott on the duties of the Y.M.C.A. and the chaplains in the coming struggle. With a deep sense of the unprecedented opportunities awaiting the Church in its relations with the Army and Navy, he took the initiative in urging the Presiding Bishop to "appoint a War Commission and get the Church moving." Bishop Tuttle at once appointed a strong commission with Lawrence as chairman, and after that there was no doubt that the Church had begun to move. What was accomplished for the soldiers and sailors, and especially for the chaplains, we have already recorded. The part which Bishop Lawrence bore was not only the raising of $800,000 but the continued oversight of every variety of war work, including service as Vice-President of the Wartime Commission which

[9] *Ibid.*, 366, 371.

represented all the Protestant Churches. Never had there been put to more fruitful use his unresting attention to detail and his rare ability to keep always several steps ahead of the needs of the hour.

When the bishop's resignation at the age of seventy-seven freed him from all responsibility for his diocese it did not leave him without varied occupation. Seldom was a retirement less retired. For fourteen years more, except in summer, he scarcely knew an idle moment. He preached often in churches throughout the diocese, and at the urgency of Bishop Sherrill, who felt for him the devotion of a son, he addressed the diocesan convention every year. At Harvard his service on the Corporation continued until he was eighty-one, and ended with the university's awarding him the degree of LL.D., a very rare instance of giving two honorary degrees to the same man.[10] It was two years afterward, when two thousand people assembled in Symphony Hall to celebrate the fortieth anniversary of his consecration, that President Lowell of Harvard paid him this tribute: "Bishop Lawrence has been right four and a half times out of five, and the other half occasion on which he may have been wrong I do not remember. He has had an uncanny faculty of being right; and, what is more remarkable, of not irritating people by being right. . . . What is the secret . . . of the wisdom he has ever shown? . . . It resides in the man himself, in his clearness of thought, his breadth of view, his disinterestedness, his attitude to life, to the many luminous threads woven into the texture of his character. He has been right so often because he has seen the present clearly in the light of the eternal." [11]

Though any full record would tell of such avocations as his work for prison reform, for the Boston Community Fund, and for the Massachusetts General Hospital, it might mislead the reader into thinking that Lawrence was concerned only with institutions. On the contrary, his thoughtful alertness was almost daily responsible for little acts of kindness and sympathy. These were so literally innumerable as to dispel any thought that he was a cool executive of the impersonal type. Not only did people turn to him in trouble or perplexity and find a welcome, but messages of gratitude and encouragement and appreciation constantly went forth to meet the varied needs of the friends he never forgot. To the very end he was instinctively and generously the pastor.

And the end came quietly when he was ninety-one years old. On November 6, 1941, he died a few hours after a heart attack. It was then that many agreed with President Lowell when he said, "Only genius has the scope to write an epitaph for such a man." Others perhaps remembered what the bishop had said to a great gathering of his friends some

[10] Lawrence had already received the degree of D.D. from Harvard in 1893.
[11] Sherrill, *William Lawrence,* 75 f. (Harvard University Press).

years before, and counted that better than any epitaph. "Consecrated to Jesus Christ, fully consecrated, I find in Him the supreme satisfaction, joy, and support of life. With this clear and final, what have I to fear from man, misfortune, disease, or sorrow? In perfect faith, one may live on toward the setting of the sun, tranquil, and in perfect serenity." [12]

CHARLES HENRY BRENT

Many-sided in character and of varied powers, Bishop Brent, in a lifetime of sixty-seven years, touched nearly every aspect of God's work in the world, and "he touched nothing that he did not adorn."

Born on April 2, 1862, in the little town of Newcastle, Ontario, where his father was rector, Brent was educated at Trinity College, Toronto. In 1887 he was ordained to the priesthood, and after brief service at St. Andrew's Mission in Buffalo, New York, he spent two years with the Society of St. John the Evangelist in Boston. For the next decade he was minister-in-charge of St. Stephen's Church in the slums of that city. In December, 1901, Brent was consecrated as the first Missionary Bishop of the Philippine Islands. Seventeen years later, after declining many calls to other dioceses, he became Bishop of Western New York. On March 27, 1929, he died at Lausanne in Switzerland.

"Great men need not that we praise them: the need is ours that we know them." Let us try to know him by remembering that he was missionary, poet, soldier, statesman, and saint. In each aspect of that abundant life we can see something of what he was and of what he did.

First and foremost he was a missionary. It is the only one of these titles that he would have claimed and the one of which he would have been proudest. The guiding watchword of his life was "Adventure for God." It is his own phrase, and it was his central motive.

One adventure for God began when he was chosen bishop and sent out in the first year of the century to found the Episcopal Church in the Philippine Islands. Rejoicing in what was sure to be an adventure, he led the Church in paths more adventurous than those of any other Christian body in the Islands—outward from the center he planned at Manila, not to the Christianized Filipinos but to the Igorot tribes of the northern mountains and to the fierce Moslems of the southern islands. To *pioneer* was always his eager vocation, and to lead where the name of Christ was unknown or the Cross of Christ an offense, remained his ideal for the missionary calling. Today in little churches among the hills of Luzon and in hospital and school among the Moro tribesmen we see one monument after another to the bishop who was everybody's bishop and whom army

[12] *Ibid.*, 78.

officers remember as the one white man who could go among the Moros unarmed—and be welcome. In his own words, "Opportunity is adjacent to peril." Because he paid the price gladly, the Church and the Islands are the richer.

But it is not every missionary who is a poet. Bishop Brent was not a poet in the usual modern sense: there is no little volume of unintelligible verses to his credit. He was a poet in the broader sense of investing all he did with the atmosphere of romance—not the romance in sentimental contrast with what is real, but the romance that sees what is real ringed with the halo of its ideal. Like the youth that at heart he was, he beheld the light and whence it flowed, "and by the vision splendid was on his way attended."

"Theology alone," he wrote, "creates an angular soul. . . . Melt your theology into poetry." And it is as poetry that we may justly count many of the writings that came from his pen, most of them in those crowded years of missionary life. Sermons, lectures, addresses, books of devotion and of prayers—nineteen volumes large and small—all are the work of one who spoke from "the mount of vision," who loved poetry, and whose style was always touched with a virile grace and charm. Those masterly Noble Lectures at Harvard on *Leadership,* the books that he called *The Revelation of Discovery, The Conquest of Trouble,* and *The Inspiration of Responsibility*—the very titles breathe his spirit of adventure and the very prefaces are romantic—dated from a steamer in the Gulf of Aden, from an army transport in the Philippine Archipelago, from a mountain rest-house in Luzon. Most of all in his written prayers he was the poet, consecrating his power of expression in a reverent offering to God.

And unlike many poets, he was a soldier. From first to last he endured hardship, keeping ever ready and fit in body, mind, and spirit, that "he might please Him who had chosen him to be a soldier." Once he prayed, "In hours of hardship preserve me from self-pity and endow me with the warrior's mind, that even in the heat of battle I may be inspired with the sense of vocation and win the peace of the victor."

As missionary, as statesman, or as saint, he was endowed with the warrior's mind. Physically he was stalwart and naturally valiant, whether mounted on the polo field or among the hazards of a missionary campaign. It was partly because he was like them, but even more because he was unlike them, that officers and men in the Army gave him their trust and admiration. From General Pershing (whom he won to Christian conviction and to Confirmation) down to the man in the ranks, they were his fast friends. And at length the time came when they could serve him and he could serve them—the days of the first World War. Early in 1918 the bishop was commissioned as Senior Headquarters Chaplain—the nearest approach then allowed by regulations to Chaplain-General of the American Expeditionary Forces. There he served for the final year of the war. With old friends and fellow-workers in every department he exerted an influence that no other American could have commanded. With the aid of others better at organizing than he himself, he gave form to the Chaplain's Corps and unconsciously endowed it with something of his own prestige. It was he who was chosen to represent our Army in Allied conferences to control the evils of prostitution and who spoke through our Commander-in-Chief on behalf of clean living and high standards. It was he who, on one memorable day, visited the British Grand Fleet at Scapa Flow and brought to officers and men the greetings of the new American Army. And to him was later awarded the Distinguished Service Medal. Whatever the citation may have been, the service that really distinguished him was to have brought something of the presence and power of Christ into a great modern army. Even in the heat of battle he was inspired with the sense of divine vocation.

If to his own Church and his own islands he was primarily the missionary and to our Army the bishop in uniform, he was better known to the world at large as statesman—an international statesman in his crusade against opium and a statesman of the Church in his crusade for Christian unity.

In a sense, the Philippines were too small for him. The reach of his vision drew him out to deal with problems of the wider Orient. Most baffling of these was the opium evil. Here indeed was opportunity beset with risk —a chance for another adventure for God. Thanks in large measure to his initiative, came the Opium Conference at Shanghai in 1909, over which he presided, and later the International Opium Conference at the Hague in 1911 to which President Taft sent him as delegate and of which he was presiding officer. Again, in 1924, he sat with the American delegation at Geneva, to throw his weight for the last time on the side of restriction and reform. A great crusade it has been, not ended yet; but when the citadel one day surrenders, the pressure of his inflexible purpose will be remembered.

In the movement toward Church unity—the last and greatest of his adventures—we see him as both missionary and statesman. At the Edinburgh Conference in 1910, which brought together eleven hundred representatives of Protestant and Anglican Missions, he was a leader. Deeply moved by that inspired gathering, he caught the vision of something higher and harder—a World Conference not avoiding faith and order but centered upon faith and order with the aim to bring nearer the union of Christendom. A prisoner of the great hope which it embodied, he devoted to its realization the best years of his life. "We rejoice," he once said, "that we are prisoners of hope. We refuse to live in today. We live in tomorrow. Our ideal enlarges as we advance. We can never rest content unless we are storming some fresh difficulty, each one more defiant than the last." How the ideal enlarged as he advanced, how every difficulty was met as it arose, and how at length so great a portion of Christendom met at Lausanne in 1927 is now part of the history of the Ecumenical Movement. In a manner almost beyond belief the Conference drew inspiration and guidance from him—ill though he was and often too weak to preside. His unresting endeavor, enlisting in its aid a host of Christian comrades, had brought to pass the first great step. For to him it was only the first step. He knew that he must leave to others the distant fulfilment. But, as pioneer in the greatest Christian adventure of our day, he had won the right to say with Bunyan's hero, Valiant-for-Truth, "I am going to my Father's, and though with great difficulty I have got hither, yet now I do not repent me of all the trouble I have been at to arrive where I am. My sword I give to him that shall succeed me in my pilgrimage, and my courage and skill to him that can get it. My marks and scars I carry with me, to be a witness for me that I have fought His battles who now will be my rewarder."

In all that he was and *after* all that he was, it is as a saint that he will live in the hearts of all who knew him—not a pale twilight saint, but a saint who could write of "the splendor of the human body," a saint of disciplined mental vigor, one whom soldiers were proud to salute and whom children were happy to play with, who could dominate a parliament and minister to an invalid, a priest and bishop who gloried in the heritage of his Church, yet who stood among all his Christian brothers as one who served. Equally at home in Lambeth Palace and in a monastery cell, in his own cathedral and in the trenches, in the Indian Viceroy's lodge and in a village of savages, he was everywhere an ambassador of Christ.

Gentle he was and humble, pure at heart like a flame, but essentially virile. Despite great inner conflict of which the world knew little, he gave the impression of a restful and massive calm, wielding power through imparting a sense of immense reserve energy—the latent force of one whose indomitable will was rooted in the divine will. He lived with Christ, and when he came to behold Him it was not as a stranger. "The saviour of others," he once wrote, "cannot be afraid to die, because having died daily, he is skilled in the practice of immortality. His large experience in adventure has revealed to him the glory of the unknown, so that he is assured that behind the last great adventure is the grandest and best part of life. The tone of triumph should dominate our farewell, for death in its Christian character is a superb victory, crowning all the victories of life." [13]

[13] The best life of Bishop Brent is that by A. C. Zabriskie.

Chapter XXVII

"FAITH AND ORDER"

STRANGELY enough, the same generation which had to endure a series of tragic and destructive conflicts between nations could rejoice in the steady development of that Ecumenical Movement [1] which was drawing the Churches into closer fellowship. During the first half of the twentieth century there was greater progress toward Church unity than in all the centuries since the Reformation; and in that advance the Anglican Communion played an honorable part, and the Christian forces in America were especially active.

It was as early as 1905 that a conference of five hundred delegates from most of the Protestant denominations formulated the constitution of the Federal Council of the Churches of Christ in America; and three years later the Council was established as a federation of Churches representing 17,000,000 communicants. The Episcopal Church did not join the Council until 1940, but during most of the intervening years it co-operated through membership in various commissions of the Council, such as those on the Church and Social Service, the Church and Race Relations, and International Justice and Goodwill. In keeping with its federal character, which preserved the complete independence of each participating body, the Council had only the mission of studying problems and only the power to offer recommendations; but as an educative force in expressing and guiding Christian public opinion, it proved more and more valuable. The fact that its utterances were occasionally thought to be too radical was but one sign of its vitality.

But leadership toward both federation and organic union was especially notable in the mission field. There the task of the Church often seems more important than its traditions, and there its future often seems

[1] This now familiar term did not come into general use until after the Oxford and Edinburgh Conferences of 1937.

of more pressing consequence than its past. As the Bishop of Dornakal declared at the Lausanne Conference in 1927, "In the West unity is something desirable; in the mission field it is a vital necessity. In the West disunion is a weakness; in the mission field it is a sin and a scandal." Though interdenominational missionary conferences had previously taken place, the first World Missionary Conference composed of official representatives of Protestant and Anglican Christendom was held in Edinburgh in 1910. After years of study and consultation commissions presented to the conference a series of reports of the highest value; and for its deliberations and its findings, and perhaps even more for its atmosphere of inspired fellowship, Edinburgh became famous. Its Continuation Committee, with John R. Mott as chairman, was responsible for organizing National Christian Councils in China, Japan, and India in 1922 and 1923. Already in 1921 there had been formed the International Missionary Council in which were represented both these regional Councils in the mission field and the federated boards of missions in the "sending countries." And this I. M. C., in its turn, brought about the successors of Edinburgh—the Jerusalem Meeting of 1928 and that of Madras in 1938. In all these groups and conferences the Church of England and the Episcopal Church were represented—often with commanding strength, as by Archbishop William Temple at Jerusalem.

In the promotion of organic union, too, the Churches in the mission field made the first ventures. In 1908 four separate missions in South India, representing the Presbyterian and Congregational communions, combined to form the United Church of South India. It was with this body that the Church of England in India began in 1919 those prolonged negotiations which were consummated nearly thirty years later—the first instance on record of the organic union of episcopal and non-episcopal Churches. Far easier was the union of Presbyterians and Congregationalists (1927) to form the Church of Christ in China. By that time, moreover, there had been achieved in Canada (1925) the United Church which comprehended not only the Presbyterian and Congregational denominations but also the Methodists.

Except in its skilful and deliberate preparations for the World Conference on Faith and Order, with which we shall deal shortly, the Episcopal Church made no valuable contribution to the Ecumenical Movement in the first quarter of the twentieth century. Two attempts in that cause proved of little value—the adoption of Canon 19 and the formation of the Concordat with the Congregationalists.

Until 1907 it had been forbidden by canon that any person should officiate in a congregation unless he had been "duly licensed or ordained to minister in this Church." In that year, however, General Convention passed an amendment to the canon (then numbered 19) to the effect that nothing in the law should be so construed as "to prevent the Bishop of a Diocese or Missionary District from giving permission to Christian men, who are not ministers of this Church, to make addresses in the church on special occasions." Though this amendment implied no recognition of non-episcopal orders and did not even concede that Protestant ministers were capable of preaching sermons, its cautious provisions created a surprising degree of alarm. Even the clause calling for episcopal permission could not allay a widespread suspicion that the Church had let down all the bars and committed itself to an "open pulpit."

As evidence of how easily the fears of orthodoxy are aroused, the House of Bishops received at the next Convention a petition signed by eleven hundred clergy begging the House to interpret the canon so as to assure the Church that its provisions did not permit men not episcopally ordained to teach in the Church's name. In reply the bishops unanimously agreed upon a statement which declared that the recent amendment "was not intended to alter and cannot fairly be interpreted as in the least degree modifying the position of the Church as expressed in the Prayer Book and Ordinal which restricts the ministry of the Word and Sacraments in our congregations to men who have received episcopal ordination." The response concluded with the remark that the canon contained "nothing to disturb the order or disquiet the peace of the Church." It was none the less made the occasion for several priests to secede to Rome. Yet after the first flurry of excitement the Church adjusted itself to the idea that men who were not priests could often express ideas that were worth listening to, and that upon occasion their messages might be of a kind not unfit to be uttered in a church.

Later in time and more ambitious in scope was the legislation supporting an agreement known as "The Concordat." In 1919 the General Convention was informed that certain bishops, priests, and laymen had been holding informal conferences with a group of Congregational ministers and laymen in the course of which there had been discussion of principles and measures which might enable Congregational ministers to receive ordination from bishops without becoming members of the Episcopal Church and without ceasing to exercise their ministry as pastors of their own congregations. This project, which bore a close resemblance to certain plans in the Muhlenberg Memorial of 1853, was set forth in a document called "Proposals for an Approach toward Unity," and among its signers were several prominent pastors in the Congregational communion. "We are agreed," the Proposals stated, "that it is our Lord's purpose that believers in Him should be one visible society. . . . It cannot be fully realized without community of worship, faith, and order, including common participation in the Lord's Supper. Such unity would be compatible with a rich diversity in life and worship." After acknowledging that Episcopalians ought not to be expected to give up the episcopate as a basis for reunion, and after agreeing at the same time that non-episcopal Churches "have been used by the Holy Spirit in bringing the world to Christ," the writers went on to say, "We desire . . . a willing acceptance of the treasures of each for the common enrichment of the united Church." A formal merger of the two Churches being confessedly impracticable at the present time, they proposed as a first step "intercommunion in particular instances," and to effectuate this they offered a canon providing for "supplementary orders."

After consideration of these propositions by committees of both Houses the Convention adopted a preamble and resolutions giving general approval to the Proposals, and appointed a Joint Committee to continue conferences with the Congregational signatories and to report to the next Convention. After meeting during the triennium with a similar Congregational committee, the Joint Committee reported to General Convention in 1922 a canon to implement the Concordat. It was an amended form of the canon first offered and it suffered further changes at the hands of the Convention, so that the canon finally adopted (then numbered 11) was at two removes from the original. It provided for the ordination of a minister not episcopally ordained who "shall desire to receive such orders from a Bishop of this Church to the Diaconate or to the Priesthood without giving up or denying his fellowship or his ministry in the Communion to which he belongs." It required that no bishop should proceed to this action until the minister's congregation had officially declared not only that it desired the ordination but also that its purpose was "to receive in future the ministrations of the Sacraments of one who shall be ordained to the Priesthood by a Bishop." This last requirement had never been agreed to by the Congregationalists and was inserted against the advice of the Joint Committee of General Convention.

Other stipulations in the canon required that the minister applying for orders should subscribe to the Creeds and should refrain from admitting to the Holy Communion any person not validly baptized. It was further demanded of him that he should conform to certain standards in administering the Sacraments; that he should agree to hold himself answerable to the bishop "in case he be called in question in respect to error of faith or of conduct"; and that he should meet with the bishop for counsel and cooperation. Ministers possessing this supplementary ordination might officiate in dioceses and missionary districts "according to the prescribed order of this Church," if licensed by the ecclesiastical authority, but they might not become rectors or ministers of any church until they had promised to conform to the doctrine, discipline, and worship of the Church. Finally, to make this canon constitutional, the Convention gave approval for the second time to a constitutional amendment which served to make the demand for subscription to the doctrine, discipline, and worship of the Church applicable only to deacons and priests to be ordained in and for the Episcopal Church.

The most significant observation that can be made upon this "Concordat" is that no Congregational or any other minister was ever ordained in accordance with its provisions. The whole proposal simply fell flat. One immediate obstacle was the demand that the congregation of the minister in question must declare its intention to receive in future the ministrations of an episcopally ordained priest. Another was the fact that no ordination service was ever properly authorized other than the full service in the Ordinal. But deeper than these causes of failure was the truth, temporarily forgotten, that this method of approach to union was just as mistaken in 1922 as it was in 1853. The only reason that it did not raise more problems than it solved was that it was never tried.

The only other approach to Protestants within our period was a resolution of the General Convention of 1928 inviting Methodists and Presbyterians to appoint commissions to confer with a similar Episcopal commission "in active study of matters of Christian morality looking toward organic unity." In 1931 this commission reported to the Convention the results of a two-day conference held in 1930 with representatives of the Methodist Church (North) and the Presbyterian Church (North). Most of the discussions dealt with such topics as the relations of Church and State, law observance, Sunday observance, the family, race relations, industrial problems, and the like. On nearly all questions cordial agreement was recorded. There is some truth, however, in the tart comment of a minority report which asserted that "the conference had no definite value in increasing mutual goodwill and understanding upon questions of morality because the measure was already full and overflowing before the conference was called to order. The subject of organic unity between the Churches represented was avoided." But the Convention of 1931 enlarged the powers of the commission to include discussion of matters other than moral, and the process of negotiation continued, with consequences of greater moment in later years.

In approaches to the Church of Sweden no progress was made. The Joint Commission on the Orders of that Church reported in 1901 that their activities were causing considerable irritation in Sweden, where the value of researches into "validity" was not appreciated. The commission asked to be discharged, and its functions were transferred to the Commission on Ecclesiastical Relations. Many years later, after the Lambeth

Conference of 1920, the Church of England came to a reciprocal understanding with the Church of Sweden by which members of each body were to be admitted to the Holy Communion at the altars of the other. But since the Swedish Church in the United States is organized without bishops similar relations did not prevail in this country.

The Episcopal Church and the Church of England, however, were in full accord in the agreement reached with the Old Catholic Church at a conference initiated at Lambeth in 1930 and held at Bonn, Germany, in July, 1931. Representatives of the three Churches there concurred on three main points: "Each communion recognizes the catholicity and independence of the other, and maintains its own. Each communion agrees to admit members of the other communion to participate in the Sacraments. Intercommunion does not require from either communion the acceptance of all doctrinal opinion, sacramental devotion, or liturgical practice characteristic of the other, but implies that each believes the other to hold all the essentials of the Christian faith." This agreement was ratified at the General Convention of 1934.

Closer relations with the Eastern Orthodox Churches were established through actions taken by several of them during this period. In 1922 the House of Bishops received from the Archbishop of Canterbury a copy of a letter written by the Patriarch of Constantinople. In this document the writer reported that the Holy Synod of his Patriarchate had adopted a resolution to the effect that Anglican Orders had the same validity as those of the Roman, Old Catholic, and Armenian Churches. Between 1923 and 1936 similar recognition was accorded by four other Orthodox bodies—the Patriarchates of Jerusalem and Alexandria, the Church of Cyprus, and the Church of Romania.[2]

Important as many of the developments we have recorded may prove to be, they must yield precedence to the most deeply significant of all ecumenical movements which the early twentieth century produced—the "Faith and Order" movement.

The Missionary Conference at Edinburgh in 1910 necessarily adopted the rule that no matters touching on faith and order should be discussed. Though recognizing the need for this restriction, Bishop Brent, as we have seen, was among those who found the fellowship at Edinburgh so inspiring that the vision arose before him of another conference in the future where those great sundering factors, faith and order, instead of being banned, should be the declared subjects of fraternal discussion and

[2] Dealings with the Eastern Churches were conducted for some ten years (1920–31) through the Foreign-born Americans Division of the Department of Missions, under the leadership of the Rev. Thomas Burgess and the Rev. W. C. Emhardt. Thereafter the responsible body has been that now known as the "Advisory Council on Ecclesiastical Relations."

frank confession. Stirred by this hope, he made a memorable speech at the General Convention of 1910, and as a consequence of his initiative the Convention adopted a resolution appointing a Joint Commission "to bring about a Conference for the consideration of questions touching Faith and Order." "All Christian communions throughout the world which confess our Lord Jesus Christ as God and Saviour" were to be asked "to unite with us in arranging for and conducting such a Conference."

The convictions which prompted this historic action and the spirit which animated it were eloquently voiced in these words: "We believe that the time has now arrived when representatives of the whole family of Christ, led by the Holy Spirit, may be willing to come together for the consideration of questions of Faith and Order. We believe, further, that all Christian Communions are in accord with us in our desire to lay aside self-will and to put on the mind which is in Christ Jesus our Lord. . . . We would place ourselves by the side of our fellow-Christians, looking not only on our own things, but also on the things of others, convinced that our one hope of mutual understanding is in taking personal counsel together in the spirit of love and forbearance. It is our conviction that such a Conference for the purpose of study and discussion, without power to legislate or to adopt resolutions, is the next step toward unity.

"With grief for our aloofness in the past, and for other faults of pride and self-sufficiency which make for schism; with loyalty to the truth as we see it and with respect for the convictions of those who differ from us, holding the belief that the beginnings of unity are to be found in the clear statement and full consideration of those things in which we differ, as well as of those things in which we are at one, we respectfully submit the following Resolution."

Then began the long and arduous process of making ready for a kind of meeting which had never before been held. Though the preparation was regrettably retarded by four years of warfare (1914–18), it began promptly and was conducted with a happy combination of prudence and enthusiasm. Little of the actual labor could be carried on by Brent, who was absent in the Philippines or with the Army in France during the next nine years. The chief burden fell upon Robert H. Gardiner of Maine, the secretary of the commission, a devout and able layman who gave a large part of the remaining fourteen years of his life to conducting the negotiations and the correspondence of growing complexity which the enterprise demanded. On the practical side the Conference owed an unlimited debt to his selfless and unwearied activity.

Operating through an executive committee and fortified by an initial gift of $100,000 from the elder J. P. Morgan, the Commission set about enlisting the cooperation of all the Churches of Christendom. The countless steps taken in this endeavor cannot be enumerated here, but among those of highest consequence we may note five. A delegation from the Episcopal Church was sent in 1912 to meet with representatives of the Church of England and to win their support—the first important move and perhaps the least difficult. In 1914 a group of American Protestant leaders went on a similar mission to the non-Anglican Churches in Great Britain. Five years later a deputation of Episcopal bishops and priests made a prolonged tour in Europe and the Near East, during which they paid successful visits to the chief authorities of Eastern Orthodox and Continental Protestant Churches and submitted to the Pope an invitation which he was not slow to decline. By the summer of 1920 it was possible to hold a preliminary meeting at Geneva, which was attended by 137 representatives from 70 Churches and 40 countries—the first inter-church conference in which the Orthodox Churches had ever participated. On this occasion there was created a Continuation Committee which met in Stockholm in 1925 and settled upon the time and place and agenda for the World Conference on Faith and Order at Lausanne in August, 1927.

During this long and trying period of preparation renewed impetus and vitality was imparted to the Ecumenical movement by the Lambeth Conference of 1920 and the Stockholm Conference of 1925. At Lambeth two hundred and fifty-two bishops issued "An Appeal to All Christian People" which expressed in moving terms the same aspirations which sustained the Faith and Order movement and the purposes which guided those who shared in it. The bishops united in affirming "We acknowledge all those who believe in our Lord Jesus Christ, and have been baptized into the name of the Holy Trinity, as sharing with us membership in the universal Church of Christ which is His Body. . . . This united fellowship is not visible in the world today. . . . We acknowledge this condition of broken fellowship to be contrary to God's will, and we desire frankly to confess our share in the guilt of thus crippling the Body of Christ and hindering the activity of His Spirit. . . . The time has come, we believe, for all the separated groups of Christians to agree in forgetting the things which are behind and reaching out towards the goal of a reunited Catholic Church. . . . The vision which rises before us is that of a Church genuinely Catholic, loyal to all Truth, and gathering into its fellowship all 'who profess and call themselves Christians,' within whose visible unity all the treasures of faith and order, bequeathed as a heritage by the past to the present, shall be possessed in common, and made serviceable to the whole Body of Christ. Within this unity Christian Communions now separated from one another would retain much that has long been distinctive in their methods of worship and service. It is through a rich diversity of life and devotion that the unity of the whole fellowship will be fulfilled."

While the Conference on Faith and Order was being evolved there were many who believed that approaches to unity were more likely to succeed if they dealt with the life and work of the Church than if they raised the divisive issues of faith and order. If not as a substitute, at least as a supplement to "Faith and Order" there was gradually organized "The Universal Christian Conference on Life and Work," which was held in Stockholm in August, 1925. There more than five hundred delegates from thirty-seven nations and from most of the Christian communions met for twelve days. The initiative for this gathering came from the Federal Council of Churches in the United States and from the archbishops and other leaders in Sweden. But though the Episcopal Church was only one of many participating bodies, it was strongly represented by Bishop Brent and seven other delegates. One of the presidents of the Conference and its guiding genius was the Archbishop of Upsala, Nathan Söderblom, a scholar of intellectual power and a character of rare nobility and charm.

In its own words the Conference aimed "to unite the different Churches in common practical work to furnish the Christian conscience with an organ of expression in the midst of the great spiritual movements of our time, and to insist that the principles of the Gospel be applied to the solution of contemporary social and international problems." For the topics considered there had been careful preparation by appointed commissions. The subjects were: 1. The Purpose of God for Humanity and the Duty of the Church. 2. The Church and Economic and Industrial Problems. 3. The Church and Social and Moral Problems. 4. The Church and International Relations. 5. The Church and Christian Education. 6. Methods of Cooperative and Federative Efforts by the Christian Communions. Instead of passing resolutions on these matters the Conference expressed its conclusions in a Message composed during its sessions. The high quality of this united declaration was everywhere recognized, and its contents were widely influential. "Life and Work," however, was not merely a meeting but a movement. After preparation by a Continuation Committee another Conference on Life and Work was held in Oxford in 1937, and in 1948 the enterprise became a part of the organization embraced by the new World Council of Churches.[3]

At length there gathered at Lausanne by the Lake of Geneva on the third of August, 1927, the assembly of Christians so long hoped and sought for. There were 399 members from 42 countries and 116 Churches —Orthodox Patriarchs from Greece and Asia Minor, doctors of divinity from China, scholars from Germany, bishops from England, Congrega-

[3] See G. K. A. Bell (ed.) *The Stockholm Conference, 1925.*

tional pastors from the United States, and scores of other varieties from every quarter of Christendom. Charles Henry Brent, Bishop of Western New York, was the chairman, and in the sermon with which the meetings began these were his opening words: "We are here at the urgent behest of Jesus Christ. We have come with willing feet. All the prayers and desires and labors of seventeen years meet in this hour."

What the Conference aimed to do and how it operated were clearly described in the Preamble to its final Reports: "We, representatives of many Christian Communions throughout the world, united in the common confession of faith in Jesus Christ the son of God, our Lord and Saviour, believing that the Spirit of God is with us, are assembled to consider the things wherein we agree and the things wherein we differ. . . . This is a Conference summoned to consider matters of Faith and Order. It is emphatically *not* attempting to define the conditions of future reunion. Its object is to register the apparent level of fundamental agreements within the Conference and the grave points of disagreements remaining; also to suggest certain lines of thought which may in the future tend to a fuller measure of agreement.

"Each subject on the agenda was first discussed in plenary session. It was then committed to one of the sections, of more than one hundred members each, into which the whole Conference was divided. The report, after full discussion in subsections, was finally drawn up and adopted unanimously or by a large majority vote by the section to which it had been committed. It was twice presented for further discussion to a plenary session of the Conference, when it was referred to the Churches in its present form." [4]

The subjects were these: 1. The Church's Message to the World—the Gospel. 2. The Nature of the Church. 3. The Church's Common Confession of Faith. 4. The Ministry of the Church. 5. The Sacraments. 6. The Unity of Christendom in Relation to Existing Churches. The nature of these topics is a sufficient guarantee that the Conference, true to its purposes, was ready to encounter difficulties and to register differences as well as agreements. The one subject which produced complete harmony was the first—the Gospel; but in considering the last topic so much trouble was encountered that the report was finally referred not (like all the others) to the Churches but to the Continuation Committee for future revision. For any account of the contents of these and the other reports we have no space. Of the use to be made of them the Conference was urgently reminded in the Concluding Statement with which they ended: "We have not finished our whole task. We have but taken a step on a long journey. The Conference was only a new starting point. What

[4] H. N. Bate (Ed.), *Faith and Order*, 459 f.

we did there will crumble into dust unless the representatives at Lausanne bring home to their several Churches the duty and responsibility of studying the Reports which they themselves received for this very purpose. The Conference should be repeated in every main ecclesiastical assembly, as well as in each separate congregation, throughout our entire Christian constituency if we are to take full advantage of the progress registered. By our presence and activity at Lausanne we are solemnly pledged to reproduce, each in his own local circle, the spirit and method which made the World Conference on Faith and Order what it was." [5]

"Lausanne" made a profound impression upon all who shared the experience it afforded. As William Temple, then Bishop of Manchester, put it, "The great thing about our Conference is that it has happened." "Inevitably," wrote another member, "there were clashes, controversies, and conflicts of opinion in plenty, but they were always chivalrous. Mutual goodwill and tolerance ruled everything." To Canon Woods of Canterbury it seemed that "the sense of a real spiritual unity, transcending formidable differences was perhaps the greatest miracle of the Conference. . . . We knew we loved the same Christ and served the same Kingdom; especially we knew it when we sang and prayed together." [6] Voicing the conviction borne in upon all who met at Lausanne that ultimate reunion must accord with the principle of *unity in diversity*, Bishop Gore wrote, "The reunited Church must be large and comprehensive enough to contain all the treasures of experience which have given their strength to the various non-episcopal communities. . . . The Conference will bear fruit exactly in proportion as those it represents acknowledge that true Catholicism is wider and more comprehensive than anything embodied in any single communion; or, more generally, that there is a true witness borne by the different Protestant communities which Catholicism as commonly understood needs for its own sake and has in history failed to realize, and on the other hand, that Protestantism needs to make its own what has been the strength and glory of Catholicism." [7]

[5] *Ibid.*, 474 f.

[6] E. S. Woods, *Lausanne, 1927*, 29.

[7] *Ibid.*, 158 f. "Faith and Order," like "Life and Work," continued to be active through a large Continuation Committee, and a second World Conference met at Edinburgh in 1937. Again like "Life and Work," the movement became part of a larger whole with the formation of the World Council of Churches in 1948.

EPILOGUE

THROUGHOUT the pages that have recorded the history of the Episcopal Church during a century and a half we have frequently noted with unsparing frankness the limitations, the failures, the faults, and even the sins of the Church. We have not overlooked, where they have appeared, the examples of its timidity and its lethargy. We have acknowledged the extent to which its numbers have been so largely restricted to the cities. We have taken no satisfaction in its high social prestige, knowing its small influence among the farmers and in the ranks of labor. We have not disguised the fact that in pursuit of the reunion of Christendom its words have spoken louder than its actions. And our story has made clear how inadequate still remain its endeavors in the missionary field, in Christian education, and in forwarding the Christian solution of social problems. Such an effort at objective honesty seemed to be demanded of any record that aimed to be not propaganda but history.

Surely, then, in closing, we have earned the right to point, with equal regard for veracity, to what is noblest in the Church—to those virtues which have given it an influence far out of proportion to its numbers, which have drawn to it new strength from other communions, and which have contributed to the enrichment of American Christianity.

The Episcopal Church has long since become *genuinely* American, but just because in many ways it is not *typically* American it can offer to religion certain elements for lack of which this country would be the poorer. In spite of distinctions from each other in which they may properly take pride, the many and obvious likenesses among Protestant denominations make all the more valuable the life and work of a Church which can transmit a Catholic heritage that is not Roman but Reformed.

From its Catholic inheritance the Church draws an interpretation of personal and social morality often at odds with the traditions of Puritanism, but by its sanity exempt from the reactions that so often have followed "the rule of the saints." By emphasizing in religion the mind and the will rather than the emotions, the Church is prepared to avoid both the excitement and the depression that attend the practices of revivalism. By its characteristic stress upon the slow processes of Christian nurture the Church has acknowledged the genuineness of the "once-born" type of Christian experience and has encouraged its development. By its respect for the achievements of intellect the Church (however tardily) has been foremost among major Christian bodies in welcoming the results of scientific advance, escaping thereby the consequences of "Fundamentalism," which can only alienate the rising generation.

In the midst of twentieth-century democracy the Church maintains the principle of authority in the tradition of the episcopate and the principle of freedom in a constitution and system of government thoroughly democratic. That same combination of authority and freedom prevails in the sphere of doctrine and teaching. The two simplest of creeds, steadfast as guides and landmarks, are consistent with wide liberty in the interpretation of theology and in the preaching of the Gospel. Indeed, the very fact that the Church is both Catholic and Reformed constitutes it a wholesome public example of the power of deep conviction to resist the passion for uniformity, to endure tension, and even to profit from it. In no other Christian body is such wide difference of opinion and temperament combined with the capacity for united corporate action and continuous fellowship. So far as the Church is true to its Anglican tradition of comprehensiveness it remains a standing rebuke to that organized uniformity which is sectarianism. It serves no less, by its very existence, as a lively encouragement to those plans for organic union which call for uniting into one body Churches primarily Catholic and Churches primarily Protestant. Having long flourished as a Church incorporating both elements, the Episcopal Church can offer itself not as the model of an ideal Church in the sight of God, but at least as an example of unity in diversity.

Finally, in its emphasis upon worship the Episcopal Church bears witness to a truth too easily ignored or forgotten among a people intensely practical—the truth that the highest privilege of the Church is worship, and that worship is not mainly instruction and exhortation. Thanks to a liturgical heritage which has drawn treasures from every age of Christian history, beauty of form and richness of content are at the disposal of the humblest congregation. And thanks to the central place increasingly accorded to the Holy Communion, worship may the more readily become so selfless and objective that it rises to its highest manifestation in adoration.

A TABLE OF DATES IN ENGLISH CHURCH HISTORY FROM 1558 TO 1799

1558 Accession of Elizabeth
1559 Act of Supremacy
Act of Uniformity
Consecration of Archbishop Parker
1559–1570 First Stage of Puritanism
1570 Beginning of Second Stage of Puritanism
Attack on Episcopacy
Pius V issues Bull of Deposition
1571 Thirty-nine Articles
1572 "Admonition to the Parliament"
First Presbytery formed
1580 Coming of the Jesuits
1581 Beginning of Third Stage of Puritanism
Rise of "Independency"
1588 Defeat of Spanish Armada
1593 Banishment of Nonconformists
1593–1597 Hooker's *Ecclesiastical Polity*
1603 Accession of James I
1604 Hampton Court Conference
Canons of 1604
1605 Gunpowder Plot
1611 Authorized Version of the Bible
1625 Accession of Charles I
1633 Laud Archbishop of Canterbury
1638 Scottish Covenant
1640 Meeting of Long Parliament
Impeachment of Laud
1641 The "Grand Remonstrance"
1642 Beginning of Civil War
1643 Solemn League and Covenant
Westminster Assembly meets
1645 Execution of Laud
1646 Modified Presbyterianism established
1649 Execution of Charles I
1653–1658 Cromwell Lord Protector
1660 Restoration of Charles II
1661 Savoy Conference
1662 Act of Uniformity
Revision of Prayer Book
1663 Ejection of Puritan Clergy
1664 Conventicle Act
1665 Five Mile Act
1672 Declaration of Indulgence
1673 Test Act
1678 Popish Plot
1685 Accession of James II
1687 Declaration of Indulgence
1688 Trial of the Seven Bishops
1689 Accession of William and Mary
Toleration Act
1691 Secession of Nonjurors
1698 Foundation of S.P.C.K.
1701 Foundation of S.P.G.
1702 Accession of Anne
1714 Accession of George I
1717 Convocation repressed
1729 Beginning of Methodism at Oxford
1739 Wesley and Whitefield begin preaching
Rise of Evangelical Movement
1799 Foundation of the Church Missionary Society

A LIST OF BOOKS REFERRED TO IN THE NOTES

Allen, A. V. G., *Life and Letters of Phillips Brooks,* New York, 1900.

Ayres, Anne, *Life and Work of W. A. Muhlenberg,* 5th ed., New York, 1894.

Bacon, L. W., *History of American Christianity,* New York, 1897.

Bate, H. N. (Ed.), *Faith and Order, Lausanne, 1927,* New York, 1928.

Bell, G. K. A. (Ed.), *The Stockholm Conference, 1925,* London, 1926.

Berrien, William, *Memoir of the Life of the Rt. Rev. John Henry Hobart, D.D.* (Vol. I in "Posthumous Works" of Hobart), New York, 1832–33.

Brewer, C. H., *History of Religious Education in the Episcopal Church to 1835,* New Haven, 1924.

Brilioth, Y. T., *Three Lectures on Evangelicalism and the Oxford Movement,* London, 1934.

Caswall, Henry, *America and the American Church,* London, 1839.

Chase, Philander, *Reminiscences,* 2 vols., 2d ed., Boston, 1848.

Cheshire, J. B., *The Church in the Confederate States,* New York, 1912.

Chorley, E. C., *Men and Movements in the American Episcopal Church,* New York, 1946.

Church Congress of 1874, *Papers and Addresses,* New York, 1874.

Clark, G. N., *The Later Stuarts, 1660–1714,* Oxford, 1934.

Cross, A. L., *The Anglican Episcopate and the American Colonies,* New York, 1902.

DeMille, G. E., *The Catholic Movement in the American Episcopal Church,* Philadelphia, 1941.

Dix, Morgan, *History of the Parish of Trinity Church in the City of New York,* 4 vols., New York, 1898–1906.

Elliot, Jonathan (Ed.), *Debates in the Several State Conventions on the Adoption of the Federal Constitution,* etc., Washington, 1836.

Evangelical Catholic Papers, First Series (compiled by Anne Ayres), New York, 1875.

Faulkner, H. V., *The Quest for Social Justice,* New York, 1931.

Fish, C. R., *The Rise of the Common Man,* New York, 1927.

Gavin, F. S. B. (Ed.), *Liberal Catholicism and the Modern World,* Vol. I, Milwaukee, 1934.

General Conventions of the Protestant Episcopal Church, Journals of, 1785–1835, edited by W. S. Perry, Claremont, N. H., 1874.

General Conventions of the Protestant Episcopal Church, Journals of, published triennially.

Gore, Charles (Ed.), *Lux Mundi,* 2d ed., New York, 1890.

Hawks, F. L., *Contributions to the Ecclesiastical History of the United States,* Vol. I, *Virginia,* Vol. II, *Maryland,* New York, 1836–39.

Henshaw, J. P. K., *Memoir of the Life of the Rt. Rev. Richard Channing Moore, D.D.,* Philadelphia, 1842.

Historical Magazine of the Protestant Episcopal Church, edited by the Rev. Walter H. Stowe, S.T.D. and published at 5 Paterson St., New Brunswick, N. J. This quarterly is an invaluable guide to all who are interested in the history of the Episcopal Church.

Hobart, J. H., *The Churchman* [N. Y., 1819], reprinted (G. W. Doane, Ed.) in Boston, 1832. Contains "The Principles of the Churchman."

Hobart, J. H., *The High Churchman Vindicated* [N. Y., 1826], reprinted (G. W. Doane, Ed.) in Boston, 1832.

Hodges, George, *The Heresy of Cain,* New York, 1894.

Hodges, George, *Three Hundred Years of the Episcopal Church in America,* Philadelphia, 1906.

Hopkins, C. H., *The Rise of the Social Gospel in American Protestantism, 1865–1915,* New Haven, 1940.

Hopkins, J. H., *Scriptural, Ecclesiastical, and Historical View of Slavery,* New York, 1864.

Howe, M. A. DeW., *Life and Labors of Bishop Hare,* New York, 1911.

Howe, M. A. DeW., *Memoirs of the Life and Services of the Rt. Rev. Alonzo Potter, D.D., LL.D.,* Philadelphia, 1871.

Huntington, Virginia E., *Along the Great River,* New York, 1940.

Huntington, W. R., *The Church-Idea* [N. Y., 1870], 5th ed., Boston, 1928.

Krout, J. A. and D. R. Fox, *The Completion of Independence,* New York, 1944.

Lambeth Conferences of 1867, 1878, and 1888, Official Reports edited by the Rt. Rev. Randall T. Davidson, rev. ed., London, 1896.

Lambeth Conference of Bishops of the Anglican Communion, July, 1897, Resolutions and Reports, London, 1897.

[Lambeth]. *Conference of Bishops of the Anglican Communion,* holden at Lambeth Palace, July 6 to August 5, 1908, London, 1908.

[Lambeth]. *Conference of Bishops of the Anglican Communion,* holden at Lambeth Palace, July 5 to August 7, 1920, London, 1920.

Lambeth Conference, 1930, *Encyclical Letter together with Resolutions and Reports,* London, 1930.

Lambeth Conference, 1948, *Encyclical Letter, together with Resolutions and Reports,* London, 1948.

Lawrence, William, *Life of Phillips Brooks,* New York, 1930

Lawrence, William, *Memories of a Happy Life,* Boston, 1926.

Liberal Evangelicalism by Members of the Church of England, London [1923?]

Living Church Annual, published by the Morehouse-Gorham Co., New York. A book of facts and figures indispensable for the historian.

McConnell, S. D., *History of the American Episcopal Church,* 3rd ed., New York, 1891.

Manross, W. W., *The Episcopal Church in the United States, 1800–1840,* New York, 1938.

Manross, W. W., *History of the American Episcopal Church,* New York, 2d ed., revised and enlarged, 1950. The best and most recent history of the Church, equipped with full bibliography.

Masterman, C. F. G., *Frederick Denison Maurice,* London, 1907.

May, Henry F., *Protestant Churches and Industrial America,* New York, 1949.

Miller, S. and J. F. Fletcher, *The Church and Industry,* New York, 1930.

Muller, J. A., *Apostle of China,* New York, 1937.

Nevins, Allan, *The Emergence of Modern America,* New York, 1927.

Newton, W. W., *Dr. Muhlenberg,* Boston, 1891.

Parsons, E. L. and B. H. Jones, *The American Prayer Book,* New York, 1937.

Perry, W. S., *History of the American Episcopal Church,* 2 vols., Boston, 1885.

Potter, Alonzo (Ed.), *Memorial Papers,* Philadelphia, 1857.

Seabury, Samuel, *American Slavery,* 2d ed., New York, 1861.

Schlesinger, A. M., *The Rise of the City,* New York, 1933.

Selwyn, E. G. (Ed.), *Essays Catholic and Critical,* New York, 1926.

Sherrill, H. K., *William Lawrence: Later Years of a Happy Life,* Cambridge, U.S.A., 1943.

Smythe, G. F., *Kenyon College: Its First Century,* New Haven, 1924.

Stone, J. S., *Memoir of the Life of the Rt. Rev. Alexander Viets Griswold, D.D.,* Philadelphia, 1844.

Sweet, W. W., *The Story of Religion in America,* rev. ed., New York, 1939.

Temple, Frederick, et al., *Essays and Reviews,* 3rd ed., London, 1860.

Tiffany, C. C., *History of the Protestant Episcopal Church,* 2d ed., New York, 1900.

Trevelyan, G. M., *England under Queen Anne,* 3 vols., London, 1931–34.

Trevelyan, G. M., *English Social History,* New York, 1942.

Tucker, H. St. G., *History of the Episcopal Church in Japan,* New York, 1938.

Tulloch, John, *Movements of Religious Thought in Britain in the Nineteenth Century,* New York, 1885.

Tuttle, D. S., *Reminiscences of a Missionary Bishop,* New York, 1906.

Visser't Hooft, W. A., *The Background of the Social Gospel in America,* Haarlem, 1928.

Wakeman, H. O., *Introduction to the History of the Church of England,* 11th ed., London, 1927.

Waylen, Edward, *Ecclesiastical Reminiscences of the United States,* New York, 1846.

White, E. A., *Constitution and Canons . . . of the Protestant Episcopal Church . . . 1789–1922, Annotated,* New York, 1924.

White, Greenough, *An Apostle of the Western Church,* New York, 1900.

White, William, *Memoirs of the Protestant Episcopal Church in the United States of America,* 3rd ed., New York, 1880.

Wilson, Bird, *Memoir of the Life of the Rt. Rev. William White, D.D.,* Philadelphia, 1839.

Woods, E. S., *Lausanne, 1927,* New York, 1927.

Worcester, Elwood, S. McComb, and I. H. Coriat, *Religion and Medicine,* New York, 1908.

Zabriskie, A. C. (Ed.), *Anglican Evangelicalism,* Philadelphia, 1943.

Zabriskie, A. C., *Bishop Brent,* New York, 1948.

Index

THE PAGE NUMBERS IN BOLD TYPE INDICATE THE MAIN ENTRIES UNDER WHICH A SUBJECT IS TREATED.